JN020893

TOEIC® L&R TEST 990点獲得 全パート難問模試

MediaBeacon
メディアビーコン

無料音声
ダウンロード付

ベレ出版

はじめに

本書は、TOEIC® L&R TESTで満点（990点）獲得を目指す方に向けた、TOEIC全パート対策書です。最終的な目標として990点獲得というところを想定していますが、あなたが900点や900点後半を目指すのなら、ぜひお使いいただきたい一冊となっています。

数年前から難化傾向にあるTOEIC公開テストでは、だれでもすぐに活用できるようなテクニックはもう通用しません。かつて990点を獲得した経験がある方も頭を抱えるほど、高く幅広い能力が求められる試験になっています。基本的な英語力はもちろん、情報を速く正確に読み取って全体の流れや状況を把握し、情報の整理や予測をする能力も高いレベルで求められるのです。

私たちは毎回のTOEIC公開テストを受験し、試験の傾向や対策を分析・研究しています。また、TOEICのコーチングを通じて、高得点を目指す学習者へ直接指導を続けてきました。そんな私たちだからこそ、最新の問題傾向に沿った質の高い問題を作成し、学習者に寄り添った教材制作を実現することができると自負しています。

私たちのノウハウを全て本書に詰め込み、高得点を目指す学習者のために心を込めて作りました。本書を徹底的に使い倒せば、990点獲得のために必要な力はきっと身に付くと信じています。ぜひ本書を通じて、これからのTOEIC L&R TESTに太刀打ちできる"本物の力"を身に付けてください。

あなたが本書を使って目標スコアを達成し、
人生の新たなチャンスを掴めるよう願っています。

メディアビーコン

TOEIC® L&R TEST 990点獲得 全パート難問模試
［目次］

TEST 1　解答・解説　正解一覧　　　　　　18

TEST 2　解答・解説　正解一覧　136

掲載画像クレジット一覧

Direction
© Mangostar/stock.adobe.com

TEST 1
1. © Syda Productions/stock.adobe.com
2. © panchaphon/stock.adobe.com
3. © JackF/stock.adobe.com
4. © Nomad_Soul/stock.adobe.com
5. © WavebreakMediaMicro/stock.adobe.com
6. © Brandon Mauth/stock.adobe.com

TEST 2
1. © Ekaterina Belova/stock.adobe.com
2. © romaset/stock.adobe.com
3. © kroshanosha/stock.adobe.com
4. © New Africa/stock.adobe.com
5. © pressmaster/stock.adobe.com
6. © starush/stock.adobe.com

本書の構成

［本冊］
- TEST 1 と TEST 2 の解答・解説
- 正解一覧
- 学習プログラム
- TOEIC 攻略アドバイス
- マークシート

［別冊］
- TEST 1 と TEST 2 の問題
- 正誤記録表

特典 1 ▶ 英語コーチによる授業動画

本書を使って英語学習をしてくださる皆さんのために、**TOEIC 満点の英語コーチによる授業動画**をご用意しています。授業動画の内容は、下記の通りです。

① TOEIC 攻略アドバイス
② 難問ポイントの解説

授業動画は、ご自身のスマートフォンで二次元バーコードをスキャンすることでご視聴いただけます。①の動画は本冊 P.12-17 の「TOEIC 攻略アドバイス」の各ページに、②の動画は本冊の問題解説ページにある 👑**Level Up！** に、二次元バーコードがございます。

■ 付属のダウンロード音声について

本書の音声は、スマートフォンやタブレット、またはパソコンで聞くことができます。音声は全て無料でお聞きいただけます。

スマートフォン・タブレットの場合

AI英語教材アプリabceed（株式会社Globee提供）
①アプリストアで「abceed」をダウンロード。
②アプリを立ち上げ、本書の名前を検索して音声を使用。

https://www.abceed.com

英語アプリmikan
①アプリストアで「mikan」をダウンロード。
②アプリを立ち上げ、「教材一覧」の検索バーで本書の名前を検索。
③音声ボタン（♫）より、音声を再生。

https://mikan.link/beret

パソコンの場合

「ベレ出版」ホームページ（https://www.beret.co.jp/）
①「ベレ出版」ホームページ内、『TOEIC® L&R TEST 990点獲得 全パート難問模試』のページへ。「音声ファイル」の「ダウンロード」ボタンをクリック。

②8ケタのコードを入力して「ダウンロード」ボタンをクリック。

ダウンロードコード　（ EzMiGUTp ）

③ダウンロードされた圧縮ファイルを解凍して、お使いの音声再生ソフトに取り込んで音声を使用。

＊ダウンロードされた音声はMP3形式となります。
＊zipファイルの解凍方法、iPod等のMP3携帯プレイヤーへのファイル転送方法、パソコン、ソフトなどの操作方法については小社での対応はできかねますこと、ご理解ください。
☞音声の権利・利用については、小社ホームページ内［よくある質問］にてご確認ください。

特典2 ▶ 「大会場バージョン」の特殊音声

リスニング試験において、「大きな試験会場だと音が反響して聞き取りにくい、音がこもって聞こえる」などと悩む学習者が多くいます。そういった声を受け、本書では、大会場の音響を再現したリスニング音声を特別にご用意しました。こちらの音声を使うことで、どんな環境でも対応できる"最強のリスニング力"を身に付けることができます。

▶「大会場バージョン」の音声は、トラック番号が"TRACK_S"で始まるものです。
　※例）TRACK_S001

本書での学習の進め方

　本書では、Part 1〜7の2回分の模試を収録しています。それぞれの模試を解き、そこで得られる知識をしっかりと自分のものにできれば、本番でも出題される「難問」に対応できる力がつきます。ただ、一度解いて終わりでは意味がありません。徹底的な復習をしながら何度も問題を解くことで、ようやく、満点を獲得するために必要な力が身に付くのです。

　本書では、1つの模試を最低4回は解くことを推奨しています。下記に、本書の各TESTを4回解くときの実際の取り組み方、復習の方法をまとめました。

1回目

①2時間測って、問題を通しで解く

　最初の1回は、必ずまとまった時間が取れるときに解きましょう。また、リスニング音声はイヤホンではなくスピーカーで聞くことをお勧めします。実際の試験となるべく同じ環境で模試を解くことがポイントです。

②答え合わせをする

　解答を確認し、丸付けをします。正誤記録表（別冊P.84〜）に結果を記録しておくと、1回ごとの進歩が見られるので、ぜひご活用ください。

③解説を読んでポイントを確認する

　解説をよく読んで、各問題のポイントや、自分が間違えてしまった原因などを確認しましょう。勘や推測で選んでたまたま合っていた可能性もあるので、正答を選べている問題も解説を読んで、全問正しく理解することが大切です。解説と一緒に 語彙チェック も確認して、知らなかった単語や表現はしっかり覚えておくようにしましょう。

　また、難しいポイントがある問題には、 👑Level Up! というコーナーを設けて解説しています。そしてその中でも特に押さえておくべきポイントに関しては、授業動画を付けています。 👑Level Up! 内の二次元バーコードをスキャンして動画を確認し、難問ポイントを押さえましょう。

2回目・3回目

①1問（または1題）ずつ問題を解く

　1回通しで解いた後は、1つずつ問題を解いて理解度を高めていきます。リーディングは、必ず時間を測って解きましょう。Part 5は1問20秒、Part 6は1題2分、Part 7は1問あたり1分が目安の解答時間です。解説ページには各問題に （解答時間） の記入欄があるので、実際に解答にかかった時間を記録しておきましょう。2回目よりも3回目の方が解答時間が速くなっていれば、復習の成果が出ていることを確認できます。

②答え合わせをする

　解答を見て丸つけをし、正誤記録表（別冊P.84〜）に記録を付けましょう。

③復習をする

　解説をざっと確認したら、精読・精聴をして徹底的に復習をしてください。Part 1、2は音声を聞きなおして、そのとき聞き逃してしまった語数を確認し、（聞き逃し単語） の記入欄に記録します。こちらも、聞き逃し単語の数がだんだんと減っていくことを目指しましょう。Part 3、4は全体の話をなんとなく理解

するだけではなく、1つ1つの文を瞬時に正しく理解できているかが大切。本書の解説ページでは、本文スクリプトをある程度のカタマリで分けて番号を振っています。そのカタマリごとに意味を瞬時に理解できたかどうか確認し、理解できたカタマリの数を カンベキ理解 の記入欄に記入しましょう。 カンベキ理解 用に、カタマリごとに区切れた音声もご用意しているのでそちらをご活用ください。

また、リスニング・リーディングともに、「音読トレーニング」が英語力アップにとても効果的です。最後に音読トレーニング法を紹介しているので、自分のレベルに合った方法で音読トレーニングをしましょう。

4回目

①2時間測って、問題を通しで解く

1回目と同様に、時間を測って全ての問題を通しで解きます。復習がしっかりできていれば、1回目の解きやすさとの違いを実感できるはずです。

②答え合わせをする

解答を見て丸つけをし、正誤記録表（別冊P.84〜）に記録を付けましょう。

③復習をする

間違えた問題を中心に、解説を読んで復習します。特に理解度が足りなそうなところは、精読や精聴、音読などのトレーニングを繰り返し行いましょう。

おすすめの音読トレーニング法 ～～～～～～～～～～～～～～～～～～～～

Lv.1：Read and Look up

まずは意味のまとまりごとに英文にスラッシュを入れます。その後、スラッシュごとに英文を見ながら音読（または黙読）して、直後に英文を見ないで音読します。慣れてきたら、1度に読む量を増やして1文ずつできるように挑戦しましょう。

Lv.2：オーバーラッピング

英文を目で追いながら、音声と一緒に声を出して音読します。スピードに追い付けるようになったら、意味を意識しながら音読しましょう。

Lv.3：シャドーイング

英文を見ずに音声だけを聞いて、それに付いていくように音読します。意味を理解しながら、できるだけ感情を込めて読むのがコツです。速度に追い付けないようなら、オーバーラッピングに戻るようにしてください。

Lv.4：瞬間英作文

日本語訳を読んで、それを1文ずつ英語で発話します。発話後すぐにスクリプトの英文を見て、抜けているところなどを確認します。何度も読んで英文を大体覚えている状態で行うと良いでしょう。

学習プログラム

本書を使い倒していただくために、「1つの模試を60日間で4回解く」学習プログラムをご用意しました。バランス良く英語力を鍛えるという目的で、1日の学習の中に必ずリーディングとリスニングの両方の学習を含めるように設計しています。毎日の学習時間がもう少し取れる方は、何日分かをまとめて進めることをお勧めします。

	Part 1	Part 2	Part 3	Part 4	Part 5	Part 6	Part 7	
Day 1			2時間測って、通しで解く					1回目
Day 2	6問 (No.1~6)				4問 (No.101~104)			2回目
Day 3		6問 (No.7~12)			4問 (No.105~108)			
Day 4		6問 (No.13~18)			4問 (No.109~112)			
Day 5		6問 (No.19~24)			3問 (No.113~115)			
Day 6		7問 (No.25~31)			3問 (No.116~118)			
Day 7			1題 (No.32~34)		3問 (No.119~121)			
Day 8			1題 (No.35~37)		3問 (No.122~124)			
Day 9			1題 (No.38~40)		3問 (No.125~127)			
Day 10			1題 (No.41~43)		3問 (No.128~130)			
Day 11			1題 (No.44~46)			1題 (No.131~134)		
Day 12			1題 (No.47~49)			1題 (No.135~138)		
Day 13			1題 (No.50~52)			1題 (No.139~142)		
Day 14			1題 (No.53~55)			1題 (No.143~146)		
Day 15			1題 (No.56~58)				SP1題	
Day 16			1題 (No.59~61)				SP1題	
Day 17			1題 (No.62~64)				SP1題	
Day 18			1題 (No.65~67)				SP1題	
Day 19			1題 (No.68~70)				SP1題	
Day 20				1題 (No.71~73)			SP1題	
Day 21				1題 (No.74~76)			SP1題	
Day 22				1題 (No.77~79)			SP1題	
Day 23				1題 (No.80~82)			SP1題	
Day 24				1題 (No.83~85)			SP1題	
Day 25				1題 (No.86~88)			DP1題	
Day 26				1題 (No.89~91)			DP1題	
Day 27				1題 (No.92~94)			TP1題	
Day 28				1題 (No.95~97)			TP1題	
Day 29				1題 (No.98~100)			TP1題	

	Part 1	Part 2	Part 3	Part 4	Part 5	Part 6	Part 7	
Day 30	6 問 (No.1~6)				4 問 (No.101~104)			3 回目
Day 31		6 問 (No.7~12)			4 問 (No.105~108)			
Day 32		6 問 (No.13~18)			4 問 (No.109~112)			
Day 33		6 問 (No.19~24)			3 問 (No.113~115)			
Day 34		7 問 (No.25~31)			3 問 (No.116~118)			
Day 35			1 題 (No.32~34)		3 問 (No.119~121)			
Day 36			1 題 (No.35~37)		3 問 (No.122~124)			
Day 37			1 題 (No.38~40)		3 問 (No.125~127)			
Day 38			1 題 (No.41~43)		3 問 (No.128~130)			
Day 39			1 題 (No.44~46)			1 題 (No.131~134)		
Day 40			1 題 (No.47~49)			1 題 (No.135~138)		
Day 41			1 題 (No.50~52)			1 題 (No.139~142)		
Day 42			1 題 (No.53~55)			1 題 (No.143~146)		
Day 43			1 題 (No.56~58)				SP1 題	
Day 44			1 題 (No.59~61)				SP1 題	
Day 45			1 題 (No.62~64)				SP1 題	
Day 46			1 題 (No.65~67)				SP1 題	
Day 47			1 題 (No.68~70)				SP1 題	
Day 48				1 題 (No.71~73)			SP1 題	
Day 49				1 題 (No.74~76)			SP1 題	
Day 50				1 題 (No.77~79)			SP1 題	
Day 51				1 題 (No.80~82)			SP1 題	
Day 52				1 題 (No.83~85)			SP1 題	
Day 53				1 題 (No.86~88)			DP1 題	
Day 54				1 題 (No.89~91)			DP1 題	
Day 55				1 題 (No.92~94)			TP1 題	
Day 56				1 題 (No.95~97)			TP1 題	
Day 57				1 題 (No.98~100)			TP1 題	
Day 58	2 時間測って、通しで解く							4 回目
Day 59	弱いところを徹底的にトレーニング!!							
Day 60				弱いところを徹底的にトレーニング!!				

満点獲得のための
TOEIC攻略アドバイス

TOEICテストの各Partの攻略アドバイスをお伝えする前に、1つご質問です。あなたの英語学習は、TOEIC対策にばかり偏っていませんか？　スコアアップしていくためには、TOEICテストの攻略法を学ぶ以前に必要な能力があります。以下の3点は、TOEIC対策だけではカバーできない重要な能力を鍛えるためのアドバイスです。「どんなにTOEIC対策をしてもスコアが上がらない」という方は特に、以下の点を参考に英語学習の仕方を見直してみることをお勧めします。

〜TOEIC対策の前に〜

1. 英語の基礎知識をしっかりつける

　TOEIC高得点者の方でも意外と、この部分が抜けている方が多いです。TOEICテストの傾向や解答テクニックばかり頭に入れているだけでは、TOEIC満点は取れません。自分はできていると思い込まずに、本当に基礎を完璧に理解できているのかを再確認し、曖昧な知識をなくしていきましょう。

2. 毎日英語に触れる

　多読多聴をして、日常的に目や耳を英語に慣らしておくことがポイント。実際のテストの時間も2時間と長いので、英語に慣れていた方が集中力も維持しやすくなります。また、ある程度の高得点を取れている方は、TOEICの英文以外の文献にも触れるようにするとより効果的ですよ。

3. ビジネスに関する知見を広げる

　TOEICテストでは、あらゆる業界のあらゆるシチュエーションが登場します。TOEICテストでの定番はあるものの、満点を獲得するためにはイレギュラーなトピックにも対応できなくてはなりません。ビジネスにまつわる海外ドラマを見る、海外のビジネスニュースを見るなど、ビジネスに関する知見を広げるための工夫を取り入れてみましょう。

〜Part 1 攻略アドバイス〜

1. Part 1特有の文法を押さえる

　Part 1は状況描写の問題なので、登場する文法はある程度限られています。特に、述語動詞の形です。be *doing*「〜しているところだ」やbe -ed「〜されている」など、写真の状況に応じて述語動詞の形が変わりますが、その種類は多くありません。それを押さえておくだけで、聞き取りや理解のスピードも速くなります。中には聞き間違えやすいものもあるので、音も一緒に把握しておくことが重要です。

2. 広い視野で写真の情報を掴む

　Part 1での難問ポイントの1つに、「写真の中の情報量が多い」という点があります。従来は情報量が少ない写真が多い傾向にありましたが、近年は要素の多い、引きの写真がよく登場するようになってきました。写真を確認するときには、1つ1つの要素だけでなく、それぞれの要素の関係性や全体の状況を把握するように意識しましょう。

3. 同じ物・状況の表し方のパターンを複数用意しておく

　写真を見て、どんな英語がくるのかを事前にある程度予測することは大切です。ただ、そのときに複数のパターンを予測しておくことがポイント。例えば写真に「車」が写っていたとき、「きっとcarがくるだろう」と予測するのではなく、「もしかしたらvehicleって言われるかも」「具体的にtruckって呼ぶ可能性もあるな」などと、頭の中に複数パターンを用意しておく、ということです。そうすれば、どんな表現がされていても瞬時に対応できるようになります。日常で目にするものを英語でどんなふうに言えるのか、複数考えてみる癖をつけるのも良いですね。

▼ 動画をCHECK！

～Part 2 攻略アドバイス～

1. 消去法を活用する

　Part 2では、直接的には質問に答えていないような応答も正解になりうります。こういった曖昧な応答が増えているからこそ、正答を選ぶためには、他の選択肢もよく確認して正解候補を削っていく必要があります。全問正解を目指すならなおさら、消去法は必須。Part 2はあくまで、選択肢の中で「最も適切な応答」を選ぶ問題なので、質問に答えてないかも…と深く悩むより、全ての選択肢を正確に聞き取って消去法をすることに力を使いましょう。

2. 最初の問いかけの文は、要約して脳内復唱

　Part 2の悩みとして、「最初の問いかけ文の内容を忘れてしまう」という声をよく聞きます。この問題の多くは、「1文まるまる覚えようとしている」「和訳を介している」といった点に原因があります。例えば、Where can I find the sales data?「販売データはどこにありますか」なら「sales data(販売データ)、where(どこ)」のように、相手の発言のキーワードを押さえることがポイント。選択肢が流れている合間も、そのキーワードだけ脳内で復唱して頭の中に刻み込むイメージで、音声を聞いていきましょう。

3. 1問ごとに頭をリセットする

　Part 2は1問が短く、問題数も多いため、1問ごとの切り替えがかなり重要になります。前の問題に迷って引きずってしまうと、次以降の問題に大きく影響してしまいます。1問解いたら、数秒目を閉じる、深呼吸をするなどして、気持ちを落ち着けてから次の問題に入ることがコツです。

〜Part 3&4 攻略アドバイス〜

1. 設問の先読みのテンポを掴む

　Part 3とPart 4は、本文の音声を聞く前の準備が何より大切。それはつまり、"設問の先読み"です。各問題の2問目の設問文が流れるまでにマークをし終えて、次の問題の先読みに移るのが時間配分の目安です。いつも決まった要領で落ち着いて解けるように、普段から先読みをしてテンポを染み込ませておきましょう。時間と気持ちに余裕があれば、選択肢も軽く先読みしておくのもお勧めですよ。

2. 状況を想像する

　細かな音の聞き取りばかりに集中しすぎるのはNG。音声を聞きながら状況を想像することを意識しましょう。根拠となる部分を聞き取っただけで正解が選べる問題もありますが、それでは安定して満点を取ることはできません。設問の先読みで得た情報を軸にしつつ、会話やトークを俯瞰して聞くのがポイントです。

3. 「読解力」をつけてから「聴解力」をつける

　聞き取りばかりをトレーニングしていても、実は「聴解力（聞いて理解する力）」以前に「読解力（読んで理解する力）」が足りていない、という可能性があります。読んで分からないものは、聞いても分かるわけがありませんよね。スクリプトで英文を確認し、今の自分はそもそも「読んで理解できている」状態なのかをまず確かめましょう。

〜Part 5&6 攻略アドバイス〜

1. 全文読んで時間内に解く

　皆さんの中には空所の前後を見て解答する方もいらっしゃるかもしれませんが、本書では、Part 5とPart 6ともに全文読んで解答することをお勧めいたします。部分的に読んでいると文構造を取り違えてしまうこともありますし、空所から離れた位置に解答の根拠がある可能性もあります。そういった穴をなくしていくことが満点獲得へのカギです。

2. 誤答の理由も説明できるように復習する

　Part 5、Part 6の復習をするときは、正答の根拠を確認するだけではまだ不十分です。誤答の選択肢も確認して、それぞれがなぜ空所に不適切なのかを説明できるようにします。それが説明できて初めて、「その問題を理解できた」と考えることが大切です。また、ある問題で誤答として出題されていたものが、別の問題で正答として登場することもあります。誤答の理由を説明するトレーニングをすることで、他の問題への応用力も高めることができるのです。

3. 文のつながりを意識する

　Part 6の英文を読むときは、1文1文の意味をバラバラで理解するのではなく、前の文とのつながりを常に意識しながら読むことがポイントです。前の内容に対して「補足しているんだな」「例外を伝えてるんだな」というように、フワッと考えるイメージ。これができれば、苦手意識を持つ人が多い文挿入問題もラクラク解けるはずです。

～Part 7 攻略アドバイス～

1. Part 7の設問の先読みを染み込ませる

　効率良く、かつ正確に正答を選ぶために、私たちは設問の先読みをすることを推奨しています。満点を獲得するためには、限られた時間の中でテンポよく正答を選んでいかなくてはなりません。設問を先読みすることで問われている情報が分かり、焦点が絞られるので、より効率的に解くことができます。Part 7の問題を解く手順を改めて確認し、日々の学習を通して先読みのテンポを染み込ませるようにしましょう。

2. 時間配分を意識して問題を解く

　テスト本番は時間との戦いです。本番で「最後まで解ききれない」「時間がなくて焦ってしまう」ということがないよう、毎日の学習でも時間配分を意識して問題を解くことを徹底してください。もちろん実際のテストでは、時間のかかる問題とすばやく解ける問題があり、そこでバランスを取って時間内に解き終えることもできます。ただ、練習の際は、全て「1問1分」の計算で目標解答時間を決めて取り組みましょう。3問付きの問題は3分、5問付きの問題は5分、ということですね。

3. 深読みしすぎない

　高得点者の方がPart 7で問題を取りこぼしている原因には、「深読みしすぎてしまう」という点があります。特に推測が必要な問題では、明確な根拠が書かれていないものも多いので、過剰にモヤモヤして心配になってしまう人が多いです。結果的に、何度も読み直して時間をかけ過ぎてしまったり、もともと正答を選んでいたのに変えてしまったり、ということが起きます。根拠がかなり曖昧なものもあるという認識を持った上で、問題を解くようにしましょう。

TEST 1

解答&解説

Part 1

問題番号	正解
1	B
2	A
3	D
4	D
5	A
6	C

Part 2

問題番号	正解
7	A
8	A
9	B
10	C
11	C
12	A
13	A
14	B
15	A
16	A
17	C
18	A
19	B
20	A
21	C
22	B
23	A
24	A
25	B
26	B
27	C
28	C
29	B
30	C
31	C

Part 3

問題番号	正解
32	A
33	B
34	C
35	C
36	A
37	D
38	B
39	D
40	D
41	B
42	C
43	B
44	A
45	A
46	D
47	D
48	C
49	A
50	A
51	C
52	B
53	D
54	A
55	D
56	B
57	D
58	D
59	C
60	B
61	C
62	A
63	C
64	B
65	A
66	C
67	C
68	D
69	D
70	B

Part 4

問題番号	正解
71	D
72	B
73	D
74	C
75	A
76	D
77	B
78	C
79	D
80	A
81	C
82	B
83	C
84	B
85	D
86	A
87	B
88	A
89	A
90	D
91	B
92	D
93	B
94	D
95	C
96	C
97	C
98	A
99	B
100	B

Part 5

問題番号	正解
101	A
102	D
103	D
104	C
105	B
106	C
107	D
108	A
109	A
110	B
111	A
112	A
113	D
114	D
115	A
116	D
117	A
118	C
119	B
120	B
121	C
122	B
123	C
124	B
125	D
126	C
127	B
128	C
129	C
130	C

Part 6

問題番号	正解
131	D
132	A
133	C
134	B
135	B
136	C
137	A
138	D
139	A
140	B
141	D
142	C
143	B
144	C
145	D
146	A

Part 7

問題番号	正解
147	A
148	D
149	B
150	C
151	C
152	D
153	B
154	C
155	B
156	A
157	C
158	D
159	A
160	D
161	A
162	C
163	C
164	A
165	C
166	B
167	B
168	C
169	D
170	B
171	B
172	C
173	C
174	A
175	B
176	A
177	B
178	B
179	C
180	C
181	B
182	A
183	D
184	D
185	B

問題番号	正解
186	A
187	B
188	A
189	C
190	D
191	C
192	D
193	B
194	D
195	A
196	B
197	A
198	D
199	D
200	B

Part 1

音読 □□□ 聞き逃し単語 語 ▶ 語

1 🇬🇧 　　　　　　　　　　正解 **B** □□□□　▶TRACK_002

(A) The man is adjusting his chef's hat.
(B) The man has thin gloves on.
(C) An oven under the countertop is wide open.
(D) Some plastic containers are being stuffed in the drawer.

(A) 男性はシェフの帽子を調節している。
(B) 男性は薄い手袋をしている。
(C) カウンター下のオーブンが大きく開いている。
(D) プラスチック容器が引き出しの中に詰め込まれているところだ。

男性が両手にゴム手袋のようなものを着用していることを言い表した(B)が正解。have ～ onの形で「～を身に着けている」という意味。

音読 □□□ 聞き逃し単語 語 ▶ 語

2 🇦🇺 　　　　　　　　　　正解 **A** □□□□　▶TRACK_003

(A) There are some street stalls put up.
(B) A tent is being assembled by a motorbike.
(C) Some people are gathering in an auditorium.
(D) Commodities are displayed indoors.

(A) 露店が出されている。
(B) テントがバイクのそばで組み立てられているところである。
(C) 何人かの人々が講堂に集まっている。
(D) 商品が屋内に展示されている。

商品を展示したテントのようなものが設置されているので、これをstreet stall「露店」と言い表している(A)が正解。put upはstreet stallsを後ろから修飾している。

👑 **Level Up !**
(B)はis beingがhas beenなら正解となる。音も似ているので聞き間違いに注意！

語彙チェック □put up ～ （テントなど）を張る　□auditorium　講堂

音読 □□□ 聞き逃し単語 語 ▶ 語

3 🇨🇦 　　　　　　　　　　正解 **D** □□□□　▶TRACK_004

(A) Plants flourish in a doorway.
(B) An industrial bucket is filled with grass.
(C) A woman is holding a bundle of sticks.
(D) A man is digging the soil with a tool.

(A) 植物が戸口で繁茂している。
(B) 業務用バケツが芝生で満たされている。
(C) 女性は木の枝の束を握っている。
(D) 男性は道具で土を掘っている。

手前の男性がシャベルで土を掘っている様子を言い表している(D)が正解。選択肢ではシャベルがtool「道具」と抽象的に表現されている。

語彙チェック □flourish　（植物が）繁茂する　□bundle　束　□dig　～を掘る

音読 ☐☐☐　聞き逃し単語　語 ▶　語

4 🇺🇸　　　　　　　　　正解 **D** ☐☐☐☐　▶TRACK_005

(A) Some watering cans are in use.
(B) Gardening supplies are being put into a cart.
(C) She's rolling up her sleeves.
(D) She's grasping the broom handle.

(A) じょうろが使用中である。
(B) ガーデニング用品がカートに入れられているところである。
(C) 彼女は袖をまくり上げているところである。
(D) 彼女はほうきの柄を掴んでいる。

中央に写っている女性の動作に注目。ほうきの柄を掴んでいる女性の様子を言い表している(D)が正解。

👑**Level Up!**
(A)には難単語は含まれていないが、後半の音がつながって少し聞き取りにくい。短い語の連鎖に気を付けよう。

語彙チェック　☐watering can　じょうろ　☐be in use　使用中である
☐roll up 〜　（袖など）を巻き上げる　☐broom　ほうき

音読 ☐☐☐　聞き逃し単語　語 ▶　語

5 🇬🇧　　　　　　　　　正解 **A** ☐☐☐☐　▶TRACK_006

(A) Some cardboard boxes are piled up irregularly.
(B) Packing tape has been applied to a wooden stool.
(C) One of the women is placing a reflective vest on a rack.
(D) One of the men is taking notes on the clip board.

(A) 段ボール箱が不揃いに積み重ねられている。
(B) 梱包用のテープが木製のスツールに貼られている。
(C) 女性の1人は棚の上に反射ベストを置いている。
(D) 男性の1人はクリップボードの上でメモを取っている。

写真中央に注目。段ボール箱がカートの上に積み重ねられている。よって、(A)が正解。

語彙チェック　☐irregularly　不揃いに　☐reflective vest　反射ベスト

音読 ☐☐☐　聞き逃し単語　語 ▶　語

6 🇨🇦　　　　　　　　　正解 **C** ☐☐☐☐　▶TRACK_007

(A) A flag is flying on the roof of a house.
(B) Blinds are covering the bay windows.
(C) A staircase is leading to a dwelling.
(D) Vines are winding around an iron fence.

(A) 旗が家の屋根の上ではためいている。
(B) 日よけが出窓を覆っている。
(C) 階段が住居につながっている。
(D) つる草が鉄製のフェンスの周りに巻きついている。

写真中央に階段が写っている。この階段は奥にある家に続いているので、これを言い表している(C)が正解。

語彙チェック　☐fly　（旗などが）はためく　☐bay window　出窓
☐dwelling　住居　☐vine　つる草
☐wind around 〜　〜に巻きつく

Part 2

音読 ☐☐☐ 　聞き逃し単語 　語 ▶ 　語

7 W🇬🇧 M🇺🇸 　　正解 **A** ☐☐☐☐ 　▶TRACK_009

How's the preparation of the sales report going? 　営業報告の準備はどうですか。

(A) I've been on a business trip for two weeks. 　(A) 私は2週間出張に行っていたんですよ。

(B) Before the annual company banquet. 　(B) 年に一度の会社の宴会の前です。

(C) Yes, for about one or two hours. 　(C) はい、1〜2時間くらいです。

How's 〜 going?の形で、報告準備の進捗を尋ねている。これに対して、「私は2週間出張に行っていた」と言うことで、出張で忙しくてまだ準備ができていないことを遠回しに伝えている(A)が正解。

語彙チェック ☐ sales report　営業報告　☐ banquet　宴会

音読 ☐☐☐ 　聞き逃し単語 　語 ▶ 　語

8 W🇨🇦 M🇦🇺 　　正解 **A** ☐☐☐☐ 　▶TRACK_010

Why has the beach cleanup been called off? 　なぜビーチ清掃は中止されたのですか。

(A) I'll forward you the details. 　(A) 詳細を転送しますね。

(B) A cancellation policy. 　(B) キャンセルポリシーです。

(C) Well, both will cost a lot. 　(C) まあ、どちらも多額の費用がかかるでしょう。

ビーチ清掃が中止された理由を尋ねている。これに対して、理由を直接答えるのではなく「詳細を転送する」と申し出ることで、遠回しに返答している(A)が正解。(C)はbothが何を指すのかが不明のため不適切。

語彙チェック ☐ cleanup　清掃　☐ call off 〜　〜を中止する　☐ forward A B　AにBを転送する

音読 ☐☐☐ 　聞き逃し単語 　語 ▶ 　語

9 M🇦🇺 W🇬🇧 　　正解 **B** ☐☐☐☐ 　▶TRACK_011

Would you like to use posters or digital signs? 　ポスターを使いたいですか、それともデジタル看板を使いたいですか。

(A) Yes, you can use either one. 　(A) はい、どちらでもご利用いただけます。

(B) We're considering video advertisement. 　(B) 私たちは動画広告を検討しています。

(C) Turn right at the stop sign. 　(C) 一時停止の標識で右に曲がってください。

質問はA or B「AあるいはB」の形を使った選択疑問文で、「ポスター」と「デジタル看板」という2つの選択肢を提示している。これに対し、「動画広告を検討している」と答えることで、動画を流すことのできる「デジタル看板」を希望していることを遠回しに伝えている(B)が正解。

👑 **Level Up !**
AかBかと聞かれているとき、どちらかをそのまま答えると思いこむのはNG。本問のように、遠回しにどちらがよいかを答えるパターンも出題される！

語彙チェック ☐ stop sign　一時停止の標識

音読 □□□ 聞き逃し単語 語 ▶ 語

10 M 🇺🇸 W 🇬🇧　　　　正解 **C** □□□□　▶TRACK_012

Is it okay if I use your mobile battery?
(A) How much is the fare?
(B) Yes, I owe her one.
(C) By all means.

あなたのモバイルバッテリーを使ってもいいですか。
(A) 運賃はいくらですか。
(B) はい、彼女に借りがあります。
(C) もちろんです。

Is it okay if ～? 「～してもいいですか」という表現を使って、相手にモバイルバッテリーの使用許可を求めている。これに対して、「もちろん」と快諾している (C) が正解。(B) は Yes か No かを聞く疑問文に対して Yes と答えているが、her の指す人物が不明のため不適切。

語彙チェック　□ fare　運賃　□ owe *A B*　A に B の借りがある

音読 □□□ 聞き逃し単語 語 ▶ 語

11 W 🇬🇧 M 🇺🇸　　　　正解 **C** □□□□　▶TRACK_013

Wasn't Mike in London for a trade show last week?
(A) Yes, I need a round-trip ticket.
(B) At a reception desk in the hotel.
(C) There was a change.

マイクは先週、見本市のためにロンドンにいたのではないのですか。
(A) はい、往復券が必要です。
(B) ホテルの受付でです。
(C) 変更があったんです。

否定疑問文で「マイクは先週、ロンドンにいたのではないのか」と尋ねている。それに対し、「変更があった」と答えることで、ロンドンに滞在する予定が変更されたことを伝えている (C) が正解。

👑**Level Up!**
否定疑問文は、"想定外の出来事"に対する驚きを表す。応答文では、その出来事に対する理由が述べられると予想することができる!

語彙チェック　□ trade show　見本市　□ round-trip　往復の　□ reception desk　受付

音読 □□□ 聞き逃し単語 語 ▶ 語

12 M 🇦🇺 W 🇨🇦　　　　正解 **A** □□□□　▶TRACK_014

I saw a repairperson on the second floor.
(A) We had our fridge fixed.
(B) No, this is my first time.
(C) Some tools and boxes.

2階で修理工を見かけました。
(A) 冷蔵庫を修理してもらいましたよ。
(B) いいえ、初めてなんです。
(C) いくつかの工具と箱です。

「2階で修理工を見かけた」という発言に対し、「冷蔵庫を修理してもらった」と答えることで、修理工を呼んだ理由を説明している (A) が正解。(C) は、repairperson「修理工」という単語から連想される tools「工具」や boxes「箱」という単語を使った、ひっかけの誤答。

語彙チェック　□ repairperson　修理工　□ fridge　冷蔵庫　□ fix　～を修理する

13　W 🇬🇧　M 🇺🇸　　正解 A □□□□　▶TRACK_015

A lot of people have already signed up for the webinar.

(A) The lecturer seems to be renowned.

(B) They don't accept returns, actually.

(C) Correct, please fold it in half.

多くの人がすでにそのウェビナーに申し込んでいます。

(A) 講師が有名な人のようです。

(B) 実は、返品を受け付けていないんです。

(C) その通りです、半分に折ってください。

「多くの人がウェビナーに申し込んでいる」という発言に対して、「講師が有名な人のようだ」と、参加率が高い理由を述べている (A) が正解。

語彙チェック　□ webinar　ウェビナー、オンラインセミナー　□ renowned　名高い　□ fold　〜を折る

14　M 🇦🇺　W 🇬🇧　　正解 B □□□□　▶TRACK_016

Will this rental video be due soon?

(A) Right, I can give you one.

(B) In two days.

(C) The monitor wasn't bright enough.

このレンタルビデオはもうすぐ返却期限になりますか。

(A) そうですね、お渡しできますよ。

(B) 2日後です。

(C) モニターの明るさが十分ではありませんでした。

レンタルビデオの返却期限を尋ねる質問に対し、「2日後」と具体的に期限を答えている (B) が正解。〈in + 期間〉は、「(今から) 〜後に」という意味を表す。

> **Level Up！**
> 質問文後半に登場する due は「期限が来て」という意味の単語。単語が短く聞き逃しやすいので、最後まで集中力を切らさないことがポイント。

語彙チェック　□ due　返却期限が来て　□ bright　明るい

15　W 🇨🇦　M 🇺🇸　　正解 A □□□□　▶TRACK_017

Have the guests arrived yet?

(A) I saw a group of people.

(B) No, the memo is two pages.

(C) Because it is a holiday season.

ゲストはもう到着しましたか。

(A) 人の集団を見かけました。

(B) いいえ、メモは2ページです。

(C) 休暇シーズンだからです。

「ゲストはもう到着したか」と尋ねているのに対し、「人の集団を見かけた」と答えることで、ゲストがすでに到着している可能性があることを遠回しに伝えている (A) が正解。

16　M 🇺🇸　W 🇬🇧　　正解 A □□□□　▶TRACK_018

You've prepared the slides, haven't you?

(A) Ann has done that for me.

(B) Actually, it shifted slightly.

(C) I have a pair of glasses with me.

あなたがスライドを用意したのですよね。

(A) アンが私のためにそれをやってくれました。

(B) 実は、少しずれたんです。

(C) 私は眼鏡を持っています。

問いかけ文は付加疑問文で、スライドを用意したかどうかを確認するもの。これに対し、「アンが私のためにそれをやってくれた」と答えている (A) が正解。done that は prepared the slides のことを指している。(B) は、it が指し示すものが不明なので不正解。

語彙チェック　□ shift　移る　□ slightly　わずかに

17 M 🇦🇺　M 🇺🇸　　正解 **C** ☐☐☐☐　▶TRACK_019

The bus isn't coming, is it?

(A) Yes, he is a qualified driver.

(B) At the gas station nearby.

(C) Shall we share a taxi?

バスが来ないですね。

(A) はい、彼は資格を持った運転手です。

(B) 近くのガソリンスタンドでです。

(C) タクシーをシェアしませんか。

付加疑問文で、バスが来ないことについて話を切り出している。これに対して、「タクシーをシェアしないか」と、バス以外の交通手段を使うことを提案している(C)が正解。Shall we 〜?は「〜しませんか」という提案の表現。

語彙チェック　☐ qualified　資格のある

18 M 🇺🇸　W 🇨🇦　　正解 **A** ☐☐☐☐　▶TRACK_020

Weren't you supposed to work the morning shift?

(A) You must be talking about Dolores.

(B) I used to work for the company.

(C) At ten A.M. on Thursday.

あなたは朝シフトで働くはずではなかったのですか。

(A) Doloresのことを言っているんでしょう。

(B) 以前その会社に勤めていました。

(C) 木曜日の午前10時にです。

問いかけ文は、be supposed to do 〜「〜することになっている」という表現を使った否定疑問文。「あなたは朝シフトで働くはずではなかったのか」という質問に対して、自分ではなく別の人（＝ Dolores）のシフトと勘違いしているに違いないと指摘している(A)が正解。

19 W 🇬🇧　M 🇦🇺　　正解 **B** ☐☐☐☐　▶TRACK_021

Do you mind if I share this photo online?

(A) Yes, I'd be happy to.

(B) Please go ahead.

(C) I don't have anything in mind.

この写真をネット上で共有してもいいですか。

(A) はい、喜んでやります。

(B) どうぞ。

(C) 何も考えがありません。

Do you mind if 〜?「〜してもいいですか」は、相手に許可を求める表現。写真をネット上で共有しても問題ないかと確認しているのに対し、「どうぞ（共有してください）」と答えている(B)が正解。

20 M 🇦🇺 W 🇬🇧 　正解 A □□□□ ▶TRACK_022

Do you want me to show you a map? 　地図をお見せしましょうか。

(A) I've been to the venue before. 　(A) 以前、その会場に行ったことがあります。

(B) At the police station. 　(B) 警察署です。

(C) Of course, here you are. 　(C) もちろん、どうぞ。

Do you want me to do ～?は「～しましょうか」という意味の定型表現。「地図を見せましょうか」という申し出に対して、「以前その会場に行ったことがある」と答えることで、地図は必要ないと伝えている(A)が正解。

👑 **Level Up !**
Do you want me to do ～?は申し出をするときの表現。Do you want to do ～?「あなたは～したいですか」という表現と混同しないように気を付けよう！

語彙チェック □ venue 会場 □ police station 警察署

21 W 🇨🇦 M 🇺🇸 　正解 C □□□□ ▶TRACK_023

Why's the cafeteria being renovated? 　なぜカフェテリアが改装されているのですか。

(A) Let's go to the café. 　(A) カフェに行きましょう。

(B) The drapes do look fine, though. 　(B) カーテンは立派に見えますが。

(C) The company has grown in size. 　(C) 会社の規模が大きくなったのです。

カフェテリアが改装されている理由を尋ねているのに対し、「会社の規模が大きくなった」と答えている(C)が正解。応答でbecauseが使われていなくても、文脈から理由を述べている文だということが分かる。

語彙チェック □ renovate ～を改装する □ drapes （厚手の）カーテン

22 M 🇦🇺 W 🇬🇧 　正解 B □□□□ ▶TRACK_024

Why don't you update the software? 　ソフトウェアを更新してみてはどうですか。

(A) You should wear protective gear. 　(A) 防護服を着用すべきです。

(B) I need to charge my laptop first. 　(B) まずノートパソコンを充電する必要があります。

(C) That up-to-date factory nearby. 　(C) 近くにあるあの最新の工場です。

Why don't you ～?は「～してはどうですか」という提案の表現。「ソフトウェアを更新してはどうか」という提案に対し、「まずノートパソコンを充電する必要がある」と、ソフトウェアの更新の前にすべきことを答えている(B)が正解。

語彙チェック □ update ～を更新する □ protective gear 防護服 □ up-to-date 最新の

23　M🇺🇸　M🇦🇺　正解 A □□□□　▶TRACK_025

Should I take over the wheel?
運転を代わりましょうか。

(A) Let's switch at the next service area.
(A) 次のサービスエリアで交代しましょう。

(B) Yes, they're very useful.
(B) はい、それらはとても便利です。

(C) Roughly 100 dollars per month.
(C) およそ月100ドルです。

「〜しましょうか」という意味のShould I 〜?という表現を使い、「運転を代わろうか」と申し出ている。これに対して、「次のサービスエリアで交代しよう」と答えることで、申し出を受け入れている(A)が正解。

語彙チェック　□ take over the wheel　運転を代わる　□ switch　交代する　□ roughly　およそ

24　M🇺🇸　W🇨🇦　正解 A □□□□　▶TRACK_026

Where's the conference going to be held?
会議はどこで開催される予定ですか。

(A) At the Beacon Hotel near the station.
(A) 駅近くのBeaconホテルでです。

(B) Our shuttle bus service is available.
(B) 弊社のシャトルバスサービスが利用可能です。

(C) I think it's on Monday.
(C) 来週の月曜日だと思います。

会議が開催される予定の場所を尋ねている。これに対して、場所を表す前置詞のatを使い、「駅近くのBeaconホテルで」と会議の開催場所を答えている(A)が正解。

25　W🇬🇧　M🇦🇺　正解 B □□□□　▶TRACK_027

Who's handling the shipping?
誰が発送を担当しているのですか。

(A) It's Mark's delivery.
(A) Markの配達物です。

(B) We're outsourcing that.
(B) 私たちはそれを外注しています。

(C) On the supposed delivery date.
(C) 想定されている配達日にです。

発送作業の担当者を尋ねている。これに対して、担当者の名前を直接伝えるのではなく、「それを外注している」と遠回しに質問に答えている(B)が正解。that は発送作業のことを指す。

👑 Level Up !
Who is が短縮され Who's になっているので、同じ音の"Whose"と聞き間違えないように気を付けよう！

語彙チェック　□ handle　〜を担当する　□ outsource　〜を外注する
　　　　　　　□ supposed　想定された

26 W 🇬🇧　W 🇨🇦　正解 **B** ☐☐☐☐　▶TRACK_028

Whose water bottle is this?

(A) Jack brought them, too.

(B) Mine is the gray one.

(C) Please water the plant.

これは誰の水筒ですか。

(A) Jack もそれらを持ってきました。

(B) 私のはグレーのものです。

(C) その植物に水をあげてください。

水筒の持ち主を尋ねているのに対し、「私のはグレーのものだ」と答えている (B) が正解。自分の水筒の色を答えることで、遠回しにその水筒が自分のものではないということを伝えている。

語彙チェック　☐ water　〜に水をやる

27 W 🇨🇦　M 🇺🇸　正解 **C** ☐☐☐☐　▶TRACK_029

What's your recommendation from the menu?

(A) Absolutely, I highly recommend it.

(B) I'm happy to go with you.

(C) This one won an award.

メニューの中であなたのおすすめは何ですか。

(A) 間違いなく、それを強くおすすめします。

(B) あなたとぜひ一緒に行きたいです。

(C) これは賞を取りました。

おすすめのメニューを尋ねている。これに対して、「これは賞を取った」と答えることで、そのメニューがおすすめであると伝えている (C) が正解。

語彙チェック　☐ recommendation　おすすめのもの

28 M 🇦🇺　W 🇨🇦　正解 **C** ☐☐☐☐　▶TRACK_030

What's this key for?

(A) Ms. Yang is the keynote speaker.

(B) We can meet at the entrance.

(C) You can open the storeroom with it.

この鍵は何のためのものですか。

(A) Yang さんが基調講演者です。

(B) 入り口で待ち合わせができます。

(C) それで物置を開けることができます。

What's 〜 for? は「〜は何のためのものですか」と、目的や用途を尋ねる表現。「この鍵は何のためのものか」という質問に対し、「それで物置を開けることができる」と使用用途を答えている (C) が正解。it は問いかけ文の this key を指している。

Level Up!

What から始まる質問は、What 〜 for?「何のために」や What time 〜?「何時」など、後ろに続く言葉によって意味合いが変わる。最後まで聞き取って判断しよう。

語彙チェック　☐ keynote speaker　基調講演者　☐ storeroom　物置

29 W 🇨🇦 M 🇺🇸 　正解 B □ □ □ □ ▶ TRACK_031

Which of the fabrics do you prefer?
(A) They took us to the brickworks.
(B) Are there more options?
(C) Because the budget is limited.

あなたはどの生地が好きですか。
(A) 彼らは、れんが工場に連れて行ってくれました。
(B) もっと他の選択肢はありますか。
(C) 予算が限られているためです。

Which of 〜 「どの〜」を使い、生地の好みを尋ねている。これに対して、「もっと他の選択肢はあるか」と、提示されている生地以外からも選ぶことができるかどうかを尋ねている (B) が正解。

語彙チェック □ fabric　生地　□ brickworks　れんが工場

30 M 🇦🇺 W 🇨🇦 　正解 C □ □ □ □ ▶ TRACK_032

How many attendees have answered the questionnaire?
(A) Attendance at the orientation is free.
(B) I need an additional ten items.
(C) The collection box is almost full.

何人の参加者がアンケートに答えてくれましたか。
(A) オリエンテーションへの参加は自由です。
(B) 追加で10点必要です。
(C) 回収箱はほぼ満杯です。

How many 〜 ? は「数」を尋ねる表現。アンケートの回答人数を尋ねる質問に対し、「回収箱はほぼ満杯だ」と答えることで、たくさんの人がアンケートに回答してくれたことを伝えている (C) が正解。

🏆 Level Up !
(B)は「数」を答えているが、アンケートの回答人数ではないので不正解。

31 W 🇬🇧 M 🇦🇺 　正解 C □ □ □ □ ▶ TRACK_033

I have a package to send.
(A) Install the light, please.
(B) I ordered office supplies yesterday.
(C) Let me weigh it then.

送りたい荷物があります。
(A) 照明を取り付けてください。
(B) 昨日、事務用品を注文しました。
(C) それなら、それの重さを量らせてください。

「送りたい荷物がある」という発言に対して、「それの重さを量らせてほしい」と答えている (C) が正解。it は a package を指しており、文末の then 「それなら、その場合は」とともに、相手の発言を受けての応答であることが分かる。

語彙チェック □ install　〜を取り付ける　□ weigh　〜の重さを量る

Part 3

音読 □□□　カンベキ理解　/11 ▶ /11

会話 ▶TRACK_035　問題 ▶TRACK_036

カンベキ理解 ▶TRACK_K01

W 🇬🇧　**M** 🇦🇺

Questions 32 through 34 refer to the following conversation.

カンベキ理解		
1	□□	W: Hi. Um... do you have a reservation for Dalton?
2	□□	I'm supposed to meet some coworkers here.
3	□□	I'm running a little late.
4	□□	M: Well, we don't take reservations on Thursdays,
5	□□	so I can't tell you whether or not they're here.
6	□□	W: I see. I lost my phone. That's why I'm late.
7	□□	I can't call them to check.
8	□□	Um... would you mind if I walked around the tables to see if they're here?
9	□□	M: Not at all.
10	□□	Just a moment.
11	□□	I'll have one of the waiters show you around.

問題32-34は次の会話に関するものです。

女性：こんにちは。ええと…Daltonの名前での予約はありますか。私はここで何人かの仕事仲間に会うことになっています。少し遅れてしまいました。

男性：そうですね、木曜日はご予約を受け付けておりませんので、いらっしゃるかどうかは分かりません。

女性：分かりました。電話を失くしたせいで遅れてしまったのです。彼らに電話をかけて確認することができません。うーん…テーブルを見て回って、彼らがここにいるかどうかを確認してもよろしいですか。

男性：構いませんよ。少々お待ちくださいませ。ウェイターの1人に案内させますね。

語彙チェック　□ be supposed to *do*　〜することになっている　□ coworker　仕事仲間、同僚　□ that's why 〜　そういうわけで〜
□ Would you mind if 〜?　〜しても構いませんか。　□ see if 〜　〜かどうか確かめる
□ show 〜 around　〜を案内して回る

32

正解 A ☐☐☐☐

Where most likely are the speakers?

(A) At a restaurant

(B) At an art gallery

(C) At a car rental agency

(D) At a fitness club

話し手たちはどこにいると考えられますか。

(A) レストラン

(B) 美術館

(C) レンタカー会社

(D) スポーツクラブ

👑 **Level Up!**
会話の場所を推測する問題は、根拠が明確に述べられるとは限らない。会話全体に散らばるキーワードから、場所をイメージして答えよう。

女性が冒頭でdo you have a reservation for Dalton?と尋ね、男性が木曜の予約は取っていないと言っている。また、女性は後半でwould you mind if I walked around the tables to see if they're here?と述べ、同僚が店内にいるかどうかを確かめるためにテーブルを見て回ってよいかを男性に聞いている。さらに、最後に男性が「ウェイターの1人に案内させる」と言っている。これらの発言から、これはレストランでの会話であると推測できるので、正解は(A)。

33

正解 B ☐☐☐☐

Why is the woman most likely late?

(A) She did not check a train schedule.

(B) She was looking for her telephone.

(C) She had some car trouble.

(D) She was in a meeting.

女性はなぜ遅れていると考えられますか。

(A) 電車の時刻表を確認しなかった。

(B) 自分の電話を探していた。

(C) 車のトラブルがあった。

(D) 会議に出席していた。

女性は会話の半ばでI lost my phone. That's why I'm late.と述べ、遅れたのは自分の電話を失くしてしまったからだと説明している。つまり、女性は電話を探すのに時間がかかって遅れたと考えられるので、正解は(B)。

34

正解 C ☐☐☐☐

What does the man say he will do?

(A) Provide a map

(B) Reschedule an appointment

(C) Call a colleague

(D) Print out some records

男性は何をするつもりだと言っていますか。

(A) 地図を渡す

(B) 予定を変更する

(C) 同僚を呼ぶ

(D) いくつかのデータを印刷する

女性は会話の後半で、テーブルを回ってお店に仕事仲間がいるかどうかを確認したいと伝えている。それに対して男性は、問題ないと述べた後、I'll have one of the waiters show you around. と答え、従業員に店内を案内させることを申し出ている。よって、正解は(C)。one of the waiters「ウェイターの1人」が、選択肢では a colleague「同僚」に言い換えられている。

語彙チェック　☐ reschedule　〜の予定を変更する　☐ record　データ、記録

M 🇺🇸　W 🇨🇦

Questions 35 through 37 refer to the following conversation.

カンベキ理解		
1	□□	M: Flanders. How can I help you?
2	□□	W: Hi. It's Margaret Wells.
3	□□	<u>I'm supposed to bring my car in for service this afternoon.</u>
4	□□	M: Yes. We're expecting you in about twenty minutes.
5	□□	W: Well, <u>I'm stuck in traffic.</u>
6	□□	<u>My map app's telling me I won't be there for an hour.</u>
7	□□	M: <u>In that case, why don't you bring it in tomorrow instead?</u>
8	□□	We'll probably be closed by the time you get here.
9	□□	W: OK. I'll come on my way to work.

問題35-37は次の会話に関するものです。

男性：Flandersです。どのようなご用件でしょうか。

女性：こんにちは、Margaret Wellsです。今日の午後、車を修理に出すことになっているのですが。

男性：はい。およそ20分後にお越しになりますよね。

女性：あの、渋滞に巻き込まれたんです。地図アプリを見る限り、1時間後でないとお店に着けなさそうです。

男性：それでしたら、今日ではなく明日お持ちになってはどうでしょうか。お客様がご到着されるころには、もう閉店しているかもしれません。

女性：分かりました。仕事の途中に寄ります。

語彙チェック　□ be supposed to *do*　〜することになっている　□ expect　（人）が来るのを待つ
　　　　　　□ be stuck in traffic　渋滞に巻き込まれる　□ bring 〜 in　〜を持ち込む　□ instead　代わりに
　　　　　　□ on *one's* way to 〜　〜に向かう途中で

35

Where does the man most likely work?
(A) At a radio studio
(B) At a doctor's office
(C) At an auto repair shop
(D) At a bakery

男性はどこで働いていると考えられますか。
(A) ラジオ番組のスタジオ
(B) 病院
(C) 自動車修理工場
(D) パン屋

冒頭で男性が店名を述べ、女性に用件を尋ねているのに対し、顧客である女性はI'm supposed to bring my car in for service this afternoon.と答えている。顧客が店に車を持ち込もうとしていることから、男性は自動車の修理関係の店で働いていると推測できる。よって、正解は(C)。

36

Why is the woman concerned?
(A) She will arrive later than expected.
(B) She does not know the man's address.
(C) Her phone battery will not last long.
(D) Her car has broken down.

女性はなぜ心配していますか。
(A) 彼女は予定より遅れて到着する。
(B) 彼女は男性の住所を知らない。
(C) 彼女の携帯電話のバッテリーは長く持ちそうにない。
(D) 彼女の車が故障した。

男性が「およそ20分後にお待ちしております」と女性に伝えている。それに対し、女性はI'm stuck in trafficと渋滞にはまっていることを伝え、My map app's telling me I won't be there for an hour.と述べている。約束していた時間より遅れて到着することを心配していると分かるので、正解は(A)。I won't be there for an hourは、「あと1時間は着くことができない」、つまり「到着までにあと1時間はかかる」ということ。

語彙チェック □ last 持ちこたえる、続く □ break down 故障する

37

What does the man say the woman should do?
(A) Call her insurance company
(B) Rent a vehicle
(C) Speak with a colleague
(D) Come on another day

男性は女性がすべきことは何だと言っていますか。
(A) 保険会社に電話する
(B) 乗り物を借りる
(C) 同僚と話す
(D) 別の日に来る

渋滞に巻き込まれ予定時間に店に到着できそうにない女性に対して、男性はIn that case, why don't you bring it in tomorrow instead? と伝え、来店を次の日にしてはどうかと提案している。よって、正解は(D)。

語彙チェック □ insurance company 保険会社 □ vehicle 乗り物 □ colleague 同僚

33

W 🇨🇦　**M** 🇦🇺

Questions 38 through 40 refer to the following conversation.

カンベキ理解	
1 □□	W: Excuse me.
2 □□	Could you tell me... Does this bus go to Valleyview?
3 □□	I can't seem to find a list of stops.
4 □□	M: I don't know either, I'm afraid.
5 □□	I'm looking for the information desk, but I can't find it.
6 □□	I have to get to Valleyview by ten A.M. for the opening of the new library.
7 □□	I suppose that's where you're headed, too.
8 □□	W: I am.
9 □□	I have to cover it for an architectural magazine.
10 □□	M: Would you like to share a taxi?
11 □□	It shouldn't cost too much.
12 □□	W: Sounds good to me.

問題38-40は次の会話に関するものです。

女性：すみません。教えていただきたいのですが…、このバスはValleyviewまで行きますか。停留所のリストが見つからないんです。

男性：あいにく私も知りません。案内所を探しているんですが、見つからないんです。新しい図書館の開館式があるので、午前10時までにValleyviewに着かなければならないんです。おそらくあなたもそこに向かうつもりかと思いますが。

女性：そうです。建築専門誌向けの取材があるんです。

男性：タクシーに相乗りするのはどうでしょうか。そんなに高くはないはずです。

女性：いいですね。

語彙チェック　□ seem to do　〜するように思われる　□ I'm afraid　残念ながら　□ be headed　向かう　□ cover　〜を取材する　□ architectural　建築の　□ share a taxi　タクシーに相乗りする　□ cost　費用がかかる

38

正解 B ▢▢▢▢

What does the man want to find?

(A) A ticket booth

(B) An information desk

(C) A food stall

(D) A news agency

男性は何を探したいと思っていますか。

(A)チケット売り場

(B)案内所

(C)屋台

(D)新聞社

「このバスはValleyviewまで行きますか」と尋ねる女性に対し、男性はI'm looking for the information desk, but I can't find it. と答え、「（バスの行き先について尋ねることができる）案内所を探している」と伝えている。よって、正解は(B)。

語彙チェック ▢ stall　屋台

39

正解 D ▢▢▢▢

Who most likely is the woman?

(A) A librarian

(B) An architect

(C) A salesperson

(D) A journalist

女性は誰だと考えられますか。

(A)図書館員

(B)建築家

(C)販売員

(D)ジャーナリスト

女性は男性に「あなたもそこ（＝新しく開館する図書館）に向かうつもりかと思いますが」と話しかけられた後、それに同意し、さらにI have to cover it for an architectural magazine. と述べ、図書館に行く目的は雑誌の取材だと伝えている。雑誌の取材という仕事から連想される女性の職業は、(D)のジャーナリスト。

Level Up!
職業を推測する問題では、業務内容に関する発言を聞き取ることがポイント。その職業ではどんな仕事をするのかを整理しておこう！

40

正解 D ▢▢▢▢

What does the man suggest?

(A) Getting something to eat

(B) Asking for assistance

(C) Checking a price

(D) Taking a taxi together

男性は何を提案していますか。

(A)何か食べるものを手に入れること

(B)助けを求めること

(C)値段を確認すること

(D)一緒にタクシーに乗ること

女性も自分と同じ目的地へ向かうということが分かった後、男性はWould you like to share a taxi? と、2人が行く図書館までタクシーに相乗りすることを提案している。よって、正解は(D)。本文のshare a taxiが、選択肢ではTaking a taxi together と言い換えられている。

語彙チェック ▢ ask for 〜　〜を求める

会話 ▶TRACK_041　問題 ▶TRACK_042
カンベキ理解 ▶TRACK_K04

M 🇦🇺　W 🇬🇧

Questions 41 through 43 refer to the following conversation.

カンベキ理解		
1	□□	M: Hi. It's Cole Whitman from Sanders Appliances calling.
2	□□	W: Oh. Hi, Mr. Whitman. I was just about to call you.
3	□□	We've already mounted the television on the wall,
4	□□	but I cannot find the remote control.
5	□□	M: Yes, that's what I was calling about.
6	□□	I'm sorry for the inconvenience.
7	□□	That one was a display model,
8	□□	and we forgot to put the remote in the box when we repackaged it.
9	□□	I was going to suggest I bring the remote to your house today.
10	□□	W: I have a meeting near your store in the afternoon.
11	□□	I can pick up the remote then.

問題41-43は次の会話に関するものです。

男性：もしもし、Sanders電化製品店のCole Whitman です。

女性：ああ、こんにちは、Whitman さん。ちょうどお電話しようと思っていたところです。我々はもう壁にテレビを取り付けたのですが、リモコンが見つからなくて。

男性：はい、そのことでお電話したんです。ご迷惑をおかけして申し訳ございません。そちらの商品はディスプレイモデルで、包装し直すときにリモコンを箱に入れるのを忘れてしまいました。今日、あなたのご自宅にリモコンをお持ちしようと思っているのですが。

女性：午後、あなたのお店の近くで会議があるんです。そのときにリモコンを受け取ることができますよ。

語彙チェック　□ be about to *do*　まさに〜しようとするところである　□ mount *A* on *B*　AをBに取り付ける
□ remote control　リモコン　□ repackage　〜を包装し直す　□ pick up 〜　〜を手に入れる

41

正解 B □□□□

What does the woman say she has done?
(A) Filled out a form
(B) Installed a device
(C) Called a store
(D) Returned an order

その女性は何をしたと言っていますか。
(A) 用紙に記入した
(B) 機器を取り付けた
(C) 店に電話をした
(D) 注文を返品した

👑 **Level Up !**
televisionのような具体的な単語が、device といった抽象的な単語に言い換えられるケースは頻出なので、しっかり押さえておこう。

女性は男性に対して、We've already mounted the television on the wall と言っている。よって、正解は (B)。本文の mounted the television「テレビを取り付けた」が、選択肢では Installed a device「機器を取り付けた」に言い換えられている。

語彙チェック □ install 〜を取り付ける □ device 機器

42

正解 C □□□□

Why is the man calling?
(A) To request some assistance
(B) To recommend some repairs
(C) To discuss a missing part
(D) To apologize for a scheduling error

男性はなぜ電話していますか。
(A) 手伝いを依頼するため
(B) 修理を勧めるため
(C) 不足している部品について話すため
(D) スケジュールの誤りに対して謝罪するため

「リモコンが見つからない」と言っている女性に対し、男性は「そのことで電話した」と述べ、we forgot to put the remote in the box when we repackaged it と続けている。男性が電話しているのは不足している部品（＝箱に入れ忘れたリモコン）について話すためだと分かるので、正解は (C)。

語彙チェック □ missing 欠けている

43

正解 B □□□□

Why does the woman say, "I have a meeting near your store in the afternoon"?
(A) To request delivery
(B) To turn down an offer
(C) To reschedule an appointment
(D) To share an address

女性はなぜ"I have a meeting near your store in the afternoon"と言っていますか。
(A) 配達を依頼するため
(B) 申し出を断るため
(C) 約束の時間を変更するため
(D) 住所を共有するため

リモコンを女性の家に持っていくことを提案している男性に対し、女性は I have a meeting near your store in the afternoon.「午後、あなたのお店の近くで会議があるんです」と言い、その後 I can pick up the remote then. と続けている。会議のついでに自分が取りに行けることから、「自宅にリモコンを届ける」という男性の申し出を断っていることが分かるので、正解は (B)。

語彙チェック □ turn down 〜 〜を断る □ reschedule 〜の予定を変更する

W 🇬🇧　M 🇺🇸

Questions 44 through 46 refer to the following conversation.

カンペキ理解	
1 ☐☐	W: We have a request from Ms. Alicia Day for special permission to host a party at our restaurant.
2 ☐☐	What do you think?
3 ☐☐	M: Well, I don't know if you know this or not,
4 ☐☐	but Ms. Alicia Day is a very well-known online video creator.
5 ☐☐	She has a vlog called *Day Trips*. She has millions of subscribers,
6 ☐☐	and the businesses she recommends usually get a lot of attention afterward.
7 ☐☐	W: I know that vlog!
8 ☐☐	This could be big for us.
9 ☐☐	M: That's what I mean.
10 ☐☐	We should let her have the party.
11 ☐☐	She'll be making a video there and uploading it next month.
12 ☐☐	I'll make up a list of conditions for her to sign.

問題44-46は次の会話に関するものです。

女性：Alicia Day さんから、私たちのレストランでパーティーを開催する特別な許可の依頼がありました。どう思いますか。

男性：ええと、ご存知かどうか分かりませんが、Alicia Day さんはとても有名なオンラインビデオクリエイターなんです。彼女は *Day Trips* というビデオブログを持っています。彼女は何百万人もの購読者がいて、彼女が薦めるビジネスはたいていその後大きな注目を浴びるんですよ。

女性：そのビデオブログ、知っています！　これは私たちにとって大きな意味を持つかもしれないですね。

男性：そういうことです。彼女にパーティーを開催してもらうべきですね。彼女は来月にそこでビデオを撮って、アップロードすることになります。彼女が署名するための条件リストを私が用意しておきますよ。

語彙チェック　☐ permission　許可　☐ well-known　よく知られた　☐ subscriber　購読者　☐ attention　注目　☐ afterward　その後で　☐ make up ～　～を用意する　☐ condition　条件

44

正解 A □□□□

What are the speakers discussing?

(A) A customer's request

(B) A news story

(C) A new regulation

(D) A party invitation

話し手たちは何について話し合っていますか。

(A)顧客からの依頼

(B)ニュース記事

(C)新しい規則

(D)パーティーの招待状

女性は冒頭で、We have a request from Ms. Alicia Day for special permission to host a party at our restaurant.と述べている。our restaurantと言っていることから話し手たちはレストランの従業員だと分かるので、Alicia Dayさんは話し手たちにとっての顧客にあたると分かる。よって、正解は(A)。話し手たちがDayさんのパーティーに誘われているわけではないので、(D)は内容と合わない。

👑 Level Up！
本問では、会話内でのMs. Alicia Dayが選択肢でcustomerと言い換えられている。明確な根拠はないが、話の流れからサービスの受け手（顧客）側なのか、提供側なのかを判断する必要がある！

語彙チェック □ regulation　規則

45

正解 A □□□□

What does the woman mean when she says, "This could be big for us"?

(A) They have been given an important opportunity.

(B) They will be very busy in preparation.

(C) They should hire some additional employees.

(D) They will have to make an extra order.

"This could be big for us"という発言で、女性は何を意図していますか。

(A)彼らは重要な機会を与えられた。

(B)彼らは準備でとても忙しくなる。

(C)彼らは何人か追加で従業員を雇うべきである。

(D)彼らは追加注文をしなければならない。

男性は会話の半ばでMs. Alicia Day is a very well-known online video creatorと述べ、さらにthe businesses she recommends usually get a lot of attention afterwardと続けている。Dayさんの知名度や影響力に関する話を受けて、女性がThis could be big for us.と発言していることから、女性は自分たちのレストランが注目を浴びる重要な機会になると考えていることが分かる。よって、正解は(A)。

語彙チェック □ be busy in ～　～で忙しい　□ preparation　準備

46

正解 D □□□□

What will Ms. Day most likely do next month?

(A) Travel overseas

(B) Sign a contract

(C) Expand her business

(D) Produce a video

Dayさんは来月何をすると考えられますか。

(A)海外旅行をする

(B)契約書に署名する

(C)事業を拡大する

(D)ビデオを制作する

男性は最後の発言で「Dayさんにパーティーを開催してもらうべきだ」と述べた後、She'll be making a video there and uploading it next month.と続けている。このSheはDayさんのことを表しているので、正解は(D)。本文のmaking a videoが、選択肢ではProduce a videoに言い換えられている。

語彙チェック □ overseas　海外に　□ sign　～に署名する　□ expand　～を拡大する

M 🇦🇺　W 🇬🇧

Questions 47 through 49 refer to the following conversation.

カンペキ理解

1	☐☐	M: Hi, this is Morris.
2	☐☐	This is embarrassing, but I need to reschedule our meeting.
3	☐☐	I can get over to the apartments at about eleven.
4	☐☐	Will that be alright?
5	☐☐	W: That's fine,
6	☐☐	but we need to get the smoke alarms installed in each apartment by three o'clock.
7	☐☐	The city is sending around an inspector at four,
8	☐☐	and if they're not in place then, the building will be fined.
9	☐☐	M: No problem. I might be there earlier.
10	☐☐	I can't find the key to the garage door at our office, though.
11	☐☐	As soon as I find it, I'll get in the truck and head over.

問題47-49は次の会話に関するものです。

男性：こんにちは、Morris です。困ったことに、待ち合わせの予定を変更する必要があります。11時ごろにアパートに行くことができますが、それで大丈夫でしょうか。

女性：それは大丈夫ですが、3時までに各アパートに煙探知機を設置しないといけないんです。4時に市から検査官が来るので、そのときに決まった場所に設置されていないと罰金が科せられてしまいます。

男性：大丈夫です。もっと早く着くかもしれません。でも、会社の車庫のドアの鍵が見つからないんです。見つかり次第すぐに、トラックに乗って向かいますね。

語彙チェック　☐ embarrassing　やっかいな、困った　☐ get over to ～　～へ行く　☐ smoke alarm　煙探知機
☐ send around ～　～を派遣する　☐ inspector　検査官　☐ in place　設置されて　☐ fine　～に罰金を科す
☐ garage　車庫　☐ head over　向かう

47

正解 D ▢▢▢▢

Why is the man calling the woman?

(A) To announce a price change

(B) To suggest some products

(C) To thank a supplier

(D) To postpone an appointment

男性はなぜ女性に電話していますか。

(A) 価格の変更を知らせるため

(B) いくつかの製品を提案するため

(C) 供給業者に感謝するため

(D) 約束を延期するため

男性は冒頭でThis is embarrassing, but I need to reschedule our meeting.と述べている。その後、予定変更が問題ないかどうか女性に尋ねており、女性は時間までに作業が終わるかを心配している。このことから、男性は待ち合わせの時間を遅らせたいと分かるので、電話した理由としてふさわしいのは(D)。本文のreschedule our meeting「待ち合わせの予定を変更する」が、選択肢でpostpone an appointment「約束を延期する」と言い換えられている。

語彙チェック   □ supplier　供給業者　□ postpone　〜を延期する

48

正解 C ▢▢▢▢

What concern does the woman have?

(A) A software is too complicated to use.

(B) Few staff members are available.

(C) An extra cost may be generated.

(D) There is a traffic congestion.

女性はどんな心配をしていますか。

(A) ソフトウェアが複雑すぎて使えない。

(B) 手の空いているスタッフがほとんどいない。

(C) 余分な費用が生じるかもしれない。

(D) 交通渋滞がある。

女性は「3時までに各アパートに煙探知機を設置しないといけない」と述べた後、4時に検査官が煙探知機の確認に来ることを伝え、if they're not in place then, the building will be finedと続けている。罰金が科せられる、つまり余分な費用が生じてしまう可能性があることを懸念していると分かるので、正解は(C)。

👑 Level Up !
罰金が科せられることがつまり「余分な費用が生じる」ということだと気付けるか、という点が試されている。単語を正確に聞き取った上で、瞬時に、そして抽象度を上げて内容を理解する力が求められる！

語彙チェック   □ complicated　複雑な　□ available　手の空いている　□ generate　〜が生じる　□ traffic congestion　交通渋滞

49

正解 A ▢▢▢▢

What will the man do next?

(A) Look for a key

(B) Repair a vehicle

(C) Check a deadline

(D) Set up some equipment

男性は次に何をするつもりですか。

(A) 鍵を探す

(B) 乗り物を修理する

(C) 締め切りを確認する

(D) 装置を据える

男性は会話の最後で、I can't find the key to the garage door at our office, though. As soon as I find it, I'll get in the truck and head over.と述べている。「鍵が見つかり次第すぐに向かう」と言っているので、男性はまず鍵を探すということが分かる。よって、正解は(A)。

語彙チェック   □ deadline　締め切り　□ equipment　装置

W1 🇬🇧　**W2** 🇨🇦　**M** 🇦🇺

Questions 50 through 52 refer to the following conversation with three speakers.

カンペキ理解		
1	☐☐	W1: Excuse me.
2	☐☐	Um... will we be able to see Harper Wylde's office during the tour?
3	☐☐	W2: We read in the *Sunday Times* that it's recently been made accessible to the general public.
4	☐☐	It's one of the reasons for our trip.
5	☐☐	M: I'm happy to say that we will be visiting the home Ms. Wylde lived in when she wrote some of her most popular novels.
6	☐☐	W1: Good.
7	☐☐	Could we see some reviews on this tour?
8	☐☐	M: There is a section on our Web site.
9	☐☐	You can get there by scanning the 2D barcode here.

問題50-52は3人の話し手による次の会話に関するものです。

女性1：失礼します。ええと…ツアー中にHarper Wyldeの事務所は見られますか。

女性2：*Sunday Times*で読んだのですが、最近一般公開されたようです。それが今回の私たちの旅の目的の1つでもあります。

男性　：うれしいことに我々は、最も人気の小説をWyldeさんが書いたときに住んでいた家を訪れることになりますよ。

女性1：いいですね。このツアーのレビューを見ることはできますか。

男性　：私たちのウェブサイトに評価の欄がございます。こちらの二次元バーコードをスキャンしていただくとご覧いただけます。

語彙チェック　☐ accessible　行くことができる　☐ general public　一般大衆　☐ scan　〜をスキャンする

50

正解 A ☐☐☐☐

What are the speakers mainly discussing?

(A) A tour of historic places
(B) A new government regulation
(C) An office renovation plan
(D) An opening of a new theater

話し手たちは主に何について話し合っていますか。

(A) 歴史上有名な場所へのツアー
(B) 新しい政府の規制
(C) 事務所の改修計画
(D) 新しい劇場の開館

1人目の女性はHarper Wyldeという人物の名前を出し、will we be able to see Harper Wylde's office during the tour? と尋ねている。さらに、同じ旅行仲間と考えられる2人目の女性は、Wyldeさんの事務所が最近一般公開されていることについて伝えている。これに対し、旅行会社の社員と思われる男性は、I'm happy to say that we will be visiting the home Ms. Wylde lived in when she wrote some of her most popular novels. と答えている。3人の話し手たちは、有名な人物であるWyldeさんにちなんだ場所へのツアーについて話し合っていると分かるので、正解は(A)。

語彙チェック　☐ historic　歴史的に有名な　☐ renovation　改修、修繕

51

正解 C ☐☐☐☐

Who most likely is Ms. Wylde?

(A) A tourist
(B) A journalist
(C) An author
(D) An entertainer

Wyldeさんは誰だと考えられますか。

(A) 観光客
(B) ジャーナリスト
(C) 作家
(D) 芸人

男性はWyldeさんについて、we will be visiting the home Ms. Wylde lived in when she wrote some of her most popular novelsと言及している。「小説を書いていた」という情報から推測できる職業は作家なので、正解は(C)。観光客とは女性2人のことなので、(A)は不正解。

52

正解 B ☐☐☐☐

What does the man say is available on a Web site?

(A) The rate for a service
(B) Comments from customers
(C) An updated schedule
(D) A registration form

男性はウェブサイトで何を見ることができると言っていますか。

(A) サービスの料金
(B) 顧客からのコメント
(C) 最新のスケジュール
(D) 登録用紙

1人目の女性がCould we see some reviews on this tour? と尋ねているのに対し、男性はThere is a section on our Web site. と答えている。ツアーを体験した顧客のレビュー欄がウェブサイト上にあると分かるので、正解は(B)。本文にあるreviewsが、選択肢ではComments from customersに言い換えられている。

語彙チェック　☐ rate　料金

M 🇺🇸　W 🇨🇦

Questions 53 through 55 refer to the following conversation.

カンベキ理解

1 □□　M: It looks like the rehearsals are going well.
2 □□　　The director seems pleased with the actors' progress.
3 □□　　Only one month until opening night, though.
4 □□　　Oh... sorry about the holdup on those new cameras.
5 □□　　I know you want them so the actors can check their performances.
6 □□　W: Yes. I heard they'll be a couple of weeks.
7 □□　　We'll have to make do with our mobile phone cameras for now.
8 □□　　The quality isn't great — especially the sound.
9 □□　M: Well, you'll love these new cameras when they get here.
10 □□　　The reviews online are really good.
11 □□　　The audio quality in particular is getting a lot of attention.
12 □□　W: Something to look forward to, then!

問題53-55は次の会話に関するものです。

男性：リハーサルは順調なようですね。演出家も俳優の成長ぶりに満足しているようです。初日まであと1カ月しかないのですが。そうでした…新しいカメラに関しては遅れが生じていてすみません。役者が自身の演技を確認できるよう、それらが欲しいということは分かっているのですが。

女性：そうなんです。2週間ほどかかると聞いています。今は携帯電話のカメラで間に合わせるしかありません。質はよくないですね─特に音質です。

男性：そうですね、これらの新しいカメラが届いたらきっと気に入りますよ。オンラインでの評判がとてもいいんです。特に音質が大きく注目されています。

女性：それは楽しみですね！

語彙チェック　□ rehearsal　リハーサル　□ progress　進歩、成長　□ holdup　遅れ　□ make do with ~　~で間に合わせる　□ audio　音声の、オーディオの　□ in particular　特に　□ attention　注目

44

53

正解 **D** ☐☐☐☐

What are the speakers discussing?

(A) Stage lights

(B) Printing machines

(C) A speaker system

(D) Video cameras

話し手たちは何について話し合っていますか。

(A) 舞台の照明

(B) 印刷機

(C) スピーカーシステム

(D) ビデオカメラ

男性は sorry about the holdup on those new cameras と述べ、「役者が自身の演技を確認できるよう、それらが欲しいということは分かっている」と続けている。その後も、カメラの質や評判について話しているので、正解は (D)。

54

正解 **A** ☐☐☐☐

What problem does the woman mention?

(A) The temporary equipment's sound quality is poor.

(B) The cost is much higher than expected.

(C) An event may be postponed due to a shipment delay.

(D) An order form was not completed.

女性は何の問題について述べていますか。

(A) 仮の機器の音質が悪い。

(B) 費用が予想よりはるかに高い。

(C) 出荷の遅れによりイベントが延期になるかもしれない。

(D) 注文書が未記入だった。

女性は We'll have to make do with our mobile phone cameras for now. と述べ、新しいカメラの代わりに今は携帯電話のカメラで間に合わせるしかないことを伝えている。そして、The quality isn't great — especially the sound. と続けている。よって、正解は (A)。間に合わせで使う携帯電話のカメラのことを、選択肢では temporary equipment と抽象的に言い換えられている。

語彙チェック ☐ temporary 仮の、一時的な ☐ postpone 〜を延期する

55

正解 **D** ☐☐☐☐

What does the man say about the new equipment?

(A) It is very durable.

(B) It is more economical.

(C) It will be shipped from overseas.

(D) It received positive reviews.

男性は新しい機器について何と言っていますか。

(A) とても耐久性がある。

(B) より経済的である。

(C) 海外から発送される予定である。

(D) 肯定的な評価を受けた。

男性は女性が新しい機器（＝カメラ）を気に入るだろうと述べ、The reviews online are really good. と伝えている。新しいカメラが肯定的な評価を受けたことが分かるので、正解は (D)。

語彙チェック ☐ durable 耐久性のある ☐ economical 経済的な、安い

W 🇬🇧　M1 🇺🇸　M2 🇦🇺

Questions 56 through 58 refer to the following conversation with three speakers.

カンベキ理解		
1	□□	W: I'm very impressed with the SRG delivery van.
2	□□	I think it'll be perfect for my business.
3	□□	Our grand opening is May sixth.
4	□□	Can you get it to me by then?
5	□□	M1: That might be a bit tight, I'm afraid.
6	□□	I think the earliest we can do is around May sixteenth.
7	□□	We might have a solution, though.
8	□□	Jeff, what do you think?
9	□□	M2: Um... Oh, I have an idea.
10	□□	We have a demonstration model that we could let you use until your van arrives.
11	□□	How about that?
12	□□	W: That sounds reasonable.
13	□□	I think I'm ready to go ahead with the purchase agreement.

問題56-58は3人の話し手による次の会話に関するものです。

女性 ：SRG社の配達用トラックにはとても感心しています。私のお店にぴったりだと思います。グランドオープンは5月6日です。それまでに車を届けていただけますか。

男性1：恐れ入りますが、それは少し厳しいかもしれません。最短でも5月16日ごろになるかと思います。解決策はあるかもしれませんが、Jeff、どう思いますか。

男性2：ええと…、あ、考えがございます。あなたのトラックが到着するまでの間、お使いいただける試乗車がございます。そちらはいかがでしょうか。

女性 ：それは合理的ですね。もう私は購入契約の手続きに進む心の準備ができたと思います。

語彙チェック　□ delivery van　配達用トラック　□ tight　きつい　□ solution　解決策　□ demonstration model　試乗車
　　　　　　　□ reasonable　合理的な、納得できる　□ I'm ready to *do*　〜する準備ができている
　　　　　　　□ go ahead with 〜　〜を進める　□ agreement　契約

56

正解 B ☐☐☐☐

What are the speakers discussing?

(A) A business idea

(B) Product availability

(C) A clothing item

(D) A menu update

話し手たちは何について話し合っていますか。

(A) 仕事のアイディア

(B) 商品の入手可能状況

(C) 衣料品

(D) メニューの更新

冒頭で女性は、SRG社の配達用トラックに感心したこと、またそれが自身のお店で使うのにぴったりであると感じたことを述べている。さらに女性はグランドオープンの日程が5月6日だと伝え、Can you get it to me by then? と続けている。1人目の男性はそれに対しI think the earliest we can do is around May sixteenth. と答え、最短でトラックを届けられる日時を示している。商品（＝トラック）がいつ女性の元へ渡るかについてやり取りをしているので、正解は(B)。

57

正解 D ☐☐☐☐

What does Jeff offer to do?

(A) Provide some instructions

(B) Introduce a colleague

(C) Reduce a price

(D) Lend a vehicle

Jeffは何をすることを申し出ていますか。

(A) 指示を与える

(B) 同僚を紹介する

(C) 値段を下げる

(D) 乗り物を貸す

女性が希望する日にちまでにトラックを届けることが難しいという状況を受けて、Jeffと呼ばれている2人目の男性は「考えがある」と述べ、We have a demonstration model that we could let you use until your van arrives. How about that? と続けている。希望のトラックが届くまで試乗車を貸すということを申し出ているので、正解は(D)。

語彙チェック ☐ instructions 指示

58

正解 D ☐☐☐☐

What will the woman probably do next?

(A) Write a product review

(B) Check a budget

(C) Place an advertisement

(D) Make a contract

女性はおそらく次に何をしますか。

(A) 製品レビューを書く

(B) 予算を確認する

(C) 広告を出す

(D) 契約をする

女性は、希望のトラックが届くまで試乗車を使うことができると聞き、I think I'm ready to go ahead with the purchase agreement. と述べている。この発言から、このあと女性は購入契約の手続きに進むと考えられるので、正解は(D)。

語彙チェック ☐ place （広告など）を出す

M 🇦🇺　W 🇨🇦

Questions 59 through 61 refer to the following conversation.

カンベキ理解		
1	□□	M: I just had a call from *The Hillford Times*.
2	□□	It's raising its advertising rates again.
3	□□	W: Oh, really?
4	□□	Our marketing budget is maxed out.
5	□□	M: Perhaps it's time to look at alternatives to print media.
6	□□	W: It has been effective, though.
7	□□	We advertised with them last Wednesday,
8	□□	and since then, air conditioner sales have been up by thirty percent.
9	□□	M: True. We need to put together a report for our weekly meeting with the CEO.
10	□□	Would you mind doing that?
11	□□	You should take a look at our monthly sales revenue and compare it with the amount we spend on advertising.
12	□□	Then, we can work out what times of the year to focus our print advertising spending on.

問題59-61は次の会話に関するものです。

男性：*The Hillford Times* から電話がありました。また広告料を値上げしようとしています。

女性：え、本当ですか？　我々のマーケティングの予算はいっぱいいっぱいです。

男性：おそらく印刷媒体に代わるものを検討する時期かもしれませんね。

女性：ですが、効果はあるんです。先週の水曜日に広告を出して宣伝しましたが、それ以来、エアコンの売り上げは30パーセント上昇しました。

男性：そうですね。社長との週次ミーティングに向けて、報告書をまとめる必要がありますね。やっていただけますか。毎月の売上収益を見て、広告費と比べてみてください。そうすれば、1年のうちのどの時期に印刷広告費を集中的に使えばよいかを考えることができます。

語彙チェック □ max out 〜　〜を最大限に達せさせる　□ alternative　代わるもの　□ print media　印刷媒体、紙媒体
□ put together 〜　〜をまとめる　□ sales revenue　売上収益　□ work out 〜　（計画・方法など）をよく考える

59

正解 C □□□□

What are the speakers mainly discussing?
(A) Shipping difficulties
(B) Work scheduling
(C) Advertising expenses
(D) Product reviews

話し手たちは主に何について話し合っていますか。
(A) 出荷の難しさ
(B) 仕事のスケジュール管理
(C) 広告宣伝費
(D) 製品レビュー

男性は It's raising its advertising rates again. と述べ、*The Hillford Times* から広告費の値上げの電話があったことを女性に伝えている。女性はそれに対し Our marketing budget is maxed out. と返しており、その後もエアコンの広告費に関してや、印刷広告費を使う時期などの話が続いている。よって、正解は (C)。

60

正解 B □□□□

What type of business do the speakers most likely work for?
(A) An accounting firm
(B) An appliance store
(C) A newspaper publisher
(D) A travel agency

話し手たちはどんな種類の企業で働いていると考えられますか。
(A) 会計事務所
(B) 家電量販店
(C) 新聞社
(D) 旅行代理店

女性は広告の宣伝効果として、air conditioner sales have been up by thirty percent と述べている。エアコンを売り出していることをヒントに考えると、正解は (B)。本文の air conditioner が、選択肢では appliance に言い換えられている。

61

正解 C □□□□

What does the man ask the woman to do?
(A) Contact a colleague
(B) Attend a conference
(C) Prepare a report
(D) Arrange an event

男性は女性に何をするよう求めていますか。
(A) 同僚に連絡する
(B) 会議に参加する
(C) 報告書を準備する
(D) イベントを手配する

会話の後半で男性は女性に対し、We need to put together a report for our weekly meeting with the CEO. Would you mind doing that? と述べている。doing that は前の文の put together a report 「報告書をまとめる」という内容を指しているので、正解は (C)。人に何かをお願いするときに使われる、Would you mind *doing* 〜？「〜していただけますか」という重要フレーズを押さえておきたい。

👑 Level Up !

話し手が依頼していることや提案していることを問う問題では、依頼や提案の定番表現を待ち構えて解こう。ただし、今回のように、依頼・提案の内容を代名詞（that や it など）で置き換えているものもあるので要注意だ。

語彙チェック □ arrange 〜を手配する

W 🇨🇦 M 🇺🇸

Questions 62 through 64 refer to the following conversation and price list.

カンペキ理解

1 ☐☐ W: Our inventory software doesn't support sales of downloadable content.
2 ☐☐   I heard the new version does,
3 ☐☐   so I'll talk to the IT department about upgrading before we start advertising our e-books.
4 ☐☐ M: Good thinking.
5 ☐☐   Before you do that, you should take a look at the business software package Madsen Tech is offering.
6 ☐☐ W: Madsen Tech?
7 ☐☐   I don't know much about them,
8 ☐☐   but I have seen their poster on the train.
9 ☐☐   Are there some benefits I should be aware of?
10 ☐☐ M: Price mostly.
11 ☐☐   I think we should consider this one.
12 ☐☐   It's over $200 a month, but it's still cheaper than what we currently spend on software — $250.

問題62-64は次の会話と価格表に関するものです。

女性：我々の在庫リストのソフトウェアはダウンロードコンテンツの販売に対応していません。新しいバージョンでは対応していると聞いたので、電子書籍の広告を始める前に、IT部門にアップグレードについて相談してみようと思います。
男性：いい考えですね。それをする前に、Madsen技術社が提供しているビジネスソフトウェア製品を見てみるべきですよ。
女性：Madsen技術社ですか。私はあまり知りませんが、電車の中でポスターを見たことはあります。何か知っておくべき利点はありますか。
男性：主に価格ですね。これは検討した方がいいと思います。月に200ドルよりも多くかかりますが、それでも現在我々がソフトウェアに支払っている250ドルよりは安いです。

語彙チェック   ☐ downloadable ダウンロードできる ☐ content コンテンツ ☐ e-book 電子書籍
     ☐ Good thinking. いい考えだね。 ☐ be aware of ~ ～を知っている ☐ mostly 主に ☐ still それでも
     ☐ currently 現在

Madsen Tech — Business Software	
Platinum Pack	$250 per month
Gold Pack	$230 per month
Silver Pack	$200 per month
Bronze Pack	$160 per month

Madsen 技術社 ―ビジネスソフトウェア	
プラチナパック	月々 250 ドル
ゴールドパック	月々 230 ドル
シルバーパック	月々 200 ドル
ブロンズパック	月々 160 ドル

62

正解 **A** ☐☐☐☐

According to the woman, why should the company update its software?

(A) It is offering new product types.

(B) It will expand its offices.

(C) There have been some malfunctions.

(D) There is a compatibility problem.

女性によると、会社はなぜソフトウェアを更新する必要がありますか。

(A) 新しい種類の製品タイプを提供する。

(B) オフィスを拡張する。

(C) 故障が発生した。

(D) 互換性に問題がある。

👑 **Level Up！**

電子書籍が会社の新しい製品とは言っていないが、「電子書籍の広告を始める前に」と言っていることから、電子書籍がnew product types「新しい種類の製品タイプ」であると理解する！

女性は冒頭で、現在のソフトウェアがダウンロードコンテンツの販売に対応していないことを述べ、その後I'll talk to the IT department about upgrading before we start advertising our e-booksと続けている。これから電子書籍という新しい製品タイプを販売し始めるため、このタイミングでソフトウェアを更新するべきだと考えていることが分かる。よって、正解は(A)。

語彙チェック ☐ malfunction 故障、機能不良 ☐ compatibility 互換性

63

正解 **C** ☐☐☐☐

What does the woman say about Madsen Tech?

(A) It has a good reputation for customer service.

(B) It is not famous around the country.

(C) It has placed train advertisements.

(D) It is a newly founded company.

女性はMadsen技術社について何と言っていますか。

(A) 顧客サービスのよさに定評がある。

(B) 全国的に有名ではない。

(C) 電車広告を出したことがある。

(D) 新しく設立された会社である。

女性はMadsen技術社について、I have seen their poster on the trainと述べている。Madsen技術社は電車広告を出しているということが分かるので、正解は(C)。place an advertisementは「広告を出す」という意味の定番フレーズ。

語彙チェック ☐ reputation 評判 ☐ found 〜を設立する

64

正解 **B** ☐☐☐☐

Look at the graphic. Which package does the man recommend?

(A) Platinum Pack

(B) Gold Pack

(C) Silver Pack

(D) Bronze Pack

図を見てください。男性はどのパックを勧めていますか。

(A) プラチナパック

(B) ゴールドパック

(C) シルバーパック

(D) ブロンズパック

会話の後半で、男性は女性に新たなパックを勧めている。男性の It's over $200 a month, but it's still cheaper than what we currently spend on software ─ $250. という発言をヒントに、月額が200ドル以上で250ドル未満のパックを図表から選ぶ。この条件にあてはまるのは月額230ドルのゴールドパックなので、正解は(B)。(A)は話し手たちの会社が現在使用しているパックと同じ価格なので不正解。over「〜を越えている、〜よりも多い」や、cheaper than 〜「〜よりも安い」などの、金額の大小を表すキーワードを聞き逃さないように注意しよう。

M 🇺🇸　W 🇬🇧

Questions 65 through 67 refer to the following conversation and catalog.

カンベキ理解

1 □□ M: Let's get a new coffee table for the <u>waiting room</u> from here.
2 □□ 　　The old one's not very nice.
3 □□ 　　A few of our <u>patients</u> have commented on it.
4 □□ W: Oh, you're looking at a catalog.
5 □□ 　　I don't like that one with the four thin legs.
6 □□ M: Neither do I.
7 □□ 　　The round ones won't work in the room, either.
8 □□ 　　Let's get this one.
9 □□ 　　<u>The thick legs and angular design match the other furniture in the room.</u>
10 □□ W: OK. <u>I'll fill out a purchase authorization form after lunch.</u>
11 □□ 　　<u>Do you think you could approve it by three o'clock?</u>
12 □□ M: Sure. You must be hoping to get it delivered tomorrow.

問題65-67は次の会話とカタログに関するものです。

男性：待合室用の新しいコーヒーテーブルをこの中から買いましょう。古いのはあまりよくありません。患者さん数人が言及していました。
女性：ああ、カタログを見ているのですね。私は、その4本の細い脚が付いたものは好きではありません。
男性：私も好きではありません。丸いのも部屋には合いませんね。これにしましょう。脚が太くて角のあるデザインだから、部屋の他の家具に合いますよ。
女性：分かりました。昼食の後に購入承認書を書いておきますね。3時までに承認していただけそうですか。
男性：もちろんです。明日には到着してほしいはずですもんね。

語彙チェック　□ patient　患者　□ comment on ～　～について意見を言う　□ thin　細い　□ round　丸い　□ thick　太い、厚い
□ angular　角のある　□ authorization form　承認書

Tables	
The Spokel	The Objectus
The Giordano	The Retronica

テーブル	
The Spokel	The Objectus
The Giordano	The Retronica

65

正解 A ☐☐☐☐

Where do the speakers most likely work?

(A) At a dentist's office

(B) At a café

(C) At a publishing house

(D) At a college

話し手たちはどこで働いていると考えられますか。

(A) 歯科医院

(B) カフェ

(C) 出版社

(D) 大学

男性の冒頭の発言に waiting room「待合室」や patients「患者」などのキーワードが含まれている。これらから、話し手たちは患者を相手にする仕事をしているということが分かる。選択肢の中で該当するのは(A)。

66

正解 C ☐☐☐☐

Look at the graphic. Which table will the speakers probably buy?

(A) The Spokel

(B) The Objectus

(C) The Giordano

(D) The Retronica

図を見てください。話し手たちはおそらくどのテーブルを購入するつもりですか。

(A) The Spokel

(B) The Objectus

(C) The Giordano

(D) The Retronica

男性はテーブルについて The thick legs and angular design match the other furniture in the room. と述べ、女性はそれに対して賛成している。よって、脚が太く角のあるデザインのテーブルである(C)が正解。女性は「4本の細い脚が付いたものは好きではない」、男性は「丸いのも部屋には合わない」とそれぞれ述べているので、他のテーブルのデザインは不正解。

👑 **Level Up !**

イラストを使った図表問題では、形や模様などの表現が登場する。本問で出てきている、thin や thick などの厚さを表す形容詞、round や angular などの形を表す形容詞を覚えておこう！

67

正解 C ☐☐☐☐

What does the woman ask the man to do?

(A) Provide a reimbursement

(B) Help load a truck

(C) Check a document

(D) Negotiate a price

女性は男性に何をすることを求めていますか。

(A) 払い戻しをする

(B) トラックに荷物を積むのを手伝う

(C) 書類を確認する

(D) 値段の交渉をする

女性は購入が決まったテーブルについて、I'll find out a purchase authorization form after lunch. と発言し、購入承認書のことを話している。その後、男性に対して Do you think you could approve it by three o'clock? と尋ねている。よって、正解は(C)。本文の a purchase authorization form や approve が、選択肢でそれぞれ a document や check に言い換えられている。

語彙チェック ☐ reimbursement 払い戻し ☐ load ～を積む ☐ negotiate ～を交渉する

W 🇨🇦　M 🇦🇺

Questions 68 through 70 refer to the following conversation and map.

カンペキ理解		
1 ☐☐	W: I understand that you'd like to move Dawson Electronics to a new location.
2 ☐☐	M: That's right.
3 ☐☐	Next year, the owner of this building is going to tear it down and put up a high-rise apartment complex.
4 ☐☐	W: I see. I've brought this map of the area.
5 ☐☐	It shows some buildings with shop space that are currently available.
6 ☐☐	There's one right across the road from our office here at FRT Real Estate.
7 ☐☐	M: Yes, but that one isn't big enough.
8 ☐☐	It is not appropriate for our business, I'm afraid.
9 ☐☐	W: I see.
10 ☐☐	The only other building with a large shop space I have listed around here is the one behind Ray's Bikes.
11 ☐☐	I have the keys.
12 ☐☐	Would you like to take a look with me?
13 ☐☐	M: Sounds great. I'll get my coat.

問題68-70は次の会話と地図に関するものです。

女性：Dawson 電器店を新しい場所に移したいということですね。

男性：そうです。来年、このビルのオーナーが取り壊しをして、高層集合住宅を建てる予定なんです。

女性：なるほど。この辺りの地図を持ってきました。この地図には、現在利用可能な店舗スペースのあるビルがいくつか示されています。私たちFRT不動産の事務所からちょうど道路を挟んだところに1つありますね。

男性：そうですね、でもあそこは広さが足りないんです。残念ながら、私たちの会社には適していません。

女性：承知しました。この辺りで私がリストに挙げた広い店舗スペースのあるビルは、Ray's Bikes の裏手のところだけです。鍵は持っていますよ。一緒に見に行かれますか。

男性：いいですね。コートを取ってきます。

語彙チェック　☐ tear 〜 down　〜を取り壊す　☐ high-rise　高層の　☐ apartment complex　集合住宅、アパート
☐ appropriate　適切な　☐ list　〜をリストに挙げる　☐ take a look　一目見る

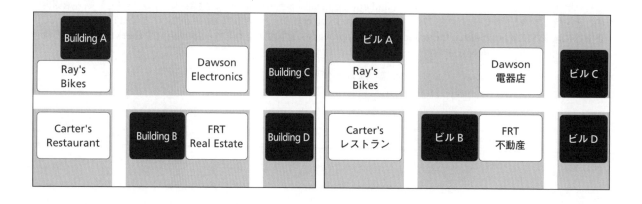

68

正解 D ☐☐☐☐

What will be constructed next year?

(A) A community college

(B) A new highway

(C) An appliance store

(D) A residential building

来年何が建設される予定ですか。

(A) コミュニティカレッジ

(B) 新しい幹線道路

(C) 家電量販店

(D) 住宅用建物

男性は Dawson 電器店を新しい場所に移す理由として、Next year, the owner of this building is going to tear it down and put up a high-rise apartment complex. と話している。高層集合住宅が建つということが分かるので、正解は (D)。すでに建っている家電量販店が取り壊されるという話なので、(C) は不正解。

語彙チェック ☐ residential 住宅用の

69

正解 D ☐☐☐☐

Look at the graphic. Which building does the man say is not appropriate?

(A) Building A

(B) Building B

(C) Building C

(D) Building D

図を見てください。男性はどのビルが適していないと言っていますか。

(A) ビル A

(B) ビル B

(C) ビル C

(D) ビル D

女性は会話の半ばで、There's one right across the road from our office here at FRT Real Estate. と述べ、それに対して男性は Yes, but that one isn't big enough. It is not appropriate for our business, I'm afraid. と答え、勧められた場所が自分の会社に適していない広さだと伝えている。女性の言葉をヒントに図を見ると、FRT 不動産の事務所からちょうど道路を挟んだところにビル D がある。よって、正解は (D)。

70

正解 B ☐☐☐☐

What will the speakers most likely do next?

(A) Review a lease agreement

(B) Tour a vacant building

(C) Measure a room

(D) Exchange contact details

話し手たちは次に何をすると考えられますか。

(A) 賃貸借契約書を確認する

(B) 空きビルを見学する

(C) 部屋の寸法を測る

(D) 連絡先を交換する

女性は会話の後半で別の空きビルを提案し、Would you like to take a look with me? と男性に提案している。それに対して男性は Sounds great. I'll get my coat. と応じているため、話し手たちはこれからその物件を見に行くと考えられる。よって、正解は (B)。

語彙チェック ☐ tour ～を見学する　☐ vacant 空いている　☐ measure ～の寸法を測る

Part 4

音読 □□□　カンペキ理解　　/9 ▶　　/9

トーク ⓘTRACK_062　問題 ⓘTRACK_063

カンペキ理解 ⓘTRACK_K14

W 🇬🇧

Questions 71 through 73 refer to the following telephone message.

カンペキ理解		
1 □□	Hi, it's Tina White from Carter Fishing Tours calling.
2 □□	We have a reservation for three under the name of Ford.
3 □□	It's for the Reef Fishing Experience.
4 □□	Um… Unfortunately, we have to cancel the tour due to the weather forecast.
5 □□	It looks like we'll have some heavy rain and strong winds on the coast today and tomorrow.
6 □□	It'd be too dangerous to be out on the water.
7 □□	We can reschedule the trip for another day.
8 □□	At the moment, we have openings for a group on May twelfth and May thirteenth.
9 □□	We expect those to fill up soon, so please let us know as soon as possible.

問題71-73は次の電話のメッセージに関するものです。

お世話になっております、Carter Fishing ToursのTina Whiteです。Ford様というお名前で3名様分のご予約を承っております。Reef Fishing Experienceのご予約の件でございます。ええと… 残念ながら、天気予報によりツアーを中止しなければなりません。今日と明日、海岸は大雨と強風になるようです。海上に出るのはかなり危険です。旅行の予定を別の日に変更することは可能です。今のところ、5月12日と5月13日のグループに空きがございます。すぐに満員になってしまうと思いますので、お早めにお知らせください。

語彙チェック　□ under the name of 〜　〜という名前で　□ reef　岩礁　□ weather forecast　天気予報　□ coast　海岸
　　　　　　　□ reschedule A for B　A（予定・約束など）をB（の時期）に変更する　□ at the moment　現在、今のところ
　　　　　　　□ opening　空き　□ fill up　満員になる

👑 Level Up！

アメリカ人の発音と、イギリス人の発音の違いに注意。本文中のreschedule（米・リスケジュール、英・リシェヂュール）など、米・英で発音が変わる単語がある。他にも、イギリス英語には「Tを強く発音する」「Rの音を弱く発音する」などの特徴がある。

71

正解 **D** ☐☐☐☐

Where does the speaker most likely work?
(A) At a travel agency
(B) At a construction firm
(C) At an accommodation provider
(D) At a tour company

話し手はどこで働いていると考えられますか。
(A) 旅行代理店
(B) 建設会社
(C) 宿泊施設
(D) ツアー会社

話し手は冒頭の Hi, it's Tina White from Carter Fishing Tours calling. で名前と会社名を伝えた後、Unfortunately, we have to cancel the tour due to the weather forecast. と述べ、天気予報が原因でツアーを中止する旨を伝えている。ここから、話し手が勤めているのはツアー会社だと推測できる。よって、正解は (D)。(A) も旅行にまつわる選択肢だが、代理店はツアーの中止を判断する立場ではないので不正解。

語彙チェック ☐ provider 販売業者、供給者

72

正解 **B** ☐☐☐☐

Why is the speaker calling?
(A) To recommend a newly released product
(B) To rearrange the date of a trip
(C) To promote a campaign for the sea
(D) To request some assistance for a volunteer

話し手はなぜ電話をかけていますか。
(A) 新しく発売された製品を薦めるため
(B) 旅行の日程を再調整するため
(C) 海のキャンペーンを宣伝するため
(D) ボランティアに手伝いをお願いするため

話し手は予定していたツアーが中止になる旨を告げ、その後 We can reschedule the trip for another day. と述べ、旅行の予定を変更することが可能だと言っている。その後さらに、具体的に空きがある日付を複数提示しているので、正解は (B)。トーク中の reschedule が、選択肢では rearrange に言い換えられている。

語彙チェック ☐ newly 新しく ☐ rearrange 〜を再調整する

73

正解 **D** ☐☐☐☐

What does the speaker want the listener to do?
(A) Organize an event
(B) Write a review
(C) Attend a banquet
(D) Indicate a preference

話し手は聞き手に何をしてほしいと思っていますか。
(A) イベントを計画する
(B) レビューを書く
(C) 宴会に出席する
(D) 選択を伝える

話し手は空きがあるツアーの日程の候補を挙げた後、We expect those to fill up soon, so please let us know as soon as possible. と述べている。ツアーはすぐに満員になることが予想されるので、話し手は、希望日を早めに教えてもらいたいと考えていることが分かる。よって、正解は (D)。

語彙チェック ☐ banquet 宴会 ☐ indicate 〜を示す ☐ preference 選択、好み

M 🇺🇸

Questions 74 through 76 refer to the following radio broadcast.

カンベキ理解		
1 ☐☐	Good morning listeners.
2 ☐☐	This is Radio 3TD and I'm the host of *Morning Matters*, Kent Grimm.
3 ☐☐	This morning, we have Mr. Ralph Arnold in the studio.
4 ☐☐	He's the award-winning author of *Future Funds*,
5 ☐☐	and he's here to talk to us about planning for our financial future.
6 ☐☐	Mr. Arnold has a new television show with the same name.
7 ☐☐	It premiered just last month, and it's getting amazing ratings.
8 ☐☐	This afternoon he's flying to London for the Regent Book Awards, for which he is one of the nominees.
9 ☐☐	So, we were very lucky to get him.
10 ☐☐	Mr. Arnold, it's a real honor to have you here with us this morning.
11 ☐☐	What can we look forward to on this week's episode?

問題74-76は次のラジオ放送に関するものです。

リスナーの皆さん、おはようございます。こちらはラジオ3TD、*Morning Matters* の司会、Kent Grimm です。今朝は Ralph Arnold さんをスタジオにお迎えしています。彼は、受賞歴のある *Future Funds* の著者で、経済的な将来の計画をたてることについて私たちに話をするために来てくださっています。Arnold さんは、同じタイトルの新しいテレビ番組に出演しています。先月初めて放送されたばかりですが、驚異的な視聴率を記録しています。今日の午後、彼は Regent Book Awards に出席するためにロンドンへ飛行機で向かう予定です。彼はその賞の候補者の1人なんです。ですから、彼をここに迎えることができたのはとても幸運なことでした。Arnold さん、今朝こちらにお越しいただけたこと、誠に光栄に思っております。今週の放送では、どんな話を楽しみにお待ちすればよろしいでしょうか。

語彙チェック　☐ award-winning　受賞歴のある　☐ financial　経済的な、金銭の　☐ ratings　視聴率
☐ nominee　候補に指名された人　☐ honor　光栄なこと　☐ episode　（テレビやラジオ番組の）1回分、1話

74

正解 C ☐☐☐☐

What is Mr. Arnold's area of expertise?

(A) Television advertising

(B) Product manufacturing

(C) Financial planning

(D) Exercise and nutrition

Arnold さんの専門分野は何ですか。

(A) テレビ広告

(B) 製品製造

(C) ファイナンシャル・プランニング

(D) 運動と栄養

話し手はラジオ番組のゲストとして Arnold さんを紹介し、He's the award-winning author of *Future Funds*, and he's here to talk to us about planning for our financial future. と述べている。お金に関する計画についての専門家であると分かるので、(C)が正解。

語彙チェック ☐ nutrition　栄養

75

正解 A ☐▪☐☐

What has Mr. Arnold recently done?

(A) Appeared on television

(B) Gone on a trip to London

(C) Retired from his job

(D) Taken a public office

Arnold さんは最近何をしましたか。

(A) テレビに出演した

(B) London に旅行をした

(C) 仕事を辞めた

(D) 公職に就いた

話し手は Arnold さんについて、放送の半ばで Mr. Arnold has a new television show with the same name. と言い、It premiered just last month と説明している。新しいテレビ番組に出演しており、それは先月放送されたということから、正解は (A)。

♛ Level Up !
トーク中で使われている動詞 premiere は、「初演される、初公開される」という意味を持つ自動詞。映画などが「封切られる」、演劇などが「初演される」といった意味で Part 3, 4 によく出てくる語なので押さえておきたい。

語彙チェック ☐ appear on ～　～に出演する　☐ public office　公職

76

正解 D ☐☐☐☐

What will the speaker most likely do next?

(A) Announce the winner

(B) Give a demonstration

(C) Explain some rules

(D) Interview a guest

話し手は次に何をすると考えられますか。

(A) 勝者を発表する

(B) 実演をする

(C) 規則を説明する

(D) ゲストにインタビューをする

話し手は放送の最後で、What can we look forward to on this week's episode? と述べ、Arnold さんに今週放映されるテレビ番組の内容について尋ねている。話し手はこれから Arnold さんにインタビューを始め、Arnold さんがそれらに答えていくと考えられるので、正解は (D)。

語彙チェック ☐ demonstration　実演

W 🍁

Questions 77 through 79 refer to the following announcement.

カンベキ理解	
1 □□	I have a brief announcement to make.
2 □□	Next Monday, we'll be turning on the new facial recognition security system.
3 □□	There are a bunch of benefits.
4 □□	The one I'll appreciate most is not having to take out a card key when I get here in the morning.
5 □□	It also means that you'll be able to come and go at any time of day.
6 □□	Naturally, we'll need photographs of everyone to register with the system.
7 □□	Please take a photograph of your face by Wednesday and send it to me by e-mail.

問題77-79は次のお知らせに関するものです。

手短なお知らせがあります。来週の月曜日、新しい顔認証セキュリティシステムを開始します。これにはさまざまな利点があります。一番ありがたいのは、朝ここに来るときにカードキーを取り出す必要がないことです。これは、いつでも出入りができるようになるということでもあります。もちろん、システムに登録するためには全員の顔写真が必要です。水曜日までに自分の顔写真を撮影して、私にEメールで送ってください。

語彙チェック □ brief 手短な □ turn on ～ （継続的な供給）を始める □ facial recognition 顔認識
□ a bunch of ～ たくさんの～ □ appreciate ～をありがたく思う □ register with ～ ～に登録する

77

正解 B ☐☐☐☐

What will happen next week?
(A) Some new employees will start work.
(B) A security system will be activated.
(C) An analyst will inspect the facility.
(D) Some new software will be installed.

来週に何が起こりますか。
(A)何人かの新入社員が働き始める。
(B)セキュリティシステムが作動する。
(C)分析官が施設を検査する。
(D)新しいソフトウェアがインストールされる。

話し手は冒頭で、Next Monday, we'll be turning on the new facial recognition security system. と述べている。よって、正解は(B)。

語彙チェック ☐ activate ～を作動させる ☐ analyst 分析官 ☐ inspect ～を検査する ☐ facility 施設

78

正解 C ☐☐☐☐

What benefit does the speaker mention?
(A) Lower running costs
(B) Fewer accounting errors
(C) Easier after-hours access
(D) More modern appearance

話し手はどのような利点を述べていますか。
(A)より安価な維持費
(B)経理ミスの少なさ
(C)勤務後の出入りのしやすさ
(D)より近代的な外観

顔認証セキュリティシステムの利点について、話し手はカードキーを取り出す必要がないことを理由の1つに挙げ、その後に It also means that you'll be able to come and go at any time of day. と続けている。よって、正解は(C)。

語彙チェック ☐ running cost 維持費 ☐ after-hours 営業時間後の ☐ appearance 外観

79

正解 D ☐☐☐☐

What are the listeners asked to do?
(A) Attend a workshop
(B) Complete a survey
(C) Read a manual
(D) Provide an image

聞き手たちは何をするよう求められていますか。
(A)研修会に参加する
(B)アンケートに記入する
(C)手引きを読む
(D)画像を提供する

話し手は聞き手たちに対して、Please take a photograph of your face by Wednesday and send it to me by e-mail. と述べ、新しく導入される顔認証セキュリティシステム用の写真を求めている。よって、正解は(D)。トーク中のphotograph「写真」が、選択肢ではより抽象的にimage「画像」と言い換えられている。

M 🇺🇸

Questions 80 through 82 refer to the following excerpt from a meeting.

カンベキ理解		
1	☐☐	As you probably know,
2	☐☐	we've been hired to build the headboards for each room of the Regis Hotel.
3	☐☐	We miscalculated the amount of fabric we needed for the padding and had to order some more from our supplier in India.
4	☐☐	It just arrived this afternoon.
5	☐☐	The team working on the project is way behind schedule,
6	☐☐	so I need everyone to work some extra hours tomorrow and the next day to catch up.
7	☐☐	We're starting at seven A.M. tomorrow, earlier than usual.
8	☐☐	I'd like as many of you as possible to come in to help.

問題80-82は次の会議の抜粋に関するものです。

ご存知かと思いますが、私たちはRegisホテルの各部屋のベッドの頭板の製作を依頼されています。パッドに必要な布の量の計算を誤ってしまったので、インドの供給業者へ追加注文する必要が生じました。その布は今日の午後に届いたばかりです。当プロジェクトに取り組んでいるチームは予定よりかなり遅れているので、遅れを取り戻すために、明日と明後日は皆さんに時間外労働をしてもらう必要があります。明日はいつもより早い朝7時から仕事開始です。できるだけ多くの人に来てもらい、手伝ってもらえたらと思います。

語彙チェック　☐ headboard　（ベッドの）頭板　☐ miscalculate　〜の計算違いをする　☐ fabric　布　☐ padding　パッド、詰め物　☐ behind schedule　予定に遅れて　☐ work extra hours　時間外労働をする　☐ catch up　遅れを取り戻す　☐ than usual　いつもより

80

正解 **A** ▢▢▢▢

Where does the speaker most likely work?

(A) At a furniture factory

(B) At a shipping firm

(C) At a hotel

(D) At a catering business

話し手はどこで働いていると考えられますか。

(A) 家具工場

(B) 配送会社

(C) ホテル

(D) 仕出し業者

冒頭の we've been hired to build the headboards for each room of the Regis Hotel より、話し手はホテルからベッドの頭板の製作を依頼されているということが分かる。話し手は家具を作る会社で働いていると推測できるので、正解は (A)。hotel という語だけを聞きとって、(C) に飛びつかないよう注意したい。

👑 **Level Up !**

直接的なキーワードである headboard「(ベッドの) 頭版」の意味を知らなくても、話し手が何かを制作するプロジェクトに関わっていると理解できれば、(A) 以外は誤答だと判断できる。消去法を駆使して解くことが、難問で点数を落とさないコツ。

81

正解 **C** ▢▢▢▢

What was the cause of the delay?

(A) The company was understaffed.

(B) A vehicle broke down.

(C) Some materials ran out.

(D) A road was closed.

遅れの原因は何でしたか。

(A) 会社は人手が足りなかった。

(B) 車両が故障した。

(C) 材料が切れた。

(D) 道路が閉鎖された。

話し手は We miscalculated the amount of fabric we needed for the padding and had to order some more from our supplier in India. と述べ、計算ミスのせいで布が足りず、供給業者へ追加注文する必要が生じたことを伝えている。そしてその後、追加の布が今日届いたばかりであることを述べ、遅れを取り戻すための解決策を提案している。よって、布が不足していたことが遅れの原因だと分かるので正解は (C)。

語彙チェック　□ understaffed　人員不足の　□ run out　（材料などが）尽きる

82

正解 **B** ▢▢▢▢

What are the listeners asked to do?

(A) Review a schedule

(B) Report to work early

(C) Order extra materials

(D) Change an estimate

聞き手たちは何をするよう求められていますか。

(A) 予定を確認する

(B) 早めに出勤する

(C) 追加の材料を注文する

(D) 見積もりを変更する

話し手は「遅れを取り戻すために、明日と明後日は皆さんに時間外労働をしてもらう必要がある」と述べた後、We're starting at seven A.M. tomorrow, earlier than usual. I'd like as many of you as possible to come in to help. と続け、早い時間に来るようにお願いしている。よって、正解は (B)。選択肢の report to ～ という表現は、「(人・組織) に直属している」という意味として使われることも多いので、あわせて押さえておきたい。

語彙チェック　□ report to work　出勤する　□ estimate　見積もり

W 🇬🇧

Questions 83 through 85 refer to the following announcement.

カンベキ理解	
1 □□	Good afternoon shoppers.
2 □□	Welcome to Dan's Discount Emporium.
3 □□	I trust you're enjoying our everyday low prices in every section of the store.
4 □□	Today we're running a promotion on Steadman brand men's shavers, aftershave lotions, soaps, and shampoos.
5 □□	All of these items will be half price.
6 □□	It's only today and tomorrow, so don't miss out!
7 □□	If you'd like to know about future special offers,
8 □□	why not sign up for our weekly catalog?
9 □□	Information about all of our newest and most heavily discounted items will be delivered to your mailbox every Thursday.

問題83-85は次のお知らせに関するものです。

お買い物客の皆さま、こんにちは。Dan'sディスカウントショップへ、ようこそお越しくださいました。皆さまには、店内全ての売り場で毎日低価格をお楽しみいただいていることと思います。本日は、Steadman製の男性用シェーバー、アフターシェーブローション、石鹸、シャンプーの販売促進キャンペーンを実施中です。これらの商品は全て、半額になります。本日と明日のみですので、どうかお見逃しなく！　今後のお得な情報を知りたい方は、当店の週刊カタログに登録してみてはいかがでしょうか。最新の商品や大幅値下げ商品全ての情報を、毎週木曜日に郵便ポストにお届けします。

語彙チェック □ shopper 買い物客　□ emporium 商店、専門店　□ section 売り場、部門
□ run a promotion プロモーションを行う　□ shaver シェーバー、ひげそり　□ aftershave ひげそり後の
□ miss out 機会を失う　□ sign up for 〜 〜に登録する　□ heavily 大いに　□ mailbox 郵便ポスト

83

正解 C ☐☐☐☐

What items are being promoted?

(A) Beverages

(B) Appliances

(C) Toiletries

(D) Decorations

何の商品が宣伝されていますか。

(A) 飲料

(B) 家電製品

(C) 洗面用品

(D) 装飾品

話し手は店内にいる買い物客へ向けて、Today we're running a promotion on Steadman brand men's shavers, aftershave lotions, soaps, and shampoos. と述べている。男性用シェーバーやアフターシェーブローション、石鹸、シャンプーなどはどれも洗面用品にあたるので、正解は(C)。

👑 Level Up !

選択肢で、抽象度の高い単語に言い換えられている問題。(A)のbeverages「飲料」や(B)のappliances「家電製品」などはこの手の問題でよく登場するが、toiletries「洗面用品」も覚えておこう！

84

正解 B ☐☐☐☐

What does the speaker say about the promotion?

(A) It is mainly intended for students.

(B) It offers a 50% discount on the items.

(C) It is conducted once a week.

(D) It will be postponed until tomorrow.

販売促進キャンペーンについて、話し手は何と言っていますか。

(A) 主に学生を対象にしている。

(B) 商品を50パーセント引きで購入できる。

(C) 週に1回実施される。

(D) 翌日に延期される。

話し手は、洗面用品の販売促進キャンペーンを行っていると述べた後、All of these items will be half price. と続け、それらの商品の価格が半額になるということを伝えている。よって、正解は(B)。トーク中のhalf price「半額」が、選択肢ではa 50% discount「50パーセント引き」に言い換えられている。

語彙チェック ☐ be intended for ～　～向けである　☐ conduct　～を行う

85

正解 D ☐☐☐☐

According to the speaker, what can customers receive in the mail?

(A) A magazine

(B) A voucher

(C) An invitation

(D) A catalog

話し手によると、顧客は郵便で何を受け取ることができますか。

(A) 雑誌

(B) クーポン券

(C) 招待状

(D) カタログ

話し手は買い物客に、If you'd like to know about future special offers, why not sign up for our weekly catalog? と呼びかけ、週刊カタログを登録することを勧めている。さらにその後、Information about all of our newest and most heavily discounted items will be delivered to your mailbox every Thursday. と述べ、商品の情報が含まれたカタログが郵便で届くと説明している。よって、正解は(D)。ちなみに、設問のin the mailは「郵便で、郵送されて」という意味で、e-mail「Eメール」とは関係ない。知識として押さえておこう。

M 🇦🇺

Questions 86 through 88 refer to the following excerpt from a meeting.

カンベキ理解

1 ☐☐	Just before we finish the meeting,
2 ☐☐	I have one more topic I'd like to discuss.
3 ☐☐	I've contacted our water supplier and canceled the contract for water delivery.
4 ☐☐	We've thrown out two bottles of water this week.
5 ☐☐	People just aren't drinking enough to make it viable.
6 ☐☐	Instead, I've ordered some small bottles of water from an online store.
7 ☐☐	We'll receive a shipment of twenty-four bottles each week.
8 ☐☐	These are for guests only.
9 ☐☐	Please make sure there are at least six chilled bottles available at all times.

問題86-88は次の会議の抜粋に関するものです。

会議を終える前に、もう1つ話したいことがあります。水供給業者に連絡して、水の配達の契約をキャンセルしました。我々は今週、水のボトルを2本廃棄しました。水の配達を続けるほど、皆は十分に水を飲んでいないのです。その代わりに、オンラインショップで小さなボトルの水をいくつか注文しました。毎週24本ずつ送られてきます。これは来客用です。少なくとも6本は常時冷えた状態にしておいてください。

語彙チェック   ☐ throw out 〜   〜を捨てる   ☐ viable   採算が取れる、(計画などが)やっていける   ☐ chilled   冷やされた
☐ at all times   常に、いつも

86

Why does the speaker say, "We've thrown out two bottles of water this week"?

(A) To explain a decision
(B) To draw attention to an error
(C) To ask for assistance
(D) To introduce a new product

話し手はなぜ "We've thrown out two bottles of water this week" と言っていますか。

(A) 決定について説明するため
(B) 間違いに注意を向けるため
(C) 支援を求めるため
(D) 新製品を紹介するため

話し手は前半で I've contacted our water supplier and canceled the contract for water delivery. と述べ、水の配達の契約をキャンセルしたと伝えている。その直後に、We've thrown out two bottles of water this week.「我々は今週、水のボトルを2本廃棄しました」と今週起こったことを述べ、さらに People just aren't drinking enough to make it viable. と続け、人々が配達された水を十分に消費していないため採算が取れていない、ということを伝えている。契約をキャンセルするという決断に至った理由を説明するためにこの発言をしたことが分かるので、正解は (A)。

語彙チェック ☐ draw attention to 〜 　〜に注意を向ける 　☐ assistance 　支援、助け

87

What does the speaker say about the newly ordered water bottles?

(A) They are a popular product.
(B) They are not for staff.
(C) They will not expire soon.
(D) They must be removed immediately.

新しく注文した水のボトルについて、話し手は何と言っていますか。

(A) 人気のある商品である。
(B) 従業員用ではない。
(C) すぐに期限切れにはならない。
(D) すぐに捨てなければならない。

話し手はオンラインショップで注文した水について、These are for guests only. と述べ、従業員用ではなく来客用であることを示している。よって、正解は (B)。

語彙チェック ☐ expire 　賞味期限が切れる 　☐ remove 　〜を取り除く 　☐ immediately 　ただちに、すぐに

88

What are the listeners asked to do?

(A) Maintain a certain number of refrigerated bottles
(B) Purchase water before scheduling large meetings
(C) Get permission before making large purchases
(D) Keep a record of water usage in the office

聞き手たちは何をするよう求められていますか。

(A) 一定の数のボトルを冷えた状態に保つ
(B) 大きな会議の予定が入る前に水を購入する
(C) 大きな買い物をする前に許可を得る
(D) 社内の水の使用量を記録する

話し手は聞き手たちに対し、Please make sure there are at least six chilled bottles available at all times. と述べ、少なくとも6本のボトルを常時冷えた状態に保ってほしいと伝えている。よって、正解は (A)。トーク中の chilled が、選択肢では refrigerated に言い換えられている。

語彙チェック ☐ maintain 　〜を保つ 　☐ refrigerated 　冷却された 　☐ keep a record of 〜 　〜を記録する 　☐ usage 　使用（量）

W 🇨🇦

Questions 89 through 91 refer to the following news broadcast.

カンペキ理解		
1 ☐☐	In local news, approval has been given for the construction of a tunnel under the Carter Bridge in Windsor.
2 ☐☐	It's not an area that has a lot of traffic at any time of day.
3 ☐☐	According to a city spokesperson,
4 ☐☐	the plan is to draw drivers away from the Vandelay Bridge.
5 ☐☐	This should help to reduce traffic there.
6 ☐☐	Work will begin in September,
7 ☐☐	and the project is expected to take two years to complete.
8 ☐☐	Since it is expected to attract more visitors to Windsor,
9 ☐☐	the City Council is considering construction of a new shopping center.
10 ☐☐	They plan to hold a meeting and gather residents' opinions about this next week.

問題89-91は次のニュース放送に関するものです。

地方のニュースでは、WindsorのCater橋の下にトンネルを建設することが承認されたそうです。この地域は、一日のどの時間帯でも交通量が多いというわけではありません。市の広報担当者によると、Vandelay橋からドライバーを減らすための計画だといいます。これによって、そこの交通量が緩和されるはずです。作業は9月から開始し、計画が完了するまでに2年かかる見込みです。またWindsorでは観光客の増加が見込まれることから、市議会は新しいショッピングセンターの建設を検討しています。市議会は来週にも説明会を開き、この件に関する住民の意見を集める予定です。

語彙チェック ☐ approval 承認 ☐ tunnel トンネル ☐ traffic 交通（量） ☐ spokesperson 広報担当者
☐ draw *A* away from *B* AをBから離す ☐ gather ～を集める ☐ resident 住民

89

正解 A ☐☐☐☐

Why does the speaker say, "It's not an area that has a lot of traffic at any time of day"?

(A) To avoid a misunderstanding
(B) To make a recommendation
(C) To correct some information
(D) To reject a suggestion

話し手はなぜ "It's not an area that has a lot of traffic at any time of day" と言っていますか。

(A) 誤解を避けるため
(B) おすすめするため
(C) 情報を訂正するため
(D) 提案を断るため

トンネル建設の話題に対して、話し手は It's not an area that has a lot of traffic at any time of day.「この地域は、一日のどの時間帯でも交通量が多いというわけではありません」と発言している。そしてその直後に、the plan is to draw drivers away from the Vandelay Bridge と述べ、This should help to reduce traffic there. とトンネルが建設される本来の目的を説明している。建設を行う理由を聞き手たちが誤解しないように発言したことが分かるので、正解は (A)。

語彙チェック ☐ misunderstanding 誤解 ☐ correct 〜を訂正する ☐ reject 〜を断る

90

正解 D ☐☐☐☐

What is the City Council planning to do?

(A) Hire additional staff
(B) Raise some money
(C) Organize a tour
(D) Build a new complex

市議会は何をするつもりですか。

(A) 追加の従業員を雇用する
(B) お金を集める
(C) 見学会を開催する
(D) 新しい複合施設を建設する

話し手は終盤で、the City Council is considering construction of a new shopping center「市議会は新しいショッピングセンターの建設を検討している」と述べている。よって、正解は (D)。トーク中の shopping center「ショッピングセンター」が、選択肢では complex「複合施設」と抽象的に言い換えられている。

語彙チェック ☐ raise （お金など）を集める

91

正解 B ☐☐☐☐

What will happen next week?

(A) Work on a construction project will begin.
(B) A plan will be discussed.
(C) New equipment will be installed.
(D) A festival will be held for residents.

来週に何が起こりますか。

(A) 建設計画の作業が始まる。
(B) 計画が検討される。
(C) 新しい機器が設置される。
(D) 住民のための祭りが開催される。

トークの後半で、話し手は市が計画している新しいショッピングセンターの建設について触れ、They plan to hold a meeting and gather residents' opinions about this next week. と伝えている。来週この建設計画について話し合われることが分かるので、正解は (B)。トーク中に9月からトンネルの建設作業が開始されるとあるが、来週が9月であるとはどこにも述べられていないため、(A) は内容と合わない。

👑 Level Up !
設問文にある next week が登場するのは会話の一番最後。next week という単語が流れる前の部分を聞き取っておかないと、この問題を正解することはできない。集中力を切らさず最後まで聞き取ろう。

M 🇦🇺

Questions 92 through 94 refer to the following talk.

カンペキ理解		
1 ☐☐	I've got an announcement from the head office.
2 ☐☐	This'll take a minute.
3 ☐☐	You should all sit down.
4 ☐☐	The regional manager has informed me that our plant will be merged with the one in Springfield.
5 ☐☐	Their plan is to shut this factory down and use the building as a storage warehouse.
6 ☐☐	The Springfield plant is much larger,
7 ☐☐	and it's currently running way below capacity.
8 ☐☐	Apparently, it makes more financial sense for us to move there.
9 ☐☐	Of course, this means a much longer commute for most of us.
10 ☐☐	The company will pay for your additional travel expenses.
11 ☐☐	It'll also affect our work responsibilities.
12 ☐☐	We'll discuss that more at a later date.

問題92-94は次の話に関するものです。

本社からお知らせがあります。少し時間がかかります。皆さんお座りください。地域マネージャーから聞いたのですが、我々の工場はSpringfieldの工場と統合されるそうです。この工場は閉鎖され、建物は保管用倉庫として使われる予定です。Springfieldの工場ははるかに大きく、現在は生産力を大幅に下回っています。どうやら、そちらに移った方が経済的に得策のようです。もちろん、私たちのほとんどは通勤時間が長くなります。その分の交通費は会社が負担してくれます。また、私たちの職責にも影響が出ます。そちらについては後日詳しく説明します。

語彙チェック　☐ head office　本社　☐ regional　地域の　☐ merge *A* with *B*　AをBと合併させる　☐ shut ～ down　～を閉鎖する
☐ storage　保管　☐ warehouse　倉庫　☐ capacity　（工場などの）生産力　☐ apparently　どうやら～らしい
☐ make financial sense　財政・経済的に意味がある、元が取れる　☐ commute　通勤時間
☐ work responsibilities　職責

92

What does the speaker mean when he says, "This'll take a minute"?

(A) A project is easy to complete.
(B) A meeting is near its end.
(C) He does not plan to attend.
(D) His talk will not be over soon.

正解 D

"This'll take a minute" という発言で、話し手は何を意図していますか。

(A)計画は簡単に完了する。
(B)会議が終わりに近づいている。
(C)彼は出席する予定ではない。
(D)彼の話はすぐには終わらない。

問われている発言は、「少し時間がかかる」という意味。話し手は冒頭で「お知らせがある」と伝え、This'll take a minute. と発言している。そしてその直後に、You should all sit down. と、聞き手たちに対して座るように伝えている。これらの内容から、座って話を聞いてもらう程度に、話す時間がかかるということが分かる。よって、正解は(D)。

語彙チェック □ over 終わって、済んで

93

Who are the listeners?

(A) Software developers
(B) Factory workers
(C) Sales representatives
(D) Product designers

正解 B

聞き手たちは誰ですか。

(A)ソフトウェア開発者
(B)工場労働者
(C)営業担当者
(D)製品設計者

トークの内容から、話し手の職業を推測する必要がある問題。中盤で、our plant will be merged、Their plan is to shut this factory down という発言があることから、工場の従業員向けに話をしているということが分かる。よって、正解は(B)。

語彙チェック □ representative 担当者

94

According to the speaker, what will the company pay for?

(A) Overnight accommodation
(B) Additional training
(C) Building repairs
(D) Transportation costs

正解 D

話し手によると、会社は何の金額を負担しますか。

(A)1泊分の宿泊費
(B)追加の研修
(C)建物の修繕費
(D)交通費

話し手は工場の統合により従業員の通勤時間が長くなるという問題点を挙げた後、The company will pay for your additional travel expenses. と続け、追加で生じた交通費は会社が負担することを伝えている。よって、正解は(D)。トーク中の travel expenses「旅費、交通費」が、選択肢では Transportation costs「交通費」に言い換えられている。

語彙チェック □ overnight 1泊の

M 🇺🇸

Questions 95 through 97 refer to the following telephone message and voucher.

カンベキ理解		
1 □□	Hi. It's Red Michaels from Sanderson Drugs.
2 □□	One of your people visited us yesterday to talk about our gardening needs.
3 □□	At the time, I told her that I was considering the six-month plan.
4 □□	After talking with our head office,
5 □□	we decided to go with the full-year plan, instead.
6 □□	If you send an updated invoice to our drug store, we'll pay it today.
7 □□	We're using that coupon, by the way.
8 □□	Oh, I just remembered — I'm looking for someone to take care of my garden at home.
9 □□	Could you send over a pamphlet with your residential services and prices?

問題95-97は次の電話のメッセージとクーポンに関するものです。

こんにちは。Sanderson 薬局の Red Michaels です。昨日、御社の担当者の方が当店へお越しになり、我々のガーデニングの必要性について話をしてくださいました。その際、6カ月プランを検討していることを彼女に伝えました。本社と相談した結果、代わりに通年プランにすることにいたしました。更新後の請求書を当薬局にお送りいただければ、本日中にお支払いいたします。ちなみに、あのクーポンを使おうとしています。あ、ちょうど思い出しました—自宅の庭の手入れをしてくれる人を探しているところなんです。住宅向けのサービスと料金が掲載された小冊子を送っていただけますか。

語彙チェック □ gardening ガーデニング、造園 □ send over 〜 〜を送る □ pamphlet 小冊子、パンフレット
□ residential 住宅向けの

Discount Coupon	割引クーポン
Indigo Garden Care	**Indigo Garden Care**
1-Month Plan ·················5% off	1 カ月プラン ··············5 パーセント割引
6-Month Plan ·················10% off	6 カ月プラン ··············10 パーセント割引
12-Month Plan ···············15% off	12 カ月プラン ·············15 パーセント割引
24-Month Plan ···············20% off	24 カ月プラン ·············20 パーセント割引
(Corporate Contracts Only)	（法人契約のみ）

95

正解 C ☐☐☐☐

Where does the speaker work?
(A) At a factory
(B) At a clinic
(C) At a pharmacy
(D) At a hotel

話し手はどこで働いていますか。
(A) 工場
(B) 診療所
(C) 薬局
(D) ホテル

話し手の If you send an updated invoice to our drug store, we'll pay it today. という発言に注目。our drug store「当（私たちの）薬局」という部分から、正解は (C)。「薬局」を表す単語には、drug store 以外にも pharmacy という単語がある。

👑 Level Up！
冒頭に Sanderson Drugs という店名は出てくるものの、our drug store という明確な根拠はかなり遅く登場する。1 問目に意識を向けすぎて、次の問題を取りこぼさないように注意。

96

正解 C ☐☐☐☐

Look at the graphic. What discount will the business receive?
(A) 5% off
(B) 10% off
(C) 15% off
(D) 20% off

図を見てください。その会社はどのような割引を受けますか。
(A) 5 パーセント割引
(B) 10 パーセント割引
(C) 15 パーセント割引
(D) 20 パーセント割引

After talking with our head office, we decided to go with the full-year plan, instead. という部分から、話し手の会社は通年プランを契約するということが分かる。図を見ると、この full-year plan「通年プラン」と同様の意味を表す、12-Month Plan「12カ月プラン」がある。その右側には 15% off「15パーセント割引」と書かれていることから、話し手の会社は 15 パーセント割引を受けることになると分かる。よって、正解は (C)。

👑 Level Up！
図表問題では、答えのキーワードとなりそうな数字が複数回発言されることもある。最初に聞こえた音に飛びつかずに、会話の流れを聞き取ってから答えよう。

97

正解 C ☐☐☐☐

What does the speaker ask the listener to do?
(A) Provide a price estimate
(B) Visit a residential address
(C) Send some promotional materials
(D) Cancel a gardening contract

話し手は聞き手に何をするよう求めていますか。
(A) 価格の見積もりを提示する
(B) 住居を訪問する
(C) 販促物を送る
(D) 造園の契約を解除する

話し手は最後に Could you send over a pamphlet with your residential services and prices? と述べ、住宅向けのサービスと料金について書かれている小冊子を送ってもらえないかと聞き手にお願いしている。よって、正解は (C)。トーク中の pamphlet「パンフレット」が、選択肢では promotional materials「販促物」に言い換えられている。

語彙チェック　☐ promotional material　販促物

W

Questions 98 through 100 refer to the following excerpt from a meeting and floor plan.

カンペキ理解		
1	□□	Good morning.
2	□□	I really appreciate you taking the time out of your busy class schedules
3	□□	to help out at the Dolby Preservation Society fundraising book sale.
4	□□	I believe this experience will provide you with valuable insights for your future career.
5	□□	Today, I need you to help me stack the shelves.
6	□□	We've placed some bookshelves down the middle.
7	□□	Most people are interested in recent releases.
8	□□	Rather than putting them in front of the door,
9	□□	I'd like to place them on the middle shelf in front of the cash register.
10	□□	That way, people will have to walk past other books to get to them.
11	□□	Now, I know it doesn't look like we have enough books at the moment,
12	□□	but we're expecting a big delivery tomorrow morning.

問題98-100は次の会議の抜粋と間取り図に関するものです。

おはようございます。お忙しい授業スケジュールの中、Dolby保存協会による資金集めブックセールをお手伝いいただき、誠に感謝しております。私はこの経験が、将来のキャリアにとって貴重な知見をあなた方に提供すると信じています。今日は、本棚に商品を積むお手伝いをしていただきます。中央に本棚をいくつか置いています。ほとんどの人が、最近発売された出版物に興味を持っています。それらを扉の前に置くのではなく、レジ前にある中央の棚に置きたいと思います。そうすれば、それらを手に入れるために、他の本の前を通らなければいけなくなりますからね。今のところ、本の数が少ないように見えますが、明日の朝にかなりの配送があります。

語彙チェック □ fundraising 資金集めの □ valuable 貴重な □ insight 洞察、理解（力） □ stack shelves 棚に商品を積む
□ bookshelf 本棚 □ release 出版物 □ place A on B AをBに置く □ cash register レジ
□ past 〜を過ぎて □ at the moment 今のところ

Dolby Community Center Entrance Hall

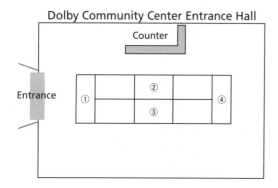

Dolby コミュニティセンター エントランスホール

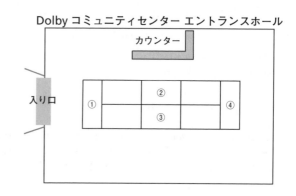

98

正解 A

Who most likely are the listeners?

(A) Students

(B) Bookkeepers

(C) Authors

(D) District center staff

聞き手たちは誰だと考えられますか。

(A) 学生

(B) 簿記係

(C) 著者

(D) 地区センターの職員

話し手は冒頭で、I really appreciate you taking the time out of your busy class schedules to help out at the Dolby Preservation Society fundraising book sale. と、授業スケジュールの合間をぬって資金集めブックセールの手伝いをしてくれることに感謝を述べている。さらにその後、I believe this experience will provide you with valuable insights for your future career. と述べている。busy class schedules「忙しい授業スケジュール」、valuable insights for your future career「将来のキャリアにとって貴重な知見」などのキーワードから、本の販売を手伝うのは学生だと考えられる。よって、正解は (A)。

語彙チェック □ district center 地区センター

99

正解 B

Look at the graphic. Where will the recent releases be displayed?

(A) On shelf 1

(B) On shelf 2

(C) On shelf 3

(D) On shelf 4

図を見てください。最近発売された出版物はどこに展示される予定ですか。

(A) 棚1

(B) 棚2

(C) 棚3

(D) 棚4

話し手は、ほとんどの人が最近発売された出版物に興味を持っていることを伝えた後、それらの本の置き場所として Rather than putting them in front of the door, I'd like to place them on the middle shelf in front of the cash register. と続けている。図を見ると、レジ前にある中央の棚は②に該当するので、正解は (B)。rather than 〜「〜よりも、〜ではなく」という表現も押さえておきたい。

100

正解 B

According to the speaker, what will happen tomorrow?

(A) An event will commence.

(B) A shipment will arrive.

(C) A hall will be closed.

(D) A message will be sent.

話し手によると、明日に何が起こりますか。

(A) あるイベントが始まる。

(B) 荷物が届く。

(C) 会場が閉鎖される。

(D) 伝言が送られる。

話し手は本の在庫について、we're expecting a big delivery tomorrow morning と述べ、明日配送が届く予定であると伝えている。よって、正解は (B)。

語彙チェック □ commence 始まる □ shipment 荷物

音読 □□□　　解答時間　　秒 ▶　　秒

101

正解 A □□□□　　▶TRACK_082

Customers have shown little ------- to take part in a satisfaction survey unless they are unhappy with some part of the service.

(A) inclination
(B) insulation
(C) consultation
(D) culmination

顧客はサービスのどこかに不満がない限り、満足度調査に参加したいという意向はほとんど示していません。

述語動詞 have shown の目的語にあたる部分に空所がある。後ろに to 不定詞が続いていることに注目。inclination to do で「〜したいという意向」という意味を表す (A) inclination を入れると、「満足度調査に参加したいという意向」となり文意が通る。(B) は「隔離」、(C) は「相談」、(D) は「最高点」という意味。

音読 □□□　　解答時間　　秒 ▶　　秒

102

正解 D □□□□　　▶TRACK_083

The ------- taken to reduce the annual running costs were more expensive to implement than was expected.

(A) measuring
(B) measurable
(C) measurably
(D) measures

年間の維持費を削減するために講じられた対策は、予想されていたよりも、実施するのに費用がかかりました。

語彙チェック　□ running cost　維持費
　　　　　　　□ implement　〜を実施する

空所前に冠詞 the、空所直後に過去分詞 taken があるため、空所には taken に修飾される名詞が入る。take measures「対策を講じる」という表現となり、文意の通る (D) measures「対策」が正解。(A) は動名詞なので名詞の働きをするが、「測定すること」を表すため、ここでは文意に合わない。

👑 Level Up！

文法的には空所に入ってしまう選択肢でも、正解になるとは限らない。文の後ろまで読んで、意味が通るかを必ず確認しよう！

音読 □□□　　解答時間　　秒 ▶　　秒

103

正解 D □□□□　　▶TRACK_084

Tuffwipes can be used to clean stubborn ------- from all kinds of kitchen appliances.

(A) interim
(B) density
(C) uptick
(D) residue

Tuffwipes は、あらゆる種類のキッチン用品の頑固な汚れを落とすのにお使いいただけます。

空所は to 不定詞句に含まれ、to clean に続く目的語となるので、直前の形容詞 stubborn「頑固な」に修飾されて意味の通るものを選ぶ。(D) residue「残留物」は stubborn residue で「頑固な残留物（＝汚れ）」となるため、空所に入れると「キッチン用品の頑固な汚れを落とす」という自然な文脈になる。(A) は「合間」、(B) は「密度」、(C) は「上昇」という意味。

音読 □□□　　解答時間　　秒 ▶　　秒

104

正解 C □□□□　　▶TRACK_085

Mr. Cooper was so happy with his new desk heater that he purchased a ------- for his desk at work.

(A) one
(B) further
(C) second
(D) maximum

Cooper さんは新しいデスクヒーターにとても満足していたので、職場のデスク用にもう1つ購入しました。

so 〜 that ...「とても〜なので…」という構文で、前半が理由、後半がその結果を表す。前半の「新しいデスクヒーターに満足していた」という内容から、その結果「（同じものを）もう1つ購入した」と考えると文意が通るので、(C) second が正解。the second は「2番目の（もの）」という意味だが、a second だと「もう1つの（もの）」という意味になる。

音読 □□□　　解答時間　　秒 ▶　　秒

105

正解 B □□□□　　▶TRACK_086

Owing to the mechanical failure, it is ------- impossible to launch the service as scheduled.

(A) barely
(B) virtually
(C) incredibly
(D) indefinitely

機械の故障が原因で、予定通りにサービスを開始することは事実上不可能です。

語彙チェック　□ owing to 〜　〜が原因で

空所直後の impossible「不可能な」という形容詞を修飾する副詞を選ぶ。virtually impossible で「事実上不可能な」という意味になり、全体の文意も通るため、(B) virtually が正解。(A) は「かろうじて」、(C) は「信じられないほど」、(D) は「漠然と」という意味。

106　正解 C　▶TRACK_087

Five candidates were interviewed for the designer position, ------- of whom had experience in home renovation.
(A) neither　　　　　　　　(C) each
(B) every　　　　　　　　　(D) any

デザイナー職の候補者5人の面接が行われましたが、いずれの候補者も住宅のリノベーション経験を持っていました。

------- of whom がカンマ以降の節の主語となっているので、空所には名詞の働きをする語が入る。whomは人を説明する関係代名詞なので、主節の主語 Five candidates「5人の候補者」を指すことが分かる。代名詞の働きを持つ (A)(C)(D) のうち、「5人の候補者それぞれが」という意味になる (C) each が正解。

👑 Level Up !
(A) neither は neither of 〜で「〜のどちらも…ない」という意味を表すが、原則「2人の人、2つのもの」に対して使う。今回の問題文では、候補者が5人いるので不適切。

音読 □□□　解答時間　秒 ▶　秒

107　正解 D　▶TRACK_088

The warranty will become ------- if any other party makes alterations to the ice cream maker in any way.
(A) waived　　　　　　　　(C) assured
(B) expired　　　　　　　　(D) void

いかなる方法でも他の人がアイスクリームメーカーに変更を加えた場合、保証は無効になります。

空所は動詞 become に続く補語となるので、主語 The warranty「保証」がどうなるのかを考える。if節では「アイスクリームメーカー（商品）に変更を加えた場合」とあるので、空所に (D) void「無効な」を入れ、「その場合は（商品の）保証が無効になる」とすると自然な文脈になる。(A) は「放棄された」、(B) は「期限が切れて」、(C) は「確かな」という意味。

音読 □□□　解答時間　秒 ▶　秒

108　正解 A　▶TRACK_089

Even after an exhaustive investigation, no one could say for sure ------- had caused the damage to the machinery.
(A) what　　　　　　　　　(C) where
(B) that　　　　　　　　　(D) how

徹底的な調査の後でさえ、何が機械の損傷を引き起こしたのかはっきりと分かる人はいませんでした。

語彙チェック □ exhaustive 徹底的な　□ for sure 確実に

選択肢には関係詞の働きを持つ語が並ぶ。空所の後ろには関係詞節の主語となる語句がないため、空所に入るのは主格の関係代名詞。(A) と (B) のうち、空所の前には先行詞となる語句がないことから、先行詞をとらない主格の関係代名詞 (A) what が正解。what節が述語動詞 say の目的語となっている。(B) を見て say that 〜「〜と述べる」という表現を作る接続詞 that だと考えた場合、that節内の主語が必要となるため不適切。

音読 □□□　解答時間　秒 ▶　秒

109　正解 A　▶TRACK_090

Mr. Antilles gave a ------- talk on the use of 3D printers to create parts for antique lamps.
(A) compelling　　　　　　(C) compel
(B) compelled　　　　　　(D) compellable

Antilles さんは、アンティークのランプの部品を作るために3Dプリンターを使用することに関して、説得力のある話をしました。

空所の前には冠詞 a があるので、空所には後ろの名詞 talk を修飾する語が入る。空所を挟んで give a talk「話をする」という表現があるので、(A) compelling「説得力のある」を入れて「説得力のある話をした」とすると文意が通る。(B)(D) も形容詞の働きをするが、(B) compelled は「強制された」、(D) compellable は「強制可能な」という意味なので、いずれも文意に適さない。

音読 □□□　解答時間　秒 ▶　秒

110　正解 B　▶TRACK_091

Max Leeman has hired a ------- publicist who has a remarkable background to help him prepare for the launch of his latest book.
(A) fatal　　　　　　　　　(C) conceivable
(B) seasoned　　　　　　　(D) stagnant

Max Leeman は自身の最新の本の発売準備を手伝ってもらうための、素晴らしい経歴を持つベテランの広報担当を雇いました。

語彙チェック □ publicist 広報担当　□ remarkable 素晴らしい

人を表す名詞 publicist を修飾する形容詞としてふさわしいのは (B) seasoned「ベテランの」。season には「（人）を成熟させる」という動詞の意味があり、seasoned で「経験豊富な、ベテランの」という意味を表す。(A) は「命にかかわる」、(C) は「考えられる」、(D) は「不活発な」という意味。

111

With this app installed, you can get access to the latest international news ------- in the world you are.

(A) wherever　　　　(C) what
(B) that　　　　　　(D) however

このアプリがインストールされていれば、世界中のどこにいても最新の国際ニュースにアクセスすることができます。

語彙チェック □ get access to 〜 （情報など）を入手する

空所前までで文の内容が完結していることから、空所以降は修飾的な内容を表す副詞節であると考えられる。正解候補は副詞節を作ることができる (A) と (D)。wherever in the world you are「（あなたが）世界中のどこにいても」となり文意が通る、(A) wherever が正解。

112

Permission to build a facility in Dolby was dismissed because the land had certain plants ------- to the local wildlife.

(A) vital　　　　　(C) vitally
(B) vitality　　　　(D) vitalize

その土地には地域の野生生物にとって不可欠な、特定の植物が生えているので、Dolby に施設を建設するための許可は却下されました。

語彙チェック □ dismiss 〜を却下する　□ wildlife 野生生物

空所が含まれる because の節にはすでに、主語（the land）・述語動詞（had）・目的語（certain plants）という要素が揃っている。よって、空所以降は直前の名詞 plants に後ろから説明を加えていると考えられるので、vital to 〜 で「〜にとって不可欠な」という意味を表す形容詞の (A) vital が適切。

113

Professional photographers from Clearshot Photography ------- at the last meeting to take all of the photographs used in this manual.

(A) have commissioned
(B) would be commissioned
(C) commissioned
(D) were commissioned

Clearshot 写真館のプロのカメラマンたちは、前回のミーティングで、この手引書に使われる全ての写真を撮るよう依頼されました。

語彙チェック □ manual 手引書

空所は文中の述語動詞の位置にあたり、選択肢には時制や態が違う語句が並ぶ。主語は Professional photographers、動詞は commission「〜に依頼をする」だが、空所後に目的語となる名詞がない。よって、この文は受動態の文だと考えられる。空所後に at the last meeting とあることから、過去時制の (D) が正解。commission A to do で「Aに〜を依頼する」という意味。

Level Up!
would は現在の推量を表すので、(B) を入れると「カメラマンたちは前回のミーティングで依頼されるだろう」となり、時制が合わない。

114

Although Mr. Porter wanted to sit in the front row, he had to content ------- with being seated in the back row.

(A) he　　　　(C) him
(B) his　　　　(D) himself

Porter さんは最前列に座りたいと思っていましたが、後列に座るしかありませんでした。

語彙チェック □ in the front row 最前列に　□ in the back row 後列に

空所の前の content は had to do という表現に続いているので、ここでは動詞として用いられている。content oneself with 〜 で「〜で満足する」という意味なので、(D) himself を入れると、これが Porter さん自身を指すことになり文意が通る。「後列に座ることで満足せざるをえなかった」ということ。

Level Up!
content A with 〜「Aを〜で満足させる」の形でも使えるので (C) も可能性があるが、この場合 him が指す Porter さん以外の人物が見当たらないため不適切。

115

Mr. Hammond keeps in touch with employees by ------- of a popular social networking app.

(A) way　　　　(C) setting
(B) place　　　(D) access

Hammond さんは人気のあるソーシャル・ネットワーキングアプリを使って従業員と連絡を取っています。

空所前後の by と of と組み合わさって、by way of 〜「〜を手段として」という表現になる (A) way が正解。Hammond さんが従業員と連絡を取る手段を説明する副詞句となり、文意が通る。(B) は「場所」、(C) は「環境」、(D) は「入手」という意味。

116

音読 □□□　解答時間　秒 ▶　秒

正解 **D** □□□□　▶TRACK_097

Mitchum no longer has the ------- force necessary to sustain a business as large as Cox Foods.

(A) laboring
(B) labors
(C) laborious
(D) labor

Mitchum社にはもはや、Cox Foods社と同じくらいの規模の事業を維持するために必要な労働力がありません。

空所は冠詞theと名詞forceの間にあるので、名詞を修飾する形容詞か、forceと組み合わさって複合名詞を作る名詞が入ると考えられる。labor force「労働力」という複合名詞になる (D) labor を入れると、「必要な労働力がない」という内容になり文意が通る。(A) laboring は「骨の折れる」、(C) laborious は「困難な」という意味の形容詞だが、いずれも文意が通らない。

117

音読 □□□　解答時間　秒 ▶　秒

正解 **A** □□□□　▶TRACK_098

Mr. Clarkson often draws ------- his experience as an engineer when doing maintenance work around the house.

(A) on
(B) about
(C) through
(D) to

Clarksonさんはその住宅の周辺のメンテナンス作業をするときに、修理工としての経験を生かすことが多いです。

空所直前の述語動詞drawsと結び付いて意味が通る前置詞を選ぶ。draw on ～で「(経験など) を生かす」という意味になる (A) on を入れると、空所後のhis experience as an engineerとも組み合わさって「修理工としての経験を生かす」という自然な文脈となる。

118

音読 □□□　解答時間　秒 ▶　秒

正解 **C** □□□□　▶TRACK_099

The East Ridge Apartment complex situated across the river ------- more than 1,000 permanent residents.

(A) house
(B) to house
(C) houses
(D) housing

川の向こう側にある East Ridge アパートは、1,000人以上の永住者を収容しています。

語彙チェック　□ permanent　永久的な

まずは文全体の述語動詞を探す。situatedがあるが、後ろに目的語がないため、これは名詞を後ろから修飾する過去分詞であると分かる。よって、この文には述語動詞となる語が必要。主語 The East Ridge Apartment complex は単数形の名詞句なので、house「～を収容する」の三人称単数現在形である (C) houses が正解。

119

音読 □□□　解答時間　秒 ▶　秒

正解 **B** □□□□　▶TRACK_100

Although Mr. Lin was not considered a ------- candidate for the CEO position, he was chosen unanimously by the board of directors.

(A) likeness
(B) likely
(C) liken
(D) like

LinさんはCEOのポジションの有力候補者とはみなされていませんでしたが、取締役会によって満場一致で彼が選ばれました。

語彙チェック　□ unanimously　満場一致で

空所は冠詞aと名詞candidate「候補者」の間にあるので、空所には形容詞が入る。(B) likely は形容詞で「有望な」という意味があるため、likely candidate で「有力候補者」という意味になり文意も通る。

120

音読 □□□　解答時間　秒 ▶　秒

正解 **B** □□□□　▶TRACK_101

The sales goal ------- is what they think is achievable considering the recent market trend.

(A) setting
(B) set
(C) to set
(D) sets

設定された売上目標は、最近の市場のトレンドを考慮すると、達成可能であると考えられるものです。

語彙チェック　□ achievable　達成可能な

空所直後には述語動詞となるbe動詞のisと、whatから始まる名詞節が続いているので、The sales goal ------- が文の主語。名詞を後置修飾する過去分詞の (B) set を入れると、what以降の内容ともつながる。

👑 **Level Up !**

setのように、複数の品詞の働きを持つ語には要注意。選択肢を見ただけで品詞を決めつけてしまわないようにしよう！

121

The store featured in MBC magazine and gaining increasing attention now has some new sports apparel ------- the window.

(A) at
(B) up
(C) in
(D) to

MBC雑誌で特集され、ますます注目を集めるその店舗は今、新しいスポーツウェアをウィンドウに展示しています。

空所の後ろの the window と結び付き、some new sports apparel「新しいスポーツウェア」がどこにあるのか説明を加える前置詞句を作るのに適切なものを選ぶ。in the window で「飾り窓に、陳列してある」という意味の表現となる (C) in を入れると、「飾り窓にある新しいスポーツウェア」となり文意が通る。

122

------- she has only been with Simpson Animation for two years, Ms. Yeardly is being considered for the CFO position.

(A) Given
(B) Even though
(C) As long as
(D) In case

Yeardly さんは Simpson アニメーションにほんの2年間しか在籍していませんが、最高財務責任者のポジションを検討されています。

語彙チェック ☐ CFO　最高財務責任者

選択肢は全て接続詞の働きをする語。カンマ前後の内容を適切につなぐ語を選ぶ。前半の「2年間しか会社に在籍していない」ことと、後半の「最高財務責任者のポジションを検討されている」ことは「逆接」の関係になっているので、(B) Even though「〜にもかかわらず」が正解。(A) は「〜を考慮すれば」、(C) は「〜である限り」、(D) は「〜の場合には」という意味。

123

Drummond Enterprises placed an advertisement online ------- to hire an engineer with experience maintaining cargo vessel engines.

(A) arranging
(B) encouraging
(C) looking
(D) recruiting

Drummond 社は貨物船のエンジン整備の経験を持った修理工を雇おうとして、オンライン上に広告を出しました。

語彙チェック ☐ cargo vessel　貨物船

空所の後ろの to 不定詞と結び付いて意味が通るものを選ぶ。(C) looking は look to do で「〜することを期待する、〜しようとする」という表現になり、ここでは「修理工を雇おうとする」と文意が通るので、(C) が正解。looking to hire から文末までは分詞構文となっている。

👑 **Level Up !**
(A) は arrange to do「〜するよう手配する」、(B) は encourage A to do「A を〜するように励ます」、(D) は recruit to do「〜するのを手伝う」のように、誤答の選択肢も to 不定詞と結び付く表現があるので注意！

124

Ms. Walters refused to give any ------- to the idea of merging with a larger company.

(A) considering
(B) consideration
(C) considerate
(D) considerably

Walters さんは、より規模の大きい会社と合併するという意見について検討することを拒否しました。

空所の前には動詞 give と形容詞 any があるので、空所には give の目的語となる名詞が必要。名詞である (B) を入れると、give consideration to 〜で「〜に配慮する、〜を考慮する」という意味の表現となり文意が通る。

125

It is important that user manuals for the photography software be thorough yet -------.

(A) reflective
(B) variable
(C) benevolent
(D) succinct

その写真ソフトウェアの利用者手引書は、詳細だが簡潔であることが重要です。

語彙チェック ☐ thorough　完全な、詳細な

空所直前の yet は、「それにもかかわらず、けれども」という意味を表す逆接の接続詞。形容詞 thorough「詳細な」と空所が yet によって並列されているので、that 節の主語である user manuals「利用者手引書」を説明する形容詞として適切なものを空所に入れる。「手引書は詳細だが簡潔である」と考えると文意が通るので、(D) succinct が正解。(A) は「考え込む」、(B) は「変化しやすい」、(C) は「善意の」という意味。

126

正解 **C** □□□□ ▶TRACK_107

The date for the annual sales conference has been pushed ------- on account of scheduling issues.

(A) away 　　　　　　　(C) back
(B) over 　　　　　　　 (D) along

年次販売会議の日程は、スケジュールの都合上延期されました。

語彙チェック □ on account of ～　～のために

空所の前には動詞 pushed、後ろには on account of ～「～のために」という前置詞句がある。空所以降は意味のまとまりとして成立しているので、空所には動詞 push と結び付いて意味が通るものを入れる。(C) back を入れると、push back ～「～を延期する」という表現を使った受動態の文となり文意が通る。

👑 **Level Up!**
誤答もそれぞれ動詞 push と結び付く表現がある。(A) は push away ～「～を払いのける」、(B) は push over「席を詰める」、(D) は push along「どんどん進む」となるので合わせて覚えておこう！

127

正解 **B** □□□□ ▶TRACK_108

The marketing team discussed their targets and ------- they reach them in the most efficient way.

(A) wherever 　　　　　(C) what
(B) how 　　　　　　　 (D) which

マーケティングチームは彼らの目標と、それらの目標を最も効率的なやり方で達成する方法について話し合いました。

空所前の接続詞 and によって their targets と空所以降が並列され、述語動詞 discussed の目的語となっていることを掴む。「～する方法」という意味の名詞節を導く (B) how が正解。先行詞となる語句がないことと、空所以降の節に文の要素が揃っていることから、(C) と (D) は不適切。また、(A) wherever は動詞の目的語となる名詞節を導く場合、「～するところならどこでも」という意味になるので文意が通らない。

128

正解 **C** □□□□ ▶TRACK_109

The client has submitted ------- that will make the arrangement unprofitable for us.

(A) demand 　　　　　　(C) demands
(B) demanding 　　　　 (D) to demand

顧客は、その取り決めを私たちにとって利益のないものにするような要求を提示しました。

語彙チェック □ unprofitable　利益のない

空所は、主語（The client）、動詞（has submitted）の後の目的語にあたる。空所前には冠詞がないため、名詞の (A) と (C) のうち、複数形である (C) が正解。demand には不可算名詞の用法もあるが、「需要」という意味になるため文意が通らない。

129

正解 **C** □□□□ ▶TRACK_110

Although the documentary filmmakers shot hundreds of hours of footage, very ------- of it was used in the series.

(A) few 　　　　　　　　(C) little
(B) nothing 　　　　　　(D) seldom

そのドキュメンタリー映画製作者たちは何百時間もの映像を撮影したにもかかわらず、シリーズ内で使われた映像はほとんどありませんでした。

空所の前には形容詞 very、後ろには前置詞句 of it があるので、空所には名詞の働きをする語が入る。of it の it はカンマ前の footage という不可算名詞を指していることから、(C) little を空所に入れると、very little of it で「それ（撮影した何百時間もの映像）のほんのわずかな時間」という意味になり文意が通る。(A) few は可算名詞の複数形を受けるときに使う。

130

正解 **C** □□□□ ▶TRACK_111

The way JMB Cooking analyzes recent market trends based on statistical data figures ------- in what is then going to be produced.

(A) inconsistently 　　　(C) prominently
(B) simultaneously 　　 (D) overly

JMB Cooking 社が統計データに基づいて最近の市場のトレンドを分析する方法は、次に何が製造されるかに深く関わっています。

語彙チェック □ figure in ～　～で重要な役割を演じる

文頭から data までがこの文の主語。述語動詞は figures で、「重要な位置を占める」という意味。これを修飾するのに適切なのは (C) prominently「深く」。figure prominently in ～「～の中で極めて重要である、～に深く関わっている」という意味の表現になる。(A) は「矛盾して」、(B) は「同時に」、(D) は「過度に」という意味。

Part 6

Questions 131-134 refer to the following memo.

To: Customer Service Staff
From: Casy Summers
Date: August 2
Subject: Get ready to welcome

This memo is to let everyone know that a new 131. is starting tomorrow. Her name is Nora Timms, and she 132. the customer service group. Please do your best to make her feel welcome. There is a morning orientation workshop for her and the other new employees. She is going to take part in the workshop with them shortly after she reports to work at 9 A.M. She is available 133. that. I am going to invite her to have lunch with us at Lancelot's. I would like as many people as possible to attend. Please let me know whether or not you can make it by 5 P.M. 134. .

問題131-134は次のメモに関するものです。

宛先：カスタマーサービス職員
差出人：Casy Summers
日付：8月2日
件名：歓迎する準備をしてください

このメモは、明日から新入社員が働き始めることをお知らせするものです。彼女の名前はNora Timmsで、カスタマーサービスグループに加わる予定です。彼女を温かく迎えるために、最善を尽くしてください。彼女とその他の新入社員のためのオリエンテーションワークショップが午前中にあります。彼女は午前9時に出社した後すぐに、他の新入社員とともにそのワークショップに参加する予定です。彼女はその後は空いています。Lancelot'sというお店で私たちと一緒に昼食をとるよう、私は彼女に依頼しようと思っています。私はできるだけ多くの人に出席してもらいたいです。出席できるかどうか、午後5時までに教えてください。*帰る前に予約しようと思います。

語彙チェック ☐ get ready to do ～するための準備をする ☐ make *A* feel welcome Aを温かく迎える
☐ shortly after ～ ～のすぐ後に ☐ report to work 出社する

131　正解 D

(A) protocol	(A) 名詞「条項」
(B) acumen	(B) 名詞「鋭さ」
(C) patron	(C) 名詞「常連」
(D) associate	(D) 名詞「同僚」

空所はメモの1文目にある。2文目に Her name is Nora Timms「彼女の名前は Nora Timms です」とあることや、続く3文目に do your best to make her feel welcome「彼女を温かく迎えるために最善を尽くす」とあることから、カスタマーサービスグループに新しく社員が加わることを既存の職員に伝えるためのメモであることが分かるので、(D) が正解。「歓迎する準備をしてください」というメモの件名もヒントになる。

132　正解 A

(A) will be joining	(A) 動詞 join「〜に加わる」の未来進行形
(B) had joined	(B) 過去完了
(C) was being joined	(C) 過去進行形の受動態
(D) joins	(D) 三人称単数現在形

空所直前にある主語の she は、Nora Timms のことを指している。1文目に tomorrow という単語があることに注目。彼女が加わるのは未来のことと分かるので (A) が正解。それ以降も、5文目に She is going to take part in 〜「彼女（＝ Nora Timms）は〜に参加する予定です」と未来の表現が使われていることもヒントになる。

♛ **Level Up !**

誤答の選択肢 (D) は現在形。現在形も未来を表すことができるが、その場合は電車など公共交通機関の発車時刻や映画の開始時刻などに対して使われることが多く、本問では不適切。

133　正解 C

(A) because of	(A) 前置詞句「〜の理由で」
(B) during	(B) 前置詞「〜の間」
(C) after	(C) 前置詞「〜の後に」
(D) along	(D) 前置詞「〜に沿って」

空所の後ろにある代名詞の that が何を指しているのかを、正確に把握することがポイント。指示代名詞の that はそれ以前に登場した単数名詞を受けるので、空所以前の文から that が指している名詞を探す。5文目に the workshop という語句があり、これは4文目の a morning orientation workshop を受けていると分かる。よって、この that は「オリエンテーションワークショップ」のこと。主語の She は Nora Timms さんのことなので、「Nora Timms さんはオリエンテーションワークショップ------- 空いている」という意味になることから、空所に (C) を入れると文意が通る。

134　正解 B

(A) We need to book tickets as early as possible.	(A) 私たちはできるだけ早くチケットを予約する必要があります。
(B) I will make a reservation before I leave.	(B) 帰る前に予約しようと思います。
(C) I will introduce her to whoever needs her help.	(C) 彼女の助けを必要とする人なら誰にでも彼女のことを紹介します。
(D) It is only open in the evenings.	(D) それは夕方しか営業していません。

空所は本文の最後にある。空所の前まででは、メモの差出人である Casy Summers さんが、新入社員の Nora Timms さんを明日ランチへ誘うつもりであることや、できるだけ多くのカスタマーサービス職員にそのランチに出席してほしいと思っていることが述べられている。そうした話を受け、空所直前の文では「出席できるかどうか、午後5時までに教えてください」と頼んでいる。出席連絡の期限を伝えている流れから、Casy Summers さんは今日帰宅する前に、明日のランチの予約をしようと思っているという文脈が自然なので、(B) が正解。(D) は主語の It が Lancelot's というお店のことを指しているとも考えられるが、そのお店にはランチに行こうとしているので、営業時間が合わない。

語彙チェック　□ as early as possible　できるだけ早く

Questions 135-138 refer to the following e-mail.

▶TRACK_113

To: Jax Ortega <jortega@wyldestalyns.com>
From: Kim Wissler <kwissler@freedomheatmix.com>
Date: May 4
Subject: Your order

Dear Mr. Ortega,

Thank you for your order of an off-peak thermal storage heater for your home. Although it is for 135. use, it weighs in excess of 50 kilograms. We have one in stock, but shipping may take up to two weeks depending on the availability of our shipping company. 136.. Please let me know if you would like us to recommend a qualified electrical technician in your area. The heater 137. in a protective plastic sheet by the manufacturer. Please be sure to remove 138. before turning it on for the first time.

問題135-138は次のEメールに関するものです。

受信者：Jax Ortega <jortega@wyldestalyns.com>
送信者：Kim Wissler <kwissler@freedomheatmix.com>
日付：5月4日
件名：ご注文

Ortega 様

ご自宅用のオフピーク蓄熱ヒーターをご注文いただき、ありがとうございます。家庭用とはいえ、それは50キログラムを超える重量です。在庫は1台ありますが、発送は運送会社の都合によっては最大2週間かかる場合があります。*ご注文に設置が含まれていないことに気が付きました。お近くの、資格を持つ電気技術者を弊社におすすめしてほしい場合は、お知らせください。ヒーターは製造業者によって保護ビニールシートに包まれていました。初めて電源を入れる前に、必ずそれを取り除いてください。

語彙チェック　□ off-peak　オフピークの　□ thermal　熱の　□ weigh　重さが〜である　□ in excess of 〜　〜より多く
□ up to 〜　（最高）〜まで　□ qualified　資格を有する　□ protective　保護用の　□ be sure to *do*　必ず〜する
□ turn 〜 on　（明かりなど）をつける

135

(A) industrial

(B) domestic

(C) limited

(D) local

(A) 形容詞「産業の」

(B) 形容詞「家庭の」

(C) 形容詞「限られた」

(D) 形容詞「地元の」

1文目から、Eメールの受信者であるOrtegaさんは、自宅用のオフピーク蓄熱ヒーターを注文したということが分かる。空所を含む文の主語itは、このan off-peak thermal storage heater「オフピーク蓄熱ヒーター」を指していることから、for your home「自宅用の」の言い換えにあたるfor domestic useという表現を作る(B)が正解。

136

(A) Unfortunately, we do not have any affiliates near you.

(B) It is light enough for one person to carry with ease.

(C) I noticed that you have not included installation in your order.

(D) As it is a used item, there is only a one-month warranty.

(A) 残念ながら、お近くに弊社の支店はございません。

(B) それは1人で楽々と運ぶのに十分な軽さです。

(C) ご注文に設置が含まれていないことに気が付きました。

(D) それは中古品なので、1カ月分の保証しかありません。

空所の後ろの文には、「電気技術者を弊社におすすめしてほしい場合は」とある。空所以前には電気技術者に関わる話題は出てきていないので、空所には電気技術者につながる情報が述べられる必要がある。installation「設置、取り付け」という単語を含む(C)に注目。注文に設置が含まれていないということは、すなわち、後ほど取り付けるのに電気技術者が必要になるかもしれないということ。よって、a qualified electrical technicianの話題へと自然につながる文脈を作る(C)が正解。

語彙チェック ☐ affiliate 支社 ☐ with ease 楽々と ☐ warranty 保証

137

(A) was wrapped

(B) had been wrapped

(C) was wrapping

(D) wraps

(A) 動詞wrap「～を包む」の過去形の受動態

(B) 過去完了の受動態

(C) 過去進行形

(D) 三人称単数現在形

主語のThe heaterは、3文目でWe have one in stock「在庫は1台ある」と述べられているヒーターのこと。選択肢の並びから、態と時制の2つの観点に沿って適切なものを選ぶ。wrap「～を包む」という他動詞の目的語となる名詞が空所の後ろにはないことと、by the manufacturer「製造業者によって」という語句があることから、受動態である(A)と(B)が正解候補。(B)の過去完了は過去のある時点を基準として、それ以前のことを言及するときに用いるので、ここでは不適切。よって、(A)が正解。

138

(A) them

(B) him

(C) one

(D) it

(A) 代名詞「それら」

(B) 代名詞「彼」

(C) 代名詞「1つ」

(D) 代名詞「それ」

空所を含む文の内容は、「初めて電源を入れる前に、必ず-------を取り除いてください」というもの。turning it onのitは、Ortegaさんが注文した「オフピーク蓄熱ヒーター」のことを指している。空所の前の文では、そのヒーターについて「製造業者によって保護ビニールシートに包まれていた」と述べられている。よって、使用を開始する前に取り除くものとして、前出のa protective plastic sheet「保護ビニールシート」を指す(D)を空所に入れると文意が通る。

> 👑 **Level Up！**
> 誤答の選択肢(C)のoneは不特定多数のものの中の1つを指すので、ここでは不適切。代名詞の用法を改めて復習しておこう。

Questions 139-142 refer to the following advertisement.

Holland Taban Power (HTP)

HTP can help your business cope with fluctuating _139._ requirements. We have a database of over 10,000 highly trained individuals with experience in all kinds of industries. Independent surveys show that HTP's clients have some of the highest satisfaction scores in the industry. _140._ , many express interest in making the situation permanent. If both parties are _141._, this can be arranged by paying a reasonable one-time introduction fee. If things are not working out as well as you would like, simply request a replacement. _142._ .

www.hollandtabanpower.com

問題139-142は次の広告に関するものです。

Holland Taban Power (HTP)

HTP社は、お客様の会社が、変動する人員配置のニーズに対処するのをお手伝いします。弊社には、あらゆる業界で経験を積んだ、1万人以上の高度な訓練を受けた人材のデータベースがあります。外部調査によると、HTP社のお客様は業界で最も高い満足度を得ているということが示されています。当然、多くのお客様はその状況を恒久化することに興味を示します。もし双方が受け入れるのであれば、一回限りのお手頃な紹介料を支払うことで、これを実現できます。もしお望みのようにうまくはいかないようでしたら、代わりの人を要請してください。*面倒な手続きや追加料金なしで、必要な手配は全て弊社が行います。

www.hollandtabanpower.com

語彙チェック □ cope with 〜　〜に対処する　□ fluctuating　変動する　□ independent　独立した、独自の
□ permanent　恒久的な　□ reasonable　（値段などが）まあまあの

139 正解 A ☐☐☐☐

(A) staffing	(A) 職員の配置
(B) parking	(B) 駐車
(C) funding	(C) 資金
(D) housing	(D) 住宅

空所があるのは広告の1文目。この内容を受けて話が展開していく2文目では、「あらゆる業界で経験を積んだ、1万人以上の高度な訓練を受けた人材のデータベースがある」と述べられている。よって、HTP社は人材派遣会社であることが分かるので、同社が提供するサービスの内容として文意が通る(A)が正解。

140 正解 B ☐☐☐☐

(A) Equally	(A) 等しく
(B) Naturally	(B) 当然
(C) In contrast	(C) 対照的に
(D) Similarly	(D) 同様に

空所前後の文脈に適したものを選ぶ。空所の前には「HTP社のお客様は業界で最も高い満足度を得ている」とある。一方、空所の後ろには、「多くのお客様はその状況を恒久化することに興味を示す」と述べられている。よって、空所以降の文は、高い満足度を得ている顧客が当然とる行動について述べていると考えると自然な文脈となるので、(B)が正解。

141 正解 D ☐☐☐☐

(A) desirable	(A) 望ましい
(B) responsible	(B) 責任がある
(C) deniable	(C) 否定できる
(D) amenable	(D) 受け入れる

空所を含む節は「もし両者が〜であれば」という意味。空所の前文までに、多くの利用者がHTP社に派遣された人材にずっと居続けてほしいと希望する、という内容が述べられている。「受け入れる」という意味の(D)を入れると、「もし双方が受け入れるのであれば（この希望が叶う）」と説明する文となり、文意が通る。

142 正解 C ☐☐☐☐

(A) You can rest assured there is no one better for your organization.	(A) あなたの組織にこれ以上適した人は誰もいませんのでご安心ください。
(B) All placements are final and no further requests will be entertained.	(B) 全ての配置は最終決定であり、いかなる要求にも応じることはできません。
(C) We will make all the necessary arrangements with no fuss or additional charges.	(C) 面倒な手続きや追加料金なしで、必要な手配は全て弊社が行います。
(D) Simply give our customer service staff your warranty number over the telephone.	(D) お電話にて、カスタマーサービス職員にあなたの保証書番号をお伝えください。

空所は本文の最後にあるので、それ以前にどんな話題が出ているかに注目する。空所の前文に「もしお望みのようにうまくはいかないようでしたら、代わりの人を要請してください」とある。よって、(C)を入れると、代わりの人を手配する手続き上の話が続くことになり、文意が通る。誤答はいずれも本文の流れに合わず、文意が通らない。

語彙チェック ☐ rest assured (that) 〜　〜に安心する　☐ entertain　（申し出など）を受け入れる　☐ fuss　厄介ごと、不満

Questions 143-146 refer to the following notice.

▶TRACK_115

NOTICE

Attention patrons,

The Moreton Public Library will be closed from April 9 to April 24. During this period, we will be accepting 143. at a mobile building parked by the fountain near the main entrance. There will be a chute by the front door for after-hours use. Librarians will be present in the office during the library's regular hours of operation. 144. . You will be able to view the online catalog and request books. 145., staff will require 24 hours to retrieve the books from the collection. Loans 146. at the previously mentioned mobile building. Further details are available on our Web site. You can view them at www.moretonpubliclibrary.com.

問題143-146は次のお知らせに関するものです。

お知らせ

利用者の皆さまへ

Moreton 公共図書館は、4月9日から4月24日まで閉館となります。この期間、正面玄関近くにある噴水のそばに停められている移動式建物で、返却を受け付ける予定です。時間外の利用に関しては、その移動式建物の玄関わきにシュートがあります。図書館の通常の営業時間内は、図書館員が事務所にいます。*残念ながら、図書館をご利用のお客様は、当館の蔵書を閲覧することができません。オンラインカタログを閲覧したり、蔵書をリクエストしたりすることは可能です。しかしながら、スタッフが蔵書の中から本を取り寄せるのには、24時間必要です。貸出は先述した移動式建物で処理されます。詳細は当館のウェブサイトでご案内しています。www.moretonpubliclibrary.com でご覧いただけます。

語彙チェック □ fountain 噴水 □ chute シュート（郵便物などを下へ滑り落とす装置） □ librarian 図書館員
□ be present （ある場所に）いる □ retrieve A from B AをBから取り戻す □ loan 貸出 □ previously 以前に

143

(A) applications
(B) returns
(C) entries
(D) submissions

(A) 申し込み
(B) 返却物
(C) 入会
(D) 提案

この文書は、図書館の一時閉館期間中のサービスの利用方法について知らせるもの。空所は、述語動詞 will be accepting の目的語の位置にある。閉館中の図書館が受け付けるものとして最も適切なのは、(B) returns「返却物」。また、続く文に「時間外の利用に関しては、シュートがある」と述べられていることからも (B) が適切と分かる。(A)(C)(D)はいずれも、これにつながる内容が文書内に述べられていないので不正解。

144

(A) They will be temporarily halting all services next week.
(B) Our policy on the use of mobile phones in the library has been updated.
(C) Unfortunately, our collection will be unavailable for library patrons to peruse.
(D) Nevertheless, a nearby parking space will be available to our visitors.

(A) 彼らは来週、一時的に全てのサービスを停止する予定です。
(B) 図書館での携帯電話の使用に関する当館の方針が更新されました。
(C) 残念ながら、図書館をご利用のお客様は、当館の蔵書を閲覧することができません。
(D) それにもかかわらず、ご来館のお客様は近くの駐車場をご利用いただけます。

空所に続く文では「オンラインカタログを閲覧したり、蔵書をリクエストしたりすることは可能」であるということが述べられている。空所に (C) を入れると、図書館の閉館中に来館者が利用できるサービスとして、「蔵書を閲覧することはできないが、オンラインカタログの閲覧や蔵書のリクエストは可能」という文意となり、自然な文脈となる。選択肢 (A) は主語の They が前文の Librarians を指すと考えることもできるが、空所に続く文に述べられているように、サービスの一部は閉館中も利用可能であることから不適切。

語彙チェック ☐ temporarily 一時的に ☐ halt 〜を停止させる ☐ peruse 〜を読む

145

(A) Accordingly
(B) Otherwise
(C) Therefore
(D) However

(A) それに応じて
(B) さもなければ
(C) それゆえに
(D) しかしながら

前後の文脈に適したものを選ぶ。一時的な閉館期間に図書館の利用客ができることとして、空所の前では「オンラインカタログを閲覧したり、蔵書をリクエストしたりすることは可能」だと述べられている。一方、空所の後ろでは「スタッフが蔵書の中から本を取り寄せるのには、24時間必要」と述べられている。よって、空所の前後は「蔵書のリクエストは可能だが、ある程度時間が必要」という逆接の関係になっていると分かるので、(D) が正解。

146

(A) will be processed
(B) have been processed
(C) processed
(D) to process

(A) 助動詞 will ＋動詞 process「〜を処理する」の受動態
(B) 現在完了の受動態
(C) 過去形・過去分詞
(D) to 不定詞

空所を含む文は「貸出は先述した移動式建物で -------」という意味。mobile building「移動式建物」というキーワードに注目する。2文目から、これは図書館の閉館期間中に利用できる施設であることが分かる。図書館が閉館するのは未来のことなので、(A) が正解。

👑 Level Up!
Part 6の時制を問う問題は、空所を含む1文だけを読んでも解くことができない。時制を問う設問を確認したら、特に時制に注意をしながら英文を読み進めることがカギ！

Part 7

Questions 147-148 refer to the following memo.

WHILE YOU WERE OUT

For: Don Ayoade

Date: Tuesday, November 10

Time: 11:23 A.M.

Caller: Helen Minter

From: Dainty Software

TEL: 216-555-8543

Message: ❶Tomorrow, Ms. Minter will interview Seth White for a position at her company. She wanted to speak to you because he has listed you as one of his character references. I told her that you were quite busy today, and she assured me that it would only take a minute. She will call back at 3:30 P.M. Otherwise, you could call her whenever you have some free time. ❷Please let me know if you would like a copy of Mr. White's personnel record. I will have someone in HR deliver it to you.

Taken By: Paul Townsend

問題147-148は次のメモに関するものです。

伝言メモ

宛先： Don Ayoade
日付： 11月10日 火曜日
時間： 午前11時23分
発信者： Helen Minter
所属： Dainty Software 社
電話番号：216-555-8543

メッセージ：明日、Minter さんが彼女の会社での職について、Seth White の面接を行います。White さんは推薦人の一人としてあなたを入れていたようなので、Minter さんがあなたと話をしたいとのことでした。今日はかなり忙しいとお伝えしたら、話はすぐに済むとおっしゃっていました。午後3時半に折り返し電話してくださるとのことですが、折り返しがなければ、お手すきの際に Ayoade さんの方からお電話いただいても問題ありません。White さんの人事記録のコピーをご希望でしたら、お知らせください。人事部の者に届けに行かせます。

受信者：Paul Townsend

語彙チェック □ list 〜をリストに入れる、〜を挙げる □ character reference 人物推薦人、人物証明書
□ assure A that 〜 確かに〜だと A に言う □ personnel record 人事記録

147

What is implied about Mr. White?

(A) He previously worked at Mr. Ayoade's company.

(B) He is currently employed at Dainty Software.

(C) He is a member of the human resources department.

(D) He has moved to a different city.

Whiteさんについて何が示唆されていますか。

(A) 彼は以前、Ayoadeさんの会社で働いていた。

(B) 彼は現在Dainty Software社で雇用されている。

(C) 彼は人事部の一員である。

(D) 彼は別の都市に引っ越した。

❶に「MinterさんがSeth Whiteという人物の面接を行う予定で、Whiteさんは推薦人の一人としてあなたを入れている」といった内容が書かれている。ここでの「あなた」とはメモの宛先であるAyoadeさんのことである。推薦状を書いてくれる推薦人は、その人物の資質を詳しく知る前職の同僚や友人、家族など、近い関係にある人。これらの情報から、WhiteさんはAyoadeさんの会社で勤めていた可能性が高いと判断できる。よって、(A)が正解。

👑Level Up！

What is implied about 〜？という問題は、根拠が明確には書かれておらず、推測をして解かなければならない問題。不安になって、時間をかけすぎないように注意しよう。

148

What does Mr. Townsend offer to do?

(A) Speak with an applicant

(B) Schedule a meeting

(C) Deliver a message to Ms. Minter

(D) Request some documents

Townsendさんは何をすることを申し出ていますか。

(A) 候補者と話をする

(B) 会議の日程を決める

(C) Minterさんに伝言を届ける

(D) 資料を要求する

Townsendさんは、❷で「Whiteさんの人事記録のコピーが必要なら、人事部の者に（Ayoadeさんの元へ）届けに行かせる」と述べている。a copy of Mr. White's personnel record「Whiteさんの人事記録のコピー」をsome documents「資料」と言い換え、「資料を（人事部に）要求する」とした(D)が正解。

Questions 149-150 refer to the following text-message chain. ▶TRACK_117

Sofia Berger 8:50 A.M.
I'm taking the day off today. ❶Would you mind watering my plants before you leave this evening?

Peter Brown 8:51 A.M.
Happy to. There is a parcel on your desk marked urgent, though. Do you want me to take a look inside?

Sofia Berger 8:53 A.M.
❷I wasn't expecting anything. You'd better open it up just in case.

Peter Brown 8:54 A.M.
It's a manual for the new 3D printer.

Sofia Berger 8:56 A.M.
That's right! ❸I had to request one because they shipped the printer without it.

Peter Brown 8:59 A.M.
Ok, I'll put it in the cabinet with the printer.

Sofia Berger 9:02 A.M.
Thanks, Peter. The plants will need a little extra water. I won't be in until Monday morning.

Peter Brown 9:03 A.M.
I'll set an alarm, so I don't forget.

問題149-150は次のテキストメッセージのやりとりに関するものです。

Sofia Berger ［午前8時50分］
今日はお休みをいただいています。今日の夕方帰宅する前に、植物に水をあげてもらえませんか。

Peter Brown ［午前8時51分］
もちろんです。あなたのデスクに緊急と書かれた小包が置いてありますが。中を見た方がいいでしょうか。

Sofia Berger ［午前8時53分］
何も受け取る予定はないのですが。念のため、開けていただいた方がいいかもしれません。

Peter Brown ［午前8時54分］
新しい3Dプリンターの説明書ですね。

Sofia Berger ［午前8時56分］
そうでした！　プリンターが説明書なしで届いたので、1部送ってもらわなければならなかったんです。

Peter Brown ［午前8時59分］
分かりました。プリンターと一緒に戸棚に入れておきますね。

Sofia Berger ［午前9時02分］
ありがとうございます、Peter。植物は少し余分に水が必要かもしれません。月曜の朝まで戻らない予定なので。

Peter Brown ［午前9時03分］
忘れないように、アラームをセットしておきます。

語彙チェック □ water 〜に水やりをする □ parcel 包み □ marked 印の付いた □ urgent 緊急の □ expect 〜を予期する

149

正解 B □□□□

What is one purpose of the text-message chain?

(A) To request time off work

(B) To ask a favor

(C) To announce some changes

(D) To provide feedback

テキストメッセージのやり取りの目的の1つは何ですか。

(A) 仕事の休みを申請すること

(B) お願いをすること

(C) 変更を知らせること

(D) フィードバックを行うこと

文書の目的を問う問題。このテキストメッセージのやり取りを始めているBergerさんは、❶でBrownさんに対して、「今日の夕方帰宅する前に、植物に水をあげてもらえないか」とお願いをしている。よって、(B)が正解。

👑 **Level Up !**

What is one purpose of ～?「～の目的の1つは何ですか」という設問の場合、文書の目的が複数ある可能性が高い。複数ある目的のうちの1つを選択肢から選べばOKなので、あまり悩みすぎないようにしよう。

語彙チェック □ ask a favor　頼みごとをする

150

正解 C □□□□

At 8:56 A.M., what does Ms. Berger mean when she writes, "That's right"?

(A) She agrees with Mr. Brown.

(B) She wants to encourage Mr. Brown.

(C) She had forgotten what she did.

(D) She knows the answer.

午前8時56分に、"That's right" という発言で、Bergerさんは何を意図していますか。

(A) 彼女はBrownさんに同意している。

(B) 彼女はBrownさんを励ましたいと思っている。

(C) 彼女は自分がしたことを忘れていた。

(D) 彼女は答えを知っている。

Brownさんが「デスクに緊急と書かれた小包が置いてある」と述べており、これに対してBergerさんは❷で「何の心当たりもない」と述べている。Brownさんが「新しい3Dプリンターの説明書だ」と説明すると、BergerさんはThat's right! と述べ、さらに❸で「プリンターが説明書なしで届いたので、1部送ってもらわなければならなかった」と、小包が届いた理由を思い出している。Bergerさんは自分がしたこと（＝説明書を1部送ってもらうよう依頼したこと）を忘れていたと分かるので、(C)が正解。

語彙チェック □ encourage　～を励ます

Questions 151-152 refer to the following notice.

▶TRACK_118

Notice to Camden Town Residents

We have received many calls about trees on public land with branches overhanging private property. Under no circumstances should you attempt to prune or cut down trees in our public parks or any public areas yourself. Town maintenance crews are addressing the issue as fast as they can. Unfortunately, it may take as long as a month before they can respond to your particular request. ❶ If you believe that the branches pose a risk to your home, you should take a photograph and send it to the director of the Parks Maintenance Department at pmddirector@ctcc.com.au. ❷ If you have trees on your property whose branches are in danger of falling onto any part of your home, you may hire a professional tree surgeon to come and remove those limbs. ❸ It is necessary, however, to receive permission from the council if you plan to remove any tree taller than five meters. Please use the form on the council Web site to request a consultation. You will typically receive a response within 24 hours.

問題151-152は次のお知らせに関するものです。

Camden町にお住まいの皆さまへのお知らせ

公有地の樹木が私有地の方に枝を張り出しているというお電話を多数いただいております。いかなる場合においても、公園や公共区域内にある樹木の剪定や伐採をご自身で行わないようにお願いいたします。町の保守員が、できる限り迅速にこの問題に対処しております。あいにく、皆さまの個々のご要望にお応えするまでに1カ月ほどかかる可能性がございます。枝がご自宅に危険を及ぼすと思われる場合は、写真を撮り、公園管理部の部長（pmddirector@ctcc.com.au）にお送りください。ご自宅のどこかに枝が落ちてくる危険のある樹木が、敷地内にある場合、専門の樹木医を雇ってそれらの大枝を除去しに来てもらうことが可能です。ただし、5メートルを超える高さの木を切り倒す場合は、地方自治体の許可が必要です。自治体のウェブサイトにあるフォームより、相談の予約を行ってください。通常、24時間以内に回答が届きます。

語彙チェック □ branch 枝 □ overhang 〜の上にかかる □ property 所有地
□ under no circumstances どんなことがあっても決して〜ない □ prune 〜を取り除く □ address 〜に取り組む
□ pose 〜を引き起こす □ fall 落ちる □ tree surgeon 樹木医 □ remove 〜を除去する □ limb 大枝
□ permission 許可 □ council 地方自治体 □ typically 通常は

151

正解 C ☐☐☐☐

What is the purpose of the notice?

(A) To announce a rule change

(B) To recommend preventative maintenance

(C) To explain a procedure

(D) To request volunteer assistance

お知らせの目的は何ですか。

(A) ルールの変更を知らせること

(B) 予防保全を勧めること

(C) 手順を説明すること

(D) ボランティアの助けを要請すること

文書全体は、町役場がCamden町の住民に対して出したお知らせであると考えられる。私有地に張り出す公有地の樹木の枝に関する対処法として、❶で「枝が自宅に危険を及ぼすと思われる場合は、写真を撮って公園管理部の部長に送るように」と、町民が取るべき行動の手順を説明している。❶以降も、さまざまな条件における対処の手順について説明を続けているので、(C)が正解。

語彙チェック ☐ preventative　予防の

152

正解 D ☐☐☐☐

What does the notice say about removing tall trees on private land?

(A) It can be scheduled using the council Web site.

(B) It must be carried out by town employees.

(C) It is required to notify the neighbors of the work.

(D) It is necessary to obtain prior official approval.

私有地の高い木を除去することについて、お知らせに書かれていることは何ですか。

(A) 地方自治体のウェブサイトでスケジュールを立てられる。

(B) 町の職員によって実施されなければならない。

(C) 作業に関して近所の人々に告知する必要がある。

(D) 事前に正式な承認を得る必要がある。

私有地の木の枝の除去については、❷以降で言及されている。そして❸では、「5メートルを超える高さの木を切り倒す場合は地方自治体の許可が必要」と述べられている。よって、(D)が正解。permission from the council「地方自治体の許可」がofficial approval「正式な承認」に言い換えられている。自治体のウェブサイトにあるフォームは木を撤去してもらう許可を得るための相談に使われるものであり、木の撤去の予約自体を行うことができるとは述べられていないので、(A)は不正解。

語彙チェック ☐ carry out 〜　〜を行う　☐ notify A of B　AにBを通知する

To:	Jim Nichol <jnichol@coolboysandthefrontman.com>
From:	Chief Organizer <co@seattlebobcoc.com>
Date:	September 2
Subject:	Are you ready?

Dear Battle of the Bands entrant,

❶ We are no longer accepting applications for the Seattle Battle of the Bands. ❷ Recipients of this e-mail should have already received acceptance letters at this stage. If you have not received official notice, please contact Dalton Walker at dwalker@seattlebobcoc.com. In total, 50 bands will take part in the competition. ❸ The event will take place between September 23 and September 27. The first round will be held online. ❹ You should upload a video of your band playing their best original song to Flixnet.com and e-mail a link to the event organizers. The appropriate e-mail address is mentioned in the aforementioned document. You have until September 20 to complete this step. You may e-mail me if you are having any difficulty with this step. ❺ Out of the 50, 25 bands will perform in front of a live audience at Kingsmill Auditorium on September 26 and 27. Please wait for announcements of rehearsal times and equipment testing.

Contestants should keep in mind that audience participation will be one of the evaluation criteria. It is important to practice your stagecraft as well as your technical musical performance. Visit the following link to view videos of previous years' competitions. This should provide an indication of the quality that is expected and provide some inspiration for your performance.

www.seattlebob.com

Good luck!

Sam Bygrave
Chief Organizer
Seattle Battle of the Bands

問題153-154は次のEメールに関するものです。

受信者：Jim Nichol <jnichol@coolboysandthefrontman.com>
送信者：主催者 <co@seattlebobcoc.com>
日付：9月2日
件名：準備はいいですか？

Battle of the Bandsの参加者の皆さま

Seattle Battle of the Bandsの応募受付は締め切らせていただきました。このEメールを受信された方は、この段階ですでに合格通知を受け取っているはずです。もし正式な通知を受け取っていない場合は、Dalton Walker（dwalker@seattlebobcoc.com）までご連絡ください。合計50組のバンドがコンテストに参加します。イベントは、9月23日から9月27日の間に開催される予定です。一次予選はオンラインで行われます。あなたのバンドが最高のオリジナル曲を演奏している動画をFlixnet.comにアップロードし、そのリンクをイベント主催者にEメールでお送りください。正しいEメールアドレスは、前で述べた書類に記載されています。9月20日までにこの手順を完了させてください。このステップに問題がある場合は、私にEメールを送っていただいてもかまいません。計50組のバンドのうち25組は、9月26日と27日にKingsmill講堂にて生の観客の前で演奏していただく予定です。リハーサルの時間や機材テストに関するお知らせをお待ちください。

出場者は、観客の参加も評価基準の1つであることを念頭に置く必要があります。技術的な演奏だけでなく、ステージの演出法も練習しておくことが大切です。以下のリンクから、過去のコンテストの動画をご覧いただくことができます。これにより期待されている水準が分かり、なおかつご自身の演奏へのヒントとなるはずです。

www.seattlebob.com

幸運をお祈りしております！

Sam Bygrave
主催者
Seattle Battle of the Bands

語彙チェック　□ recipient　受取人　□ acceptance letter　合格通知　□ take part in ～　～に参加する　□ first round　1回戦
□ appropriate　適切な　□ aforementioned　前述の　□ evaluation　評価　□ criteria　基準
□ stagecraft　演出法　□ indication　兆候　□ inspiration　着想の源

153

正解 B ☐☐☐☐

According to the e-mail, how can readers find the appropriate e-mail address to send video links to?

(A) By downloading the attached document
(B) By checking their acceptance letters
(C) By calling the organizing committee
(D) By visiting the official Web site

Eメールによると、読者はどのようにして動画リンクを送るための正しいEメールアドレスを見つけることができますか。

(A) 添付の書類をダウンロードすることによって
(B) 合格通知を確認することによって
(C) 組織委員会に電話することによって
(D) 公式のウェブサイトにアクセスすることによって

Battle of the Bandsの参加者に対し、主催者は❹で「動画をアップロードし、そのリンクをEメールで送るように」「正しいEメールアドレスは、前述の書類に記載されている」と述べている。前述の書類とは、❷に出てくるacceptance letters「合格通知」のことだと考えられる。よって、正解は(B)。❹の2文目に出てくる形容詞aforementioned「前述の」を見て、それよりも前で述べられている内容から正解を探すことができるかどうかが試される問題だ。

154

正解 C ☐☐☐☐

What is NOT implied about the competition?

(A) Only half of the bands will be invited to perform live.
(B) All of the participants have been decided.
(C) The winners will be selected by the audience.
(D) It will be held over multiple dates.

コンテストについて示唆されていないことは何ですか。

(A) 演奏ライブに招待されるのは半数のバンドだけである。
(B) 参加者全員が決定している。
(C) 観客によって優勝者が選ばれる。
(D) 複数の日程で開催される。

❺に「計50組のバンドのうち25組が生の観客の前で演奏する予定」とあるため、(A)は述べられている。また❶に「Seattle Battle of the Bandsの応募受付は締め切った」とあることから、参加者全員が決定したと述べられている(B)も示唆されている。さらに❸には「（コンテストは）9月23日から9月27日の間に開催される」とあり、(D)に述べられている複数日程での開催も示唆されていることが分かる。優勝者の決め方については述べられていないので、残った(C)が正解。

👑 **Level Up !**

What is NOT implied about 〜？「〜について示唆されていないことは何ですか」という設問は、いかに時間をかけずに解くかがカギ。文書と選択肢をすばやく照合させよう。

語彙チェック ☐ multiple 複数の

Questions 155-157 refer to the following article.

MOSCOW (February 7) — ❶Popular social media personality Helga Sanchez has recently announced that she will be moving from New York to Moscow. She informed the five million subscribers to her video blog on Wednesday by broadcasting live from in front of the famous Baranov Theater. She rode on a bus from there to her new apartment in Ananenko Tower all the while talking about her plans for the future direction of her video channel. ❷The tower is one of Moscow's most prestigious addresses. It is famously home to the fashion designer Joe Akimov and international soccer sensation Ivan Oleksiy.

❸According to one Moscow real estate agent, landlords typically ask between $10,000 and $15,000 per month to rent apartments in the building. So, we can assume that Ms. Sanchez is doing quite well for herself. In recent months, she has switched from touting the products of her sponsors to selling her own line of cosmetics and fashion accessories. Various reports claim that she has more than doubled her monthly income. Her publicist Danny Madsen said that Ms. Sanchez has always wanted to live in Moscow. "This is a permanent arrangement, and ❹she's already quite fluent in the language," he explained. "❺She plans to create many videos exploring Russian culture and food from her new base here in Moscow." Whether or not she is successful remains to be seen. Her move is an unusual one, but that might work to her advantage. Russia is a largely unexplored region for western video bloggers. Ms. Sanchez has a reputation for being original and extremely entertaining. Undoubtedly, others will be following in her footsteps in the coming years.

問題155-157は次の記事に関するものです。

Moscow（2月7日）— ソーシャルメディアの人気タレントであるHelga Sanchezは最近、New YorkからMoscowに引っ越すことを発表した。彼女は水曜日に、有名なBaranov劇場の前から生中継で、自身のビデオブログの登録者500万人に知らせた。彼女はそこからバスに乗ってAnanenkoタワーにある新居に向かい、その間にビデオ・チャンネルの今後の方向性について語った。Ananenkoタワーは、Moscowでも有数の高級住宅地である。ファッションデザイナーのJoe Akimovや世界的に評判の良いサッカー選手のIvan Oleksiyが住んでいることでも知られている。

あるMoscowの不動産業者によると、家主は通常そのビル内にあるアパートの賃借代として、月に1万ドルから1万5000ドルを請求するという。つまり、Sanchezさんは相当うまくいっていることが推測できる。ここ数カ月、彼女はスポンサーの製品を売り込むことから、自分の化粧品やファッションアクセサリーを販売することに切り替えた。さまざまな報道によれば、彼女の月収は2倍以上になったという。彼女の広報であるDanny Madsenは、SanchezさんはずっとMoscowに住みたいと思っていたと語った。「これは半永久的な計画であり、彼女はすでに流暢に言葉を話しています」と彼は説明した。「彼女はここMoscowの新しい拠点から、ロシアの文化や食べ物を探求する多くの動画を作っていく予定です」。彼女が成功するか否かは、まだ我々の知るところではない。彼女の引っ越しは異例だが、それが有利に働くかもしれない。ロシアは、欧米のビデオブロガーにとってほとんど未開拓の地域だ。Sanchezさんはオリジナリティがあり、非常に面白いという評判がある。間違いなく、今後数年のうちに彼女の後に続く人が出てくることだろう。

語彙チェック　☐ broadcast 〜を放送する　☐ prestigious 名声のある　☐ sensation 大評判　☐ switch 切り換える
☐ tout 〜をしつこく推奨する　☐ permanent 永久的な　☐ fluent 流暢な　☐ unexplored 探索されていない
☐ undoubtedly 疑いの余地なく　☐ follow in *one's* footsteps （人）の例にならう

155

正解 **B** ☐☐☐☐

What is the subject of the article?

(A) A business opportunity for readers

(B) An influencer's recent activities

(C) The popularity of a video streaming site

(D) The rising cost of accommodations in Moscow

記事の主題は何ですか。

(A) 読者にとってのビジネスチャンス

(B) あるインフルエンサーの最近の活動

(C) 動画配信サイトの人気の高まり

(D) Moscowにおける宿泊費の高騰

第1段落の冒頭❶を見ると、「ソーシャルメディアの人気タレントであるHelga Sanchezは最近、New YorkからMoscowに引っ越すことを発表した」「彼女は生中継で、それ（＝引っ越し）について自身のビデオブログの登録者に知らせた」と、インフルエンサーであるSanchezさんの最近の活動が述べられている。さらに第2段落では今後の彼女の方向性について周りの人たちが提供する情報が述べられていることから、(B)が適切。Sanchezさんが動画配信をしたことは述べられているものの、動画配信サイトの人気がテーマではないので、(C)は不適切。

語彙チェック ☐ streaming 配信

156

正解 **A** ☐☐☐☐

What is suggested about Ananenko Tower?

(A) It is an expensive place to live.

(B) It is the headquarters of a tech company.

(C) It is close to Baranov Theater.

(D) It is advertised in online videos.

Ananenkoタワーについて何が分かりますか。

(A) 住むのに高価な場所である。

(B) 技術会社の本社である。

(C) Baranov劇場の近くにある。

(D) オンライン動画で宣伝されている。

第1段落より、AnanenkoタワーとはSanchezさんが新しく住み始めたアパートのことである。第2段落冒頭の❸にはそのアパートの家賃に関する情報があり、「Sanchezさんは相当うまくいっていることが推測できる」と述べられている。このことから、Ananenkoタワーは住むのに高価な場所であると判断できる。よって、正解は(A)。

157

正解 **C** ☐☐☐☐

What is NOT implied about Ms. Sanchez?

(A) She plans to try Russian cuisine.

(B) She has studied Russian.

(C) She moves on a yearly basis.

(D) She has some famous neighbors.

Sanchezさんについて示唆されていないことは何ですか。

(A) 彼女はロシア料理に挑戦するつもりである。

(B) 彼女はロシア語を勉強してきた。

(C) 彼女は年単位で引っ越しをしている。

(D) 彼女には有名な隣人が何人かいる。

❺に「ロシアの文化や食べ物を探求する多くの動画を作る予定」とあることからロシア料理に挑戦することが推測できるので、(A)は示唆されている。❹には「すでに流暢に言葉を話している」とあり、さらにSanchezさんの引っ越し先はロシアのMoscowであるということが❶から分かるので、ロシア語を勉強してきたという(B)の内容も示唆されている。さらに❷にはAnanenkoタワーに住む住人として「ファッションデザイナーのJoe Akimovや世界的に評判の良いサッカー選手のIvan Oleksiy」の2名について触れられており、(D)の内容も示唆されている。引っ越しの頻度について本文では言及されていないので、(C)が正解。

Important Announcement
From
Redmond Chang, Vice President of Planning and Marketing

We need product testers.

❶ Anval Inc. is almost ready to start production of its latest Wi-Fi routers. Before we do so, we would like to test the products in the homes of actual consumers. We are looking for 100 households that are willing to install and use our new routers exclusively for a full month. ❷ In order to make this a win-win proposition, we are willing to let participants keep the routers valued at around $500 free of charge. Naturally, if we find any bugs or defects, we will provide updates to make sure you are using fully functional equipment.

There are a couple of conditions. First, this offer is not for the households of company employees. As a matter of course, we want to test the products in demanding environments. ❸ We need households with four or more members that generate high-volume data traffic. In particular, we are looking for large families with a variety of Internet-connected devices. We are also interested in testing the coverage of our routers. Households making use of their attic, basement, or even a shed are of particular interest. This offer is not limited to the extended families of Anval employees. You are welcome to suggest the opportunity to family friends and acquaintances. Please make it clear, though, that we will be analyzing their usage statistics and keeping logs of errors and anomalies reported by the routers. ❹ They will also be asked to take part in a very brief online interview to assess their satisfaction with the devices.

Please ask anyone interested in taking part to contact my assistant Steve Spektor. He will assess their suitability and proceed with their enrollment into the program. We are trying to get the products onto the market by the start of the holiday season, so we hope that you will make this a priority in the coming days.

問題158-160は次のお知らせに関するものです。

重要なお知らせ
企画・マーケティング本部長 Redmond Chang より

消費者モニターを募集しています。

Anval社は、最新のWi-Fiルーターの生産開始を間近に控えています。生産を行う前に、実際の消費者の自宅で製品をテストしていただきたいと考えております。1カ月間、弊社のルーターのみを設置しご使用いただけるご家庭を100世帯募集しています。互いに利益があるように、約500ドル相当のルーターを無料で使い続けていただけます。もちろん、バグや不具合が見つかった際は最新情報をお伝えし、モニターの皆さんが完全に機能する機器をお使いいただけているようにいたします。

モニター参加にはいくつか条件がございます。まず、このキャンペーンは会社に勤めるご家庭には適用されません。当然ながら、厳しい環境下でのテストも行いたいと考えております。大量のデータ通信量が発生する、4人かそれ以上の人数のご家庭が必要です。特に、インターネットに接続された機器が多い、大所帯を探しております。また、弊社はルーターが受信する範囲もテストしたいと考えています。屋根裏部屋や地下室、さらには物置までを活用されているご家庭には、特に関心を持っております。このキャンペーンは、Anval社の社員のご家族に限ったものではありません。ご家族のご友人やお知り合いにも、この機会をお勧めください。ただし、利用統計の分析や、ルーターから報告されるエラーや異常のログを記録することを明確にしていただくようお願いいたします。また、機器に対する満足度を評価してもらうために、簡単なオンラインインタビューにご協力いただきます。

参加に関心を持っている方には、私のアシスタントであるSteve Spektorにご連絡いただくようお声掛けください。彼が適性を判断し、プログラムへの登録を進めてまいります。休暇の時期が始まる前までには製品を市場に出すことを目指していますので、今後数日はこちらを優先的に考えていただけますと幸いです。

語彙チェック □ bug 欠陥 □ high-volume 大量の □ data traffic データ通信量 □ coverage 範囲 □ make use of ~ ~を活用する □ attic 屋根裏部屋 □ shed 物置 □ extended 広範囲にわたる □ statistic 統計値 □ anomaly 異常 □ brief 短時間の □ suitability 適性

158

正解 **D** ☐☐☐☐

Who is organizing the program described in the announcement?

(A) A real estate agency

(B) An appliance store

(C) An Internet service provider

(D) An electronics manufacturer

お知らせの中で紹介されているプログラムを主催しているのは誰ですか。

(A) 不動産会社

(B) 家電量販店

(C) インターネットサービスプロバイダー

(D) 電子機器メーカー

お知らせの冒頭❶に「Anval社は最新のWi-Fiルーターの生産開始を間近に控えている」とあり、続けて「生産の前に消費者の自宅で製品をテストしてほしい」「1カ月間（Anval社の）ルーターを設置できる家庭を100世帯募集する」と、Anval社が主催するプログラムの内容が紹介されている。Wi-Fiルーターを製造する業種としては最も適切なのは(D)。(B)の「家電量販店」は生産ではなく販売を行う業種なので不適切。

語彙チェック ☐ electronic　電子機器

159

正解 **A** ☐☐☐☐

What is a benefit for interested individuals?

(A) Free product samples

(B) Time off work

(C) Additional bonus payments

(D) Expert technical support

協力希望者への特典は何ですか。

(A) 無料の商品見本

(B) 休暇

(C) 追加ボーナスの支給

(D) 専門家による技術サポート

❷に「約500ドル相当のルーターを無料で使い続けてもらえる」と述べられている。協力者はテストで使った商品をその後も使い続けられるということが分かるので、正解は(A)。

160

正解 **D** ☐☐☐☐

What is one condition of participation?

(A) People must commit to a year of monitoring.

(B) Homes must have both an attic and a basement.

(C) Households must have a minimum of five members.

(D) People must give their feedback online.

参加条件の1つは何ですか。

(A) 1年間のモニタリングに協力しなければならない。

(B) 屋根裏部屋と地下室の両方が自宅になければならない。

(C) 最低5人以上の世帯でなければならない。

(D) オンラインでフィードバックをしなければならない。

商品モニターへの参加条件として、❹に「機器に対する満足度評価のため、オンラインインタビューに協力してもらう」と述べられている。これを、「オンラインでのフィードバック」と抽象的に言い換えた(D)が正解。(B)については、Anval社が屋根裏部屋や地下室を活用している家庭に特に関心を持っていることは言及されているものの、それが参加の必須条件であるとまでは述べられていないので不適切。(C)は、❸で最低の世帯人数は4人と述べられているので不適切。

語彙チェック ☐ minimum　最低限

Questions 161-163 refer to the following letter.

Bakersfield Film Appreciation Society
21 Archer Lane, Suite D
Marsden, 80225

May 7

Jack Phipps
134 Sugarwood Road
Woodhill, CO 89237

Dear Mr. Phipps,

❶ This year, the Bakersfield Festival of Film will be held from July 17 to July 19. The Bakersfield Film Appreciation Society is once again fulfilling the role as the event's organizing committee. —[1]—. Last year, when we learned that the rain damage to Thornton Theater would make the venue unusable, we were thrown into a panic. ❷ I am sure that if you had not generously offered Carter School of Design's main auditorium for our screenings, we would have been forced to cancel the event. —[2]—.

To show our appreciation for your kind offer, we would like to invite you back this year as a special guest. A special dinner will be held on the first night to welcome representatives of the various production companies. ❸ I hope you will agree to sit at a table reserved for friends of the festival. —[3]—. We have also taken the liberty of naming one of the festival awards after you — the Jack Phipps Award for Excellence in Set Design. ❹ We would be honored if you would present it to the winner on the final night of the festival. I hope you will agree to say a few words at that time. —[4]—.

Please let me know as soon as possible whether or not you can attend.

Sincerely,

Frida Kruger

Frida Kruger
Chairperson — Bakersfield Film Appreciation Society

問題161-163は次の手紙に関するものです。

Bakersfield 映画鑑賞会
Archer通り21番地、スイートD
Marsden、80225

5月7日

Jack Phipps 様
Sugarwood通り134番地
Woodhill、Colorado州 89237

Phipps 様

今年は、7月17日から7月19日にかけて Bakersfield の映画祭が開催されます。今年も Bakersfield 映画鑑賞会が当イベントの実行委員会としての役割を果たします。昨年、Thornton 劇場の雨の被害で会場が使えなくなることが分かり、当委員会は大混乱に陥りました。もし Carter デザインスクールの大講堂を上映会場として寛大にも提供していただかなかったら、イベントを中止せざるを得なかったことと思います。

ご親切な申し出に対する感謝として、今年もあなたを特別ゲストとしてお招きしたいと思います。初日の夜には、各制作会社の代表をお迎えして、特別な夕食会を開催いたします。映画祭の後援者の方々のために用意された席に座ることを承諾していただけると幸いです。*あなたは Max Colby、Leanne Hester、またその他数名の重要な貢献者の方々と同じ席になります。また誠に勝手ながら、映画祭の賞の1つをあなたの名前にちなんで付けさせていただき、セットデザイン部門の優秀賞として Jack Phipps 賞、といたしました。映画祭の最終日の夜に、受賞者にこの賞を授与していただければ光栄です。その際、一言ご挨拶をいただけると幸いです。

出席の可否はなるべくお早めにお知らせください。

敬具

Frida Kruger（署名）

Frida Kruger
会長—Bakersfield 映画鑑賞会

語彙チェック □ appreciation 鑑賞 □ unusable 使用できない □ throw 〜を陥れる □ auditorium 講堂
□ screening 上映 □ force 〜を強いる □ take the liberty of *doing* 勝手に〜する

161

正解 **A** ☐☐☐☐

Who most likely is Mr. Phipps?

(A) A business owner

(B) A film club leader

(C) A film producer

(D) A committee member

Phippsさんは誰であると考えられますか。

(A) 事業主

(B) 映画クラブのリーダー

(C) 映画プロデューサー

(D) 委員会のメンバー

本文は、映画鑑賞会の会長であるKrugerさんがPhippsさんに宛てた手紙である。Krugerさんは❷でPhippさんに対し、「もしCarterデザインスクールの大講堂を上映会場として提供してもらえなかったら、イベントを中止せざるを得なかったと思う」と述べている。このことから、PhippsさんはCarterデザインスクールの大講堂を会場として貸し出した人物、つまりCarterデザインスクールを経営する事業主であるということが推測できる。よって、正解は(A)。

👑**Level Up！**
実行委員会の役割を果たすのはKrugerさんを含むBakersfield映画鑑賞会なので、(D)は不正解。設問でどの人物について聞かれているかを見落とさないように注意しよう。

162

正解 **C** ☐☐☐☐

When will Mr. Phipps be asked to speak in public?

(A) On July 16

(B) On July 17

(C) On July 19

(D) On July 20

Phippsさんはいつ公の場で話すよう求められていますか。

(A) 7月16日

(B) 7月17日

(C) 7月19日

(D) 7月20日

Phippsさんは、❹で「映画祭の最終日の夜に受賞者に賞を授与し、一言挨拶してほしい」とお願いされている。映画祭の日程については、❶に「7月17日から7月19日にかけてBakersfieldの映画祭が開催される」とある。つまり、映画祭の最終日とは7月19日のことだと分かるので、正解は(C)。

👑**Level Up！**
具体的な日程が本文に登場する場合、その日付に関連した設問が出題される可能性が高い。文書を読むときに、いつも頭のどこかで日付を意識しながら読むようにしよう！

163

正解 **C** ☐☐☐☐

In which of the positions marked [1], [2], [3], and [4] does the following sentence best belong?

"You will be joined by Max Colby, Leanne Hester, and a few other significant contributors."

(A) [1]

(B) [2]

(C) [3]

(D) [4]

[1]、[2]、[3]、[4]と記載された箇所のうち、次の文が入るのに最もふさわしいのはどれですか。

「あなたはMax Colby、Leanne Hester、またその他数名の重要な貢献者の方々と同じ席になります」

(A) [1]

(B) [2]

(C) [3]

(D) [4]

挿入文のYou will be joined by 〜は、ここでは「〜と同席になります」という意味。これに関連しそうな記述を本文から探す。第2段落❸には、「映画祭の後援者のために用意された席に座ってほしい」とある。この後に文を挿入すると、「映画祭の後援者のために用意された席に座ってほしい」「Max ColbyやLeanne Hesterと同席になる予定だ」と、2文の内容が自然につながる。よって、(C)が正解。

語彙チェック ☐ significant 重要な ☐ contributor 貢献者

Questions 164-167 refer to the following e-mail.

▶TRACK_123

To:	Stella Evans <sevans@bransonanddavies.co.uk>
From:	Harry Sutherland <hsutherland@stallardem.com>
Date:	23 March
Subject:	Conference

Dear Ms. Evans,

❶Thank you for agreeing to speak at the upcoming GTX Engineering Conference in London. The work your company has been doing on the Bristol Oil Pipeline project has been gathering a lot of attention, **and I am sure attendees will be excited to hear about your progress.** ❷We have allocated you 90 minutes on the evening of the first day of the conference. ❸You will be in Room A, which is the biggest of the three rooms we have booked. We imagine you will attract the largest crowd in the time slot.

❹I understand that you will be coming down to London on the previous day and staying at the Berger Inn across the road. I am sorry to hear that you cannot stay over 11 April for the second day of the conference. ❺Of course, Stallard Event Management will pay for all of your accommodations and transportation. Please remember to send me a copy of the receipts after the conference. ❻As I will be in town on the day before the conference starts to help set up, I was wondering if you would like to have dinner together. **If you will be too busy preparing, I understand.** I was hoping to discuss an event we are holding in Paris in July. We are looking for a keynote speaker to talk about integrating new technologies into major projects. I think you would be perfect for it. We are offering a very attractive compensation package.

Please let me know if you are interested.

Sincerely,

Harry Sutherland
Stallard Event Management

問題164-167は次のEメールに関するものです。

受信者：Stella Evans <sevans@bransonanddavies.co.uk>
送信者：Harry Sutherland <hsutherland@stallardem.com>
日付：3月23日
件名：会議

Evans様

Londonで近々開催されるGTXエンジニアリング会議での講演をお引き受けいただき、ありがとうございます。貴社のBristol石油配管計画は大きな注目を浴びておりますので、参加者が進展を聞いたらわくわくすることでしょう。会議の初日の夕方、あなたに90分間の時間を割り当てました。予約をした3つの会場のうち、最も大きなA会場で講演いただきます。この時間枠の中で、あなたが最も多くの参加者を集めることでしょう。

前日にLondonにお越しになり、道路を挟んだ向かいのBergerホテルにご宿泊とのこと、承知しております。会議2日目のために4月11日にご宿泊いただけないことは誠に残念です。もちろん、宿泊費と交通費はStallardイベント管理局が全額負担いたします。会議終了後、領収書のコピーを忘れずにお送りください。会議が始まる日の前日、私は設営を手伝うために街にいるので、一緒に夕食をとりませんか。ご準備で忙しければ構いません。7月にParisで開催するイベントの話ができればと思っていたところです。我々は、新しいテクノロジーを大掛かりなプロジェクトに取り入れることについてお話しいただける基調講演者を探しております。私は、あなたこそが適任だと考えているのです。私たちは非常に魅力的な待遇を提供する予定です。

ご興味がおありでしたら、ぜひご一報ください。

敬具

Harry Sutherland
Stallardイベント管理局

語彙チェック   □ gather 〜を集める   □ allocate *A B*   AにBを割り当てる   □ time slot 時間帯   □ come down 来る
□ accommodations 宿泊設備   □ keynote speaker 基調演説者   □ compensation package 待遇

164

正解 A ☐☐☐☐

Who most likely is Ms. Evans?

(A) An engineer

(B) An event organizer

(C) A physician

(D) An advertising expert

Evansさんとは誰のことだと考えられますか。

(A) エンジニア

(B) イベントの主催者

(C) 医師

(D) 広告の専門家

EメールはStallardイベント管理局のSutherlandさんからEvansさんに対して宛てたものである。Eメールの冒頭❶で、「近々開催されるGTXエンジニアリング会議での講演を引き受けてくれてありがとう」と述べられている。選択肢の中でエンジニアリング会議での講演者として最も可能性が高いのは(A)。イベントの主催者とはSutherlandさんのことなので、(B)は不正解。

165

正解 C ☐☐☐☐

What is implied about the conference?

(A) It will be held over three days.

(B) It will attract attendees from around the world.

(C) Several speakers will be presenting simultaneously.

(D) The venue provides discount accommodations.

会議について何が示唆されていますか。

(A) 3日間に渡って開催される。

(B) 世界中から参加者が集まる。

(C) 複数の講演者が同時に発表する。

(D) 会場が割引価格で宿泊施設を提供する。

❸でSutherlandさんはEvansさんに対し、「あなたには最も大きなA会場で講演してもらう」「この時間枠の中で、あなたが最も多くの参加者を集めるだろう」と述べている。これらの内容から、講演者はEvansさん1人ではなく、他にも同じ時間枠での講演者がいることが示唆されていると分かる。よって、正解は(C)。国外からも参加者が集まるとは述べられていないので、(B)は不適切。

語彙チェック ☐ simultaneously 同時に

166

正解 B ☐☐☐☐

What is one purpose of the e-mail?

(A) To announce a change of schedule

(B) To discuss a reimbursement procedure

(C) To explain a reservation error

(D) To ask about a venue preference

Eメールの目的の1つは何ですか。

(A) 予定変更を知らせること

(B) 払い戻しの手続きについて話すこと

(C) 予約ミスを説明すること

(D) 会場の希望について尋ねること

❺で「宿泊費と交通費はStallardイベント管理局が全額負担する」「会議終了後、領収書のコピーを忘れずに送ってほしい」と、会議に参加するにあたり発生する金額の精算について説明している。これをdiscuss a reimbursement procedure「払い戻しの手続きについて話す」と表した(B)が正解。

語彙チェック ☐ reimbursement 返済 ☐ preference 選択、好み

167

正解 B ☐☐☐☐

When will Ms. Evans and Mr. Sutherland most likely dine together?

(A) On March 23

(B) On April 10

(C) On April 11

(D) On April 13

EvansさんとSutherlandさんはいつ一緒に食事をすると考えられますか。

(A) 3月23日

(B) 4月10日

(C) 4月11日

(D) 4月13日

Sutherlandさんは❻で、「会議が始まる日の前日に、一緒に夕食をとらないか」とEvansさんを誘っている。この時点では具体的な日付が分からないので、その他の箇所から正解の根拠を探す必要がある。まず❷に「会議の初日の夕方、あなたに90分間の時間を割り当てた」とあることから、Evansさんは1日目の会議で講演を行うことが分かる。さらに❹から、Evansさんが「会議の前日にLondonに来てBergerホテルに宿泊する」こと、「4月11日の夜、（次の日に行われる）2日目の会議のために宿泊することはできない」という情報が手に入る。つまり、会議の初日は4月11日で、2日目は4月12日となる。これらの情報より、2人が一緒に夕食をとるのは会議初日の前日である、4月10日だと推測できる。

Questions 168-171 refer to the following online chat discussion.

Clinton Sanchez [4:25 P.M.]:
Hi guys. I'm on the way to a party in Spring Hill. The van has broken down, and I have a load of food that needs to get delivered as soon as possible.

Hans Ranganathan [4:26 P.M.]:
❶ Thanks for the update, Clinton. Can you tell us where you are? Are there any landmarks?

Clinton Sanchez [4:28 P.M.]:
Sorry. I'm at Plum Street. Right in front of Benin Bank.

Maxine Dagmar [4:29 P.M.]:
❷ I've just unloaded my van at an office building just down the road from there. We need three wait staff for this event, though.

Hans Ranganathan [4:33 P.M.]:
Right. Maxine, stay there. ❸ I'm on the phone with a trucking company.

Dana Patel [4:35 P.M.]:
❹ Won't that be expensive?

Hans Ranganathan [4:38 P.M.]:
That's not important right now, Dana. ❺ Clinton, a small truck from JJ Shipping is on its way.

Clinton Sanchez [4:45 P.M.]:
Wow, it's already here! Thanks.

Hans Ranganathan [4:46 P.M.]:
❻ That's my job. Let me know when you get there.

Clinton Sanchez [4:59 P.M.]:
❼ Just getting there now. Right on time!

問題168-171は次のオンラインチャットの話し合いに関するものです。

Clinton Sanchez [午後4時25分]:
やあ、皆さん。Spring Hillのパーティーに向かっています。バンが故障してしまったのですが、すぐに配達しなければならない食事がたくさんあるんです。

Hans Ranganathan [午後4時26分]:
報告ありがとうございます、Clinton。今どこにいるか教えてもらえますか。何か目印になるものはあるでしょうか。

Clinton Sanchez [午後4時28分]:
すみません。今、Plum通りにいます。ちょうどBenin銀行の前です。

Maxine Dagmar [午後4時29分]:
そこから下ってすぐのオフィスビルで、ちょうどバンから荷物を降ろしたところです。ただ、このイベントには給仕スタッフが3人必要なんです。

Hans Ranganathan [午後4時33分]:
分かりました。Maxine、そこにいてください。今トラック運送会社と電話しているところなので。

Dana Patel [午後4時35分]:
高くつかないですか。

Hans Ranganathan [午後4時38分]:
Dana、今はそんなことは重要ではないんです。Clinton、JJ Shippingの小さなトラックが向かっているところです。

Clinton Sanchez [午後4時45分]:
おお、もう来ました！　ありがとうございます。

Hans Ranganathan [午後4時46分]:
これが私の仕事ですから。着いたら教えてください。

Clinton Sanchez [午後4時59分]:
今ちょうど着くところです。時間通りですね！

語彙チェック ☐ break down 故障する ☐ a load of ~ 大量の~ ☐ landmark 目印 ☐ unload ~から荷を降ろす ☐ on the phone 電話中で

168

正解 **C** □□□□

Who most likely is Mr. Ranganathan?

(A) A delivery driver

(B) A kitchen worker

(C) A dispatch operator

(D) A banquet participant

Ranganathanさんとは誰だと考えられますか。

(A) 配達員

(B) 厨房の従業員

(C) 配車係

(D) 宴会の参加者

Ranganathanさんの発言に主に注目し、どんな職業かを推測する。バンが故障し食事が配達できないと述べるSanchezさんに対し、Ranganathanさんは❶で現在地を尋ねている。また❸で「今トラック運送会社と電話している」と述べ、さらに❺で「JJ Shippingの小さなトラックが向かっているところ」と、代車を手配していることが分かる。さらに、代車が来たことに感謝を述べるSanchezさんに対し、❻で「これが私の仕事だ」と述べている。これらの情報から、Ranganathanさんは配車係と考えるのが自然。よって、正解は(C)。

語彙チェック □ dispatch operator 配車係

169

正解 **D** □□□□

At 4:29 P.M., what does Ms. Dagmar imply when she writes "We need three wait staff for this event, though"?

(A) She needs some additional help.

(B) A budget is not high enough.

(C) The event may not go smoothly.

(D) She will work as a server.

午後4時29分に、"We need three wait staff for this event, though" という発言で、Dagmarさんは何を示唆していますか。

(A) 彼女はさらなる助けを必要としている。

(B) 予算が十分でない。

(C) イベントがうまくいかないかもしれない。

(D) 彼女は給仕係として働く予定だ。

バンが故障し困っているSanchezさんに対し、Dagmarさんは❷で「そこから下ってすぐのオフィスビルで、ちょうど荷物を降ろしたところ」と、すぐ近くにいることを伝えている。その直後に「ただ、このイベントには給仕スタッフが3人必要だ」という発言が続いているので、Dagmarさんは「（Sanchezさんを助けたいが）この後は給仕係として働く予定がある（ので難しい）」、ということを示唆していることが分かる。よって、正解は(D)。

語彙チェック □ smoothly 円滑に □ server 給仕係

170

正解 **B** □□□□

What is Mr. Patel concerned about?

(A) The distance

(B) The cost

(C) The time

(D) The reputation

Patelさんは何を懸念していますか。

(A) 距離

(B) 費用

(C) 時間

(D) 評判

RanganathanさんがトラックR運送会社に電話して車を手配しようとしているのに対し、Patelさんは❹で「高くつかないか」と、値段を心配している。よって、(B)が正解。Patelさんはオンラインチャットの中で一度しか発言していないので、午後4時35分の発言のみを見れば答えを導くことができる。

171

正解 **B** □□□□

What is probably true about Mr. Sanchez?

(A) He will apologize to his customers.

(B) He had a 5:00 P.M. appointment.

(C) He managed to fix his van.

(D) He will help Ms. Dagmar.

Sanchezさんについておそらく正しいことは何ですか。

(A) 彼はお客さんに謝るつもりである。

(B) 彼は午後5時に約束があった。

(C) 彼はなんとかバンを修理することができた。

(D) 彼はDagmarさんを助けるつもりである。

Ranganathanさんが手配した代車に乗ったと考えられるSanchezさんは、❼で「今ちょうど着くところ。時間通りだ」と発言している。この発言の時刻を見ると「午後4時59分」とあるので、Sanchezさんはおそらく午後5時に約束があったということが推測できる。よって、正解は(B)。Sanchezさんは自身でバンを修理したわけではないので、(C)は不正解。

語彙チェック □ fix ～を修理する

Questions 172-175 refer to the following article.

Meteor One to Star Francine Lee

LOS ANGELES (February 9) — ❶ Fred J Klause's popular science fiction novel *Meteor One* is finally being adapted for the big screen. A press release from Velveteen Production Company announced that it has procured the rights in a $7,000,000 deal. ❷ According to the agreement, Klause gets the right of final approval on the cast and the film's creative team. —[1]—. ❸ The screenplay is to be written by Odette Xenedez, who was responsible for other high-profile screen adaptations such as *Marionette* and *Double Trouble*. These two films went on to have amazing success making their directors world-famous. ❹ *Meteor One* will be helmed by Scott Eastman, a frequent collaborator with Velveteen Production Company.

Production is set to begin in July this year. Because the story is set almost entirely in space, ❺ it will be filmed at Velveteen's studios in Middleton, which are currently being used to shoot a television series. —[2]—. ❻ Release dates in other countries will be available on the Web site as soon as they are known. You can go to www.meteoronemovie.com although there is currently very little to see.

A few of the cast members have already been announced. Francine Lee will play Dr. Gina Rhodes, and she will be supported by Vance Modine and Pete Cunningham. ❼ Extras will be recruited from the community around the studio. Typically, these opportunities are advertised on social media and in local newspapers. —[3]—.

The book has a huge fanbase, which the producers expect to benefit from. However, this can work against the film. If it does not live up to fans' expectations, they may react negatively online discouraging others from seeing it. Mr. Eastman will be under a lot of pressure to keep that group satisfied. —[4]—.

問題172-175は次の記事に関するものです。

Francine Lee 主演の *Meteor One*

LOS ANGELES（2月9日）―Fred J Klause の人気 SF 小説 *Meteor One* が、ついに映画化される。Velveteen 製作会社のプレスリリースによると、同社は700万ドルの契約で権利を獲得したという。契約によると、Klause はキャストと映画のクリエイティブ・チームに対して最終承認権を得る。脚本は、*Marionette* や *Double Trouble* など話題となった映画化作品を手がけた、Odette Xenedez によって書かれる予定だ。この2作品は、監督たちを世界的に有名にするほどの大成功を収めた。*Meteor One* は、Velveteen 製作会社と頻繁にコラボレーションしている Scott Eastman によって監督される予定である。

製作は今年7月に開始される予定である。舞台がほとんど宇宙の物語であるため、現在テレビシリーズの撮影に使われている Middleton の Velveteen のスタジオで撮影される予定だ。*全てが計画通りに進めば、米国では12月下旬の学校休暇に間に合うように映画が公開される予定である。その他の国での公開日については分かり次第、ウェブサイトで確認できるようになる。現在は見ることができる情報はほとんどないが、www.meteoronemovie.com からアクセス可能だ。

すでに数名のキャストは発表されている。Francine Lee が Gina Rhodes 博士を演じ、Vance Modine と Pete Cunningham がそれをサポートする。エキストラは、スタジオ周辺の地域から募集される予定である。通常、これらの機会はソーシャルメディアや地元新聞を通じて宣伝される。

その本には多くのファンがおり、製作者はその恩恵を受けることを期待している。しかし、これは映画にとって不利に働くことも考えられる。ファンの期待に応えられないと、彼らはネット上で否定的な反応を示し、他の人の鑑賞意欲をそぐようなことをしかねない。Eastman 氏は、ファン集団を満足させ続けなければならないという大きなプレッシャーにさらされることになるだろう。

語彙チェック　□ adapt 〜を改作する　□ procure 〜を獲得する　□ right 権利　□ deal 商取引、契約　□ agreement 契約　□ cast キャスト、配役　□ screenplay 映画脚本　□ high-profile 注目を集める　□ adaptation 改作物　□ helm 〜を監督する　□ frequent 頻繁な　□ collaborator 共同作業者　□ production 製作　□ shoot 〜を撮影する　□ recruit 〜を募集する　□ typically 通常は　□ fanbase ファン層　□ benefit 利益を得る　□ work against 〜 〜に不利に働く　□ live up to 〜 〜に沿う　□ discourage 〜を思いとどまらせる

172

正解 **C** ☐☐☐☐

What is implied about *Double Trouble*?

(A) It was directed by Mr. Eastman.

(B) It was filmed at a studio in Middleton.

(C) It was first published as a book.

(D) It was criticized online by fans.

*Double Trouble*について何が示唆されていますか。

(A) Eastmanさんによって監督された。

(B) Middletonのスタジオで撮影された。

(C) 最初に本として出版された。

(D) オンラインでファンから批判を受けた。

まず記事冒頭❶で、人気SF小説*Meteor One*が映画化されるという内容が述べられている。この内容を踏まえ、同段落の❸で「脚本は、*Marionette*や*Double Trouble*など話題となった映画化作品を手がけた、Odette Xenedezによって書かれる」と、*Double Trouble*の映画化についても述べられている。これらの情報から、*Meteor One*同様に*Double Trouble*も本から映画へ改作されたということが推測できるので、(C)が正解。

語彙チェック ☐ direct 〜を監督する ☐ criticize 〜を批判する

173

正解 **C** ☐☐☐☐

What is probably true about Mr. Eastman?

(A) He has never worked for Velveteen Production Company before.

(B) He has been allocated a budget of just $7,000,000.

(C) His participation was authorized by the writer.

(D) His reputation has spread internationally.

Eastmanさんについておそらく正しいことは何ですか。

(A) 彼はこれまでにVelveteen製作会社で働いたことがなかった。

(B) 彼にはちょうど700万ドルの予算が割り当てられている。

(C) 彼の参加は作家によって許可された。

(D) 彼の評判は国際的に広まっている。

❹より、Eastmanさんは今後*Meteor One*を監督する予定であることが分かる。また、同段落の❷には「Klauseはキャストと映画のクリエイティブ・チームに対して最終承認権を得る」と述べられているので、Klauseさんが、Eastmanさんが映画を監督することを許可したことが推測できる。❶よりKlauseさんは*Meteor One*の作者だと分かるので、正解は(C)。

語彙チェック ☐ authorize 〜を許可する ☐ spread 広がる

174

正解 **A** ☐☐☐☐

According to the article, how can people find out about appearing in the film?

(A) By subscribing to a Middleton newspaper

(B) By attending an information session

(C) By sending an e-mail to Velveteen Production Company

(D) By visiting the production company Web site

記事によると、人々は映画へ出演することについてどのように知ることができますか。

(A) Middletonの新聞を購読することによって

(B) 説明会に参加することによって

(C) Velveteen製作会社にEメールを送ることによって

(D) 製作会社のウェブサイトにアクセスすることによって

映画の出演者については第3段落で詳しく述べられており、❼に「エキストラはスタジオ周辺の地域から募集される」「通常、ソーシャルメディアや地元新聞を通じて宣伝される」とある。さらに1つ前の第2段落❺では、「(映画は) MiddletonのVelveteenのスタジオで撮影される予定」と述べられている。つまり、「スタジオ周辺の地域」「地元」とはMiddletonのことであり、Middletonで発行される新聞にエキストラの募集が掲載されると考えると自然である。よって、正解は(A)。

175

正解 **B** ☐☐☐☐

In which of the positions marked [1], [2], [3], and [4] does the following sentence best belong?

"If everything goes according to plan, the film should be in cinemas in time for the school holidays in late December in the US."

(A) [1]   (C) [3]

(B) [2]   (D) [4]

[1]、[2]、[3] 、[4]と記載された箇所のうち、次の文が入るのに最もふさわしいのはどれですか。

「全てが計画通りに進めば、米国では12月下旬の学校休暇に間に合うように映画が公開される予定である」

(A) [1]   (C) [3]

(B) [2]   (D) [4]

挿入文は、アメリカでの映画の公開時期に関する内容である。❻にRelease dates in other countriesとあるのに注目。この直前の[2]に文を挿入すると、アメリカでの公開日とその他の国の公開日について述べる流れになり、自然。よって、正解は(B)。

Questions 176-180 refer to the following article and e-mail.

GALVESTON (June 19)— Galveston's accommodation shortage is about to be slightly alleviated with the opening of the Tristar Hotel on Sheffield Street. The grand opening will be held on Sunday, June 23. People will be able to view the hotel interior, dine in the restaurants, and even make use of the wellness center and other amenities, but reservations for accommodations will not be taken for dates before July 1. In the meantime, staff will be undergoing intensive training and working to find and resolve any problems before the first overnight guests arrive.

All Tristar Hotels including this one are rated four stars. The Galveston location is unique in that it has the country's largest rooftop swimming pool. The glass walls of the pool allow swimmers to enjoy magnificent views of the city as they relax in the heated water.

To:	Randy Slade
From:	Denis Wainwright
Date:	June 21
Subject:	Update
Attachment:	PWainwright

Dear Mr. Slade,

I trust things are going smoothly in New York. I can't wait to get back.

I am currently inspecting our Maine location, making sure that the service and facilities meet Tristar's high standards. Naturally, I have not informed the staff that I am a hotel employee or of the purpose of my trip. I think the manager here should be commended for her excellent work. Every member of the staff whom I have encountered has been extremely professional, and my room was immaculate. The same goes for their restaurants. I will be here for one more night. I will send a full report in my next e-mail.

The next hotel I will be inspecting is the new one in Galveston. I cannot get a reservation for the next week and a half, so I have decided to take some time off to catch up with my family in Boston. Naturally, this will require me to purchase an additional airline ticket. I have attached the purchase permission request to this e-mail. Please authorize it as soon as possible because there are only a few seats left.

Sincerely,

Denis

問題176-180は次の記事とEメールに関するものです。

GALVESTON (6月19日)—Sheffield通りにTristarホテルがオープンすることで、Galvestonの宿泊施設不足は少し緩和しそうだ。グランドオープンは6月23日の日曜日に行われる予定である。ホテル内の見学やレストランでの食事、またウェルネスセンターやその他の施設の利用までもが可能となるが、7月1日以前の宿泊予約については受け付けていない。その間、スタッフは集中的なトレーニングを受け、最初の宿泊客が来るまでに問題点を洗い出し解決に努める予定である。

このホテルを含む全てのTristarホテルは4つ星評価である。Galvestonにあるホテルは、国内最大の屋上プールを備えているという点で際立っている。プールはガラス張りになっているので、利用者は温水でリラックスしながら市の壮大な景色を楽しむことができる。

語彙チェック □ accommodation 宿泊設備 □ shortage 不足 □ slightly わずかに □ alleviate ～を緩和する □ interior 内装 □ dine 食事をする □ wellness center ウェルネスセンター □ amenity 娯楽施設 □ undergo ～を経験する □ intensive 集中的な □ resolve ～を解決する □ rate ～を評価する □ rooftop 屋上の □ magnificent 壮大な

受信者：Randy Slade
送信者：Denis Wainwright
日付：6月21日
件名：最新情報
添付：⦿PWainwright

Sladeさん

New Yorkでは順調にいっていることでしょう。私は早く戻りたいと思っています。

私は今Maineのホテルを視察し、サービスと設備がTristarの高い基準を満たしているか確認しているところです。もちろん、スタッフには私がホテルの従業員であることも、出張の目的も伝えていません。ここのマネージャーは、素晴らしい仕事ぶりを称賛されるべきだと思います。私が出会ったスタッフは皆、非常にプロらしく、部屋は汚れ一つありませんでした。レストランについても同じことが言えます。私はもう1泊するつもりでいます。次のEメールで詳しいレポートを送りますね。

次に視察するのは、Galvestonにある新しいホテルです。今後1週間半は予約が取れないので、少し休暇を取りBostonの家族に会いに行くことにしました。当然、このためには航空券を追加で購入する必要が生じます。このEメールに購入許可申請書を添付しました。残席がわずかですので、なるべく早く承認いただきたいです。

よろしくお願いいたします。

Denis

語彙チェック □ smoothly 円滑に □ meet ～を満たす □ purpose 目的 □ commend ～を褒める □ encounter ～に偶然出会う □ extremely とても □ immaculate 少しも汚れていない □ catch up with ～ ～と近況を話し合う □ authorize ～を許可する

正解 **A** ☐☐☐☐

According to the article, what problem does Galveston have?

(A) There are not enough hotel rooms.

(B) The transportation system is inconvenient.

(C) The restaurants are too crowded.

(D) The accommodations are not highly rated.

記事によると、Galvestonはどんな問題を抱えていますか。

(A) ホテルの部屋数が足りない。

(B) 交通機関が不便である。

(C) レストランが混雑しすぎている。

(D) 宿泊施設の評価が高くない。

記事の冒頭❶で「Tristarホテルがオープンすることで、Galvestonの宿泊施設不足が少し緩和しそうだ」と述べられている。このことから、現状Galvestonにはホテル（の部屋数）が足りないということが分かる。よって、正解は(A)。

語彙チェック ☐ inconvenient 不便な ☐ be highly rated 高く評価される

正解 **B** ☐☐☐☐

When is the final day of intensive training at the Galveston Tristar Hotel?

(A) June 23

(B) June 30

(C) July 1

(D) July 2

Galvestonの Tristar ホテルにおける集中トレーニングの最終日はいつですか。

(A) 6月23日

(B) 6月30日

(C) 7月1日

(D) 7月2日

❷に「（Tristarホテルは）7月1日以前の宿泊予約を受け付けていない」「その間、スタッフは集中的なトレーニングを受ける」と述べられている。7月1日から宿泊予約を受け付けるということは、集中トレーニングはその前日まで行われているということが分かるので、正解は(B)。(A)はTristarホテルのグランドオープンの日なので不正解。

正解 **B** ☐☐☐☐

What is implied about Mr. Wainwright?

(A) He interviewed a hotel manager.

(B) He is staying in a four-star hotel.

(C) He is Mr. Slade's supervisor.

(D) He has trained hotel staff in Maine.

Wainwright さんについて何が示唆されていますか。

(A) 彼はホテルの支配人にインタビューをした。

(B) 彼は4つ星ホテルに滞在している。

(C) 彼はSladeさんの上司である。

(D) 彼はMaineにあるホテルのスタッフを訓練したことがある。

Wainwrightさんは2文書目のEメールの送信者。Wainwrightさんは❹で、「今Maineのホテルを視察し、サービスと設備がTristarの高い基準を満たしているか確認しているところだ」と述べている。ここで記事の❸に戻ると、「この（＝Galvestonの）ホテルを含む全てのTristarホテルは4つ星評価だ」と述べられているので、Maineという場所にもTristarホテルがあり、それは4つ星評価であるということが分かる。Wainwrightさんは4つ星ホテルに滞在していると判断できるので、正解は(B)。(C)の内容につながる記述はない。

179

正解 C □□□□

What is indicated about the Tristar Hotel in Maine?

(A) It has a rooftop swimming pool.

(B) It is in the city center.

(C) It has more than one restaurant.

(D) It has several vacancies.

Maineにある Tristar ホテルについて示されていることは何ですか。

(A) 屋上にプールがある。

(B) 街の中心部にある。

(C) 2つ以上のレストランがある。

(D) 空室がいくつかある。

👑 **Level Up !**

屋上にプールがあるのは Galveston にある Tristar ホテルのことなので、(A) は不正解。どちらにある Tristar ホテルのことを指しているのか混同しないように注意しよう。

Eメールの第2段落で Wainwright さんは、自身が泊まった部屋がきれいであったことを称賛し、❺で「レストランについても同じことが言える」と述べている。their restaurants と、restaurant が複数形になっていることに注目。このことから、Maine にある Tristar ホテルにはレストランが1つではなく複数あるということが読み取れる。よって、(C) が正解。more than one は「1つよりも多く」、つまり「2つ以上」を表す。

語彙チェック □ vacancy 空室

180

正解 C □□□□

Where most likely is Mr. Wainwright's next destination?

(A) New York

(B) Galveston

(C) Boston

(D) Maine

Wainwright さんの次の目的地はどこだと考えられますか。

(A) New York

(B) Galveston

(C) Boston

(D) Maine

Wainwright さんは❻で「次に視察するのは Galveston にある新しいホテル」と目的地を述べ、直後で「今後1週間半は（Galveston のホテルの）予約が取れないので、少し休暇を取り Boston の家族に会いに行く」と続けている。つまり、Galveston の前にまず Boston へ向かうということが判断できる。よって、正解は (C)。

Questions 181-185 refer to the following online order receipt and e-mail.   ▶TRACK_127

Online Order Receipt

Thank you for your order, dated April 4 at 10:20 P.M. The following items are included:

Item	Quantity	Price
McGillicutty Desk Lamp	1	$230.00
Christof Knife Set	1	$120.00
❶Hanlan Fountain Pen (Blue)	2	$112.00
Giordano Leather Gloves	1	$85.00
❷Overnight shipping		$26.00
	TOTAL	$573.00

❸These items should arrive on April 6. They have been sent using the following shipping details;

Ms. Donna Tanner
23 Hillview Road
Flint, MI 48006

NOTE: I hope you can take the time to write reviews regarding whether or not you are completely satisfied with your items. ❹Reviewers who leave comments of 500 words or more will be sent free product samples. They are under no obligation to recommend the products to others, and they may also choose to return the products to us at our expense.

To:	Donna Tanner <dtanner@silvergoose.com>
From:	Miles Poe <mpoe@hanlansm.com>
Date:	April 7
Subject:	Your review

Dear Ms. Tanner,

I hope you do not mind my contacting you directly. ❺I am a member of the sales and marketing team at Hanlan. ❻Beacons Online Shopping has provided me with your e-mail address <u>per</u> your preferences in the service agreement.

❼Today, I read the review you left on the Beacons Online Shopping Web site. Such a glowing review is sure to affect our future sales.

In the review, you mentioned that the product color did not accurately match the color shown in the product description. Please allow me to apologize for this. ❽Our marketing team is using some new photography equipment which has not been properly calibrated. We will immediately retake the photographs and upload them again. I hope this small difference did not cause too much disappointment.

❾Lastly, we would be more than happy if you could write a little longer review in the future. We would like you to have a chance to try our free product samples.

Sincerely,

Miles Poe

問題181-185は次のオンライン注文領収書とEメールに関するものです。

オンライン注文領収書

4月4日午後10時20分のご注文、誠にありがとうございます。以下の商品が含まれております：

商品	数	価格
McGillicutty社 デスクランプ	1	230.00ドル
Christof社 ナイフ一式	1	120.00ドル
Hanlan社 万年筆（青）	2	112.00ドル
Giordano社 革製手袋	1	85.00ドル
	翌日配送	26.00ドル
	合計	573.00ドル

これらのお品物は4月6日に到着予定です。以下の発送先情報を使用し、お送りいたしました。

Donna Tanner様
Hillview通り 23番地
Flint、Michigan州 48006

注：お品物に完全にご満足いただけたかどうか、ぜひレビューをお書きください。
500語以上のコメントを残してくださったレビュー者の方には、無料の製品サンプルをお送りいたします。その製品について、他者に使用を勧める義務はございません。また、弊社の負担で商品を返品いただくことも可能です。

語彙チェック □ fountain pen　万年筆　□ regarding　～に関して　□ completely　完全に　□ satisfied　満足した
□ leave　～を残す　□ obligation　義務　□ at *one's* expense　～の負担で

受信者：Donna Tanner <dtanner@silvergoose.com>
送信者：Miles Poe <mpoe@hanlansm.com>
日付：4月7日
件名：あなたのレビュー

Tanner様

直接のご連絡をお許しください。私はHanlan社の販売マーケティングチームに所属しております。サービス契約書における希望に従って、Beacons Online Shopping社があなたのEメールアドレスを提供してくれました。

本日、Beacons Online Shopping社のウェブサイトであなたが残してくださったレビューを読みました。このような素晴らしいレビューは、私たちの今後の売り上げに影響を与えること間違いありません。

レビューの中で、商品の色が商品詳細のページで確認できる色と正確に一致していないとのご指摘がございました。この点につきまして、お詫び申し上げます。弊社のマーケティングチームは新しい撮影機材を使用しており、それはピントが正しく調整されておりませんでした。すぐに写真を撮り直し、再度アップロードいたします。この小さな違いが、あまりに大きなご不満を引き起こしていないことを願っております。

最後になりますが、今後はもう少し長いレビューを書いていただけますと大変ありがたいです。無料の製品サンプルをお試しできる機会をぜひ獲得していただきたいと思っております。

よろしくお願い申し上げます。

Miles Poe

語彙チェック □ mind　～をいやだと思う　□ preference　選択、好み　□ glowing　称賛に満ちた　□ accurately　正確に
□ match　～と一致する　□ description　説明　□ properly　適切に　□ calibrate　～の目盛りを調整する
□ immediately　ただちに　□ retake　～を撮り直す

When was Ms. Tanner's order most likely shipped?

(A) On April 4

(B) On April 5

(C) On April 6

(D) On April 7

Tanner さんの注文はいつ発送されたと考えられますか。

(A) 4月4日

(B) 4月5日

(C) 4月6日

(D) 4月7日

1文書目は領収書で、Tanner さんが注文した商品が表で一覧になっている。表の下の❸には、「これらの品物は4月6日に到着予定」と商品の到着予定日が記されている。さらに表内の❷では翌日配送料が加算されており、Tanner さんは翌日配送サービスを受けたということが分かるので、発送自体は商品が届く予定である4月6日の1日前、つまり4月5日に行われたということが推測できる。よって、正解は (B)。

> 👑 **Level Up!**
>
> overnight shipping や overnight delivery といった表現が表内に含まれている場合、これに絡めて商品の発送日や到着日を問う問題が出題されることが多い。

In the e-mail, the word, "per" in paragraph 1, line 2 is closest in meaning to

(A) in accordance with

(B) by means of

(C) for each one

(D) in turn

E メールの第1段落・2行目にある "per" に最も意味が近いのは

(A) 〜に従って

(B) 〜を用いて

(C) それぞれ

(D) 順番に

per を含む1文である❻に注目。per の前には「Beacons Online Shopping 社が E メールアドレスを提供してくれた」とあり、後ろには「サービス契約書における希望」とある。「サービス契約書における希望に従って E メールアドレスが提供された」とすると意味が通るので、この per は (A) in accordance with「〜に従って」の意味になる。per your request「あなたの要望に従って」、per your advice「あなたの助言に従って」などの表現が同様の例。

What kind of item did Ms. Tanner leave a review for?

(A) Fashion

(B) Cutlery

(C) Appliances

(D) Stationery

Tanner さんはどんな種類の商品に対してレビューを残しましたか。

(A) ファッション

(B) カトラリー

(C) 電化製品

(D) 文房具

E メールの❺で、Poe さんは Tanner さんに「私は Hanlan 社の販売マーケティングチームに所属している」と挨拶をし、その後❼で Tanner さんが書いたレビューを読んだと述べている。Hanlan 社とは領収書の❶より Fountain Pen「万年筆」を売っている会社のことだと分かるので、Tanner さんは文房具に対するレビューを残したということが分かる。よって、正解は (D)。

184

正解 D □□□□

What is suggested about Ms. Tanner's review?

(A) It was written on April 7.

(B) It is entirely complimentary.

(C) It was posted anonymously.

(D) It has less than 500 words.

Tannerさんのレビューについて何が分かりますか。

(A) 4月7日に書かれた。

(B) 全て肯定的な内容である。

(C) 匿名で投稿された。

(D) 500語よりも少なかった。

領収書の❹に「500語以上のコメントを残したレビュアーには無料の製品サンプルを送る」と記載がある。一方、Hanlan社のPoeさんからTannerさんに宛てたEメールの❾には「無料製品サンプルを試してほしいので、今後はもう少し長いレビューを書いてもらえるとうれしい」と記載がある。つまり、Tannerさんは500語よりも少ない文字数でレビューを書いたということが推測できる。よって、正解は(D)。Eメールの第3段落より、Tannerさんは注文した商品の色が想定したものと違ったとレビューに書いていたことが分かるので、(B)は不正解。

語彙チェック □ entirely　すっかり　□ complimentary　称賛を表す　□ post　〜を投稿する　□ anonymously　匿名で

185

正解 B □□□□

In the e-mail, what is mentioned about the equipment the business is using?

(A) It is state-of-the-art.

(B) It was not correctly adjusted.

(C) It will be replaced shortly.

(D) It contains a product defect.

Eメールの中で、会社が使っている機器について言及されていることは何ですか。

(A) 最先端のものである。

(B) 正しく調整されていなかった。

(C) まもなく交換される予定である。

(D) 製品に欠陥がある。

会社が使っている機器とは、Hanlan社が商品の写真を撮る際に使っている新しい撮影機材のことである。❽でPoeさんは「弊社のマーケティングチームは新しい撮影機材を使用しており、それはピントが正しく調整されていなかった」と述べている。よって、(B)が正解。

👑 **Level Up！**

新しい機材に関連して、(A)を選んだ人がいるかもしれない。state-of-the-artとは「最新技術の、最先端の」を意味する。本文には「(前と違う)新しい撮影機材を使用している」と述べられているだけで、最先端の機器を使っているとまでは言及されていないので不正解。

語彙チェック □ state-of-the-art　最先端の　□ shortly　まもなく　□ defect　欠陥

Questions 186-190 refer to the following Web site, notice, and review.

目標5:00

音読 □□□ 解答時間 : ▶ :

TRACK_128

https://www.guttenbergprc.com ▶

Guttenberg Painting Restoration and Conservation

Guttenberg Painting Restoration and Conservation is one of Britain's most trusted names for preserving valuable paintings. Our clients include the Baumgartner Museum of Art, Styles Gallery, and Holden Art Fund.

❶ Our highly trained staff can restore your valuable artwork to its original splendor while also ensuring that the art is preserved for many years to come. It is important to do this correctly because paintings preserved using outdated techniques may become damaged by the chemicals used to protect them. **We can also correct poorly restored paintings in certain cases.**

❷ One of our new services is to create ultra-high resolution digital copies of valuable artwork that can outlive their physical counterparts. This is a free service for artwork at public galleries.

As paintings are restored on a case-by-case basis, it is impossible to publish our rates. Please contact our customer service department to schedule an estimate. We can arrange secure shipment by a special transportation service. ❸ We will only come to your location in cases where paintings are particularly valuable or fragile. **This will be assessed by analyzing video of your item.**

問題186-190は次のウェブサイト、お知らせ、レビューに関するものです。

https://www.guttenbergprc.com

Guttenberg絵画修復・保存社

Guttenberg絵画修復・保存社は、貴重な絵画の保存に関してイギリスで最も信頼の名が付く会社の1つです。私たちのお客様には、Baumgartner美術館、Stylesギャラリー、Holden芸術基金などが挙げられます。

高度な訓練を受けたスタッフが、お客様の大切な美術品が元の輝きを取り戻せるように修復し、またそれが今後何年も長持ちすることを保証いたします。時代遅れの技術を用いて保存された絵画は、保護するために使用される化学薬品によって損傷する可能性があるため、正しく行うことが重要です。また場合によっては、修復が不十分な絵画を修正することも可能です。

弊社は新サービスとして、実物よりも長く残すことができるように、貴重な絵画の超高解像度デジタルコピーの作成を始めました。こちらは、公共のギャラリーに展示されている作品を対象にした無料のサービスです。

絵画の修復は1つ1つ個別に行われるため、料金を掲載することはできません。お見積もりのご予約は、弊社カスタマーサービスまでご連絡ください。特別な輸送サービスによって、確実な発送をご手配いたします。特に貴重な絵画や壊れやすい絵画の場合のみ、お客様のもとへお伺いいたします。この場合は、お品物の動画を解析し、査定させていただきます。

語彙チェック
☐ restoration　修復　☐ preserve　〜を保つ　☐ valuable　貴重な　☐ restore　〜を修復する　☐ splendor　輝き
☐ ensure　〜を保証する　☐ outdated　時代遅れの　☐ chemicals　化学薬品　☐ correct　〜を修正する
☐ poorly　不十分に　☐ ultra-high　きわめて高い　☐ resolution　解像度　☐ outlive　〜より長く残る
☐ physical　実際の　☐ counterpart　対応するもの　☐ rate　料金　☐ secure　確実な　☐ fragile　壊れやすい

NOTICE

❹Princeton Gallery regrets that *Battle of Montague* by Daniel Forbes is not available for public viewing. It is currently being restored by a professional from Guttenberg Painting Restoration and Conservation. ❺You can view the progress of the work from a window in the studio on the first floor. The restorer is only active between the hours of 1:00 P.M. and 3:00 P.M. from Monday to Friday.

WORD OUT!

Honest reviews of theaters, galleries, museums, and other attractions.

Princeton Gallery ★ ★ ★ ☆

I would have given Princeton Gallery five stars, but I was unable to properly enjoy *Battle of Montague* — the very painting I was most interested in. ❻I think galleries should use their Web sites to let visitors know when certain works are unavailable. I would have rescheduled my visit. ❼Thankfully, I was able to see two talented restoration workers cleaning the work from a studio window, so it wasn't a complete loss.

❽Overall, this is one of the best public galleries I have ever visited.

By We Ying Yang

お知らせ

あいにくではございますが、PrincetonギャラリーはDaniel Forbesによる*Battle of Montague*の一般公開を中止していることをお知らせいたします。現在、Guttenberg絵画修復・保存社の専門家による修復が行われているところです。皆さまには、1階のスタジオの窓から作業の進捗状況をご覧いただけます。修復師は、月曜日から金曜日の午後1時から3時までの間のみ作業しております。

語彙チェック □ currently 現在 □ progress 経過 □ restorer 修復専門家 □ active 活動中の

あなたの声を広めよう！

劇場、ギャラリー、美術館、その他施設の正直なレビュー

Princetonギャラリー★★★★☆
Princetonギャラリーには5つ星を付けたかったのですが、一番興味を持っていた絵画である*Battle of Montague*をきちんと楽しむことができませんでした。特定の絵画の鑑賞ができない場合、ギャラリーはウェブサイト上で来訪者に知らせるべきだと思います。知っていたら、訪問の予定を変更していました。幸いなことに、スタジオの窓から2人の有能な修復作業員が作品を洗浄しているところを見ることができたので、完全に損した、というわけではありませんでした。

総合的に、ここは私がこれまで訪れた中で最も素晴らしい公共ギャラリーの1つです。

レビュー者 We Ying Yang

語彙チェック □ honest 正直な □ attraction 遊戯設備、人を引き付けるもの □ properly きちんと □ very まさにその □ talented 有能な □ loss 損失

What is one benefit of using the service described on the Web site?

(A) Paintings will be less likely to deteriorate over time.

(B) The business offers cheaper rates than its competitors.

(C) Artwork will be easier for investors to sell.

(D) It provides training for gallery employees.

ウェブサイトに記載されているサービスを利用するメリットの1つは何ですか。

(A) 絵画が経年劣化する可能性が低くなる。

(B) 同業他社よりも安い料金である。

(C) 投資家にとって作品を売りやすい。

(D) ギャラリー従業員への教育を行っている。

1文書目は、Guttenberg絵画修復・保存社のサービスについて述べられたウェブサイト。❶で「美術品が元の輝きを取り戻せるように修復し、今後何年も長持ちすることを保証する」とサービス内容が述べられている。メリットは経年劣化の可能性が低くなることであると分かるので、(A)が正解。

語彙チェック ☐ deteriorate 劣化する

What is implied about *Battle of Montague*?

(A) It is on loan from another art gallery.

(B) It was too delicate for transportation.

(C) It is a privately owned artwork.

(D) It will be sold at auction.

*Battle of Montague*について何が示唆されていますか。

(A) 他のギャラリーから借りてきたものである。

(B) 繊細すぎて運ぶことができなかった。

(C) 個人所有の美術品である。

(D) オークションで売られる予定である。

2文書目のお知らせ❹から、*Battle of Montague*はGuttenberg絵画修復・保存社の専門家による修復が行われているところであると分かる。さらに、❺から修復作業はPrincetonギャラリーで行われていることが分かる。また、ウェブサイトの❸には「(絵画修復の際に)特に貴重な絵画や壊れやすい絵画の場合のみ、お客様のもとへお伺いする」と述べられている。よって、正解は(B)。too ～ for …は直訳すると「…には～すぎる」、つまり、「～すぎて…できない」という否定の意味になる。

語彙チェック ☐ on loan 借用中で ☐ delicate 壊れやすい ☐ own ～を所有している ☐ auction オークション

Why is Ms. Yang disappointed?

(A) Some information was not published online.

(B) A piece of art was not preserved properly.

(C) The art gallery was closed during her visit.

(D) A shipment did not arrive on time.

Yangさんはなぜがっかりしていますか。

(A) ある情報がオンラインで公開されていなかったから。

(B) 美術品が適切に保管されていなかったから。

(C) 訪れた際にギャラリーが閉鎖されていたから。

(D) 荷物が時間通りに届かなかったから。

Yangさんは、3文書目のレビューを書いた人物。Yangさんは❻で「特定の絵画の鑑賞ができない場合、ギャラリーはウェブサイト上で来訪者に知らせるべきだと思う」と不満を述べ、さらに「知っていたら予定を変更していた」と続けている。Yangさんがっかりしているのは、事前に情報がオンラインで公開されていなかったことについてだと分かるので、正解は(A)。

語彙チェック ☐ publish ～を発表する ☐ preserve ～を保存する

189

正解 **C** ☐☐☐☐

What is suggested about Ms. Yang?

(A) She has a yearly membership at Princeton Gallery.

(B) She viewed an online video of *Battle of Montague*.

(C) She visited Princeton Gallery on a weekday.

(D) She attended an event at Baumgartner Museum of Art.

Yangさんについて何が分かりますか。

(A) Princeton ギャラリーの年間会員である。

(B) *Battle of Montague* のオンラインビデオを見た。

(C) 平日に Princeton ギャラリーを訪れた。

(D) Baumgartner 美術館で行われたイベントに参加した。

Yangさんが書いたレビューの❼に、「スタジオの窓から2人の修復作業員が作品を洗浄しているところを見られた」と述べられている。これに関連した内容として、お知らせの❺に「（Princeton ギャラリーの訪問者は）1階のスタジオの窓から作業の進捗状況を確認できる」「修復師は月曜日から金曜日までのみ作業している」と述べられている。よって、Yangさんは月曜日から金曜日までのいずれかの平日に Princeton ギャラリーを訪れていたことが分かる。よって、正解は(C)。

語彙チェック ☐ membership　会員であること

190

正解 **D** ☐☐☐☐

What is indicated about Princeton Gallery?

(A) It is affiliated with the Holden Art Fund.

(B) It received huge funding from Daniel Forbes.

(C) It temporarily misplaced an item in its collection.

(D) It is entitled to receive a digital copy of paintings in its collection.

Princeton ギャラリーについて示されていることは何ですか。

(A) Holden 芸術基金と提携している。

(B) Daniel Forbes から巨額の資金援助を受けた。

(C) 一時的に所蔵品を紛失した。

(D) 所蔵する絵画のデジタルコピーを受け取る権利がある。

ウェブサイトの❷に、「新サービスとして、実物よりも長く残すことができるように、貴重な絵画の超高解像度デジタルコピーの作成を始めた」「これは公共のギャラリーに展示されている作品を対象にした無料のサービス」と、絵画修復に関するサービス内容が述べられている。さらにレビューの❽より、Princeton ギャラリーが公共のギャラリーであるということが分かる。これらの情報を総合的に考えると、Princeton ギャラリーは絵画のデジタルコピーを受け取る権利があると判断できる。よって、正解は(D)。

語彙チェック ☐ be affiliated with ～　～と提携している　☐ funding　資金　☐ misplace　～を失くす
☐ be entitled to *do*　～する権利がある

Questions 191-195 refer to the following article, advertisement, and e-mail.

⏵TRACK_129

BOSTON (January 21)—❶The Annual Tiny Home Trade Show will be held in Boston again this year. The term "tiny home" generally refers to homes under 37 square meters. Typically, they can be moved from place to place on wheels built into their bases.

As real estate prices rise, and people's values change, tiny homes are becoming a more and more popular alternative to traditional housing. The market is divided into three main sectors; owner builders, readymade homes, and bespoke homes. ❷At the inaugural Tiny Home Trade Show held last year, Wilson Builds received a lot of interest from the press and the general public. As a manufacturer of readymade homes, Wilson Builds mass produces its homes and sells them at relatively low prices. "Although our homes are readymade, there are a lot of designs for people to choose from," explained CEO Matt Wilson, "❸No matter which one you choose, you can enjoy the benefits of a fully-equipped, bathroom, kitchen, and laundry."

This year, Wilson Builds will have a lot more competition. Manufacturers from around the United States will be displaying their tiny homes in the Bluewave Convention Center. Manufacturers are not the only businesses the trade show is attracting. A variety of other businesses have sprung up to support the growing community of tiny house enthusiasts. ❹There are building courses people can enroll in, construction plans to buy, and even tiny house rentals available for people who want to experience the lifestyle before they commit. ❺All but the last have been invited to attend this year's trade show.

問題191-195は次の記事、広告、Eメールに関するものです。

BOSTON（1月21日）―タイニーホーム年次展示会が、今年もBostonで開催される。タイニーホームとは、一般的に37平方メートル未満の住宅を指す。通常、土台に組み込まれた車輪であちこちに移動することができる。

不動産価格の上昇や人々の価値観の変化に伴い、タイニーホームは従来の住居に代わる選択肢として人気を集めている。市場は3つの主要な分野に分けられ、オーナー建築、レディメイド住宅、オーダーメイド住宅がある。昨年開催された第1回タイニーホーム展示会では、Wilson Builds社が報道機関や一般の人々から多くの関心を集めた。レディメイド住宅のメーカーとして、Wilson Builds社は住宅建設を大量に行い、比較的低価格で住宅を販売している。「弊社の住宅は既製品ですが、多くのデザインからお選びいただけます」と、CEOのMatt Wilsonは説明した。「どの家をお選びいただいても、バスルーム、キッチン、洗濯場などの設備が完備されたメリットをご享受いただけます」

今年のWilson Builds社は、より激しい競争に巻き込まれることだろう。全米各地のメーカーが、Bluewaveコンベンションセンターでタイニーホームを展示する予定だ。展示会が誘致しているのは、メーカーだけではない。拡大しつつあるタイニーハウス愛好家のコミュニティを支援するために、他のさまざまな企業が立ち上がっている。参加ができる建築コースや、購入できる建築プラン、さらには、本格的に住み始める前にタイニーハウスのライフスタイルを体験してみたい人のためのレンタルまでもがある。今年の展示会には、最後の1つを除く全くが招待されている。

語彙チェック □ tiny　ごく小さい　□ generally　一般に　□ refer to ～　～を指す　□ from place to place　あちこちに
□ on wheels　車輪付きの　□ values　価値観　□ alternative　代わるもの　□ housing　住宅
□ divide A into B　AをBに分ける　□ readymade　既製の　□ bespoke　あつらえの　□ inaugural　最初の
□ relatively　比較的　□ benefit　利益　□ fully-equipped　完全装備の　□ spring up　急に現れる
□ enthusiast　熱中している人

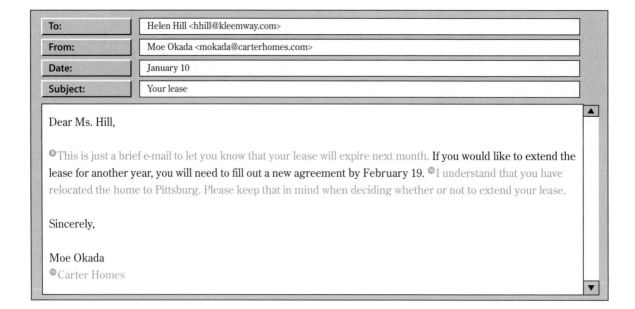

Carter Homes

⑥ Carter Homes has a wide range of tiny homes for rent on short and long-term leases. ⑦ We can deliver and retrieve them for free to addresses in Boston, Chicago, Dallas, or Sacramento and for a reasonable fee, to anywhere else in the United States. ⑧ Our supplier Wilson Builds won the Builder-of-the-Year award at this year's Tiny Home Trade Show in Boston.

To:	Helen Hill <hhill@kleemway.com>
From:	Moe Okada <mokada@carterhomes.com>
Date:	January 10
Subject:	Your lease

Dear Ms. Hill,

⑨ This is just a brief e-mail to let you know that your lease will expire next month. **If you would like to extend the lease for another year, you will need to fill out a new agreement by February 19.** ⑩ I understand that you have relocated the home to Pittsburg. Please keep that in mind when deciding whether or not to extend your lease.

Sincerely,

Moe Okada
⑪ Carter Homes

Carter住宅会社

Carter住宅会社では、短期および長期の賃貸用タイニーホームを幅広く取り揃えています。Boston、Chicago、Dallas、Sacramentoの住所には無料で、それ以外の米国内の住所にはお手頃な料金で、お引き渡しと回収を承っております。弊社の供給会社であるWilson Builds社は、Bostonで開催された今年のタイニーホーム展示会でBuilder-of-the-Year賞を受賞しています。

語彙チェック □ a wide range of 〜　広範囲の〜　□ lease　賃貸契約　□ retrieve　〜を回収する　□ reasonable　手頃な
　　　　　　　□ fee　料金

受信者：Helen Hill <hhill@kleemway.com>
送信者：Moe Okada <mokada@carterhomes.com>
日付：1月10日
件名：あなたの賃貸契約

Hill様

これは、あなたの賃貸契約が来月で終了することをお知らせするためにお送りしている手短なEメールです。もし、もう1年契約を延長する場合は、2月19日までに新しい契約書にご記入いただく必要がございます。あなたがPittsburgにお住まいを移されたということは承知しております。賃貸契約を延長するかどうか決める際には、そのことを念頭に置いていただければと思います。

よろしくお願い申し上げます。

Moe Okada
Carter住宅会社

語彙チェック □ brief　短い　□ expire　終了する　□ agreement　契約書　□ extend　〜を延長する

正解 C ☐☐☐☐

What is implied about the Annual Tiny Home Trade Show?

(A) It only caters to traditional homes.

(B) It has reduced its exhibition fees.

(C) It was held in Boston the first time.

(D) It will attract fewer exhibitors this year.

タイニーホーム年次展示会について、何が示唆されていますか。

(A) 伝統的な住宅のみを対象にしている。

(B) 出展料を引き下げた。

(C) Boston で初回が開催された。

(D) 今年は出展者が少なくなる。

記事の❶で「タイニーホーム年次展示会が今年も Boston で開催される」と、Boston で展示会が複数回開催されてきたことが述べられている。さらに❷の「昨年開催された第1回タイニーホーム展示会では」より、展示会を初めて開催したのは去年であると判断できる。これらの情報から、Boston で初回の展示会が開催されたということが分かる。よって、正解は (C)。

語彙チェック ☐ cater to ～ ～に応ずる ☐ reduce ～を減少させる

正解 D ☐☐☐☐

In the article, the word "commit" in paragraph 3, line 7 is closest in meaning to

(A) allocate

(B) promise

(C) take into account

(D) go all out

記事の第3段落・7行目にある "commit" に最も意味が近いのは

(A) ～を割り当てる

(B) 約束する

(C) ～を考慮に入れる

(D) 本腰を入れる

commit には、「本腰を入れる、本格的にやり始める」という意味がある。❹にこの意味をあてはめると、「本格的に住み始める前に、タイニーハウスのライフスタイルを体験してみたい人のためのレンタルがある」となり、文意が自然に通る。この commit と同じ意味を表す (D) の go all out が正解。

正解 B ☐☐☐☐

What is indicated about Carter Homes?

(A) It won the Builder-of-the-Year award.

(B) It was not eligible for inclusion in the Annual Tiny Home Trade Show.

(C) It manufactures bespoke homes for its clients.

(D) It does not have a customer service office in Boston.

Carter 住宅会社について示されていることは何ですか。

(A) Builder-of-the-Year 賞を受賞した。

(B) タイニーホーム年次展示会に参加する資格がなかった。

(C) 顧客にオーダーメイドの住宅を製造している。

(D) Boston にはお客様相談室がない。

Carter 住宅会社とは、広告の❻より「短期および長期の賃貸用タイニーホームを幅広く取り揃えている」会社。次に記事を見ると、❹に「(タイニーホーム年次展示会では) 参加ができる建築コースや、購入できる建築プラン、さらには、本格的に住み始める前にタイニーハウスのライフスタイルを体験してみたい人のためのレンタルまでもがある」とあり、続けて❺に「今年の展示会には、最後の1つを除く全てが招待されている」とある。❺の「最後の1つ」とは、❹で最後に挙げられている「タイニーハウスのレンタル」のことであると分かる。これは Carter 住宅会社が提供しているサービスのことなので、Carter 住宅会社はタイニーホーム年次展示会への参加資格がなかったと判断できる。よって、正解は (B)。

語彙チェック ☐ eligible 資格のある ☐ inclusion 包括されること

194

正解 D ☐☐☐☐

Why most likely does Ms. Okada mention Pittsburg?

(A) Her company will build an office there.

(B) It is the location of the next Trade Show.

(C) It is outside the approved usage zones.

(D) There will be a relocation fee.

OkadaさんはなぜPittsburgについて言及していると考えられますか。

(A) 彼女の会社がそこにオフィスを建設する予定であるため。

(B) 次の展示会の開催地であるため。

(C) 使用許可区域外であるため。

(D) 移動費用がかかるため。

Eメール⑩で、Carter住宅会社のOkadaさんはHillさんがPittsburgに引っ越したことについて触れ、「賃貸契約を延長するかどうか決める際にはこれを念頭に置いて」と述べている。次にCarter住宅会社の広告の❼を見ると、「Boston、Chicago、Dallas、Sacramentoの住所には無料で、それ以外の米国内の住所にはお手頃な料金で、引き渡しと回収を承っている」と述べられている。これらの情報から、Pittsburgは無料で引き渡し・回収可能なエリア外だということが分かるので、Okadaさんは家の移動費用がかかるということを示唆していると考えられる。よって、正解は(D)。

語彙チェック　☐ usage　使用　☐ zone　区域　☐ relocation　移転

195

正解 A ☐☐☐☐

What is probably true about the home Ms. Hill is renting?

(A) It has a laundry area.

(B) It was constructed in Boston.

(C) It was rented on a short-term lease.

(D) It has its own power supply.

Hillさんが借りている家について、おそらく正しいことは何ですか。

(A) 洗濯場がある。

(B) Bostonに建設された。

(C) 短期間のリース契約で貸し出された。

(D) 自家用電源がある。

Eメールの❾と⓫より、HillさんはCarter住宅会社で賃貸契約をしていることが分かる。広告の❽より、Carter住宅会社の供給会社がWilson Builds社であることが分かる。さらに記事の❸には「どの家にもバスルーム、キッチン、洗濯場などの設備が完備されている」とある。つまり、Hillさんが借りている家には洗濯場が完備されているということが推測できるので、(A)が正解。短期と長期どちらの賃貸契約かは本文では述べられていないので、(C)は不正解。

語彙チェック　☐ power supply　電源装置

目標5:00

音読 □□□   解答時間

: ▶ :

Questions 196-200 refer to the following information, memo, and meeting notes.

▶TRACK_130

TRF Business Software

❶TRF Business Software is an all-in-one accounting, inventory, and payroll package that can help businesses discover inefficiencies and inconsistencies in their workflow. Over time, it can save you millions in wasted time and resources.

We do not provide free evaluation versions of the software, but we do have an informative video that you can watch to see whether or not TRF is right for your business. ❷You are also welcome to read the positive customer testimonials on our Web site.

❸Subscriptions are paid quarterly, and our rates are reasonable and easy to calculate. We charge $1,500 for the first hundred users and $1,000 for each additional hundred.

Many of our larger clients have dedicated departments constantly monitoring logs and looking for ways to improve profits. ❹For businesses with under a thousand employees, it is generally more economical to hire a consultant with expertise in TRF Business Software. A good consultant will save a company far more money than it costs to hire them. We recommend the following firms:

Osprey Consultants
LeadMax Associates
MDO Analytics

問題196-200は次の案内、メモ、会議メモに関するものです。

TRF ビジネスソフトウェア

TRF ビジネスソフトウェアは、会計、在庫、給与計算のオールインワンパッケージで、ワークフローにおける非効率性や矛盾を企業が発見するお手伝いをいたします。経年的に、無駄な時間や資源を何百万ドルも節約することができます。

ソフトウェアの無料お試し版は提供していませんが、TRF 社があなたのビジネスに適しているかどうかをご確認いただける、有益なビデオをご用意しております。また、弊社のウェブサイトに掲載されているお客様の好意的な声もぜひご一読ください。

定額利用料は四半期ごとにお支払いいただく形となり、料金はお手頃で計算しやすくなっています。最初の100ユーザーまでは1,500ドル、それ以降は追加の100ユーザーごとに1,000ドル請求させていただきます。

大企業のお客様の多くが、常にログを監視し、利益向上のための方法を模索する専門部署をお持ちでいらっしゃいます。従業員数が1,000人未満の企業では、一般的にTRF ビジネスソフトウェアの専門知識を持ったコンサルタントを雇う方がより経済的です。優秀なコンサルタントは、雇用にかかるコストよりもはるかに多くの金額を企業に節約させることができます。弊社は以下の会社を推薦いたします：

Osprey コンサルティング会社
LeadMax 社
MDO 分析会社

語彙チェック　□ all-in-one　必要なものが一体に組み込まれた　□ inefficiency　非能率　□ inconsistency　不一致　□ workflow　仕事の流れ　□ save *A B*　AのBを節約する　□ wasted　無駄な　□ informative　有益な　□ testimonial　お客様の声　□ subscription　定額利用料　□ quarterly　四半期ごとに　□ calculate　〜を計算する　□ dedicated　専用の　□ constantly　絶えず　□ monitor　〜を監視する　□ log　ログ　□ expertise　専門知識

MEMO

To: All Crackersnap Department Heads
From: James Rayhman
Date: October 3
Subject: Consultant

It's been just about two weeks since we hired a consultant from Leadmax Associates. Given the number of our company's employees, I assume it was the right decision to make. The financial benefit of his recommendations will soon exceed the consulting fee.

From September 20 to October 1, the consultant Col Jones immediately reviewed the TRF logs and identified areas that need attention. Please view the advice and write a report on what measures you plan to put in place to solve the issues.

The report is due on the day of our monthly department head meeting. Please submit it to me by e-mail. The contents will be discussed at the meeting.

Sincerely,

James Rayhman

MEETING NOTES

October Meeting of Crackersnap Department Heads

Compiled by Trevor Menzies — Personal Assistant to Mr. Rayhman

Date: October 15   Time: 3:00 P.M. ~ 5:00 P.M.

• Mr. Rayhman reminded department heads of the upcoming employee satisfaction survey.

We must distribute the survey using the TRF Business Software and inform employees that it is to be anonymous. Surveys must be submitted by October 18. The data will be processed by Mr. Jones, and he will present the findings the following week.

メモ

宛先：Crackersnap社 部門長各位
差出人：James Rayhman
日付：10月3日
件名：コンサルタント

Leadmax社のコンサルタントを雇ってから、ちょうど2週間程度が経ちました。当社の従業員の数を考えると、この決断は正しかったと思います。彼の提案によって生み出される経済的利益は、まもなくコンサルティング料を上回ることでしょう。

9月20日から10月1日までの期間で、コンサルタントのCol Jonesは早速TRFのログを確認し、注意が必要な点を見つけ出してくれました。アドバイスを見て、課題解決のためにどのような対策を導入する予定か、レポートを書いてきてください。

レポートの提出期限は、毎月の部門長会議の日です。メールで私に提出してください。内容は会議で検討するつもりです。

よろしくお願いいたします。

James Rayhman

語彙チェック □ assume　〜を本当だと思う　□ recommendation　提案、助言　□ exceed　〜を上回る
□ immediately　ただちに　□ identify　〜をつきとめる　□ measures　対策　□ put 〜 in place　〜を導入する
□ solve　〜を解決する　□ submit　〜を提出する

会議メモ
10月開催Crackersnap社部門長会議

編集：Trevor Menzies— Rayhmanさんの個人秘書
日付：10月15日　時間：午後3時〜午後5時

• Rayhmanさんから各部門長に対して、近々実施される従業員満足度調査についてのお知らせがありました。
我々はTRFビジネスソフトウェアを使ってアンケートを配布し、さらにそれが匿名である旨を従業員に伝えなければなりません。アンケートの提出締切は10月18日です。データはJonesさんによって処理され、その翌週に調査結果を発表していただく予定です。

語彙チェック □ upcoming　もうすぐやって来る　□ anonymous　匿名の　□ process　〜を処理する　□ present　〜を発表する
□ findings　発見　□ following　次の

正解 B ☐☐☐☐

What is NOT mentioned about TRF Business Software?

(A) It has been praised by its users.
(B) Updates are published regularly.
(C) Customers are charged four times a year.
(D) It enables businesses to improve their work efficiency.

TRF ビジネスソフトウェアについて言及されていないことは何ですか。

(A) ユーザーから称賛されている。
(B) 定期的にアップデートが公開されている。
(C) 顧客は年4回支払う必要がある。
(D) 企業の業務の効率化を可能にする。

TRF ビジネスソフトウェアに関する案内である、1文書目に注目。❷に「ウェブサイトに掲載されたお客様の好意的な声もご一読ください」とあることから、(A)は言及されている。また❸に「定額利用料は四半期ごとにお支払いいただく」とあることから、(C)も言及されている。さらに❶に「TRF ビジネスソフトウェアはワークフローにおける非効率性や矛盾を企業が発見する手伝いをする」とあるので、(D)も述べられている。よって、正解は(B)。本文には定期的なアップデートについての記載はない。

語彙チェック ☐ praise 〜を称賛する ☐ efficiency 効率

正解 A ☐☐☐☐

What is probably true about Crackersnap?

(A) It has fewer than a thousand employees.
(B) It has provided one of the testimonials on the Web site.
(C) It produced the video mentioned in the information.
(D) It is using a free version of TRF Business Software.

Crackersnap 社についておそらく正しいことは何ですか。

(A) 従業員数が1,000人未満である。
(B) ウェブサイト上に顧客の声を投稿した。
(C) 案内の中で紹介されているビデオを制作した。
(D) TRF ビジネスソフトウェアの無料版お試し版を使用している。

Crackersnap 社はメモの❺で Leadmax 社のコンサルタントを雇ったことを述べ、「当社の従業員の数を考えると、この決断は正しかったと思う」「経済的利益は、まもなくコンサルティング料を上回ることだろう」と続けている。ここで Leadmax 社について述べられた1文書目の案内に戻ると、❹に「従業員数が1,000人未満の企業では、TRF ビジネスソフトウェアの専門知識を持ったコンサルタントを雇う方がより経済的」「雇用にかかるコストよりもはるかに多くの金額を企業に節約させられる」との記載がある。よって、Crackersnap 社は従業員数が1,000人未満であるため、この案内に従いコンサルタントを雇ったということが推測できる。正解は(A)。

語彙チェック ☐ testimonial お客様の声

正解 D ☐☐☐☐

When is the deadline for the report mentioned in the memo?

(A) September 20
(B) October 1
(C) October 3
(D) October 15

メモで言及されているレポートの締め切りはいつですか。

(A) 9月20日
(B) 10月1日
(C) 10月3日
(D) 10月15日

メモを見ると、❼に「レポートの提出期限は毎月の部門長会議の日」と述べられている。具体的な日付が分からないので、部門長会議の日がいつかを探そう。会議メモの❽に「10月開催 Crackersnap 社部門長会議」とあるのでこの文書を見ていくと、❾に「日付：10月15日」と、部門長会議の日付が書かれている。よって、レポートの提出期限は10月15日だと分かる。正解は(D)。

199

正解 **D** ☐☐☐☐

What do the meeting notes say about the survey?

(A) It must be filled out by October 20.

(B) Department heads are not required to submit one.

(C) It is carried out on a yearly basis.

(D) Staff are not required to write their names on it.

会議メモには、アンケートについて何が書かれていますか。

(A) 10月20日までに記入されなければならない。

(B) 部門長は提出する必要がない。

(C) 年単位で実施される。

(D) 従業員は自分の名前を書く必要はない。

会議メモの❿を見ると、「我々はそれ（＝アンケート）が匿名である旨を従業員に伝えなければならない」と述べられている。anonymous「匿名の」を not required to write their names「名前を書く必要がない」と言い換えた(D)が正解。部門長のアンケート提出の有無については本文で記載がないので、(B)は不正解。

語彙チェック　☐ on a yearly basis　年に1回

200

正解 **B** ☐☐☐☐

Which company will process the survey data?

(A) Osprey Consultants

(B) LeadMax Associates

(C) MDO Analytics

(D) Crackersnap

アンケートデータはどの会社が処理しますか。

(A) Osprey コンサルティング会社

(B) LeadMax社

(C) MDO分析会社

(D) Crackersnap社

会議メモの⓫に「データはJonesさんによって処理される」とあるので、Jonesさんが所属する会社名を探す必要がある。メモの❻に「コンサルタントのCol Jones」とJonesさんの名前が言及されており、さらにその前の❺で「Leadmax社のコンサルタントを雇ってから、ちょうど2週間程度が経った」と述べられている。つまり、JonesさんはLeadmax社に所属する人物だと分かるので、正解は(B)。

TEST 2

解答＆解説

Part 1

問題番号	正解
1	B
2	A
3	D
4	C
5	C
6	D

Part 2

問題番号	正解
7	B
8	A
9	C
10	B
11	A
12	A
13	C
14	B
15	A
16	A
17	C
18	C
19	A
20	B
21	C
22	A
23	A
24	B
25	A
26	B
27	C
28	C
29	B
30	C
31	B

Part 3

問題番号	正解
32	A
33	B
34	C
35	C
36	A
37	D
38	B
39	D
40	D
41	C
42	B
43	C
44	A
45	D
46	A
47	D
48	C
49	A
50	A
51	B
52	C
53	D
54	A
55	D
56	B
57	D
58	D
59	C
60	B
61	C
62	C
63	C
64	B
65	B
66	B
67	D
68	D
69	A
70	B

Part 4

問題番号	正解
71	D
72	B
73	A
74	A
75	B
76	D
77	C
78	C
79	D
80	B
81	C
82	A
83	A
84	C
85	A
86	C
87	B
88	D
89	A
90	B
91	A
92	A
93	C
94	B
95	C
96	C
97	A
98	B
99	D
100	B

Part 5

問題番号	正解
101	C
102	B
103	B
104	A
105	C
106	A
107	D
108	A
109	C
110	C
111	B
112	B
113	D
114	C
115	A
116	B
117	D
118	C
119	D
120	B
121	A
122	D
123	C
124	D
125	B
126	B
127	A
128	B
129	D
130	C

Part 6

問題番号	正解
131	D
132	C
133	A
134	B
135	C
136	B
137	A
138	D
139	A
140	D
141	B
142	C
143	C
144	B
145	D
146	A

Part 7

問題番号	正解
147	A
148	A
149	C
150	B
151	C
152	D
153	B
154	C
155	B
156	D
157	C
158	D
159	A
160	C
161	A
162	A
163	D
164	A
165	B
166	C
167	B
168	C
169	D
170	B
171	B
172	A
173	C
174	A
175	C
176	A
177	D
178	C
179	C
180	B
181	A
182	D
183	B
184	B
185	A

問題番号	正解
186	D
187	B
188	A
189	C
190	B
191	D
192	B
193	C
194	B
195	D
196	B
197	A
198	C
199	B
200	D

Part 1

1 🇬🇧　正解 **B** ☐☐☐☐　▶ TRACK_132

(A) Some people are strolling along a riverbank.
(B) Some rounded tables are arranged in a double line.
(C) Chairs are being moved into a corner of the café.
(D) A roof has been covering the deck.

(A) 何人かの人々が川岸沿いを散歩している。
(B) 円卓が2列に並べられている。
(C) 椅子がカフェの隅に移動させられているところである。
(D) 屋根がデッキを覆っている。

> 屋外の写真。店の外に円卓が2列に並べられているので、これを言い表している (B) が正解。

語彙チェック　☐ stroll　散歩する　☐ riverbank　川岸　☐ deck　デッキ

👑 Level Up!
写真に写っている要素が多いときは、主語に注意して、写真のどの部分に言及しているのかを照らし合わせながら聞こう。

2 🇦🇺　正解 **A** ☐☐☐☐　▶ TRACK_133

(A) A man is trimming a tree with shears.
(B) A man is taking care of the roof of a shed.
(C) A stepladder has been folded up.
(D) Some trees are casting shadows on the patio.

(A) 男性は大ばさみで木を刈り込んでいる。
(B) 男性は物置の屋根を手入れしている。
(C) 脚立が折り畳まれている。
(D) 木が中庭に影を落としている。

> はさみを手に持った男性が木の手入れをしている様子を言い表した (A) が正解。写真に写っている場所は中庭ではないので、(D) は不適切。

語彙チェック　☐ shears　大ばさみ　☐ shed　物置　☐ stepladder　脚立
☐ cast a shadow　影を落とす

3 🇺🇸　正解 **D** ☐☐☐☐　▶ TRACK_134

(A) One of the women is walking through the hallway.
(B) A bunch of flowers is being placed on the ground.
(C) The street surface is filled with fallen petals.
(D) Sunshades are lined up at the same height.

(A) 女性の1人は廊下を歩いて通り抜けている。
(B) 花束が地面に置かれているところである。
(C) 道路の表面が落ちた花びらでいっぱいである。
(D) 日よけが同じ高さに並べられている。

> 写真の奥の方に、いくつかの日よけが並べられている。これらは全て同じ高さになっているので、(D) が正解。

語彙チェック　☐ hallway　廊下　☐ bunch　束　☐ petal　花びら

4 🏴

正解 **C** ☐☐☐☐　▶TRACK_135

(A) A pile of cups are loaded in a dishwasher.
(B) An apron has been hung from a rack.
(C) He's pouring some liquid from a pitcher.
(D) He's stirring boiling water to let it cool.

(A) たくさんのコップが食洗機の中に積まれている。
(B) エプロンが棚からつるされている。
(C) 彼は水差しから液体を注いでいる。
(D) 彼は沸騰したお湯を冷やすためにかき混ぜている。

男性の手元に注目。男性は水差しを手に持っており、その中の液体を別の容器に移し替えている最中である。よって、これを言い表している(C)が正解。写真左手にコップは写っているが、食洗機の中にあるわけではないので(A)は不適切。

👑 **Level Up!**
(A)は、文末で読み上げられる「場所」だけが間違い。途中まで聞いて正答だと思われる選択肢も、最後まで集中して聞き取ろう。

語彙チェック ☐pour　〜を注ぐ　☐stir　〜をかき混ぜる

---

5 🇺🇸

正解 **C** ☐☐☐☐　▶TRACK_136

(A) They're looking at a spool of thread.
(B) They're repairing an electrical appliance.
(C) One of the men is grasping the rope's end.
(D) One of the men is pointing at a sign.

(A) 彼らは一巻きの糸を見ている。
(B) 彼らは家電を修理している。
(C) 男性の1人はロープの端を握っている。
(D) 男性の1人は看板を指さしている。

奥の男性の手元に注目。男性はロープの端を握っているので、この動作に言及した(C)が正解。手前の男性が指をさしている先に看板は写っていないため、(D)は不適切。

👑 **Level Up!**
(A)で使われている表現 a spool of 〜は「一巻きの〜」という意味。Part 1では、他にも a pair of 〜「1組の〜」や a bunch of 〜「1房の〜」など、「数」を表す表現が登場するので要チェック！

語彙チェック ☐spool　糸巻き　☐thread　糸　☐grasp　〜を握る

---

6 🇨🇦

正解 **D** ☐☐☐☐　▶TRACK_137

(A) A dish drainer has been placed in a sink.
(B) A faucet has been installed in front of an outlet.
(C) An iron kettle is located beside some fruit.
(D) A cabinet door has been vertically opened.

(A) 水切りかごがシンクの中に置かれている。
(B) 蛇口がコンセントの正面に設置されている。
(C) 鉄製のやかんがフルーツのそばに置かれている。
(D) 棚の扉が垂直に開けられている。

写真の上部にある棚の扉が、垂直方向に開けられたままになっている。これを現在完了の受動態の形で表している(D)が正解。

語彙チェック ☐dish drainer　水切りかご　☐faucet　蛇口
☐outlet　コンセント　☐kettle　やかん　☐vertically　垂直に

Part 2

音読 □□□ 聞き逃し単語 語 ▶ 語

7 M 🇦🇺 W 🇬🇧　　　　　　　　　　正解 **B** □□□□　▶TRACK_139

Who's going to give the presentation?　　　　誰がプレゼンテーションを行う予定ですか。
(A) It needs to be repaired.　　　　　　　　　(A) それは修理が必要です。
(B) I think Aziz is.　　　　　　　　　　　　　(B) Aziz だと思います。
(C) I've reserved a conference room.　　　　　(C) 会議室を予約しました。

プレゼンテーションを行う人物を尋ねられているので、Azizさんという人名を
挙げて答えている (B) が正解。Aziz is の後ろに going to give the presentation
が省略されている。

> **👑 Level Up!**
> Azizのような、聞き取りにくい人名には要注意。聞き慣れない単語でも、文構造から人名だと判断する力が必要！

語彙チェック □ reserve 〜を予約する

音読 □□□ 聞き逃し単語 語 ▶ 語

8 M 🇺🇸 W 🇬🇧　　　　　　　　　　正解 **A** □□□□　▶TRACK_140

I have a dentist appointment on the day of the　　セミナーの日に歯医者の予約があるんです。
seminar.
(A) It will be recorded.　　　　　　　　　　(A) 録画されますよ。
(B) OK, let's rearrange the room.　　　　　　(B) よし、部屋の模様替えをしましょう。
(C) That was a windy day.　　　　　　　　　(C) その日は風の強い日でした。

歯医者の予約がセミナーの日と被っていることを伝えている。それに対し、「(セミナーは) 録画される」と答えること
で、出席できなくても後でセミナーの内容を映像で確認できるということを伝えている (A) が正解。dentistは、アメリカ
英語で早口で発音されると「デニス」のように聞こえることもあるため要注意。

語彙チェック □ dentist 歯医者　□ rearrange 〜を再配置する　□ windy 風の強い

音読 □□□ 聞き逃し単語 語 ▶ 語

9 M 🇦🇺 W 🇨🇦　　　　　　　　　　正解 **C** □□□□　▶TRACK_141

Should we choose a white couch or a black one?　白いソファを選ぶべきでしょうか、それとも黒いソファを選ぶべき
　　　　　　　　　　　　　　　　　　　　　でしょうか。
(A) Maybe some new patterns.　　　　　　　(A) もしかすると新しい柄です。
(B) Yes, you should do that.　　　　　　　　(B) はい、そうするべきですよ。
(C) Beige could be an option.　　　　　　　(C) ベージュも選択肢に入るかもしれませんね。

ソファの色について尋ねている。「白か黒か」という質問に対して、「ベージュ」
という別の選択肢を提示している (C) が正解。

> **👑 Level Up!**
> 冒頭の Should we だけを聞くと、(B) が正解のように思える。Part 2で全問正解を目指すなら、最後まで聞く癖をつけよう。

語彙チェック □ couch ソファ　□ pattern 模様　□ beige ベージュ
　　　　　　　□ option 選択肢

10　W 🇨🇦　M 🇺🇸　正解 B □□□□　▶TRACK_142

Is this your laptop?

(A) No, use the microphone.

(B) Where did you find it?

(C) Yes, they wrapped the package.

これはあなたのノートパソコンですか。

(A) いいえ、マイクを使ってください。

(B) どこで見つけましたか。

(C) はい、彼らは荷物を包んでくれました。

ノートパソコンが自分のものかどうかを尋ねられている。それに対し、自分のものかそうでないかは答えず、代わりに見つけた場所を尋ねている(B) が応答として最も適切。

語彙チェック　□ laptop　ノートパソコン　□ microphone　マイク　□ wrap　〜を包む　□ package　荷物

11　M 🇮🇳　W 🇬🇧　正解 A □□□□　▶TRACK_143

Didn't you take the day off today?

(A) The project I work on is behind schedule.

(B) Submit the necessary documents in advance.

(C) It'll be about one hour and a half.

今日は休みを取ったのではなかったのですか。

(A) 取り組んでいるプロジェクトが予定より遅れているんです。

(B) 必要な書類を事前に提出してください。

(C) 1時間30分くらいかかります。

今日は休みを取っているはずのあなたがなぜ仕事をしているのか、といった意図を含む質問。それに対し、「(自分が) 取り組んでいるプロジェクトが予定より遅れている」と答えることで、遅れを取り戻すために今は休んでいられない、と伝えている(A) が応答として適切。

語彙チェック　□ day off　休日　□ behind schedule　予定より遅れて　□ in advance　事前に

12　W 🇬🇧　W 🇨🇦　正解 A □□□□　▶TRACK_144

Why don't you try the hoodie on?

(A) It's not quite my style.

(B) Because I am pretty full.

(C) At another clothing store.

パーカーを試着してみませんか。

(A) あまり好みではありません。

(B) かなりお腹がいっぱいだからです。

(C) 別の洋服屋でです。

Why don't you 〜?は「〜しませんか」と提案・勧誘をする表現。内容から、洋服屋での会話だと考えられる。パーカーの試着を勧められているのに対し、「好みではない」と答えることで、試着を断っている(A) が正解。

👑 **Level Up!**
Why don't you 〜?は提案の表現。文頭のWhy「なぜ」だけを聞き取り、Becauseから始まる(B) を選ばないように注意!

語彙チェック　□ try 〜 on　〜を試着する　□ hoodie　パーカー　□ pretty　かなり　□ full　お腹がいっぱいの

13 M 🇺🇸 W 🇨🇦 正解 C □□□□ ▶TRACK_145

Mari was absent from the meeting, wasn't she?
(A) In the supply room.
(B) Sure, let's do that.
(C) She should be better soon.

Mariはミーティングを欠席していましたよね。
(A) 備品室の中です。
(B) もちろんです、それをやりましょう。
(C) 彼女はすぐ良くなるはずです。

付加疑問文で、Mariという人物がミーティングを欠席していたことを確認している。それに対し、「彼女はすぐ良くなるはずだ」と答えることで、体調不良でミーティングを欠席していたと思われるMariさんの状況を話している(C)が応答として自然。

語彙チェック □ be absent from 〜 〜を欠席する □ supply room 備品室

14 W 🇬🇧 M 🇦🇺 正解 B □□□□ ▶TRACK_146

What time is the plumber supposed to arrive?
(A) The launch took place at eleven.
(B) She's fixing the pipe just now.
(C) The photocopier on the third floor.

配管工は何時に到着することになっていますか。
(A) 販売開始は11時でした。
(B) 彼女はちょうど今パイプを修理しているところです。
(C) 3階のコピー機です。

質問はbe supposed to do「〜することになっている」という表現を使い、配管工の到着時間を確認している。(B)のShe「彼女」がthe plumber「配管工」を指すと考えると、「彼女はちょうど今パイプを修理している」と答えることで、配管工がすでに到着していると伝えていることになるため、(B)が正解。

語彙チェック □ plumber 配管工 □ be supposed to do 〜することになっている

15 M 🇦🇺 W 🇬🇧 正解 A □□□□ ▶TRACK_147

Where's the stapler?
(A) That should be in the drawer.
(B) You can meet him at the station.
(C) At three P.M. every Wednesday.

ホッチキスはどこにありますか。
(A) 引き出しの中にあるはずです。
(B) 駅で彼に会うことができますよ。
(C) 毎週水曜日、午後3時にです。

ホッチキスの場所を尋ねているのに対し、「引き出しの中にあるはずだ」と場所を答えている(A)が正解。Thatはthe stapler「ホッチキス」を指す。

語彙チェック □ stapler ホッチキス □ drawer 引き出し

16 W 🇨🇦 M 🇺🇸　正解 **A** □□□□　▶TRACK_148

We're planning to throw a farewell party for John.

(A) I could help you organize that.

(B) I'm well, thanks.

(C) Here is your itinerary.

私たちはJohnの送別会を開く計画をしています。

(A) それを企画するのを手伝いますよ。

(B) 元気です、ありがとうございます。

(C) こちらがあなたの旅程表です。

同僚と思われるJohnさんの送別会について話している。「計画をしている」と聞いて、「手伝いますよ」と伝えている (A) が応答として自然。

語彙チェック　□ throw　（パーティーなど）を開く　□ farewell party　送別会　□ organize　〜を企画する、〜を準備する
□ itinerary　旅程表

17 W 🇬🇧 W 🇨🇦　正解 **C** □□□□　▶TRACK_149

This is the first time I've been to this restaurant.

(A) During the spring, I believe.

(B) Yes, we accept credit cards.

(C) That's why I brought you here.

このレストランに来たのはこれが初めてです。

(A) 春の間だと思います。

(B) はい、クレジットカードをご利用いただけます。

(C) だから私はあなたをここに連れてきたんです。

レストランにいると考えられる会話。「このレストランに来たのが初めてだ」という発言に対して、「（来たことがないと知っていて、）だから連れてきたんだ」と伝えている (C) が正解。

語彙チェック　□ bring　〜を連れてくる

18 M 🇺🇸 W 🇨🇦　正解 **C** □□□□　▶TRACK_150

Why did you leave the office early yesterday?

(A) The office building across the road.

(B) It's on your left, probably.

(C) The ward office closes at five P.M.

なぜあなたは昨日オフィスを早く出たのですか。

(A) 道路の向かいのオフィスビルです。

(B) おそらく左側にありますよ。

(C) 区役所が午後5時に閉まるんです。

相手が早めにオフィスを出た理由を尋ねている。それに対し、「区役所が午後5時に閉まる」と答えることで、区役所に用があって、そこが閉まる前に行かなくてはならなかったためだと説明している (C) が正解。

👑Level Up！

Why「なぜ」という質問に対し、Because「なぜなら」で始まらない選択肢が正解になることも多い。理由を問う質問文が流れたら、自分の脳内でBecauseを補って選択肢を聞くようにしよう。

語彙チェック　□ probably　おそらく　□ ward office　区役所

19 W 🇨🇦 M 🇦🇺　正解 **A** □□□□　▶TRACK_151

Which desk is yours?

(A) The one that faces the window.

(B) On the top shelf.

(C) There're a few chairs in the room.

あなたのデスクはどれですか。

(A) 窓に面しているものです。

(B) 一番上の棚の上です。

(C) 部屋には椅子がいくつかあります。

どのデスクがあなたのものかと尋ねているのに対し、「窓に面しているものだ」と答えている (A) が正解。one は desk を指す。

👑 **Level Up !**
質問文で登場した名詞 desk を、(A) では代名詞の one に置き換えている。代名詞を使っている文は、瞬時に意味を取りづらいので注意！

語彙チェック □ face 〜に面している

20 M 🇦🇺 W 🇬🇧　正解 **B** □□□□　▶TRACK_152

How long does this flower last?

(A) Bake it for twenty minutes.

(B) This is artificial.

(C) About two meters away.

この花はどのくらい持ちますか。

(A) 20分間焼いてください。

(B) これは人工のものですよ。

(C) 約2メートル離れたところです。

花屋での会話だと考えられる。ある花について、どのくらい長持ちするのかを尋ねているのに対し、「これ（この花）は人工のものだ」と相手の誤解を正している (B) が正解。

語彙チェック □ last 持続する、持つ　□ bake 〜を焼く　□ artificial 人工の

21 W 🇨🇦 M 🇺🇸　正解 **C** □□□□　▶TRACK_153

How do we send this fragile item?

(A) By working as a receptionist.

(B) Here is the employee satisfaction survey.

(C) Use the cushioning material in the cabinet.

この壊れやすい商品はどうやって送りますか。

(A) 受付係として働くことによってです。

(B) こちらは従業員満足度調査書です。

(C) キャビネットにある緩衝材を使用してください。

壊れやすい商品の送付方法を尋ねている。それに対し、「緩衝材を使うように」と具体的な方法を伝えている (C) が応答として適切。

語彙チェック □ fragile 壊れやすい　□ receptionist 受付係　□ cushioning material 緩衝材

22　W 🇬🇧　M 🇦🇺　　正解 A □□□□　▶TRACK_154

Have you seen the exhibition at that museum?

(A) Absolutely, it was superb.

(B) Yes, I'm looking forward to it.

(C) There's an exit in the rear.

あなたはその美術館の展示を見ましたか。

(A) もちろんです、素晴らしかったです。

(B) はい、それを楽しみにしています。

(C) 後方に出口があります。

ある美術館の展示について、もう見たのかどうかを尋ねている。それに対し、「もちろん」とその展示をすでに見たことを伝え、感想を付け加えている(A)が正解。

語彙チェック　□ absolutely　もちろん　□ superb　素晴らしい　□ exit　出口　□ rear　後部

23　M 🇦🇺　W 🇨🇦　　正解 A □□□□　▶TRACK_155

Did your customers like the Web page I designed?

(A) The engagements have been high.

(B) The designer is very famous.

(C) The webinar was a great success.

あなたの顧客は、私がデザインしたウェブページを気に入ってくれましたか。

(A) エンゲージメントは高いです。

(B) そのデザイナーはとても有名です。

(C) ウェビナーは大成功でした。

ウェブページデザイナーと考えられる人が、自分のデザインしたウェブページに対する顧客の反応について尋ねている。それに対して「エンゲージメントは高い」と答え、良い評価を伝えている(A)が正解。

👑 **Level Up !**
本問の正答(A)は、「（きっとそうです。なぜかと言うと、）エンゲージメントが高いです」というような意味合いが含まれていると考えよう。

語彙チェック　□ engagement　（ソーシャルメディアなどの）エンゲージメント
※ある投稿に対する反応

24　W 🇨🇦　M 🇺🇸　　正解 B □□□□　▶TRACK_156

Do you prefer to report to work or work from home?

(A) My specialty is online marketing.

(B) I like talking with people in person.

(C) It should be submitted to the manager.

あなたは、出社するのと在宅勤務をするのとではどちらが好きですか。

(A) 私の専門はオンラインマーケティングです。

(B) 私は人と直接話すのが好きです。

(C) それは部長に提出するべきです。

出社と在宅勤務の2つの働き方を挙げ、好みを尋ねている。それに対し、「人と直接話すのが好き」と答えることで、在宅勤務より出社する方が好きだということを暗に示している(B)が正解。

語彙チェック　□ report to work　出社する　□ specialty　専門　□ in person　直接

25　M 🇦🇺　W 🇬🇧　　正解 A □□□□　▶TRACK_157

Mark is out of the office, isn't he?

(A) Is there anything to tell him?

(B) Sorry, it's missing now.

(C) The office will be relocated soon.

Markは外出中ですよね？

(A) 何か彼に伝えることがあるのですか。

(B) すみません、それは今見つからないのです。

(C) オフィスは近々移転する予定です。

付加疑問文で、Markさんがオフィスにいるかどうかを確認している。それに対し、「何か彼（Markさん）に伝えることがあるのか」と用件を尋ねている(A)が会話として自然。

👑 **Level Up !**

本問のように、問いかけに対して質問で返す応答には要注意。質問の背景や相手の意図を確認するための応答で、直接的に答えていないので難易度が高い。

語彙チェック　□ missing　見つからない　□ relocate　〜を移転させる

26　W 🇬🇧　M 🇦🇺　　正解 B □□□□　▶TRACK_158

Didn't you arrive at the venue on time?

(A) Because they offered me discounts.

(B) The roads were frozen.

(C) Yes, every two hours.

あなたは時間通りに会場に到着しなかったのですか。

(A) 彼らが割引をしてくれたからです。

(B) 道路が凍結していたんです。

(C) はい、2時間ごとです。

相手が時間通りに会場に到着しなかったことについて、事実を確認している。それに対し、「道路が凍結していた」と答え、遅刻した理由を伝えている(B)が正解。

語彙チェック　□ venue　会場　□ on time　時間通りに　□ frozen　寒さで凍った、氷の張った

27　M 🇺🇸　W 🇨🇦　　正解 C □□□□　▶TRACK_159

Do you want me to replace your glasses frame?

(A) Oh, it overlooks the bridge.

(B) I've met the repairer before.

(C) I'm fine with the current one.

眼鏡のフレームを交換いたしますか。

(A) ああ、そこから橋が見渡せます。

(B) 私は以前、その修理業者に会ったことがあります。

(C) 今のもので大丈夫です。

Do you want me to do 〜? は、「〜しましょうか」と提案・申し出をするときの表現。眼鏡屋の店員と思われる人が、眼鏡のフレーム交換をしたいかどうかを尋ねている。それに対し、「今のもので大丈夫」と答え、フレーム交換を断っている(C)が正解。one は glasses frame「眼鏡のフレーム」を指す。

語彙チェック　□ replace　〜を取り替える　□ overlook　〜を見渡せる　□ current　現在の

28　W 🇬🇧　M 🇺🇸　正解 C　□□□□　▶TRACK_160

What type of vehicle would you like to rent?

(A) It's too far from here to walk.

(B) This is a copy of my driver's license.

(C) Anything that can hold six of us.

どのような種類の車両をレンタルされますか。

(A) ここからは歩くには遠すぎます。

(B) これが私の運転免許証のコピーです。

(C) 6人を収容できるものであれば何でもいいです。

What type of 〜「どのような種類の〜」で、あるものの種類を尋ねることができる。内容から、レンタカー店の店員と客の会話だと考えられる。店員がレンタルする車の種類を尋ねているのに対し、「6人乗れる車がいい」と条件を伝えている(C)が正解。

語彙チェック　□ rent　〜を賃借する　□ driver's license　運転免許証　□ hold　〜を収容する

29　W 🇨🇦　M 🇦🇺　正解 B　□□□□　▶TRACK_161

When are we launching our VR goggles?

(A) Let's have dinner together.

(B) Haven't you gotten the updates?

(C) At the electronics store.

VRゴーグルはいつ発売しますか。

(A) 一緒に夕食を食べましょう。

(B) 最新情報を聞いていないのですか。

(C) 電気屋でです。

製品の発売日を尋ねている。それに対し、発売日を答えるのではなく、「最新情報を聞いていないのか」と質問を返して確認している(B)が正解。

👑**Level Up !**
冒頭の When are we の部分は、音がつながって聞き取りづらいので注意しよう！

語彙チェック　□ update　最新情報

30　M 🇺🇸　W 🇬🇧　正解 C　□□□□　▶TRACK_162

Where can I buy the product?

(A) Only if they have some in stock.

(B) Usually at the end of the month.

(C) It's an online exclusive.

その製品はどこで購入できますか。

(A) 在庫がある場合に限ります。

(B) 通常は月末です。

(C) それはオンライン限定商品です。

ある製品について、どこで入手できるのかを尋ねている。それに対し、「それはオンライン限定商品だ」と答えることで、店舗などではなくオンラインでしか買えないことを伝えている(C)が正解。

語彙チェック　□ only if 〜　〜でありさえすれば　□ have 〜 in stock　〜が在庫にある　□ exclusive　制限された

31　M 🇦🇺　M 🇺🇸　正解 B　□□□□　▶TRACK_163

Why don't we have lunch at this eatery?

(A) A cup of coffee woke me up.

(B) Unless there is a long line.

(C) You should deliver it right away.

このレストランで昼食を取りませんか。

(A) 一杯のコーヒーで目が覚めました。

(B) 長い列がなければ、ですね。

(C) すぐにそれを届けるべきです。

Why don't we 〜?は「〜しませんか」と提案するときの表現。レストランで昼食を取る提案をしているのに対し、「長い列がなければ（＝待ち時間がなければ）賛成だ」と伝えている(B)が正解。unless「〜でない限り」は条件を示すときに使う。

語彙チェック　□ eatery　レストラン、軽食堂　□ wake 〜 up　〜を起こす　□ unless　〜でない限り　□ line　列

TEST 1

TEST 2

Part 3

音読 □□□　　カンペキ理解　　/11 ▶　　/11

会話 ▶TRACK_165　問題 ▶TRACK_166

カンペキ理解 ▶TRACK_K24

M 🇺🇸　W 🇨🇦

Questions 32 through 34 refer to the following conversation.

カンペキ理解		
1	□□	M: I need a large box for some tools I'm sending to Minnesota by priority mail.
2	□□	Oh, I'll also need some packing materials and some shipping labels.
3	□□	W: I'm sorry, but we just ran out of the large boxes.
4	□□	We won't have any in until tomorrow.
5	□□	I know they have some at the Cleveland branch,
6	□□	and it's only a ten-minute drive from here.
7	□□	M: I walked here, so it'll take a bit longer than that.
8	□□	That's OK, though.
9	□□	I'll be back tomorrow.
10	□□	I'll just get a packet of business envelopes for now.
11	□□	Um... the ones with the window in the front.

問題32-34は次の会話に関するものです。

男性：Minnesotaに送る道具を入れる大きな箱が欲しいのですが、優先郵便で送っていただけますか。ああ、包装材と配送ラベルもお願いします。

女性：申し訳ありませんが、ちょうど大きい箱の在庫が切れてしまいました。明日まで入荷がないのです。Cleveland支店にいくつかあるのを知っております。ここから車でたった10分くらいの場所にございます。

男性：私は歩いてここに来たので、もう少しかかりそうです。でも大丈夫です。明日、また来ます。とりあえず、ビジネス封筒を一束買っていきます。ええと…封筒の正面に窓が付いているものです。

語彙チェック　□ priority mail　優先郵便　□ shipping label　配送ラベル　□ run out of 〜　〜を切らしている
□ a packet of 〜　〜の一束　□ envelope　封筒　□ window　封筒の窓

32

正解 A ☐☐☐☐

Where most likely are the speakers?

(A) In a post office

(B) In a hardware store

(C) At a car repair garage

(D) At a hospital

話し手たちはどこにいると考えられますか。

(A) 郵便局

(B) 金物店

(C) 車の修理工場

(D) 病院

冒頭で男性は女性に対し、I need a large box for some tools I'm sending to Minnesota by priority mail.と優先郵便で送りたいものがあることを述べている。それに対し、女性は資材の在庫がないことを伝え、他の支店への案内をしている。ここから、女性は郵便局員で、2人は郵便局にいると分かる。よって、正解は(A)。

33

正解 B ☐☐☐☐

What does the woman suggest?

(A) Buying in bulk

(B) Visiting a different location

(C) Trying a new product

(D) Attending a workshop

女性は何をすることを提案していますか。

(A) 大量に買うこと

(B) 別の場所を訪れること

(C) 新しい製品を試すこと

(D) ワークショップに参加すること

会話中盤で女性は、男性が必要としている箱の在庫が切れていると伝えている。女性はそれに続けて、I know they have some at the Cleveland branch, and it's only a ten-minute drive from here.と述べ、在庫があるCleveland支店に行くことを提案している。よって、正解は(B)。

語彙チェック ☐ in bulk　大量に

34

正解 C ☐☐☐☐

What does the man request?

(A) Some directions

(B) A product demonstration

(C) Some stationery

(D) A schedule

男性は何を頼んでいますか。

(A) 指示

(B) 製品の実演

(C) 文房具

(D) 予定

男性は会話の最後で、I'll just get a packet of business envelopes for now.と言い、ビジネス封筒を一束買いたいと女性に伝えている。これをstationery「文房具」と抽象的に言い換えた(C)が正解。

W 🇬🇧 M 🇦🇺

Questions 35 through 37 refer to the following conversation.

カンベキ理解

1	□□	W: We have to pay the pool cleaners for their work on the filters by today.
2	□□	I don't have time to go to the bank,
3	□□	so I'm planning to do it using the online banking system.
4	□□	Do you have the password?
5	□□	M: If you give me the bill, I'll take care of it for you.
6	□□	W: Thanks. It's not ready yet, though.
7	□□	There was a mistake on the one they sent,
8	□□	so I'm waiting for them to send over a new one.
9	□□	They said it'd take them about an hour.
10	□□	Do you mind waiting?
11	□□	M: Well, I have to go to the post office to mail a package after lunch,
12	□□	but I'll be back at two.
13	□□	You can give it to me then.

問題35-37は次の会話に関するものです。

女性：今日までに、プールの清掃業者にフィルターの作業代を支払わなければなりません。銀行に行く時間がないので、オンラインバンキングシステムを使って支払おうと思っています。パスワードは分かりますか。

男性：請求書を渡してもらえれば、私が代わりに処理しますよ。

女性：ありがとうございます。ただ、まだ準備ができていません。送られてきた請求書に間違いがあったため、新しいものを送ってもらえるのを待っているところなんです。1時間くらいかかると言っていました。待っていただいてもよいでしょうか。

男性：ええと、昼食後に郵便局に荷物を出しに行かなければならないのですが、2時には戻ってきます。そのときに私に渡してください。

語彙チェック   □ pool cleaner　プール清掃業者　□ filter　フィルター、ろ過器
　　　　　　　□ online banking　オンラインバンキング（ネット上で行う銀行の金融取引サービス）　□ bill　請求書
　　　　　　　□ send over ～　～を送る　□ mail　～を郵送する　□ package　荷物

35

正解 **C** ☐☐☐☐

What is the topic of the conversation?
(A) A cleaning product
(B) A Web site update
(C) A bank transaction
(D) A computer malfunction

会話の主題は何ですか。
(A) 掃除用具
(B) ウェブサイトの更新
(C) 銀行取引
(D) コンピュータの不具合

女性は冒頭で、プールの清掃業者に対してフィルターの作業代を支払わなければならないことを述べ、I don't have time to go to the bank, so I'm planning to do it using the online banking system. と続けている。その後も銀行取引・支払いに関する会話が続いているので、正解は(C)。

語彙チェック　☐ transaction　取引

36

正解 **A** ☐☐☐☐

What is the woman waiting for?
(A) An invoice
(B) Some technical assistance
(C) An estimate
(D) Some instruction manuals

女性は何を待っていますか。
(A) 請求書
(B) 技術的な支援
(C) 見積書
(D) 取扱説明書

男性はIf you give me the bill, I'll take care of it for you.「請求書を渡してもらえれば、私が代わりに処理する」と申し出ている。それに対し、女性はThere was a mistake on the one they sent, so I'm waiting for them to send over a new one.と答え、a new one「新しいもの（＝請求書）」を待っているところだと伝えている。よって、正解は(A)。

♛Level Up !
女性に関する設問だが、男性の発言も聞き取って話の流れを理解しないと解けない。設問にあるキーワードだけを待ち受けるのではなく、話の流れを頭の中で整理しながら聞こう。

37

正解 **D** ☐☐☐☐

What will the man do after lunch?
(A) Attend a seminar
(B) Meet some clients
(C) Purchase some tools
(D) Send a package

男性は昼食後に何をするつもりですか。
(A) 研修会に参加する
(B) 顧客に会う
(C) 工具を購入する
(D) 荷物を送る

男性は会話の最後で、I have to go to the post office to mail a package after lunch と述べている。よって、正解は(D)。本文のmail a packageが、選択肢ではsend a packageに言い換えられている。

W 🇬🇧 M 🇺🇸

Questions 38 through 40 refer to the following conversation.

カンベキ理解		
1	□□	W: This is the Hibiscus Room.
2	□□	The stage will be set up at the far end.
3	□□	We usually set up about ten tables here,
4	□□	but we can fit as many as eighteen.
5	□□	M: I'm sorry, but I just don't think this will be big enough.
6	□□	I know it's a bit late to make changes,
7	□□	but could you check and see if there are any larger rooms available?
8	□□	W: I'm pretty sure the Lilac Room is available,
9	□□	but I'll give the manager a call to make sure.
10	□□	M: Thanks.
11	□□	Can you let me know if there will be any extra costs, too?

問題38-40は次の会話に関するものです。

女性：こちらはハイビスカスルームです。舞台は一番奥に設置されます。普段ここには10卓ほどご用意していますが、最大18卓まで入れることができますよ。

男性：申し訳ないのですが、これでは大きさが足りないと思うのです。変更するには少し遅いとは思いますが、もっと広い部屋がないか調べていただけませんか。

女性：ライラックルームが空いているのは間違いありませんが、念のため部長に電話してみます。

男性：ありがとうございます。追加料金が発生するかどうかも教えていただけますか。

語彙チェック □ set up 〜 〜を設置する □ at the far end 一番奥に □ fit 〜を入れる
□ I'm pretty sure that 〜 〜であると確信している □ give 〜 a call 〜に電話をする

38

What are the speakers discussing?
(A) Room renovation
(B) Possible event venues
(C) A construction project
(D) A furniture shipment

話し手たちは何について話し合っていますか。
(A)部屋の改修
(B)イベント会場の候補
(C)建設計画
(D)家具の出荷

冒頭で女性はとある部屋を紹介し、The stage will be set up at the far end. と舞台の配置について説明している。さらに、その部屋にどれくらいのテーブルが置けるかを補足している。それに対し男性は、I'm sorry, but I just don't think this will be big enough. と述べ、広さの問題から部屋の変更を頼んでいる。これらの会話から、話し手たちはイベント会場の候補について話し合っていると判断できる。よって、正解は(B)。本文のroomやtablesという語につられて、(A)や(D)を選ばないように注意したい。

語彙チェック □ possible 見込みのある □ venue 会場

39

正解 D □□□□

What does the woman say she will do?
(A) Refund some money
(B) Provide a discount
(C) Reschedule an event
(D) Speak with a colleague

女性は何をするつもりだと言っていますか。
(A)お金を払い戻す
(B)割引をする
(C)イベントのスケジュールを変更する
(D)同僚と話をする

女性は「ライラックルームが空いているはず」と述べた上で、but I'll give the manager a call to make sure と続けている。女性はこの後、同僚である部長に電話をするつもりだと分かるので、正解は(D)。本文のgive the manager a callが、選択肢ではSpeak with a colleagueに言い換えられている。

語彙チェック □ refund ～を返金する □ reschedule ～の予定を変更する

40

正解 D □□□□

What does the man ask the woman to do?
(A) Make a payment
(B) Arrange a meeting
(C) Help set up a device
(D) Provide some information

男性は女性に何をするよう求めていますか。
(A)支払いをする
(B)会議を準備する
(C)機器を設置するのを手伝う
(D)情報を提供する

男性は会話の最後に Can you let me know if there will be any extra costs, too? と言い、部屋を変えることで追加料金が発生するかどうかを女性に尋ねている。この、追加料金についての情報を伝えることを provide some information と表した(D)が正解。

👑 Level Up！
何を求めているかが問われる問題では、本文中の依頼表現を聞き逃さないように注意したい。今回は、Can you ～？「～してもらえますか」というフレーズが正解を選ぶカギ。

W 🇨🇦 **M** 🇦🇺

Questions 41 through 43 refer to the following conversation.

カンペキ理解

1	W: Hi. It's Wendy Varga from Gold's Cleaning Company.
2	We requested a shipment of polishing pads for our floor polishers yesterday.
3	They were supposed to be here by noon.
4	M: Hello, Ms. Varga. It's Robin speaking.
5	I am sorry for the delay.
6	I took that order yesterday, and it will be coming from Innesvale.
7	Our system sends it there because that's our closest office to you.
8	I'll have to look into it for you.
9	W: I see. How soon do you think you can get them delivered?
10	M: It's hard to tell.
11	I'd have to find out what's causing the delay first.
12	You'll know as soon as I do.

問題41-43は次の会話に関するものです。

女性：こんにちは、Gold's 清掃会社の Wendy Varga です。昨日、床磨き機用の研磨パッドの発送をお願いいたしました。それらは正午までに届くはずだったのですが。

男性：こんにちは、Varga さん。Robin と申します。遅れが生じており申し訳ございません。昨日注文をお受けいたしましたので、Innesvale から届く予定です。あなたに最も近い場所でしたので、弊社システムはその営業所に注文を送りました。お調べいたしますね。

女性：なるほど。どのくらいで届けていただけそうですか。

男性：予測するのは難しいです。まずは、何が原因で遅れているのかを調べる必要があります。確認次第、すぐに判明いたします。

語彙チェック □ polishing pad 研磨パッド □ floor polisher 床磨き機 □ be supposed to *do* ～することになっている
□ look into ～ （問題など）を調査する □ cause ～を引き起こす

41

正解 **C** ☐☐☐☐

What problem does the woman mention?
(A) Her office is overly busy.
(B) Some cleaning work was not carried out.
(C) She has not received an order.
(D) She has discovered a product defect.

女性はどんな問題について述べていますか。
(A) 彼女の会社は非常に忙しい。
(B) 一部の清掃作業が実施されなかった。
(C) 彼女は注文品を受け取っていない。
(D) 彼女は製品の欠陥を発見した。

女性は冒頭でWe requested a shipment of polishing pads for our floor polishers yesterday. と述べ、床磨き機用の研磨パッドを頼んでいたと話している。さらに女性は続けてThey were supposed to be here by noon. と述べ、「正午までに届くことはずだった」、つまり「(予定していたのに) 届かなかった」ことを説明している。商品を受け取れなかったことが問題点だと分かるので、正解は(C)。

語彙チェック ☐ overly　非常に　☐ carry out 〜　〜を実施する　☐ defect　欠陥

42

正解 **B** ☐☐☐☐

What does the man say about the office in Innesvale?
(A) The staff there are very helpful.
(B) It is located near the woman's office.
(C) It was understaffed yesterday.
(D) Some guests are headed there.

男性はInnesvaleの営業所について何と言っていますか。
(A) 従業員がとても親切である。
(B) 女性の会社の近くにある。
(C) 昨日は人手が足りなかった。
(D) 何人かの顧客が向かっている。

男性はInnesvaleにある営業所について、Our system sends it there because that's our closest office to you. と述べている。女性が勤めるGold's清掃会社に近いということが分かるので、正解は(B)。

語彙チェック ☐ understaffed　人員不足の

43

正解 **C** ☐☐☐☐

Why does the man say, "It's hard to tell"?
(A) He has some unfortunate news.
(B) The situation is very complicated.
(C) He does not know an answer.
(D) A colleague is absent from work.

男性はなぜ "It's hard to tell" と言っていますか。
(A) 彼には不幸な話がある。
(B) 状況が非常に複雑である。
(C) 彼は答えを知らない。
(D) 同僚が会社を休んでいる。

どのくらいで商品が届くか尋ねられた男性は、It's hard to tell. と発言した後、I'd have to find out what's causing the delay first. と述べている。現時点で男性は、注文品の遅延の原因が何か分かっていない。つまり、女性の質問に答えられないと分かるので正解は(C)。

語彙チェック ☐ unfortunate　不幸な　☐ complicated　複雑な

W 🇨🇦　M 🇺🇸

Questions 44 through 46 refer to the following conversation.

カンペキ理解

1 □□ W: Good morning. I'm Kelly Lancaster.

2 □□ 　 I have an appointment to have routine maintenance carried out on my car this morning.

3 □□ M: Nice to see you, Ms. Lancaster.

4 □□ 　 Oh, I see you've brought the service logbook.

5 □□ 　 Thanks for that.

6 □□ 　 If you don't have anywhere you need to be,

7 □□ 　 you can wait over there until we're finished.

8 □□ W: Oh, when did you put in this waiting area?

9 □□ 　 There're sofas and a drink machine.

10 □□ 　 That's surprising because that wasn't here last time!

11 □□ 　 I'll be over there reading one of the magazines, then.

問題44-46は次の会話に関するものです。

女性：おはようございます。私はKelly Lancasterです。今朝、車の定期点検の予約をしているのですが。

男性：お待ちしておりました、Lancasterさん。ああ、点検記録簿を持ってきてくださいましたね。ありがとうございます。もし何かご用事がなければ、作業が終了するまであちらでお待ちください。

女性：あら、いつからこの待合室はできたのですか。ソファもあるし、飲み物の自動販売機もありますね。前回はなかったので驚きです！　では、私はあそこで雑誌を読んでいますね。

語彙チェック　□ routine maintenance　定期点検　□ logbook　記録簿　□ waiting area　待合室

156

44

正解 **A**

Why is the woman at the car dealership?

(A) To have her vehicle serviced

(B) To purchase a new vehicle

(C) To test-drive a car

(D) To pick up some parts

女性はなぜ車の販売代理店にいますか。

(A) 車の点検修理をしてもらうため

(B) 新しい車を購入するため

(C) 車を試乗運転するため

(D) 部品を取りに行くため

女性は冒頭で、I have an appointment to have routine maintenance carried out on my car this morning. と述べている。車の定期点検をしてもらうためにお店を訪れたことが分かるので、正解は(A)。本文のcarが選択肢ではvehicleに言い換えられている。

語彙チェック □ service ～の点検修理をする □ test-drive ～を試乗運転する

45

正解 **D**

What has the woman brought with her?

(A) An electronic device

(B) A bicycle

(C) A beverage

(D) Some documentation

女性は何を持ってきましたか。

(A) 電子機器

(B) 自転車

(C) 飲み物

(D) 資料

男性は女性に対し、I see you've brought the service logbookと述べている。service logbookは、ここでは「点検記録簿」という意味。つまり男性はSome documentation「資料」を持ってきたということが分かるので、正解は(D)。

46

正解 **A**

Why is the woman surprised?

(A) A customer lounge is available.

(B) She has to wait longer than expected.

(C) Her appointment was changed.

(D) The price has been reduced.

女性はなぜ驚いていますか。

(A) 顧客用のラウンジが利用できる。

(B) 彼女は予想していたよりも長く待つ必要がある。

(C) 彼女の予約が変更された。

(D) 値段が安くなった。

女性は最後の発言で、when did you put in this waiting area? と述べ、前回お店を訪れたときはなかった待合室に驚いている。よって、正解は(A)。waiting area「待合室」が、選択肢ではlounge「ラウンジ」と言い換えられている。waitingという語につられ、うっかり(B)を選ばないように注意。

語彙チェック □ lounge ラウンジ、待合室

会話 ▶TRACK_175　問題 ▶TRACK_176
カンベキ理解 ▶TRACK_K29

M 🇺🇸　W 🇬🇧

Questions 47 through 49 refer to the following conversation.

カンベキ理解	
1 □□	M: Helen, we just got the earthmover back from the renters.
2 □□	The guys down in the warehouse say it has some damage to the hydraulics.
3 □□	They say it was just wear and tear.
4 □□	Unfortunately, we can't rent it out again until it's been repaired.
5 □□	W: OK. Well, you'd better take it off the Web site so that no one tries to rent it until it's working again.
6 □□	M: OK, I will. Another customer is coming to pick it up this afternoon.
7 □□	I'll call and let him know it won't be available.
8 □□	W: Let's see if we can source one from somewhere else, first.
9 □□	I'd hate to let him down on such short notice.

問題47-49は次の会話に関するものです。

男性：Helen、貸し手からブルドーザーがちょうど戻ってきたところです。倉庫にいた人たちは、油圧装置に損傷があると言っています。ただの損耗だったそうです。残念ながら、修理が済むまでは再び貸し出すことができません。

女性：分かりました。では、作動するようになるまで誰も借りることを試みないよう、ウェブサイトから削除した方がいいですね。

男性：分かりました、そうします。今日の午後、別のお客さんが受け取りに来ます。電話をして、使えなくなることを伝えておきますね。

女性：まず、どこか他のところから調達できないか確認してみましょう。急なお知らせでその方をがっかりさせるのは嫌ですから。

語彙チェック　□ earthmover　ブルドーザー、大型車両　□ warehouse　倉庫　□ hydraulics　油圧装置
　　　　　　　□ wear and tear　（通常の使用による）損耗　□ source　（ある供給源から）〜を調達する

47

正解 D ☐☐☐☐

What is the conversation mainly about?

(A) A contract bid

(B) Warehouse cleaning

(C) A moving service

(D) Damaged equipment

会話は主に何についてですか。

(A) 契約の入札

(B) 倉庫の清掃

(C) 引っ越しサービス

(D) 破損した装置

男性は、貸し手から戻ってきたブルドーザーについて、The guys down in the warehouse say it has some damage to the hydraulics. と述べ、油圧装置に損傷があったと聞いたことを伝えている。その後も破損した装置について話が展開しているため、正解は (D)。

Level Up!
earthmover という単語を知らないと状況が掴みづらいが、それでも問題は解ける。「損傷がある」「修理をする」といった情報から推測することがポイント！

語彙チェック ☐ bid　入札　☐ damaged　損傷を受けた

48

正解 C ☐☐☐☐

What does the woman ask the man to do?

(A) Increase a budget

(B) Order some merchandise

(C) Update a Web site

(D) Change a company policy

女性は男性に何をするよう求めていますか。

(A) 予算を増やす

(B) 商品を注文する

(C) ウェブサイトを更新する

(D) 会社の方針を変更する

ブルドーザーの修理が済むまで貸し出せないということが分かった女性は、男性に対して you'd better take it off the Web site so that no one tries to rent it と述べている。つまり、ウェブサイトの記載内容を変更し、ブルドーザーを借りられないようにすることを求めていると分かる。これを言い換えた (C) が正解。

語彙チェック ☐ merchandise　商品

49

正解 A ☐☐☐☐

What does the woman suggest doing?

(A) Searching for an alternative

(B) Requesting a quotation

(C) Placing an advertisement

(D) Offering a discount

女性は何をすることを提案していますか。

(A) 代替物を探すこと

(B) 見積もりを依頼すること

(C) 広告を出すこと

(D) 値引きすること

男性がブルドーザーを予約していた顧客に借りられない旨を連絡しようとしているのに対し、女性は Let's see if we can source one from somewhere else, first. と述べ、まず他のところから代わりのブルドーザーを調達できないかと提案している。よって、正解は (A)。

語彙チェック ☐ alternative　代替物　☐ quotation　見積もり

M 🇦🇺　W1 🇬🇧　W2 🇨🇦

Questions 50 through 52 refer to the following conversation with three speakers.

カンベキ理解		
1 □□	M:	Hi, Kate. Do you know where I can find Don Hoffman?
2 □□		I was contacted by one of his clients.
3 □□	W1:	He left last week to start his own firm.
4 □□	M:	Oh, I see.
5 □□		It's a previous client, so Don must not have let them know about his plans.
6 □□		Who's his replacement?
7 □□		I need someone to contact her.
8 □□	W1:	Kelly Neuman, but she won't be able to help.
9 □□		She's still learning the ropes.
10 □□	W2:	Excuse me for cutting in, Jack.
11 □□		You'd better let me handle this.
12 □□		If I can't sort it out, I'll call Don.
13 □□	M:	Thanks, Betty.
14 □□		I'll forward you the client's contact details by e-mail.
15 □□		Perhaps you should speak with her directly.

問題50-52は3人の話し手による次の会話に関するものです。

男性　：こんにちは、Kate。Don Hoffmanがどこにいるか分かりますか。彼の顧客のうちの1人から連絡があったんです。
女性1：彼は先週、自分の会社を立ち上げるために退職しましたよ。
男性　：ああ、そうですか。前の顧客だから、Donは自分の計画について知らせていなかったんでしょうね。彼の後任は誰ですか。彼女に連絡する人が必要なんですが。
女性1：Kelly Neumanです。でも彼女では無理でしょう。彼女はまだ仕事の要領を得ようとしているところですから。
女性2：割り込んでごめんなさい、Jack。この件は私に任せてください。解決できなかったらDonに電話します。
男性　：ありがとうございます、Betty。顧客の連絡先をEメールで転送しておきますね。おそらく直接話した方がいいと思います。

語彙チェック　□ leave　退職する　□ firm　会社　□ previous　前の　□ replacement　後任
　　　　　　　□ learn the ropes　仕事の要領を得る　□ cut in　割り込む　□ handle　～をこなす、～をさばく
　　　　　　　□ sort ～ out　～を解決する　□ forward A B　AにBを転送する

👑 Level Up !
この会話は3人の人物の間で行われていることに加えて、話の中でDon HoffmanやKelly Neumanなどの人物も登場している。設問を先読みする際に、人名もチェックして準備しておこう。

50

正解 A ☐☐☐☐

What does Kate say about Don Hoffman?

(A) He has left the company.

(B) He was recently promoted.

(C) He was an important client.

(D) He has returned from his vacation.

Kate は Don Hoffman ついて何と言っていますか。

(A) 彼は会社を辞めた。

(B) 彼は最近昇進した。

(C) 彼は重要な顧客だった。

(D) 彼は休暇から戻ってきた。

会話の冒頭で、男性は Hi, Kate. と挨拶し、Don Hoffman がどこにいるのか尋ねている。それに対し、1人目の女性（Kate）は He left last week to start his own firm. と答えている。よって、正解は (A)。

51

正解 B ☐☐☐☐

What does Betty offer to do?

(A) Search for a lost item

(B) Contact a previous client

(C) Hire a temporary worker

(D) Put together a plan

Betty は何をすることを申し出ていますか。

(A) 紛失物を探す

(B) 前の顧客に連絡する

(C) 臨時の従業員を雇う

(D) 計画をまとめる

会話の後半で男性が Thanks, Betty. と発言していることから、設問文の主語 Betty は2人目の女性であると分かる。会話の中盤で男性が Hoffman さんの前の顧客に連絡する必要があると述べた後、Betty は You'd better let me handle this. と言って、自分が前の顧客に連絡することができると伝えている。よって、正解は (B)。

👑 Level Up！
設問に含まれる Betty というキーワードが後から登場する、超難問！

語彙チェック ☐ temporary 臨時の ☐ put together ～ ～をまとめる

52

正解 C ☐☐☐☐

What will the man do next?

(A) Call an ex-employee

(B) Conduct a training workshop

(C) Send an e-mail

(D) Rename a company division

男性は次に何をするつもりですか。

(A) 元社員に電話をする

(B) 研修会を行う

(C) E メールを送る

(D) 会社の部署名を変更する

男性は Hoffman さんに連絡することを申し出た Betty に感謝を述べた後で、I'll forward you the client's contact details by e-mail. と続けている。Betty に対して前の顧客の連絡先を E メールで転送するつもりだということが分かるので、正解は (C)。前の顧客に連絡をするのは Betty の役目なので、(A) は不正解。

語彙チェック ☐ ex-employee 元社員 ☐ rename ～を新たに命名する

W 🇨🇦　M 🇦🇺

Questions 53 through 55 refer to the following conversation.

カンベキ理解

1 ☐☐　W: This is the fourth apartment I've shown you this morning.
2 ☐☐　　Which one do you like the best?
3 ☐☐　M: Definitely this one, but I can't really afford it to be honest.
4 ☐☐　W: It's under $700 a week.
5 ☐☐　M: I know.
6 ☐☐　　I didn't realize that I'd have to rent the parking space separately.
7 ☐☐　W: It was stated in the description, but there was a lot to read.
8 ☐☐　M: Oh, I didn't notice that.
9 ☐☐　　Well, would you mind taking me back to the one we visited first?
10 ☐☐　　I'd like to measure the kitchen.

問題53-55は次の会話に関するものです。

女性：今朝あなたにお見せしたアパートは、こちらで4軒目です。どのアパートが一番気に入っていますか。

男性：間違いなくこの部屋なのですが、正直申し上げますと、そんなに払う余裕はありません。

女性：週700ドル以下ですよ。

男性：分かっています。駐車場を別で借りなければならないとは気付いていなかったです。

女性：物件明細書には書いてありましたが、読むべきところが多かったですね。

男性：ああ、それは気が付きませんでした。ええと、最初に見学したアパートにもう一度連れて行っていただけますか。台所の寸法を測りたいです。

語彙チェック　☐ definitely　間違いなく　☐ afford　〜を手に入れる金銭的余裕がある　☐ to be honest　正直に言うと　☐ separately　別に　☐ description　明細書の記載、説明　☐ measure　〜の寸法を測る

53

正解 D ☐☐☐☐

What problem does the man mention about the apartment?

(A) The rooms are too small.

(B) It is too far from the city.

(C) The area is too noisy.

(D) The rent is too expensive.

男性はアパートについてどんな問題を述べていますか。

(A)部屋が狭すぎる。

(B) 都会から遠すぎる。

(C) 周囲がうるさすぎる。

(D)家賃が高すぎる。

一番気に入ったアパートを尋ねられた男性は、4軒目のアパートについて、Definitely this one, but I can't really afford it to be honest. と伝え、値段が高くて払う余裕がないということを問題点として述べている。よって、正解は(D)。but などの逆接から始まる内容が正解の根拠となることは多々あるので、聞き逃さないように注意したい。

54

正解 A ☐☐☐☐

What does the woman imply when she says, "there was a lot to read"?

(A) Some information was not obvious.

(B) Ample literature was supplied.

(C) A process takes a long time.

(D) People can enjoy various books.

"there was a lot to read" という発言で、女性は何を示唆していますか。

(A)一部の情報は目立っていなかった。

(B) 豊富な文献が供給された。

(C) 処理には長い時間がかかる。

(D)人々はさまざまな本を楽しむことができる。

家賃とは別に駐車場を借りなければならないことに気付かなかったと述べる男性に対し、女性は It was stated in the description と前置きし、(but) there was a lot to read「(でも) 読むべきところが多かったですね」と続けている。文字が多すぎて駐車場代に関する情報が目立たなくなってしまった、という意図で発言したと分かるので、正解は(A)。

語彙チェック ☐ obvious 明らかな ☐ ample 豊富な、余るほど十分な

55

正解 D ☐☐☐☐

What does the man ask the woman to do?

(A) Negotiate with a landlord

(B) Help him find a parking space

(C) Choose some cooking appliances

(D) Return to a previous apartment

男性は女性に何をするよう求めていますか。

(A)大家と交渉する

(B) 駐車場を探すのを手伝う

(C) 調理器具を選ぶ

(D)前のアパートに戻る

男性は、会話の最後で would you mind taking me back to the one we visited first? と女性に頼んでいる。最初に内見をしたアパートに再度戻ることを要求していると分かるので、正解は(D)。Would you mind *doing* 〜? という依頼の表現がポイント。

語彙チェック ☐ negotiate with 〜 〜と交渉する ☐ landlord 大家 ☐ cooking appliance 調理器具

会話 ▶TRACK_181 問題 ▶TRACK_182
カンペキ理解 ▶TRACK_K32

W 🇬🇧 M1 🇺🇸 M2 🇦🇺

Questions 56 through 58 refer to the following conversation with three speakers.

カンペキ理解		
1	☐☐	W: Good morning. Are you here for Mr. Ogilvy's seminar?
2	☐☐	M1: I'm not sure.
3	☐☐	We're here to attend a seminar on improving enthusiasm in office workers.
4	☐☐	M2: Hang on. I have the tickets here.
5	☐☐	The seminar leader's name is on it.
6	☐☐	W: No, that's fine.
7	☐☐	You're in the right place.
8	☐☐	Just head down the hall.
9	☐☐	It's in Conference Room A.
10	☐☐	M1: OK, thanks.
11	☐☐	We're a bit early,
12	☐☐	so we were thinking of having something to drink downstairs first.
13	☐☐	W: Sure, but don't stay there too long.
14	☐☐	Tickets have sold out.
15	☐☐	If you come at the last minute, you might not be able to sit together.

問題56-58は3人の話し手による次の会話に関するものです。

女性　：おはようございます。Ogilvyさんの研修会でお越しでしょうか。
男性1：確かではありません。我々は、会社員の熱意向上に関する研修会に参加しに来ました。
男性2：お待ちください。チケットがここにあります。研修会の指導者の名前が書いてあります。
女性　：いえ、結構です。あなた方は正しい場所にお越しになっています。ただ廊下を進んでください。会議室Aでございます。
男性1：分かりました、ありがとうございます。ちょっと時間が早いので、まず階下で何か飲み物を飲もうと思っています。
女性　：もちろんです、でもあまり長居はなさらないでくださいね。チケットは売り切れています。開始直前にいらっしゃると、一緒にご着席
　　　　いただけないかもしれませんので。

語彙チェック ☐ enthusiasm 熱意 ☐ Hang on. 待ってください。 ☐ head down 〜 〜を通って進む ☐ downstairs 階下で
☐ at the last minute 直前になって

56 正解 B ▢▢▢▢

What is the topic of the seminar?
(A) Hiring effective workers
(B) Boosting employee morale
(C) Attracting wealthy clients
(D) Reducing running costs

研修会のテーマは何ですか。
(A)有能な労働者を採用すること
(B) 従業員の士気を高めること
(C)富裕層の顧客を獲得すること
(D)維持費を削減すること

1人目の男性は We're here to attend a seminar on improving enthusiasm in office workers. と述べている。よって、正解は (B)。本文の improving enthusiasm in office workers「会社員の熱意を向上させること」が、選択肢では Boosting employee morale「従業員の士気を高めること」と言い換えられている。

語彙チェック ▢ effective 有能な ▢ boost ～を高める ▢ morale 士気 ▢ running costs 維持費

57 正解 D ▢▢▢▢

Where will the men most likely go next?
(A) To a conference room
(B) To a ticket booth
(C) To a hotel
(D) To a café

男性たちは次にどこに行くと考えられますか。
(A)会議室
(B) チケット売り場
(C) ホテル
(D)カフェ

1人目の男性が We're a bit early, so we were thinking of having something to drink downstairs first. と述べていることに注目。男性たちは研修会が始まるまでの時間で、飲み物を飲みに階下に降りようと考えていたことが分かる。飲み物が手に入る場所はカフェだと考えられるので、正解は (D)。

👑 Level Up!
本問のように、発言から推測して「選択肢の中で最もありえそうなものを選ぶ」というタイプの問題が時々出題される。4つの選択肢を比較して、一番可能性が高いものを選ぼう。

58 正解 D ▢▢▢▢

What does the woman say about the seminar?
(A) It has been rescheduled.
(B) It is held every weekend.
(C) It includes teamwork activities.
(D) It was fully booked.

女性は研修会について何と言っていますか。
(A)予定が変更になった。
(B) 毎週末に開催されている。
(C)チームで行うアクティビティを含んでいる。
(D)予約が埋まった。

飲み物を飲みに階下へ向かおうとした男性2人に対して、女性は「あまり長居しないように」と注意喚起した後、Tickets have sold out. と続けている。「チケットが売り切れた」とはつまり、「予約が埋まった」ということなので、正解は (D)。

M 🇦🇺 　 W 🇨🇦

Questions 59 through 61 refer to the following conversation.

カンベキ理解		
1	□□	M: I've been noticing that more experienced people are not always the best performers.
2	□□	Perhaps we should use different criteria when choosing candidates.
3	□□	W: I've noticed the same thing.
4	□□	If we're making a change, we should do it soon.
5	□□	We need to hire some new people
6	□□	since our auto parts orders have doubled since last quarter.
7	□□	M: I'll interview some of our more productive people to find out what they have in common.
8	□□	We can use that information to improve our criteria.
9	□□	W: Good idea.
10	□□	Let me know what you find out.

問題59-61は次の会話に関するものです。

男性：より経験豊富な人が、必ずしも業績が良い人であるとは限らないことに気付きました。候補者を選ぶときに、異なる基準を使うべきかもしれないですね。

女性：私も同じことを思いました。もし変更するのであれば、すぐに行うべきです。自動車部品の注文が前四半期の2倍になったので、何人か新しい人を雇う必要があります。

男性：生産性の高い人たちにインタビューして、彼らの共通点を探ってみますね。基準を改善するのに、その情報が使えますよ。

女性：いい考えですね。分かったことを教えてください。

語彙チェック 　□ experienced　経験豊富な　□ best performer　業績が良い人　□ criteria　基準　□ candidate　候補者
□ auto parts　自動車部品　□ double　2倍になる　□ quarter　四半期　□ productive　生産性の高い
□ find out ～　～を発見する　□ have ～ in common　～を共通で持っている

59

正解 C ☐☐☐☐

What are the speakers mainly discussing?
(A) Vacation timing
(B) Sales reports
(C) Hiring policies
(D) Running costs

話し手たちは主に何について話し合っていますか。
(A) 休暇の時期
(B) 営業報告書
(C) 採用方針
(D) 維持費

男性は冒頭で I've been noticing that more experienced people are not always the best performers. Perhaps we should use different criteria when choosing candidates. と述べ、別の採用基準を導入すべきだと提案している。女性はそれに対して同意し、その後も採用に関する会話が続いているので、正解は (C)。

60

正解 B ☐☐☐☐

Which industry do the speakers most likely work in?
(A) Temporary staffing
(B) Car manufacturing
(C) Clothing design
(D) Real estate

話し手たちはどの業界で働いていると考えられますか。
(A) 人材派遣
(B) 自動車製造
(C) 服飾デザイン
(D) 不動産

女性は中盤で We need to hire some new people since our auto parts orders have doubled since last quarter. と発言しているので、話し手たちは自動車の部品を作っている会社に勤めているということが推測できる。よって、正解は (B)。

👑**Level Up！**

全体としては採用関係の話をしているだけなので、本問は auto parts「自動車部品」という単語を聞き逃してしまうと正解できない。さらに推測も必要となる超難問！

61

正解 C ☐☐☐☐

What will the man probably do next?
(A) Place an advertisement
(B) Call an applicant
(C) Conduct a survey
(D) Reserve a room

男性はおそらく次に何をしますか。
(A) 広告を出す
(B) 応募者に電話をする
(C) 調査を行う
(D) 部屋を予約する

異なる採用基準を導入すべきだという流れを受け、男性は I'll interview some of our more productive people to find out what they have in common. と女性に伝えている。「生産性の高い人たちにインタビューして、彼らの共通点を探ってみる」ということは「調査を行う」ことだと言えるので、正解は (C)。採用に関わる話はしているが、応募者に電話をするとは一切述べられていないので (B) は不正解。

語彙チェック　☐ conduct　〜を行う

167

会話 ▶TRACK_185　　問題 ▶TRACK_186

カンペキ理解 ▶TRACK_K34

W 🇬🇧　M 🇦🇺

Questions 62 through 64 refer to the following conversation and table.

カンペキ理解	
1 □□	W: I purchased the new mattresses for the beds in the guest rooms.
2 □□	I felt that we needed one with a ten-year warranty.
3 □□	Five wouldn't be long enough.
4 □□	They didn't have any of the white ones, unfortunately.
5 □□	Anyway, they were sixteen hundred dollars each.
6 □□	M: That's great. When will they arrive?
7 □□	W: I didn't check.
8 □□	Millionways usually delivers the following day,
9 □□	so I imagine they'll be here tomorrow.
10 □□	M: OK. I'll have the staff take the old ones off the beds this afternoon.
11 □□	I don't think we can sell them.
12 □□	I'm worried about how much it'll cost to get rid of them.
13 □□	Can you ask around?

問題62-64は次の会話と表に関するものです。

女性：客室のベッドに新しいマットレスを購入しました。10年保証のものが必要だと感じたからです。5年では長さが足りません。残念ながら、白いマットレスはありませんでした。それはさておき、それぞれ1,600ドルだったんです。

男性：それはすごいですね。いつ届く予定ですか。

女性：確認していませんでした。Millionways社は通常翌日に配達をするので、明日には届くのではないかと思います。

男性：分かりました。今日の午後、スタッフに古いマットレスをベッドから取り外してもらいます。古いものは売れないかと思います。処分するのにいくらかかるか心配です。周りの人に聞いてみてくれませんか。

語彙チェック　□ mattress　マットレス　□ warranty　保証　□ the following day　翌日　□ take A off B　AをBから取り除く
□ get rid of ～　～を処分する　□ ask around　尋ねて回る

Model	Price	Color	Warranty
Regent A	$1,200	Black	5 years
Regent B		White	5 years
Galant A	$1,600	Black	10 years
Galant B		White	10 years

型	値段	色	保証
Regent A	1,200 ドル	黒	5 年
Regent B		白	5 年
Galant A	1,600 ドル	黒	10 年
Galant B		白	10 年

62

正解 **C** ☐☐☐☐

Look at the graphic. Which item did the woman most likely buy?

(A) Regent A
(B) Regent B
(C) Galant A
(D) Galant B

図を見てください。女性はどの商品を購入したと考えられますか。

(A) Regent A
(B) Regent B
(C) Galant A
(D) Galant B

👑 **Level Up!**

会話の中では「白色がなかった」という言い方をしているので、Galant A につながる black ではなく white という単語が使われている。聞こえてきた単語だけで判断してしまわないように注意しよう。

女性は冒頭の部分で購入したマットレスについて、I felt that we needed one with a ten-year warranty. と述べ、さらに They didn't have any of the white ones, unfortunately. と男性に伝えている。10年保証のマットレスが必要だと感じていたこと、また白色がなかったという2つの情報をもとに図表を確認する。女性は10年保証かつ黒色のマットレスである、Galant A を購入したと考えられるので、正解は(C)。

63

正解 **C** ☐☐☐☐

What does the man ask about?

(A) A storage plan
(B) A shipping cost
(C) A delivery date
(D) An advertising media

男性は何について尋ねていますか。

(A) ストレージのプラン
(B) 送料
(C) 配達日
(D) 広告媒体

男性は女性が購入した新しいマットレスに対して、When will they arrive? と述べ、マットレスの配達日を尋ねている。よって、正解は(C)。

語彙チェック ☐ storage　ストレージ、記憶装置

64

正解 **B** ☐☐☐☐

What does the man ask the woman to do?

(A) Get help installing some mattresses
(B) Investigate disposal charges
(C) Request a corporate discount
(D) Send in an invoice

男性は女性に何をするよう求めていますか。

(A) マットレスの取り付けを手伝ってもらう
(B) 廃棄処分料を調べる
(C) 法人割引を要求する
(D) 請求書を送る

男性は「スタッフに古いマットレスをベッドから取り外してもらう」と述べた後、I'm worried about how much it'll cost to get rid of them. Can you ask around? と、処分にいくらかかるかを調べるよう女性にお願いしている。よって、正解は(B)。

語彙チェック ☐ investigate　〜を調べる　☐ disposal charge　(不要物の) 処分料　☐ corporate　法人の
☐ send in 〜　(郵便で) 〜を送付する

会話 ▶TRACK_187　問題 ▶TRACK_188

カンベキ理解 ▶TRACK_K35

M 🇺🇸　W 🇨🇦

Questions 65 through 67 refer to the following conversation and graph.

カンベキ理解		
1	□□	M: This graph shows our current revenue streams.
2	□□	They're very stable every year,
3	□□	so losing our only government contract is a big deal.
4	□□	It's going to have a significant effect on our profits.
5	□□	Thankfully, we still have our residential contracts to fall back on.
6	□□	W: Are we going to downsize, or look at other sources of revenue?
7	□□	M: If there were any other obvious sources, I'd have pursued them already.
8	□□	It's time to sell some equipment and vehicles and put a pause on hiring any new staff.
9	□□	W: OK. What about moving to a building with cheaper rent?
10	□□	It'll cost us a bit upfront, but we'll save in the long run.
11	□□	M: Good idea.
12	□□	I'll talk with a real estate agent tomorrow.

問題65-67は次の会話とグラフに関するものです。

男性：このグラフは、現在の収入源を示しています。毎年ほとんど変動がないので、たった1件しかない政府機関との契約を失うのは大ごとです。収益には大幅な影響を与えるでしょう。ありがたいことに、住宅関連の契約がよりどころとしてまだ残っていますが。

女性：規模を縮小するか、それとも他の収益源を探しますか。

男性：他に明らかな収益源があるのであれば、すでに追求していましたよ。設備や車両を売却して、新しい従業員の雇用を一時的に止める時ですね。

女性：分かりました。より賃料が安い物件に引っ越したらどうでしょうか。初期費用は少しかかりますが、長い目で見れば節約になりますよ。

男性：いい考えですね。明日、不動産屋と話してみます。

語彙チェック　□ revenue stream　収入源　□ stable　安定した、変化のない　□ contract　契約　□ big deal　大した事・もの　□ have an effect on 〜　〜に影響を与える　□ significant　大幅な　□ thankfully　ありがたいことに　□ residential　居住の　□ fall back on 〜　〜を当てにする、に頼る　□ downsize　規模を縮小する　□ sources of revenue　収入源　□ pursue　〜を追求する　□ put a pause on 〜　〜を一時中止する　□ upfront　前金として、前もって　□ in the long run　長期的に見れば　□ real estate agent　不動産業者

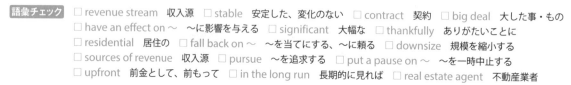

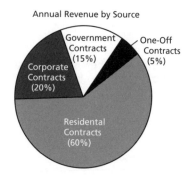

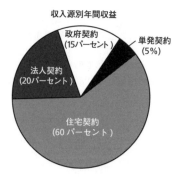

65

正解 B ☐☐☐☐

Look at the graphic. According to the man, what percentage of revenue will likely be lost over the next 12 months?

(A) 5 percent

(B) 15 percent

(C) 20 percent

(D) 60 percent

図を見てください。男性によると、今後12カ月間で収入の何パーセントが失われる可能性がありますか。

(A) 5パーセント

(B) 15パーセント

(C) 20パーセント

(D) 60パーセント

男性は会社の収入源に関して、They're very stable every year, so losing our only government contract is a big deal. と述べ、政府機関との契約を失う可能性があることを示唆している。ここで収入源の内訳が示された図を見ると、Government Contracts「政府契約」は15パーセントとあるので、正解は (B)。

66

正解 B ☐☐☐☐

What does the man say the business must do?

(A) Advertise a vacancy

(B) Sell some assets

(C) Negotiate with a client

(D) Reduce its rates

男性は会社がしなければならないことは何だと言っていますか。

(A) 欠員募集の広告を出す

(B) 資産の一部を売却する

(C) 顧客と交渉する

(D) 料金を引き下げる

会社の財政が厳しい状況を受けて、男性は It's time to sell some equipment and vehicles and put a pause on hiring any new staff. と述べている。some equipment and vehicle「設備や車両」を some assets「資産の一部」と言い換えた、(B) が正解。

語彙チェック ☐ vacancy 欠員 ☐ assets （会社の）資産、財産

67

正解 D ☐☐☐☐

What does the woman suggest spending money on?

(A) Advertising their services

(B) Getting financial advice

(C) Investing in real estate

(D) Relocating the business

女性は何にお金を使うことを提案していますか。

(A) サービスを宣伝すること

(B) 財務に関する助言を受けること

(C) 不動産に投資すること

(D) 会社を移転すること

女性は会話の最後で、What about moving to a building with cheaper rent? と述べ、より賃料が安い物件に引っ越すことを提案している。よって、正解は (D)。相手に提案する際の定番フレーズである、What about *doing* 〜?「〜したらどうですか」が使われている。

語彙チェック ☐ financial 財務の ☐ relocate 〜を移転させる

W 🇬🇧 **M** 🇺🇸

Questions 68 through 70 refer to the following conversation and message.

カンベキ理解		
1	☐☐	W: Norman, I've got another error message on my computer.
2	☐☐	Today the IT support personnel are attending an all-day seminar,
3	☐☐	so none of them are available.
4	☐☐	M: 662... That's a new one.
5	☐☐	I wouldn't shut it down, because you'd lose any unsaved data.
6	☐☐	Choose this one.
7	☐☐	It'll hold it in its current state until we can work out what to do.
8	☐☐	In the meantime, you can use another computer.
9	☐☐	W: Thanks. By the way, I was thinking of going to Harper's for lunch today.
10	☐☐	Are you in?
11	☐☐	M: I'd love to, but I've got to catch up
12	☐☐	because I took a couple of days off earlier in the week.
13	☐☐	I'll have lunch at my desk today.

問題68-70は次の会話とメッセージに関するものです。

女性：Norman、またコンピュータにエラーメッセージが出ました。今日、ITサポート課の職員は終日研修会に出席しているので、誰も都合がつかないんです。

男性：662… それは新しいですね。私なら電源を落としません、未保存のデータを失うことになりますから。こちらを選んでください。どうすればいいか分かるまで、今の状態のままが保持されます。それまでの間、他のコンピュータを使ってください。

女性：ありがとうございます。ところで、今日の昼食にHarper'sに行こうと考えていました。一緒に行きませんか。

男性：ぜひ行きたいのですが、週の初めに何日か休んだので、遅れを取り戻さないといけないんです。今日は自分のデスクで昼食をとることにします。

語彙チェック ☐ personnel 職員 ☐ all-day 終日の ☐ shut ～ down ～の電源を切る ☐ unsaved 未保存の ☐ state 状態 ☐ work out ～ ～の答えを見つけ出す ☐ in the meantime それまでの間 ☐ I've got to *do* (= I have to *do*) ～しなければならない ☐ catch up 遅れを取り戻す ☐ take ～ off ～の休みを取る

Error Code 662
Recovery Menu:
001 Suspend Program
002 Restart Program
003 Shut Down Program
004 Reboot Computer

エラーコード 662
復元メニュー：
001 プログラムの一時停止
002 プログラムの再開
003 プログラムのシャットダウン
004 コンピュータの再起動

68

正解 **D** ☐☐☐☐

Why are the IT support personnel unavailable?

(A) It is a national holiday.

(B) It is outside office hours.

(C) They are taking a lunch break.

(D) They are at a seminar.

ITサポート課の職員はなぜ不在ですか。

(A)国民の休日である。

(B) 営業時間外である。

(C) 彼らは昼休みをとっている。

(D)彼らは研修会に参加している。

女性は冒頭の発言で、Today the IT support personnel are attending an all-day seminar, so none of them are available. と述べている。研修会に参加していることが不在の理由だと分かるので、正解は(D)。

69

正解 **A** ☐☐☐☐

Look at the graphic. Which menu option does the man recommend?

(A) Option 001

(B) Option 002

(C) Option 003

(D) Option 004

図を見てください。男性はどのメニューオプションを勧めていますか。

(A)オプション001

(B) オプション002

(C)オプション003

(D)オプション004

男性は女性のコンピュータのエラーメッセージを確認した上で、Choose this one. It'll hold it in its current state until we can work out what to do. と述べている。つまり、現状維持のためにプログラムを一時停止することを勧めていると分かるので、正解は(A)。本文のholdという語が、メッセージではsuspendに言い換えられている。男性は「未保存のデータが失われるから電源は落とさない」と述べているので、(C)のオプション003は不正解。

70

正解 **B** ☐☐☐☐

What does the man say he did this week?

(A) Completed a project

(B) Took a vacation

(C) Purchased a new desk

(D) Interviewed an applicant

男性は今週何をしたと言っていますか。

(A) プロジェクトを完了させた

(B) 休暇を取った

(C)新しい机を買った

(D)応募者の面接をした

「(昼食に)一緒に行かないか」という女性の誘いに対して、男性は最後の発言でI'd love to, but I've got to catch up because I took a couple of days off earlier in the week. と女性に伝え、誘いを断る理由として週の初めに何日か休みを取ったことを伝えている。よって正解は(B)。

Part 4

音読 □□□ カンベキ理解 /8 ▶ /8

トーク ▶TRACK_192 問題 ▶TRACK_193
カンベキ理解 ▶TRACK_K37

M 🇺🇸

Questions 71 through 73 refer to the following telephone message.

カンベキ理解	
1 □□	Hi. My name is Rod Robinson.
2 □□	I am the head of marketing at Stephenson Inc.
3 □□	I'm calling you because our records show that you carried many of our products in the past.
4 □□	Stephenson Inc. has been working on revamping its perception among consumers.
5 □□	We've switched to an environmentally sustainable manufacturing process,
6 □□	and our new designs are testing extremely well with young people.
7 □□	We've invested heavily,
8 □□	and we believe this will be the beginning of a bright new future for us.

問題71-73は次の電話のメッセージに関するものです。

こんにちは、私はRod Robinsonです。Stephenson社の宣伝部長です。私どもの記録によると、御社には過去に弊社製品の多くを販売いただいておりましたため、お電話をおかけしています。Stephenson社は消費者の方々の認識をより良いものに変えるべく、日々努力しております。弊社は製造工程をより環境面で地球にやさしいものに変えまして、新しいデザインは若い方々にとても好評をいただいております。私たちは大きな投資を行いましたが、これは私たちにとって明るい新しい未来の始まりであると信じています。

語彙チェック □ the head （部などの)長 □ carry （店が商品）を置いている □ revamp 〜をより良くする □ perception 認識 □ switch to 〜 〜に切り替える □ environmentally 環境面で □ sustainable 地球にやさしい、持続可能な □ extremely 非常に、とても □ invest 投資する □ bright 明るい

👑 Level Up !

本問のトーク文には抽象的な表現が多く出てくるので、話の内容が掴みづらい。設問で問われている情報を押さえながら聞き取ろう。

71 正解 D ☐☐☐☐

Where does the listener work?

(A) At a manufacturing company

(B) At an advertising firm

(C) At a newspaper

(D) At a retail store

聞き手はどこで働いていますか。

(A)製造会社

(B)広告代理店

(C)新聞社

(D)小売店

I'm calling you because our records show that you carried many of our products in the past. の部分に注目。話し手が「（聞き手側が）自分たちの会社の製品の多くを販売してくれた」と述べていることから、聞き手は話し手の会社が製造した製品を売る小売店であるということが分かる。よって、正解は(D)。

👑 **Level Up !**
(A)は話し手側の業種なので、うっかり選ばないように注意！　トーク文が流れる前に設問を先読みして、「聞き手の働いている場所」を聞かれていることを意識しながらトークを聞こう。

72 正解 B ☐☐☐☐

According to the speaker, what does Stephenson Inc. intend to do?

(A) Expand into foreign markets

(B) Renew its public image

(C) Reduce its product diversity

(D) Announce a change of ownership

話し手によると、Stephenson社は何をするつもりですか。

(A)海外市場に進出する

(B)世間のイメージを一新する

(C)製品の多様性を縮小する

(D)所有者の変更を発表する

話し手は Stephenson Inc. has been working on revamping its perception among consumers. と述べ、製品に対する消費者のイメージを変える努力をしているということをアピールしている。よって、正解は(B)。本文中の revamping its perception among consumers「消費者の方々の認識をより良いものに変える」という箇所が、選択肢では Renew its public image「世間のイメージを一新する」に言い換えられている。

語彙チェック　☐ diversity　多様性　☐ ownership　所有者

73 正解 A ☐☐☐☐

What does the speaker mean when he says, "We've invested heavily"?

(A) His company has confidence in its products.

(B) His company is short of funds.

(C) His company will lose a lot of money.

(A) His company has taken a significant risk.

"We've invested heavily" という発言で、話し手は何を意図していますか。

(A)彼の会社は製品に自信を持っている。

(B)彼の会社は資金が不足している。

(C)彼の会社は大きな損失を被るだろう。

(A)彼の会社はかなりのリスクを冒した。

話し手は We've invested heavily「私たちは大きな投資を行った」という発言の後、続けて we believe this will be the beginning of a bright new future for us と述べている。大きな投資を行ったことが会社にとって明るい新しい未来の始まりであると信じている、と話をまとめていることから、話し手は製品に自信を持ち、期待をかけて投資を行ったということが分かる。よって、正解は(A)。

語彙チェック　☐ have confidence in ～　～に自信がある　☐ be short of ～　～が不足している　☐ take a risk　リスクを冒す

W 🇨🇦

Questions 74 through 76 refer to the following announcement.

カンペキ理解

1 □□　Good afternoon, travelers.
2 □□　This is a message for passengers traveling on flight TF742.
3 □□　One of our connecting flights will be arriving late,
4 □□　and this will push back our departure about twenty minutes.
5 □□　The new estimated departure time will be three P.M.
6 □□　The airline regrets any inconvenience this might cause.
7 □□　Please relax and make use of the free internet service and device charging terminals in the waiting lounge.
8 □□　Another announcement will be made when it's time to board.

問題74-76は次のお知らせに関するものです。

旅行者の皆さま、こんにちは。こちらは、TF742便にご搭乗いただく乗客の皆さまへのお知らせでございます。接続便の到着が遅れるため、出発が20分ほど先送りになる見込みです。新たな出発予定時刻は午後3時です。これにより発生するいかなるご不便につきまして、お詫び申し上げます。どうかおくつろぎになり、待合室の無料のインターネットサービスやデバイスの充電端末をご利用くださいませ。搭乗時刻になりましたら、改めてご案内いたします。

語彙チェック　□ connecting flight　接続便、乗継便　□ push back 〜　〜を延期する、〜を先送りにする　□ estimated　推定の
□ departure time　出発時刻　□ regret　〜を悔やむ、〜を遺憾とする　□ inconvenience　不便、迷惑
□ make use of 〜　〜を利用する　□ charging terminal　充電端末　□ waiting lounge　待合室
□ board　搭乗する

74

正解 A ☐☐☐☐

What has caused the delay?

(A) A late connecting flight

(B) Difficulty with the boarding gate

(C) A technical malfunction

(D) Some missing luggage

何が遅延を引き起こしていますか。

(A)接続便の遅延

(B) 搭乗ゲートの不具合

(C) 技術的な不具合

(D)一部の手荷物の紛失

話し手は One of our connecting flights will be arriving late, and this will push back our departure about twenty minutes. の部分で、TF742便の出発が20分ほど先送りになる原因として、接続便の到着が遅れることを述べている。よって、正解は(A)。

語彙チェック ☐ malfunction　不具合、不調　☐ missing　紛失している

75

正解 B ☐☐☐☐

According to the speaker, what is available to passengers?

(A) Some refreshments

(B) An internet connection

(C) Discount coupons

(D) Hotel accommodations

話し手によると、乗客は何を利用することができますか。

(A)軽食

(B) インターネット接続

(C) 割引券

(D)ホテルへの宿泊

話し手は Please relax and make use of the free internet service and device charging terminals in the waiting lounge. と述べ、乗客が利用できるものとして無料のインターネットサービスとデバイスの充電端末を挙げている。無料のインターネットサービスを意味する(B)が正解。

語彙チェック ☐ refreshments　軽食　☐ accommodations　宿泊設備

76

正解 D ☐☐☐☐

What will most likely be the topic of the next announcement?

(A) The weather conditions

(B) The immigration clearance

(C) The airport's internet service

(D) The flight's boarding sequence

次のお知らせの話題は何だと考えられますか。

(A)天候

(B) 入国手続き

(C) 空港のインターネットサービス

(D)飛行機の搭乗手続き

話し手は最後に Another announcement will be made when it's time to board. と述べ、搭乗時刻になったら改めて乗客に案内する旨を伝えている。よって、次のお知らせ内容として考えられるのは(D)。

語彙チェック ☐ sequence　順序、進行

W 🇬🇧

Questions 77 through 79 refer to the following excerpt from a meeting.

カンペキ理解	
1 ☐ ☐	I think everyone's here, so I'll start the meeting.
2 ☐ ☐	Thanks for coming on such short notice.
3 ☐ ☐	I've heard from several people that the parking situation is becoming problematic.
4 ☐ ☐	We've had to close off part of the car park
5 ☐ ☐	to provide room for the construction crews building the new wing.
6 ☐ ☐	This situation won't end soon.
7 ☐ ☐	We've got six months left in a year-long construction project.
8 ☐ ☐	Now, while it's far from ideal,
9 ☐ ☐	we've managed to get approval for staff to park in a vacant plot of land on Timms Street.
10 ☐ ☐	It's a bit far for a lot of people to walk.
11 ☐ ☐	We can't afford to provide a shuttle bus service,
12 ☐ ☐	so we're offering employees in certain departments the option to telecommute.

問題77-79は次の会議の抜粋に関するものです。

皆さん揃ったようですので、会議を始めます。急なお願いにもかかわらず、お集まりいただきありがとうございます。何人かの方から、駐車場の状況が問題になっていると聞いています。新館を建設している作業員の場所を空けるために、駐車場の一部を閉鎖せざるを得なくなりました。この状況はすぐには終わらないでしょう。1年間続く建設プロジェクトもあと6カ月残っていますからね。現在、理想とはほど遠い状態ですが、従業員の皆さんがTimms通りの空き地に駐車することができる認可をなんとか得たところです。多くの方にとって、歩くにはやや遠いです。シャトルバスを出す余裕はないので、特定の部署の従業員の皆さんには、在宅勤務の選択肢を提供します。

語彙チェック　☐ short notice　急な知らせ　☐ problematic　問題のある　☐ close off ～　～を閉鎖する　☐ car park　駐車場
☐ provide room for ～　～のための場所を提供する　☐ construction crew　建設作業員
☐ wing　(建物の)拡張部分、棟　☐ a year-long　1年間続く　☐ ideal　理想　☐ approval　認可、承認
☐ vacant　空いている　☐ plot　(土地などの)区画　☐ land　土地　☐ afford to *do*　～する金銭的余裕がない
☐ telecommute　在宅勤務をする

77

正解 **C** ☐☐☐☐

What are some employees concerned about?

(A) Career development opportunities

(B) Noise pollution in the workplace

(C) Insufficient parking spaces

(D) Ongoing staffing shortages

一部の従業員が懸念していることは何ですか。

(A) キャリア開発の機会

(B) 職場の騒音公害

(C) 不十分な駐車スペース

(D) 継続的な人手不足

話し手は I've heard from several people that the parking situation is becoming problematic. と述べ、続けて We've had to close off part of the car park と述べている。既存の駐車スペースの一部を閉鎖しなければならなくなったことで、駐車スペースが不十分となったことが問題だと分かる。よって、(C) が正解。car park は「駐車場」を表すイギリス英語。

語彙チェック ☐ career development　キャリア開発　☐ pollution　公害　☐ insufficient　不十分な　☐ ongoing　継続的な
☐ shortage　不足

78

正解 **C** ☐☐☐☐

When does the speaker say a project will probably be completed?

(A) In two weeks

(B) In two months

(C) In six months

(D) In a year

話し手は、プロジェクトはおそらくいつ完了すると言っていますか。

(A) 2週間後

(B) 2カ月後

(C) 6カ月後

(D) 1年後

話し手は、話の中盤で We've got six months left in a year-long construction project. と述べている。「1年間続く建設プロジェクトがあと6カ月残っている」ということは、あと6カ月でプロジェクトが終わるということなので、正解は (C)。

👑 **Level Up !**

a year-long「1年間続く」という単語だけを拾って、うっかり (D) を選ばないように注意。in a year-long construction project の部分は、あくまでもプロジェクト全体の長さを示している。

79

正解 **D** ☐☐☐☐

What temporary arrangements have been made for employees?

(A) Corporate gym memberships

(B) Staggered work hours

(C) A shuttle bus service

(D) Work-from-home options

従業員のために用意された一時的な取り計らいは何ですか。

(A) 法人向けスポーツジム会員権

(B) 時差出勤

(C) シャトルバスのサービス

(D) 在宅勤務の選択肢

話し手は最後の部分で、we're offering employees in certain departments the option to telecommute と述べ、従業員に在宅勤務の選択肢を提供することを伝えている。よって、正解は (D)。本文中の telecommute という動詞が、選択肢では work-from-home という形容詞に言い換えられている。「シャトルバスを出す余裕はない」と述べられているので、(C) は不正解。

語彙チェック ☐ corporate　法人の　☐ staggered　時間をずらした　☐ work-from-home　在宅勤務の

M 🇺🇸

Questions 80 through 82 refer to the following talk.

カンペキ理解		
1	□□	Good morning, everyone.
2	□□	I'm Nelly Cunningham, the newly appointed director of the Normandy Art Gallery.
3	□□	I'm honored to be able to address you all like this.
4	□□	Without your generous contributions, none of this would have been possible.
5	□□	My assistant is handing out information packs.
6	□□	Inside, you'll find various documents including a map of the facility.
7	□□	In a few moments, as we tour the building,
8	□□	you'll notice that the various spaces are dedicated to your businesses.
9	□□	The size of the contribution is directly related to the size of the exhibition space.

問題80-82は次のトークに関するものです。

皆さま、おはようございます。Normandy 美術館の新館長に任命された Nelly Cunningham です。このように皆さまにご挨拶できることを光栄に思います。皆さまの寛大な寄付がなければ、何事も不可能でした。今、私の助手が資料を配布しています。中には、施設の地図をはじめ、さまざまな資料が入っています。しばらくした後、館内を見学する際、さまざまなスペースが皆さんの事業に特化していることにお気付きになるかと思います。寄付金の大きさは、展示スペースの大きさに直接関係しています。

語彙チェック　□ newly　新しく　□ appointed　任命された　□ address　〜に演説する、〜に向けて話す　□ generous　寛大な
□ contribution　寄付（金）　□ hand out 〜　〜を配布する　□ information pack　（情報をまとめた）資料
□ including　〜を含んだ　□ facility　施設　□ tour　〜を見学する　□ be dedicated to 〜　〜に特化している

80

正解 B ☐☐☐☐

Who are the listeners?

(A) Art experts

(B) Corporate donors

(C) New gallery guides

(D) Government employees

聞き手たちは誰ですか。

(A) 美術専門家

(B) 企業の寄付者

(C) 新しい美術館の案内人

(D) 政府職員

美術館の新館長である話し手は、Without your generous contributions, none of this would have been possible. と述べ、聞き手たちに感謝を述べている。さらに後半では、In a few moments, as we tour the building, you'll notice that the various spaces are dedicated to your businesses. と述べている。これらの情報から、聞き手たちは美術館に対して寄付を行った、各企業の寄付者であるということが分かる。よって、正解は (B)。

語彙チェック ☐ corporate 企業の ☐ donor 寄付者

81

正解 C ☐☐☐☐

What are the listeners about to receive?

(A) Refreshments

(B) Name tags

(C) Information folders

(D) Uniforms

聞き手たちは何を受け取ろうとしていますか。

(A) 軽食

(B) 名札

(C) 資料パンフレット

(D) ユニフォーム

話し手は My assistant is handing out information packs. Inside, you'll find various documents including a map of the facility. と述べ、助手が施設の地図などを含む資料を配っていることを聞き手たちに伝えている。本文中の information packs を Information folders「資料パンフレット」と言い換えた (C) が正解。

82

正解 A ☐☐☐☐

What will the listeners do next?

(A) Walk around a building

(B) Take a break

(C) Watch a video

(D) Meet a representative

聞き手たちは次に何をしますか。

(A) 建物内を歩き回る

(B) 休憩する

(C) ビデオを見る

(D) 担当者に会う

In a few moments, as we tour the building の部分より、聞き手たちはこの後、美術館内を見学するということが分かる。よって、正解は (A)。tour という単語は、「（旅行の）ツアー」という意味の名詞だけでなく、「美術館や博物館などを見て回る」という意味の動詞として使われるということも押さえておきたい。

語彙チェック ☐ representative 担当者

M 🇦🇺

Questions 83 through 85 refer to the following advertisement.

カンベキ理解

1 □□　Hillview Film and Television College is Queensland's only vocational school specializing in careers in the film and television industry.

2 □□　From next year, we'll be offering a two-year course specializing in video production for online advertising.

3 □□　This course is the first of its kind in Australia,

4 □□　and it was designed in response to demand from the video production industry.

5 □□　Graduates from Hillview Film and Television College hold important positions in several of the nation's major production companies.

6 □□　Many of them have had exceptional careers as award-winning directors and producers here and abroad.

7 □□　Order a prospectus from the Web site.

問題83-85は次の広告に関するものです。

Hillview Film and Television 学校は、Queensland州で唯一の、映画・テレビ業界でのキャリアに特化した専門学校です。来年からは、オンライン広告用の映像制作に特化した2年制の課程が開講される予定です。この課程はオーストラリアで初めてで、映像制作業界からの要望に応えて作られたものです。Hillview Film and Television 学校の卒業生は、国内の大手制作会社数社で重要な地位に就いています。彼らの多くは、国内外で受賞歴のあるディレクターやプロデューサーとして、素晴らしいキャリアを積んでいます。パンフレットはウェブサイトからお申し込みください。

語彙チェック　□ vocational school　専門学校　□ specialize in 〜　〜に特化した
□ the first of its kind　今までに類を見ないもの、はじめてのもの　□ in response to 〜　〜に応えて
□ graduate　卒業生　□ hold an important position　要職に就く　□ nation　国　□ major　主要な、大手の
□ exceptional　素晴らしい　□ award-winning　受賞歴のある　□ here and abroad　国内外で
□ prospectus　案内書、パンフレット

83

正解 A ☐☐☐☐

What is being advertised?

(A) A new course

(B) Discount tuition

(C) An open house

(D) Job vacancies

何が宣伝されていますか。

(A)新しい課程

(B)割引された授業料

(C)一般公開日

(D)求人情報

話し手は冒頭で専門学校のことを簡単に紹介し、その後From next year, we'll be offering a two-year course specializing in video production for online advertising.と述べている。これから新たな課程が開講されることが分かるので、正解は (A)。

語彙チェック ☐ tuition　授業料　☐ open house　（住宅・学校・施設などの）一般公開日　☐ vacancy　空き、欠員

84

正解 C ☐☐☐☐

What is the college known for?

(A) Its small classes

(B) Its excellent equipment

(C) Its famous graduates

(D) Its central location

専門学校は何で有名ですか。

(A)少人数制のクラス

(B)優れた設備

(C)有名な卒業生

(D)中心地に位置していること

話し手は専門学校の卒業生について、Graduates from Hillview Film and Television College hold important positions in several of the nation's major production companies. Many of them have had exceptional careers as award-winning directors and producers here and abroad.と述べている。「重要な地位に就いている」「国内外で受賞歴のあるディレクターやプロデューサーとしてキャリアを積んでいる」などの情報から、正解は(C)だと分かる。

85

正解 A ☐☐☐☐

According to the speaker, what can the listeners do on a Web site?

(A) Order a brochure

(B) See student testimonials

(C) Watch a commercial

(D) Enroll in a course

話し手によると、聞き手たちはウェブサイトで何ができますか。

(A)パンフレットを取り寄せる

(B)受講者の声を見る

(C)宣伝を見る

(D)課程に登録する

話し手はOrder a prospectus from the Web site.と述べている。prospectusとは「パンフレット」を表すイギリス英語。聞き手たちはパンフレットをウェブサイトで注文できるということが分かるので、正解は(A)。

語彙チェック ☐ testimonial　（商品やサービスを利用した）顧客の声　☐ enroll in ～　～に登録する

W 🇬🇧

Questions 86 through 88 refer to the following instructions.

1 □□ Thank you all for coming.
2 □□ This announcement is about tomorrow's workshops for employees taking positions at our international offices from next month.
3 □□ The workshops will be held in Room D.
4 □□ You'll need to bring something to write with — a tablet computer is fine.
5 □□ I trust you all have the results from your health examination.
6 □□ Make sure you bring those along.
7 □□ Um... tomorrow will be a lot of fun.
8 □□ You'll be working with a buddy who's from the country you will be living in.
9 □□ It should be a very educational experience for all of you.

問題86-88は次の説明に関するものです。

皆さん、お越しくださりありがとうございます。今回は、来月から海外拠点に勤務する社員を対象とした、明日の研修会についてお知らせします。研修会はD室で行います。何か書くものをご持参ください―タブレット端末でも構いません。皆さんは健康診断の結果をお持ちだと思います。必ず持参してください。ええと…明日は楽しいことがたくさんあります。皆さんが暮らすことになる国から来たパートナーと、一緒に仕事をしていただきます。皆さん全員にとって、非常に勉強になるはずです。

語彙チェック □ take a position at ～ ～で働く □ trust きっと～だと思う □ health examination 健康診断
□ bring ～ along ～を一緒に持ってくる □ buddy 仲間、パートナー □ educational 教育に役立つ、ためになる

86

正解 C ☐☐☐☐

According to the speaker, what are the workshops about?

(A) Changing services
(B) Advertising vacancies
(C) Taking foreign postings
(D) Choosing domestic suppliers

話し手によると、研修会は何についてですか。

(A) サービスを変更すること
(B) 求人広告を出すこと
(C) 海外赴任をすること
(D) 国内の供給業者を選ぶこと

話し手は冒頭で聞き手たちに対し、This announcement is about tomorrow's workshops for employees taking positions at our international offices from next month. と述べている。海外拠点に勤務する社員を対象とした研修会だと分かるので、正解は(C)。

👑 **Level Up !**
正答の選択肢(C)に含まれるpostingは、ここでは「任命、配属」という意味。「郵送、配送」といった意味で学ぶことが多いので、意味を取り違えないように気を付けよう！

語彙チェック ☐ posting （職務の）任命、配属 ☐ domestic 国内の

87

正解 B ☐☐☐☐

What should the listeners bring with them?
(A) Flight confirmations
(B) Health information
(C) Identification cards
(D) Trip reports

聞き手たちが持参すべきものは何ですか。
(A) フライトの確認書
(B) 健康情報
(C) 身分証明書
(D) 旅行報告書

話し手は聞き手に対して、I trust you all have the results from your health examination. Make sure you bring those along. の部分で、健康診断の結果を持ってくるよう伝えている。よって、正解は(B)。本文中のexaminationという単語は、「（教育分野の）試験、テスト」という意味だけでなく、「（患者の）検査・診察」という意味でも用いられる。

語彙チェック ☐ confirmation 確認書 ☐ identification 身分証明

88

正解 D ☐☐☐☐

What will the listeners do tomorrow?
(A) Take a trip
(B) Roleplay situations
(C) Fill out forms
(D) Work in pairs

聞き手たちは明日何をしますか。
(A) 旅行に行く
(B) 状況のロールプレイをする
(C) 用紙に記入する
(D) 2人1組で仕事をする

話し手はtomorrow will be a lot of funと述べ、明日について言及した後、You'll be working with a buddy who's from the country you will be living in. と続けている。work with a buddy「パートナーと一緒に仕事をする」という表現を、work in pairs「2人1組で仕事をする」と言い換えた(D)が正解。

語彙チェック ☐ roleplay 〜のロールプレイをする、〜を実際に演じる ☐ fill out 〜 〜に記入する

トーク ▶TRACK_204　問題 ▶TRACK_205
カンペキ理解 ▶TRACK_K43

M 🇺🇸

Questions 89 through 91 refer to the following excerpt from a meeting.

カンペキ理解	
1 □□	The head office is demanding that we raise our production goals by ten percent this month.
2 □□	The factory workers are already under a lot of pressure,
3 □□	and many of us are already working additional hours each week.
4 □□	I'm going to pay headquarters a visit and suggest that we hire more people.
5 □□	Considering what they're demanding in terms of output,
6 □□	I'd like each of you to go back to your departments
7 □□	and work out how many additional people you would need to achieve the new goals.

問題89-91は次の会議の抜粋に関するものです。

本社は、今月から生産目標を10パーセント上げるよう要求しています。工場の従業員は以前から大きなプレッシャーにさらされており、すでに私たちの多くは毎週、追加の時間で働いています。私は本社を訪ねて、もっと人を雇うように提案するつもりです。彼らが要求する生産量を鑑みて、皆さんには各部門に戻って、新しい目標を達成するために何人の増員が必要か算出していただきたいと思います。

語彙チェック　□ demand that ~　~を要求する　□ raise　~を上げる　□ under a pressure　プレッシャーの下で
□ pay ~ a visit　~を訪問する　□ headquarters　本社　□ considering　~を考慮に入れると
□ in terms of ~　~の観点から　□ output　生産量　□ work out ~　~を算出する　□ achieve　~を達成する

89

正解 **A** ▢▢▢▢

What does the speaker mean when he says, "many of us are already working additional hours each week"?

(A) The company is expecting too much.

(B) It is costing a lot to pay for overtime work.

(C) Staff are excited to work on a project.

(D) The employees will quickly complete some work.

"many of us are already working additional hours each week" という発言で、話し手は何を意図していますか。

(A)会社は多くを期待しすぎている。

(B)残業代が多くかかっている。

(C)スタッフは計画に取り組むことにわくわくしている。

(D)従業員はすぐに仕事を完了させる予定である。

話し手は The factory workers are already under a lot of pressure と述べ、(生産目標を上げるという要求により)工場の従業員が以前から大きなプレッシャーにさらされていることについて言及している。そして、その直後 many of us are already working additional hours each week という発言で、従業員にさらに負荷がかかっていることを示している。会社の要求が多いという意図で発言したということが伺えるので、正解は(A)。

語彙チェック □ overtime work　残業

90

正解 **B** ▢▢▢▢

What does the speaker say he will do?

(A) Check an employee handbook

(B) Take a trip to the head office

(C) Promote current employees

(D) Cover transportation expenses

話し手は何をすると言っていますか。

(A)従業員マニュアルを確認する

(B)本社に出向く

(C)現在の従業員を昇進させる

(D)交通費を負担する

話し手は I'm going to pay headquarters a visit and suggest that we hire more people. と述べている。人員を増やすことを提案するために本社を訪れるつもりだということが分かるので、正解は(B)。本文中の pay 〜 a visit が選択肢では take a trip to 〜に、さらに headquarters は head office に言い換えられている。

語彙チェック □ handbook　手引き、マニュアル　□ expenses　(特定の用途のための)経費

91

正解 **A** ▢▢▢▢

Who most likely are the listeners?

(A) Section chiefs

(B) Business investors

(C) City inspectors

(D) Equipment suppliers

聞き手たちは誰だと考えられますか。

(A)部長

(B)企業の投資家

(C)市の検査官

(D)機器の供給業者

話し手は I'd like each of you to go back to your departments and work out how many additional people you would need to achieve the new goals. の部分で、各部門に戻って新しい目標を達成するために必要な増員数を算出するよう、聞き手たちに頼んでいる。このことから、聞き手たちは社内で各部門を取りまとめる立場だと推測できる。よって、正解は(A)。

語彙チェック □ investor　投資家　□ inspector　検査官

W 🇨🇦

Questions 92 through 94 refer to the following telephone message.

カンベキ理解

1　□□　Hi. It's Rebecca Savage from Starfoods.
2　□□　One of our storage refrigerators needs some urgent repairs.
3　□□　We have a huge delivery of ingredients arriving this afternoon,
4　□□　and unless the refrigerator is working,
5　□□　it'll spoil before we can distribute it to restaurants on Thursday and Friday.
6　□□　I'd appreciate it if you could get back to me as soon as you hear this.
7　□□　A lot of businesses are relying on us.
8　□□　If we can't supply them with the ingredients they need,
9　□□　they may not be able to honor their reservations.

問題92-94は次の電話のメッセージに関するものです。

Starfoods 社の Rebecca Savage です。私どもの保管用冷蔵庫の1台に、緊急修理が必要です。今日の午後に大量の食材が届くのですが、冷蔵庫が動かないことには、木曜日と金曜日にレストランに配送する前に傷んでしまいます。この伝言をお聞きになり次第、すぐに連絡していただけるとありがたいです。多くの会社が私どもを頼りにしております。必要な食材を供給できない場合、彼らは予約に応じられないかもしれません。

語彙チェック　□ storage　保管　□ refrigerator　冷蔵庫　□ urgent　緊急の　□ huge　大量の　□ ingredient　食材、材料　□ unless　〜しない限り　□ spoil　傷む　□ distribute A to B　AをBに配送する　□ appreciate　〜をありがたく思う　□ rely on 〜　〜に頼る　□ supply A with B　AにBを供給する　□ honor　（約束など）を守る

92

正解 **A** ☐☐☐☐

What type of business does the speaker work for?
(A) A food distributor
(B) A health club
(C) A furniture warehouse
(D) An appliance manufacturer

話し手はどんな種類の企業で働いていますか。
(A) 食品流通業者
(B) 健康クラブ
(C) 家具卸売店
(D) 家電製造業者

話し手は冒頭でOne of our storage refrigeratorsと言っているので、保管用冷蔵庫を所有していることが分かる。さらに、We have a huge delivery of ingredients arriving this afternoon, and unless the refrigerator is working, it'll spoil before we can distribute it to restaurants on Thursday and Friday. という発言から、届いた食材をレストランに配送するという情報が得られる。よって、正解は(A)。

語彙チェック ☐ distributor 販売業者 ☐ warehouse 卸売店、問屋 ☐ appliance 器具

93

正解 **C** ☐☐☐☐

What does the speaker ask the listener to do?
(A) Make a reservation
(B) Post an online review
(C) Repair some equipment
(D) Provide some contact information

話し手は聞き手に何をするよう求めていますか。
(A) 予約をする
(B) オンラインのレビューを投稿する
(C) 備品を修理する
(D) 連絡先を提供する

話し手は One of our storage refrigerators needs some urgent repairs. と述べ、保管用冷蔵庫の1台に緊急修理が必要だという状況を聞き手に伝えている。さらにその後、I'd appreciate it if you could get back to me as soon as you hear this. と述べ、伝言を聞いた後すぐに連絡してほしいと伝えている。話し手は聞き手に冷蔵庫の修理を頼んでいるということが分かるので、正解は(C)。本文中のrefrigerator「冷蔵庫」という具体的な語が、選択肢ではequipment「備品」という抽象的な語に言い換えられている。

語彙チェック ☐ post 〜を投稿する

94

正解 **B** ☐☐☐☐

Why does the speaker say, "A lot of businesses are relying on us"?
(A) To show that her business has a good reputation
(B) To explain the seriousness of a situation
(C) To offer an excuse for a slow response
(D) To demonstrate the dependability of an appliance

話し手はなぜ "A lot of businesses are relying on us"? と言っていますか。
(A) 自分の会社が良い評判を得ていることを示すため
(B) 事態の深刻さを説明するため
(C) 対応の遅れについて弁解するため
(D) 家電製品の信頼性を証明するため

冷蔵庫の故障で食材を冷やせないというトラブルに対し、話し手はA lot of businesses are relying on us.「多くの会社が私どもを頼りにしております」という発言の後、If we can't supply them with the ingredients they need, they may not be able to honor their reservations. と続けている。冷蔵庫を修理できないことによって多くの会社が被害を被る、という事態の深刻性を伝えようとしていることが分かる。よって、正解は(B)。

語彙チェック ☐ reputation 評判 ☐ seriousness 深刻さ ☐ excuse 弁解、言い訳 ☐ demonstrate 〜を証明する ☐ dependability 信頼性

M 🇦🇺

Questions 95 through 97 refer to the following announcement and map.

カンペキ理解

1 ☐☐ OK, everyone. I've completed checking you in.
2 ☐☐ I know you must be tired after all the sightseeing we did today.
3 ☐☐ I'll hand you all your room keys in just a moment.
4 ☐☐ In the case along with your keys, you'll find a voucher for dinner at Maddison's.
5 ☐☐ Your reservation is for seven P.M.
6 ☐☐ Please keep in mind that the elevator doesn't actually stop on the floor of your restaurant.
7 ☐☐ You need to get off on the twelfth floor and take the stairs from there.

問題95-97は次のお知らせと地図に関するものです。

それでは、皆さん。皆さんのチェックインを済ませたところです。今日は観光でお疲れのことと思います。今、部屋の鍵をお渡しいたします。ケースの中に鍵と一緒にMaddison'sでの夕食券が入っています。予約は午後7時です。エレベーターは、そのレストランの階には止まりませんのでご注意ください。12階で降りて、そこから階段を使う必要があります。

語彙チェック ☐ sightseeing 観光　☐ hand *A B*　AにBを手渡す　☐ along with 〜　〜と一緒に
☐ voucher （商品・サービスの）引換券　☐ keep in mind that 〜　〜ということを覚えておく　☐ actually 実際は
☐ get off 降りる　☐ take the stairs 階段を使う

Gettysburg Hotel Restaurant Map		
13	Maddison's	
12	Cheers	
	Guest Rooms	
4		
3	Red Rock	
2		
Golden Road	1	Reception

Gettysburg ホテル レストラン地図		
13	Maddison's	
12	Cheers	
	客室	
4		
3	Red Rock	
2		
Golden Road	1	フロント

95

正解 C ▢▢▢▢

Who most likely is the speaker?

(A) A hotel porter

(B) A restaurant worker

(C) A tour guide

(D) A company executive

話し手は誰だと考えられますか。

(A) 荷物運搬人

(B) レストランの従業員

(C) ツアーガイド

(D) 会社の重役

話し手は冒頭で、I've completed checking you in. I know you must be tired after all the sightseeing we did today. と述べている。聞き手たちの宿泊場所のチェックインを行っていること、彼らに対して「観光で疲れているだろう」と気遣っていることなどから、話し手は観光客を案内するツアーガイドであると推測できる。よって、正解は (C)。

語彙チェック ☐ porter ポーター、（駅・空港・ホテルなどの）荷物運び ☐ executive 重役

96

正解 C ▢▢▢▢

According to the speaker, what will the listeners receive?

(A) A car key

(B) An itinerary

(C) A meal ticket

(D) A product sample

話し手によると、聞き手たちは何を受け取りますか。

(A) 車の鍵

(B) 旅程表

(C) 食券

(D) 商品サンプル

話し手は In the case along with your keys, you'll find a voucher for dinner at Maddison's. の部分で、部屋の鍵と一緒に Maddison's というレストランで使える夕食券が入っていることを伝えている。よって、正解は (C)。voucher は coupon「クーポン」と同じ意味合いで、無料のサービスや割引が受けられる券のことを指す。

97

正解 A ▢▢▢▢

Look at the graphic. On which floor will the listeners have dinner?

(A) The 13th Floor

(B) The 12th Floor

(C) The 3rd Floor

(D) The 1st Floor

図を見てください。聞き手たちはどの階で夕食をとりますか。

(A) 13階

(B) 12階

(C) 3階

(D) 1階

you'll find a voucher for dinner at Maddison's の部分から、聞き手たちは Maddison's という名前のレストランで夕食をとる予定であることが分かる。図を見ると、Maddison's は13階にあるので、正解は (A)。

♛ Level Up !

本文中に twelfth floor「12階」という数字が出てくるが、問われていることとは関係がない。聞こえた数字にすぐに飛びつかず、内容をしっかり聞き取ることを意識しよう。

191

W 🇬🇧

Questions 98 through 100 refer to the following excerpt from a meeting and graph.

カンペキ理解

1 ☐☐　Next, please take a look at this graph.
2 ☐☐　It shows the sales results for last quarter and the current one.
3 ☐☐　Around 160 million dollars in sales is normal in the third quarter.
4 ☐☐　At the start of this quarter,
5 ☐☐　Mr. Simms promised that we'd all get an extra bonus if sales exceeded 150 million dollars,
6 ☐☐　and a trip to a corporate retreat if we broke 200 million dollars.
7 ☐☐　The fourth quarter is traditionally our slowest sales period for farming machinery,
8 ☐☐　so his expectations were probably not so high.
9 ☐☐　Now, I'd like to invite Ms. White
10 ☐☐　to talk about the positives and negatives of her department's promotional strategies.
11 ☐☐　When she's finished, we'll adjourn to a nearby restaurant for lunch.
12 ☐☐　We'll resume our meeting at two this afternoon.

問題98-100は次の会議の抜粋とグラフに関するものです。

次に、このグラフをご覧ください。こちらは前四半期と今四半期の売上実績を示しています。第3四半期は1億6千万ドル前後の売り上げが普通です。今期の初めにSimms社長が、売上高が1億5千万ドルを超えたら臨時ボーナスを出す、そして2億ドルを上回ったら社員旅行に行けると約束しました。第4四半期は、伝統的に農機具の販売が最も低迷する時期なので、彼の期待はおそらくそれほど高くはなかったのでしょう。さて、ここでWhiteさんに、自身の部署の販売戦略のプラス面とマイナス面について話してもらいたいと思います。それが終わったら、近くのレストランに移動して昼食休憩をとりましょう。午後2時から会議を再開します。

語彙チェック　☐ take a look at ～　～を見る　☐ quarter　四半期　☐ current　現在の　☐ normal　通常、平均
☐ bonus　ボーナス　☐ exceed　～を超える　☐ corporate retreat　社員旅行　☐ break　(記録) を上回る
☐ traditionally　伝統的に　☐ farming machinery　農機具　☐ expectation　期待　☐ positive　長所、良い面
☐ negative　短所、否定的側面　☐ promotional strategy　販売戦略
☐ adjourn to ～　(休憩するために) ～に移動する　☐ resume　～を再開する

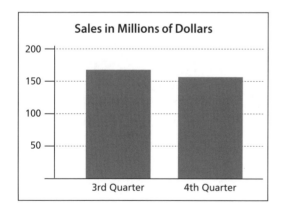

Sales in Millions of Dollars

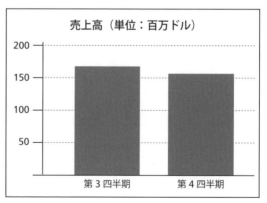

売上高（単位：百万ドル）

98

正解 B □□□□

Look at the graphic. What will happen at the company this quarter?
(A) Sales will exceed last quarter's.
(B) An additional bonus will be paid.
(C) Employees will attend a corporate retreat.
(D) A sales target will be revised.

図を見てください。今四半期、会社では何が起こりますか。
(A) 売上高が前四半期を上回る。
(B) 追加のボーナスが支払われる。
(C) 従業員は社員旅行に参加する。
(D) 売上目標が修正される。

話し手は冒頭で、前四半期と今四半期の売上実績を示すグラフについて紹介したあと、At the start of this quarter, ～の部分で、Simms 社長が売上高が1億5千万ドルを超えたら臨時ボーナスがあることを約束したと述べている。トークの内容とグラフを照らし合わせると、last quarter が3rd quarter、this quarter が4th quarter であることが分かる。グラフから、今期の売上実績が1億5千万ドルを超えていることが読み取れるので、正解は(B)。社員旅行ができるのは売上高が2億ドルを超えたらという条件なので(C)は不正解。

語彙チェック □ target 目標 □ revise ～を修正する

99

正解 D □□□□

Who most likely is Ms. White?
(A) The president of a machinery manufacturer
(B) A writer from a magazine publisher
(C) The chief of the company's accounting section
(D) The manager of the marketing department

White さんは誰だと考えられますか。
(A) 機械製造業者の社長
(B) 雑誌出版社のライター
(C) 会社の経理課長
(D) マーケティング部長

話し手は Now, I'd like to invite Ms. White to talk about the positives and negatives of her department's promotional strategies. と述べ、White さんに販売戦略のプラス面とマイナス面について話してもらおうとしている。販売戦略について詳しいということは、White さんはマーケティング部長だと推測することができる。よって、正解は(D)。

語彙チェック □ publisher 出版社 □ accounting 経理 □ section 課、部

100

正解 B □□□□

What will the listeners do after Ms. White speaks?
(A) Vote for a spokesperson
(B) Take a break
(C) Share ideas
(D) Speak with a journalist

White さんが話した後、聞き手たちは何をしますか。
(A) 広報担当者に投票をする
(B) 休憩する
(C) 意見を共有し合う
(D) ジャーナリストと話す

話し手は聞き手たちに対し、When she's finished, we'll adjourn to a nearby restaurant for lunch. と述べ、White さんの話が終わったら近くのレストランに移動して昼食休憩をとる予定だと伝えている。よって、正解は(B)。

👑 **Level Up !**
本文中の adjourn は、「（会議など）を休会する、延期する」という他動詞の意味に加え、adjourn to ～「（休憩するために）～に移動する」という自動詞としての意味もある。

語彙チェック □ vote for ～ ～に投票する

音読 □□□　　解答時間　　秒 ▶　　秒

101

正解 C　□□□□　▶ TRACK_212

The ------- of employment outlined in the employee handbook explain what is expected of workers in various situations.

(A) condition　　　　　　　(C) conditions
(B) conditional　　　　　　(D) conditionally

従業員ハンドブックに概略が述べられている雇用条件は、さまざまな状況において従業員に期待されることを説明しています。

冠詞theと前置詞ofの間にある空所には名詞が入る。述語動詞はexplainで三人称単数現在形のsは付いていないので、可算名詞の複数形の(C) conditionsが正解。なお、文の前半にoutlinedという単語があるが、これは主語に後ろから説明を加える過去分詞として用いられているので述語動詞ではない。

音読 □□□　　解答時間　　秒 ▶　　秒

102

正解 B　□□□□　▶ TRACK_213

The museum has an ------- collection of artifacts from local indigenous cultures.

(A) insolvent　　　　　　　(C) ultimate
(B) eclectic　　　　　　　　(D) instantaneous

その美術館には、土着の文化から生まれた工芸品の種々のコレクションが収蔵されています。

後ろの名詞collectionを修飾するのに適切な形容詞を選ぶ。collection of artifacts「工芸品のコレクション」を修飾するのにふさわしいのは(B) eclectic「種々の」。(A)は「破産した」、(C)は「究極の」、(D)は「即座の」という意味。

語彙チェック　□ artifact　工芸品
　　　　　　　□ indigenous　（ある土地に）固有の

音読 □□□　　解答時間　　秒 ▶　　秒

103

正解 B　□□□□　▶ TRACK_214

According to Ms. Smith's -------, the factory lost power after the new machinery was turned on for the first time.

(A) accountancy　　　　　　(C) accountably
(B) account　　　　　　　　(D) accountable

Smithさんの報告によると、工場は新しい機械が初めて電源を入れられた後に停電しました。

according to 〜「〜によると」から始まる前置詞句内にあり、直前にMs. Smith's「Smithさんの」という所有格の表現があることから、空所には名詞が入る。名詞の(A)と(B)のうち、(A)は「Smithさんの会計事務によると」となるため不自然。よって、(B) account「報告」が正解。

音読 □□□　　解答時間　　秒 ▶　　秒

104

正解 A　□□□□　▶ TRACK_215

Buffalo brand carpet detergent is ------- most frequently endorsed by industry professionals in light of its quality.

(A) the one　　　　　　　　(C) its
(B) what　　　　　　　　　(D) one of

Buffaloブランドのカーペット用洗剤は、その質の高さから業界のプロによって最も頻繁に推薦される洗剤です。

空所前のisが、この文の主語Buffalo brand carpet detergentに対応する動詞。空所後の過去分詞endorsedによって修飾される語が、空所に必要。よって、正解は(A)。(C)と(D)はともに空所後に名詞の役割をする語が必要。(B)のwhatは関係代名詞として名詞節を作るが、endorseは他動詞なので、その場合はendorsedの後ろに目的語となる名詞が必要。

語彙チェック　□ detergent　洗剤　□ endorse　〜を推薦する
　　　　　　　□ in light of 〜　〜の観点から

音読 □□□　　解答時間　　秒 ▶　　秒

105

正解 C　□□□□　▶ TRACK_216

Although sales are below expectations, the new kitchenware is ------- a reputation for excellent usability online.

(A) supplying　　　　　　　(C) enjoying
(B) granting　　　　　　　　(D) dedicating

売上高は予想を下回っていますが、新しい台所用品は使い勝手の良さに関してオンライン上で評判を得ています。

空所はbe動詞isの直後にあり、後ろには名詞a reputationがあるので、これを目的語にとって意味の通るものを選ぶ。enjoy a reputationで「評判を得る」という意味を表すので、(C) enjoyingを入れると文意が通る。(A)は「〜を供給する」、(B)は「〜を与える」、(D)は「〜をささげる」という意味。

👑 Level Up !

earn a reputation「評判を得る」、establish a reputation「名声を確立する」も同様の表現として問われるので、セットで覚えておこう。

音読 ☐☐☐　解答時間　秒 ▶　秒

106

正解 **A** ☐☐☐☐　▶TRACK_217

The company has arranged a banquet to show employees ------- appreciative it is of their hard work this year.

(A) how

(B) that

(C) however

(D) when

従業員に対して、今年の彼らの懸命な働きにどれくらい感謝しているのかを示すために、会社は宴会を手配しました。

語彙チェック ☐ banquet 宴会
☐ appreciative of ～ ～に感謝する

空所は show *A B*「AにBを示す」のBにあたるので、空所から文末までは名詞節の働きをする関係詞節になると分かる。空所直後に形容詞の appreciative があることから、〈how ＋形容詞＋ S ＋ V〉という形で「どれほど～しているか」という意味を表す (A) how が正解。

👑 **Level Up！**

(C)は名詞節を作ることはできない。また、(B)が名詞節を導く接続詞だとしても、直後に形容詞を続けた語順にはならないため不適切。

音読 ☐☐☐　解答時間　秒 ▶　秒

107

正解 **D** ☐☐☐☐　▶TRACK_218

------- stated in the product specifications, the device should be stored in a dry room at below 20 degrees Celsius.

(A) At

(B) While

(C) For

(D) As

製品仕様書に記載されているように、その機器は20℃以下の乾燥室に保管されなければなりません。

空所の直後には、他動詞 state「～をはっきり述べる」の過去分詞 stated がある。選択肢のうち (D) As には「～（する）ように」という意味があり、空所に入れると As stated in ～で「～に述べられているように、～に記載されているように」という意味になる。カンマ以降の内容が製品仕様書に書かれているという自然な文脈となるので、(D)が正解。

音読 ☐☐☐　解答時間　秒 ▶　秒

108

正解 **A** ☐☐☐☐　▶TRACK_219

Some of the board members ------- disapproved of the idea that reduces the development cost.

(A) mildly

(B) narrowly

(C) unanimously

(D) closely

取締役会のメンバーの中には、開発コストを削減するという意見に、やんわりと反対した人もいました。

語彙チェック ☐ disapprove of ～ ～に反対する

空所の後ろには述語動詞の disapproved があるので、これを修飾する副詞として適切なものを選ぶ。ある意見に対し、一部の人たちがどのように反対したのかと考えると、(A) mildly を入れて mildly disapproved of ～「～にやんわりと反対した」とするのが適切。主語が Some of the board members なので、(C) unanimously「満場一致で」は不適切。(B)は「かろうじて」、(D)は「密接に」という意味。

音読 ☐☐☐　解答時間　秒 ▶　秒

109

正解 **C** ☐☐☐☐　▶TRACK_220

Dalton Productions whose latest works are of good repute ------- a documentary on the farming industry every day unless the weather is unfavorable.

(A) to film

(B) have filmed

(C) is filming

(D) filming

最新の作品が良い評判を得ている Dalton プロダクションズは、天候が好ましくない場合を除いて、農業に関するドキュメンタリー映画を毎日撮影しています。

語彙チェック ☐ unfavorable 好ましくない

問題文には文の述語動詞となりえる語句がないので、空所に入る語句は述語動詞として用いることができる (B) と (C) の2つに絞られる。文の後半に every day という表現があるので、現在完了形の(B)は不適切。よって、(C) is filming が正解。

👑 **Level Up！**

現在進行形には「今まさに進行中の動作」だけでなく、「一定の期間の幅があり、その期間の中でくり返し行われている動作」を示す用法がある！

音読 ☐☐☐　解答時間　秒 ▶　秒

110

正解 **C** ☐☐☐☐　▶TRACK_221

HR employees usually begin job interviews with general questions and move ------- to the ones about candidates' prior experience.

(A) over

(B) in

(C) on

(D) for

人事部の従業員は通常、一般的な質問で就職面接を開始し、その後候補者の前職の経験に関する質問へ移ります。

move の前には接続詞の and があるので、この move は begin と並列された文全体の述語動詞であり、move ------- to でひとかたまりの意味を成していることが分かる。よって、move on to ～「（新しい話題など）に移る」という表現を作る (C) on を空所に入れるのが適切。and の前後で「面接での質問が一般的なものから前職の経験に関するものに移る」という自然な文脈となる。

111

Mr. Romanov's ------- to the event attendees was about improving customer satisfaction levels.

(A) addressed　　　　　　(C) addressing
(B) address　　　　　　　(D) addresses

イベントの出席者へのRomanovさんの講演は、顧客満足度を向上させることについてでした。

語彙チェック　□ customer satisfaction level　顧客満足度

空所の前にはMr. Romanov's「Romanovさんの」という所有格の表現、後ろには前置詞toがある。また、さらに後ろにはwasという述語動詞がある。よって、Mr. Romanov's ------- to the event attendeesは文全体の主語であり、空所には所有格によって修飾される名詞が入ると分かる。(B)と(D)の2つの正解候補のうち、主述の一致の観点から、単数形の(B) addressが正解。

112

A committee has been commissioned to ------- a plan that will help the business head off competition from international suppliers.

(A) desire　　　　　　　(C) dread
(B) craft　　　　　　　　(D) instill

委員会は、その企業が国際的な販売会社との競争を避けるのに役立つ計画を立てる権限を与えられました。

空所はcommission A to do「Aに〜する権限を与える」という表現のto不定詞の位置にあるので、空所直後の名詞a planを目的語にとり、文意が通る動詞を選ぶ。選択肢はどれも他動詞の働きを持つ動詞だが、planと結び付いて意味を成すのは(B) craft「〜を念入りに作る」のみ。craft a planで「計画を立てる」という意味の表現になる。(A)は「〜を強く望む」、(C)は「〜を恐れる」、(D)は「〜を教え込む」という意味。

113

The editor requires that the first drafts of articles for the September issue be submitted by August 17 ------- the very latest.

(A) on　　　　　　　(C) with
(B) in　　　　　　　(D) at

その編集者は、どんなに遅くとも8月17日までに9月号の記事の初稿が提出されることを要求しています。

空所以降がなくても文の要素は全て揃っているので、空所はthe very latestと結び付いて文に補足説明を加える前置詞句を作ると考えられる。at the latest「遅くとも」という表現に、その度合いや程度を強調するveryが付け加えられた形だと見抜けるかがポイント。「どんなに遅くとも8月17日までに初稿を提出してほしい」という自然な文脈となるので、(D) atが正解。

114

------- of the movie production company's directors has experience in a variety of fiction and non-fiction genres.

(A) Some　　　　　　(C) Each
(B) Every　　　　　　(D) Both

その映画製作会社の監督はそれぞれが、フィクションとノンフィクションのさまざまなジャンルの経験を持っています。

語彙チェック　□ a variety of 〜　さまざまな〜

空所は文頭にあり、後ろには述語動詞hasと目的語となる名詞句があるので、------- of the movie production company's directorsが文の主語であると判断できる。述語動詞がhasと三人称単数現在形になっているので、単数扱いの代名詞である(C) Eachが正解。

👑**Level Up !**
代名詞の用法は混ざって覚えてしまいがち。そのあいまいな理解をついてくる問題を取りこぼさないよう、改めておさらいしておこう。

115

A ------- number of drivers using the road will be compelled to take a detour to lower congestion near the construction area.

(A) respectable　　　　(C) respectability
(B) respectably　　　　(D) respective

その道路を利用するかなりの数のドライバーが、工事現場近くの混雑を緩和するために遠回りすることを強いられるでしょう。

語彙チェック　□ compel A to do　Aに無理やり〜させる
□ take a detour　遠回りする

空所は冠詞aと名詞numberの間にあるので、このnumberに説明を加える語が入ると考えられる。形容詞の(A)と(D)が正解候補となるが、文意を考えるとA respectable number of driversで「かなりの数のドライバー」という意味になる(A) respectable「かなりの」が正解。(D) respectiveは「それぞれの」という意味なので、意味が通らない。

116

Mr. Abby, whose first award-winning novel is now getting attention, is planning to hold a talk ------- available online.

(A) substantially　　　　(C) timely
(B) readily　　　　　　　(D) considerably

初めて賞を受賞した自身の小説が今注目を集めているAbbyさんは、オンラインですぐに視聴できる講演を開催する予定です。

空所直後にavailableという形容詞があるので、これを修飾して文意が通る副詞を選ぶ。(B) readily「すぐに」はreadily availableで「すぐに利用できる」となる。a talk readily available online「オンラインですぐに利用できる（視聴できる）講演」という名詞句となり、文意が通るので(B)が正解。(A)は「相当に」、(C)は「間に合って」、(D)は「かなり」という意味。

117

Test audiences for Mick Dunhill's latest film found the production less than -------.

(A) satisfied　　　　　(C) satisfy
(B) satisfaction　　　　(D) satisfying

Mick Dunhill社の最新映画のテスト観客は、その作品が決して満足のいくものではないと分かりました。

語彙チェック □ less than 〜　決して〜でない

空所は、find A B「AがBであると分かる」という表現のBの一部にあたる。つまり、Aにあたるthe production「その作品（＝Mick Dunhill社の最新映画）」がless than ------- であると分かった、となる。(D) satisfying「満足のいく」が空所に入ると、映画が満足のいくものではないと分かった、という文意が通る。

118

Freeman Gym members get 24-hour access and free training consultations, ------- location they choose to use.

(A) where　　　　　(C) whichever
(B) its　　　　　　(D) whose

どの店舗を利用しようとも、Freemanジムの会員は24時間アクセス可能であり、かつ無料のトレーニング相談を受けることができます。

カンマまでに文の要素は揃っており、空所直後には名詞location、さらにその後ろには主語と述語動詞を含む節が続いている。よって、空所にはカンマ前の内容に補足説明を加える副詞節を作る関係詞が入る。「どの〜であろうと」という譲歩の副詞節を作る(C) whicheverを空所に入れると、カンマ以降が「どの店舗を利用しようとも」となり文意が通る。(A) whereは空所直後の名詞locationと結び付かない。

119

Customers spending over $100 ------- to receive a free set of body towels.

(A) accept　　　　　(C) entitle
(B) contribute　　　　(D) deserve

100ドル以上お支払いのお客様は、無料のボディータオルを一式受け取ることができます。

主語は「100ドル以上お支払いのお客様」、to不定詞以降は「無料のボディータオルを一式受け取る」という内容。この内容から、deserve to doで「〜する権利がある」という意味を表す(D) deserveを入れると文意が通る。

👑 **Level Up!**

動詞の語法に注意しよう。(B)は「〜に貢献する」の意味で後ろに前置詞のtoを伴うので、toの後ろに動詞が入る場合は-ing形となる。(C)はentitle A to do「Aに〜する権利を与える」という表現があるが、後ろにAにあたる目的語が必要。

120

Harper Industries has a vacancy at its Waterford Plant for a chemical engineer ------- by the Queensland Industrial Standards Commission.

(A) qualifying　　　　　(C) having qualified
(B) qualified　　　　　(D) was qualified

Harper工業には、Queensland産業基準委員会によって認定された化学エンジニアのポジションの空きがWaterford工場にあります。

この文の主語はHarper Industriesで、述語動詞はhasである。空所前までで目的語となる要素も揃っているので、空所以降は直前の名詞句a chemical engineer「化学エンジニア」を後ろから修飾すると考えられる。「Queensland産業基準委員会によって認定された」と説明を加える形になる、過去分詞の(B) qualifiedが正解。

121

SRT abandoned its plans to expand into Asia ------- concerns that there was not enough demand for its products there.

(A) amid

(B) within

(C) across

(D) through

SRT社は、そこに製品に対する十分な需要がないという懸念の中で、アジアへ進出する計画を断念しました。

語彙チェック ☐ abandon 〜を断念する

空所直後には名詞concerns「懸念」があるので、これと結び付いて意味が通る前置詞を選ぶ。(A) amid「〜の中で」を入れると、amid concernsで「懸念の中で」という意味になり、文意が通る。

👑 **Level Up!**
(B)は距離や期間、程度の範囲内を意味するので、本問では「懸念」と結び付かず不適切。(C)は方向や運動、位置関係など、(D)は場所や時間、手段などを表すので、やはり本問では文意が通らない。

122

Departmental budgets will be decided by the finance director by the end of this week and ------- on January 10.

(A) publishing

(B) publish

(C) publisher

(D) published

部署の予算は今週の終わりまでには財務取締役によって決められ、1月10日には公表されます。

語彙チェック ☐ finance director 財務取締役

空所の前にあるandがポイント。andの前後で何がどう並列されうるかを考える。「(部署の予算は) 決められる→そして公表される」という流れが自然なので、andの後ろに続く語は述語動詞will be decidedのdecidedと並列されると判断できる。よって、過去分詞の(D) publishedが正解。

123

Many of the items in the exhibition are on ------- from the Metropolitan Museum of Antiquity in Boise.

(A) care

(B) display

(C) loan

(D) position

その展覧会の展示品の多くは、Boiseにある Metropolitan 古代博物館から借用中です。

語彙チェック ☐ antiquity 古代

Many of the items in the exhibition が主語、areが述語動詞、空所を含む前置詞on以降は主語の説明をする補語の働きをしている。(C) loan「貸し出し」を入れると、空所前後の前置詞と結び付いてon loan from 〜「〜から借用中で、〜からレンタルして」という意味の表現となり、全体の文意が通る。(B)は前置詞のonと結び付いてon display「展示されて、陳列されて」という意味になるが、from以降とつながらない。(A)は「世話」、(D)は「位置」という意味。

124

In order to boost ------- popularity among young people, Transameri Corp. hired a marketing agency with a reputation for innovation.

(A) that

(B) each

(C) those

(D) its

若者の間での人気を高めるために、Transameri社はイノベーションに定評のあるマーケティング代理店を雇いました。

語彙チェック ☐ boost 〜を高める

空所は動詞boostと名詞popularityの間にあることから、空所は名詞popularityを修飾すると考える。popularityは不可算名詞なので、可算名詞の単数形を修飾する(B) eachと、可算名詞の複数形を修飾する(C) thoseは不適切。(A)は不可算名詞を修飾することもできるが、ここではthatが指す語句がない。よって、所有格の代名詞の(D) itsが正解。its popularityとは、すなわち「Transameri社の人気」のこと。

125

Reception staff should monitor the supply of bottled water in the refrigerator and ------- it whenever necessary.

(A) alert

(B) replenish

(C) observe

(D) dwindle

受付スタッフは冷蔵庫の中にあるボトルに入った水の供給量をチェックして、必要なときはいつでもそれを補充しなければなりません。

接続詞andがあるので、空所には (should) monitorと並列される述語動詞が入ると分かる。空所には主語であるReception staffが取るべき行動として自然な文脈となるものを入れる。直後のitがbottled waterを指していると考え、(B) replenish「〜を補充する」を入れると、「ボトルに入った水を補充する」という内容になり文意が通る。(A)は「〜に注意喚起する」、(C)は「〜を観察する」、(D)は「〜を縮める」という意味。

126

正解 B □□□□　▶TRACK_237

HGT's decision to relocate will affect employees, many of ------- purchased their homes after being hired there.

(A) who　　　　　　(C) which
(B) whom　　　　　 (D) that

移転するという HGT 社の決断は、多くの人が同社に雇用された後に自宅を購入しているので、従業員に影響を及ぼすでしょう。

カンマ以降の節には述語動詞 purchased と、その目的語 their homes はあるが、主語が見当たらない。よって、空所には many of ------- の形で節の主語となる関係代名詞が入ると分かる。前置詞 of の目的語として使える (B) と (C) が正解候補。先行詞は人を表す employees「従業員」なので、(B) whom が正解。

👑 Level Up !
前置詞を伴う関係代名詞の場合 (A) who は使えない。some of や both of などに続く場合も、who ではなく whom を使うことを覚えておこう。

127

正解 A □□□□　▶TRACK_238

Despite its ------- population, Marsden was chosen as the location for the new manufacturing plant.

(A) sparse　　　　　(C) impartial
(B) imminent　　　　(D) acute

まばらな人口にもかかわらず、Marsden は新しい製造工場の建設場所として選ばれました。

文頭に前置詞 despite「～にもかかわらず」があることから、空所を含む前置詞句は、カンマ以降の内容とは逆接の関係になる。よって、(A) sparse「まばらな」を空所に入れると、「人口がまばらなのに建設場所に選ばれた」となり意味が通る。(B) は「差し迫った」、(C) は「公平な」、(D) は「鋭い」という意味。

128

正解 B □□□□　▶TRACK_239

A new dress code policy ------- employees to wear casual clothes except when meeting clients will be effective as of March 8.

(A) is enabling　　　(C) enabled
(B) enabling　　　　(D) enables

顧客と会う場合を除き、従業員がカジュアルな服装をすることを許可する新しい服装規定は、3月8日から有効になります。

後半に will be という述語動詞があるので、clients までがこの文の主語にあたる部分。空所の前には主語となる名詞句 A new dress code policy「新しい服装規定」があるので、空所以降はこれを後ろから修飾していると考えられる。空所の後ろに名詞 employees があるため、これを目的語にとる現在分詞の (B) が正解。

語彙チェック　□ dress code　服装規定
　　　　　　　　 □ effective as of ～　～から有効な

👑 Level Up !
この問題は主語が長く、文構造を見抜くのが難しい。語句は難しくなくても文構造が理解できずに間違えてしまう難問も出題されるので、日頃から素早く文構造を掴む練習をしておこう。

129

正解 D □□□□　▶TRACK_240

Ms. Dalton's ------- action saved the company a lot of money and helped preserve its good reputation.

(A) time　　　　　　(C) timer
(B) timing　　　　　(D) timely

Dalton さんの時宜を得た行動によって、会社は資金を大幅に節約し、良い評判を保つことができました。

空所の前には Ms. Dalton's「Dalton さんの」という所有格の表現、後ろには名詞 action がある。(D) timely「時宜を得た」を入れると Ms. Dalton's timely action「Dalton さんの時宜を得た行動」という名詞句となり、文意が通る。名詞の働きを持つ (A)(B)(C) はいずれも、action と結び付いて意味を成さない。

語彙チェック　□ preserve　～を保つ、～を失わないようにする

130

正解 C □□□□　▶TRACK_241

Survey respondents expressed ------- interest in receiving e-mail updates on special offers from the hotel.

(A) few　　　　　　(C) little
(B) each　　　　　　(D) any

アンケートの回答者は、ホテルからの特別割引に関する最新情報を E メールで受け取ることにほとんど関心を示しませんでした。

空所は述語動詞 expressed の目的語に含まれ、後ろには名詞 interest があるので、空所には interest を修飾して文意が通るものを選ぶ。ここでは interest が「関心」という意味の不可算名詞として用いられているので、不可算名詞を修飾することができる (C) little「ほとんどない」が正解。

Part 6

目標2:00

音読 □ □ □　解答時間 ：　▶　：

Questions 131-134 refer to the following e-mail.

▶TRACK_242

To: Molly Chiang <mchiang@freeducks.com>
From: Greg Smythe <gsmythe@carterindustries.com>
Date: March 23
Subject: Update

Thank you for 131. at Carter Industries. I am happy to inform you that you passed the first stage of the interview process. We would like to invite you back to meet with the head of our technical writing department. We have a couple of 132. available. You can come between 9:00 A.M. and 11:00 A.M. on March 25 or between 1:00 P.M. and 3:00 P.M. on March 26. Please be advised that your appointment will be made on a first come, first served basis as we are currently in contact with other candidates. 133. . When you come, you should remember to bring your parking receipt from last time. We 134. you for the cost of parking.

問題131-134は次のEメールに関するものです。

受信者：Molly Chiang <mchiang@freeducks.com>
送信者：Greg Smythe <gsmythe@carterindustries.com>
日付：3月23日
件名：最新情報

Carter工業にご応募いただきありがとうございます。あなたが一次面接を通過したことをお知らせいたします。テクニカルライティング部門の責任者と面会していただくために、私たちはあなたを再度お招きしたいと思います。空いている時間の枠が2つございます。3月25日の午前9時から午前11時の間か、3月26日の午後1時から午後3時の間にお越しいただくことが可能です。他の候補者の方と現在連絡をとり合っているため、ご予約は先着順とさせていただきますことをご了承ください。*できるだけ早くご希望をお知らせください。お越しの際は、前回の駐車場の領収書を忘れずに持参してください。駐車場代を払い戻しさせていただきます。

語彙チェック　□ appointment　（面会の）予約　□ on a first come, first served basis　先着順で
□ be in contact with ～　～と連絡をとっている　□ candidate　候補者　□ receipt　領収書

131 　正解 **D** ☐☐☐☐

(A) looking
(B) staying
(C) working
(D) applying

(A) 動詞「見る」の動名詞
(B) 動詞「滞在する」の動名詞
(C) 動詞「働く」の動名詞
(D) 動詞「申し込む」の動名詞

「受信者」と「送信者」の欄から、空所の後ろに続く Carter Industries「Carter 工業」に勤める Smythe さんから Chiang さんに送られた E メールだと分かるので、Chiang さんと Carter 工業との関係を把握する。Smythe さんは2文目で、Chiang さんが一次面接を通過したことを伝えている。よって、Chiang さんは Carter 工業の求人に応募したと考えられるので、(D) を空所に入れると文意が通る。誤答は全て空所直後の前置詞 at と結び付く表現を持つが、いずれも文意が通らない。

> 👑 **Level Up !**
>
> 次の面接の案内をしていることから、まだ面接を受けている段階であることが分かるので、(C) は不適切。Part 6 や Part 7 の文書を読むときは、「いつの話をしているのか」「今現在はどういう状況なのか」を意識しながら読むのがコツ。

132 　正解 **C** ☐☐☐☐

(A) vehicles
(B) devices
(C) slots
(D) locations

(A) 名詞「車両」の複数形
(B) 名詞「装置」の複数形
(C) 名詞「(決められた) 時間、枠」の複数形
(D) 名詞「場所」の複数形

空所の直前の a couple of 〜は「2つの〜」という意味の表現。空所の後ろに続く文を見ると接続詞の or があり、日時について2つの選択肢が与えられていることが分かる。よって、「(決められた) 時間、枠」という意味の (C) を入れると、「面接の日時について2つの時間枠から選ぶことができる」という自然な文脈となる。

133 　正解 **A** ☐☐☐☐

(A) Please let me know your preference as soon as possible.
(B) At present we are not looking for a new technical writer.
(C) We will keep your résumé on file in case another position becomes vacant.
(D) We will have our driver pick you up just before noon.

(A) できるだけ早くご希望をお知らせください。
(B) 現在は新しいテクニカルライターは募集していません。
(C) 別のポジションが空いた場合に備えて、あなたの履歴書をファイルに保管しておきます。
(D) ちょうど正午前に、私たちの運転手にあなたを車で迎えに行ってもらう予定です。

空所の前までの話の流れに適したものを選ぶ。次の面接の日時を2つの時間枠から選べることを伝えたあと、空所の直前の文では「他の候補者とも現在連絡をとり合っているため、予約は先着順になる」ということが述べられている。よって、希望の時間帯をできるだけ早く知らせてほしいという旨を伝える、(A) が正解。

語彙チェック ☐ look for 〜　〜を探す　☐ on file　ファイルに保管されて　☐ in case 〜　〜の場合に備えて

134 　正解 **B** ☐☐☐☐

(A) have reimbursed
(B) will reimburse
(C) reimbursed
(D) have been reimbursing

(A) 動詞 reimburse「〜に払い戻す」の現在完了
(B) 助動詞＋動詞の原形
(C) 動詞の過去形
(D) 現在完了進行形

reimburse は他動詞で、reimburse A for B で「A に B を払い戻す」という意味を表す。空所の直後に目的語となる you があるので、能動態が適切であると分かる。また、空所の直前の文から、「払い戻す」のは Chiang さんが次に Carter 工業に面接に来たとき、すなわち未来のことであると分かる。動詞の態と時制の両方の観点から (B) が正解。

Questions 135-138 refer to the following advertisement.

The Scarborough Inn

The Scarborough Inn is Aberdeen's most 135. hotel. Constructed over a hundred years ago, it boasts an elegance and charm unlike any other 136. provider in the area. With only 10 guest rooms, we can afford our guests special attention. This is something our competitors simply cannot 137. . Near the center of town, we are only 500 meters from Aberdeen Greens Golf Course and a short train ride from Tullamore Castle. 138. . Visit the Web site to make a reservation or read reviews from our hundreds of satisfied guests.

www.thescarboroughinn.com
TEL 555 2342

問題135-138は次の広告に関するものです。

Scarborough ホテル

Scarborough ホテルは、Aberdeen で最も豪華なホテルです。100年以上前に建てられたこのホテルは、この地域の他のいかなる宿泊施設とも違った優雅さと魅力を持っています。客室が10部屋しかないので、お客様に特別な配慮をすることができます。これは、競合他社にはとても真似のできないことです。町の中心部の近くに位置し、Aberdeen Greens ゴルフコースからたったの500メートル、Tullamore 城から電車ですぐのところにあります。*後者の入場料は、宿泊費に含まれています。予約をしたり、満足した何百人ものお客様のレビューを読んだりするためには、当ホテルのウェブサイトをご覧ください。

www.thescarboroughinn.com
電話番号 555 2342

語彙チェック □ inn　ホテル　□ boast　（誇らしいもの）を持っている　□ elegance　優雅　□ provider　供給者
□ afford A B　AをBに与える　□ attention　配慮　□ competitor　競合他社　□ hundreds of ~　何百もの~

135 正解 C ▢▢▢▢

(A) modern
(B) sizable
(C) luxurious
(D) secluded

(A) 形容詞「現代の」
(B) 形容詞「かなり大きな」
(C) 形容詞「豪華な」
(D) 形容詞「人里離れた」

👑 **Level Up!**
(A)(B)(D)の不正解の根拠は文書中に散らばっているため、空所の時点では正解を絞れない。全文を読んでから確実な答えを選ぶことがポイント！

空所には、Scarboroughホテルがどのようなホテルなのかについて、適切に説明する形容詞を入れる。2文目の主語itは1文目のThe Scarborough Inn「Scarboroughホテル」を指しており、it boasts an elegance and charm「それ（＝Scarboroughホテル）は優雅さと魅力を持っている」と述べられている。よって、このホテルの特徴を言い換えた(C)が正解。2文目に「100年以上前に建てられた」とあることから(A)は不適切。また、3文目に「客室が10部屋しかない」とあるので、(B)も不適切。さらに、5文目には「町の中心部の近くに位置し」とあることから、(D)も不適切。

136 正解 B ▢▢▢▢

(A) entertainment
(B) accommodation
(C) transportation
(D) amusement

(A) 名詞「娯楽」
(B) 名詞「宿泊設備」
(C) 名詞「輸送」
(D) 名詞「楽しみ」

空所の少し前にあるunlikeは「〜と違って」という意味の前置詞。主語のitは「Scarboroughホテル」のことを指しているので、空所を含むany other ------- provider「他のいかなる ------- 供給者」の部分は、Scarboroughホテルと比較されていることが分かる。よって、accommodation providerで「宿泊設備の供給者」、すなわち「宿泊施設」という意味を表すことができる(B)が正解。

137 正解 A ▢▢▢▢

(A) match
(B) charge
(C) spare
(D) retain

(A) 動詞「〜に匹敵する」
(B) 動詞「〜を請求する」
(C) 動詞「〜を取っておく」
(D) 動詞「〜を保持する」

3文目では「客室が10部屋しかないので、お客様に特別な配慮をすることができる」と述べられている。空所を含む4文目の主語Thisは、この3文目の内容を受けている。文脈から、これはScarboroughホテルの特長であり、お客さんにとっての利点として述べられていることが分かるので、(A)が正解。「客室の少なさゆえにお客様に特別な配慮ができる」ことは、競合他社がScarboroughホテルに敵わない部分である、という大意になり、文意が通る。

138 正解 D ▢▢▢▢

(A) Neither is accessible from The Scarborough Inn.
(B) The grand opening is scheduled for May 10.
(C) Those who book a room during this period will be offered discounts.
(D) Admission to the latter is included with your stay.

(A) どちらもScarboroughホテルからアクセスできません。
(B) グランドオープンは5月10日に予定されています。
(C) この期間に部屋を予約した人には、割引が提供されます。
(D) 後者の入場料は、宿泊費に含まれています。

空所の直前の文では接続詞のandを使って、(only 500 meters from) Aberdeen Greens Golf Course「Aberdeen Greensゴルフコース（からたったの500メートル）」と、(a short train ride from) Tullamore Castle「Tullamore城（から電車ですぐ）」の2つが並列されている。the latter「後者」、すなわち「Tullamore城」を指し、「（ホテルからアクセスの良い）Tullamore城への入場料が宿泊費に含まれている」ことを述べる(D)を空所に入れると、文意が通る。空所の直後の文では宿泊予約に関する話題も出ているので、この点からも宿泊費に言及している(D)は話の流れとして適切。(C)も予約に関する話題だが、during this period「この期間」を指すものが本文にないため、ここでは不適切。

語彙チェック ▢ accessible アクセス可能な ▢ book 〜を予約する ▢ admission 入場料 ▢ the latter 後者

Questions 139-142 refer to the following information.

▶TRACK_244

Wilson Engineering provides some 139. to promote productivity. These can include additional bonus payments or time off work. This only applies to employees who complete their work 140. it is due. In addition to early submissions, you may also obtain favorable evaluations through work quality and general attitude. Supervisors maintain an ongoing record of employee performance. This 141. to determine eligibility for rewards. 142. . A more thorough description of the evaluation criteria and the process is available in the employee handbook.

問題139-142は次の案内に関するものです。

Wilsonエンジニアリング社は、生産性を高めるためにいくつかのインセンティブを提供しています。これらにはボーナスの追加支給や休暇が含まれることがあります。これは、期日前に仕事を完了させた従業員にのみ適用されます。また、早期の提出に加え、仕事の質や総合的な態度によっても、好意的な評価を得ることができるかもしれません。上司は従業員の業績の継続的な記録をつけます。これは、報酬を受ける資格を判断するために利用されます。*もし自身の評価に不満がある場合は、人事部に連絡することも可能です。評価基準とその方法のより詳細な説明は、従業員ハンドブックに記載されています。

語彙チェック □ apply to〜 〜にあてはまる、〜に適用される □ due 期限が来て □ obtain 〜を得る □ favorable 好意的な □ supervisor 上司 □ ongoing 継続的な □ determine 〜を判断する □ eligibility 適格 □ reward 報酬 □ thorough 詳細な □ description 説明 □ criteria 基準

139

(A) incentives
(B) penalties
(C) laws
(D) installments

正解 **A** ☐☐☐☐

(A) 名詞「インセンティブ」の複数形
(B) 名詞「ペナルティー」の複数形
(C) 名詞「法律」の複数形
(D) 名詞「分割払い込み金」の複数形

Wilson エンジニアリング社が、生産性を高めるために何を提供しているのかを文脈から把握する。選択肢には全て名詞の複数形が並んでいるので、2文目の主語Theseは空所に入る名詞を指していることが分かる。2文目の内容は「これらにはボーナスの追加支給や休暇が含まれることがある」というもの。よって、「ボーナスの追加支給」や「休暇」が空所に入る名詞の具体例として述べられていると考えられるので、これを抽象的に言い換えた(A)が正解。

140

(A) while
(B) when
(C) once
(D) before

正解 **D** ☐☐☐☐

(A) 接続詞「～している間に」
(B) 接続詞「～するときに」
(C) 接続詞「いったん～すると」
(D) 接続詞「～する前に」

空所は、インセンティブが与えられるのはどのような従業員なのかを説明する、関係代名詞節のwhoの中にある。空所の後ろのitは their workを指していることに注意。インセンティブが与えられるのは、「期日が来る前に」仕事を完了させた従業員である、という意味になる(D)を空所に入れると文意が通る。

141

(A) was being used
(B) is used
(C) has used
(D) is using

正解 **B** ☐☐☐☐

(A) 動詞use「～を利用する」の過去進行形の受動態
(B) 現在形の受動態
(C) 現在完了
(D) 現在進行形

主語のThisは、前文のan ongoing record of employee performance「従業員の業績の継続的な記録」を指している。useは「～を利用する」という他動詞だが、空所の後ろに目的語となる名詞がないので、ここでは「記録は利用される」という意味の受動態の文ではないかと考える。正解候補は(A)と(B)に絞られるが、空所までの動詞の時制や話の内容から、現在形の(B)が正解。空所の後ろのto不定詞は、従業員の業績の記録を利用する「目的」を表している。

142

(A) This generally makes our suppliers more competitive in terms of service and pricing.
(B) Unfortunately, the company cannot provide any financial benefits at this time.
(C) You may contact human resources if you are unsatisfied with your assessment.
(D) We are unable to share the details about how this decision is made.

正解 **C** ☐☐☐☐

(A) サービスと価格設定の点から、これは全般的に私たちの供給業者をより競争力のあるものにします。
(B) 残念ながら今回は、会社は金銭的な利益を提供することができません。
(C) もし自身の評価に不満がある場合は、人事部に連絡することも可能です。
(D) この決定がどのようになされるかについて、詳細を共有することはできません。

空所の前後の流れに適したものを選ぶ。空所の前まででは、インセンティブの評価に関わる項目として、「仕事を早く仕上げること」や「仕事の質」、「総合的な態度」、さらには「上司によってつけられる従業員の業績の記録」などが述べられている。一方、空所の後ろの文では、「評価基準とその方法のより詳細な説明は、従業員ハンドブックに記載されている」とある。よって、assessment「評価」について述べられている(C)が正解。

👑 **Level Up!**
空所の前文のdetermine「～を判断する、～を決定する」につられて、this decision「この決定」という言葉を含む(D)に惑わされないように注意！

語彙チェック ☐ competitive 競争力のある ☐ in terms of ～ ～の点で ☐ assessment 評価

Questions 143-146 refer to the following notice.

Notice

143.. We apologize for the short notice. We sincerely regret any inconvenience this causes our regular customers. Fortunately, the kitchen will remain operational 144. the closure. Therefore, there will be no interruption to take-out orders. 145., we will still be accepting delivery orders from our partners at Deliverystar and NomNoms. You may call our reservations line to make table bookings, which will be available from June 18. We hope that you come and enjoy our all-new interior and amenities. To celebrate the improvements, we 146. 20 % off all menu items until the end of June.

問題143-146は次のお知らせに関するものです。

お知らせ

＊Seashellsレストランは、6月2日から6月17日の間は営業しません。急なお知らせに関してお詫び申し上げます。これによって常連のお客様にご迷惑をおかけし、誠に申し訳ございません。幸いにも、厨房は閉店中もずっと稼働しております。したがって、テイクアウトの注文には中断はございません。さらに、DeliverystarやNomNomsのパートナースタッフによる宅配注文も、変わらず受け付ける予定です。お席のご予約は予約受付窓口へのお電話にて承りますが、そちらは6月18日より利用可能になります。ご来店いただき、当店のまったく新しいインテリアや快適な設備をお楽しみください。建物のリフォームを記念して、6月末まで全メニュー20パーセント割引を提供いたします。

語彙チェック　□ short notice　急な知らせ　□ sincerely　心から　□ inconvenience　迷惑　□ fortunately　幸いにも　□ interruption　休止、中断　□ all-new　まったく新しい　□ amenities　快適な設備

143

正解 C ☐☐☐☐

(A) Circle Bookstore is moving to a new location on Hillview Road.
(B) Arena Furniture is looking to hire temporary staff for the first week of June.
(C) Seashells restaurant will not be open between June 2 and June 17.
(D) Crystal Café is proud to announce the opening of its second location.

(A) Circle 書店は、Hillview 通りにある新しい店舗に移転する予定です。
(B) Arena 家具店は、6月の最初の週に臨時職員を雇うつもりです。
(C) Seashells レストランは、6月2日から6月17日の間は営業しません。
(D) Crystal カフェは2つ目の店舗の開店をお知らせいたします。

空所は文書の冒頭にあるので、空所の後ろの文から正解の根拠を探す。4文目に、the kitchen という単語が出てくることに注目。ここから(C)の「レストラン」と(D)の「カフェ」に正解を絞ることができる。また、4文目には the closure という単語もあり、これが2・3文目で述べられているお客さんへの謝罪の理由であると考えられることから、一定期間閉店することを伝えている(C)が正解。

語彙チェック ☐ move to 〜　〜に移転する　☐ temporary　臨時の

144

正解 B ☐☐☐☐

(A) by
(B) during
(C) among
(D) ever since

(A) 前置詞「〜によって」
(B) 前置詞「〜の間中」
(C) 前置詞「〜の間に」
(D) 「それ以来ずっと」

空所を含む4文目の文頭に Fortunately「幸いにも」とあることに注目。これは、3文目の inconvenience this causes our regular customers「このことが常連のお客様にもたらすご迷惑」を受け、そのような状況下でもお客さんにとって良いニュースとなり得る内容が、4文目に述べられているということのヒントになる。よって、「厨房は閉店中もずっと稼働している」という意味になる(B)が正解。これは閉店期間中の良いニュースであると考えられ、文頭の Fortunately とも合う。

145

正解 D ☐☐☐☐

(A) Nevertheless
(B) In contrast
(C) Finally
(D) Furthermore

(A) 副詞「それにもかかわらず」
(B) 「対照的に」
(C) 副詞「最後に」
(D) 副詞「さらに」

空所の前後の流れから、文脈に適したものを選ぶ。空所の前の3・4文目では、「閉店中も厨房はずっと稼働していること」と、それによって「テイクアウトの注文は閉店中も利用可能であること」が述べられている。一方、空所の後ろでは、「宅配注文も変わらず受け付ける予定であること」について述べられている。よって、空所前後は閉店中に利用できるサービスの説明が列挙されているということが分かるので、「テイクアウトの注文」に加えて「宅配注文」も利用できるという文脈になる(D)が正解。

146

正解 A ☐☐☐☐

(A) will be offering
(B) had offered
(C) have been offering
(D) will be offered

(A) 助動詞＋動詞 offer「〜を提供する」の進行形
(B) 過去完了
(C) 現在完了の進行形
(D) 助動詞＋受動態

offer は「〜を提供する」という意味の他動詞。空所の後ろには目的語となる名詞句があるので、ここでは受動態ではなく能動態が適切だと分かる。正解候補の(A)(B)(C)は全て時制が異なるので、時制の観点から正解を絞っていく。空所の前の文に「ご来店いただき、当店のまったく新しいインテリアや快適な設備をお楽しみください」とあり、the improvements はこれを指していると分かる。また、さらにその前の文では、「予約は6月18日から可能になる」ことが未来を表す助動詞 will を使って述べられている。よって、空所には未来を表す時制が適切だと分かるので、(A)が正解。

Part 7

目標2:00

音読 □□□ 解答時間 : ▶ :

Questions 147-148 refer to the following e-mail.

▶TRACK_246

From:	Starwing Online Shopping — Customer Service
To:	Ralph Bennis
Date:	23 June
Subject:	Your order

Hello Ralph,

Have you made up your mind? ❶Your Try-Before-You-Buy one-week try-on period ends tomorrow. ❷If you are not completely happy with your order, you have until 11:59 P.M. tomorrow to send back the unwanted item or items. Otherwise, we'll assume you are satisfied with your items and have decided to keep them. You will be charged accordingly.

Quantity	Description	Unit Price	Item Total
1	❸Business Shoes	$76.00	$76.00
2	Leather Belt	$34.00	$68.00
1	Business Shirt	$25.00	$25.00
2	Winter vest	$17.00	$34.00
	Merchandise Subtotal:		$203.00
	Goods and Services Tax:		$10.15
	TOTAL:		$213.15

*❹Please note that this does not apply to footwear. Purchases in this category are final and refunds are only issued in cases where the products are defective.

問題147-148は次のEメールに関するものです。

送信者：Starwing オンラインショッピング ― カスタマーサービス
受信者：Ralph Bennis
日付：6月23日
件名：ご注文の件

Ralph 様

もうお決まりでしょうか。ご購入前の1週間のお試し期間は明日で終了します。もしご注文に完全に満足いただけない場合は、明日の午後11時59分までに、不要な商品をご返送ください。そうでなければ、商品に満足してお引き取りいただいたと判断いたします。それに応じた請求がなされます。

数量	品目	単価	項目合計
1	ビジネスシューズ	76.00ドル	76.00ドル
2	革ベルト	34.00ドル	68.00ドル
1	ビジネスシャツ	25.00ドル	25.00ドル
2	冬用ベスト	17.00ドル	34.00ドル
	商品小計：		203.00ドル
	商品およびサービス税：		10.15ドル
	合計：		213.15ドル

*こちらは履物には適用されませんのでご注意ください。このカテゴリーでのご購入は最終的なものであり、返金は商品に欠陥がある場合のみ行われます。

語彙チェック □ make up *one's* mind 決心する □ completely 完全に □ unwanted 不必要な □ assume ～を想定する
□ accordingly それに応じて

147

正解 A ☐☐☐☐

What is the purpose of the e-mail?

(A) To remind a customer of a deadline

(B) To announce that a shipment has taken place

(C) To notify a customer of a product recall

(D) To issue a refund for some goods

Eメールの目的は何ですか。

(A) 顧客に締め切りを思い出させること

(B) 出荷が行われたことを知らせること

(C) 製品回収をお客様に通知すること

(D) 商品の返金を行うこと

送信者の欄から、このEメールはオンラインショッピングのカスタマーサービスからであると分かる。また、受信者の欄と件名の「ご注文の件」から、Ralphという顧客に向けてのEメールであることも分かる。本文を見ていくと、❶で「ご購入前の1週間のお試し期間は明日で終了する」と商品のお試し期間の期限を伝えており、❷では「明日の午後11時59分までに、不要な商品を返送してほしい」とある。よって、このEメールの目的は締め切りを再確認させることだと判断できるので、(A)が正解。❹で返金について言及しているが、返金の手続きを行っているわけではないので(D)は不正解。

語彙チェック ☐ remind *A* of *B* AにBを思い出させる ☐ notify *A* of *B* AにBを通知する ☐ recall （欠陥商品の）回収

148

正解 A ☐☐☐☐

According to the e-mail, how much has Mr. Bennis already been charged?

(A) $76.00

(B) $68.00

(C) $203.00

(D) $213.15

Eメールによると、Bennisさんはすでにいくら請求されていますか。

(A) 76.00ドル

(B) 68.00ドル

(C) 203.00ドル

(D) 213.15ドル

❹の1文目のthisとは「ご購入前の1週間のお試し期間」のサービスのことであり、このお試し期間は「履物には適用されない」とある。続く2文目には、「このカテゴリーでの購入は最終的なものであり、返金は商品に欠陥がある場合のみ行われる」とあり、履物のお試し期間はなく、購入済みとみなされると述べられている。表では、履物は❸のビジネスシューズのみ。よって、すでに76.00ドルが請求されていると分かり、(A)が正解。

Questions 149-150 refer to the following text-message chain.

▶TRACK_247

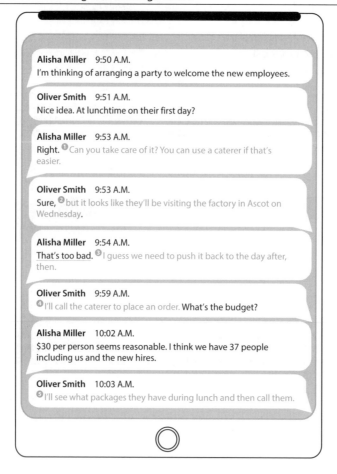

問題149-150は次のテキストメッセージのやりとりに関するものです。

Alisha Miller [午前9時50分]
新入社員を歓迎するパーティーを企画しようかと考えているんです。

Oliver Smith [午前9時51分]
いい考えですね。初日のお昼休憩にですか。

Alisha Miller [午前9時53分]
そうです。あなたに任せてもいいですか。ケータリングを使う方が楽であればそれでも構いません。

Oliver Smith [午前9時53分]
もちろんです、ですが彼らは水曜日にAscotの工場を訪問するみたいです。

Alisha Miller [午前9時54分]
それは残念ですね。それなら、翌日に延期した方がよさそうですね。

Oliver Smith [午前9時59分]
ケータリング会社に電話して注文します。予算はいくらですか。

Alisha Miller [午前10時02分]
一人あたり30ドルが妥当だと思います。私たちと新入社員を含めて37人だと思うのですが。

Oliver Smith [午前10時03分]
昼食の間にどんなパッケージがあるか調べてみて、それから電話します。

語彙チェック □ arrange　〜を準備する　□ take care of 〜　〜を引き受ける　□ caterer　ケータリング業者
□ push 〜 back　〜を延ばす

149

正解 **C** □□□□

At 9:54 A.M., why does Ms. Miller write, "That's too bad"?

(A) The business is understaffed.
(B) There is a problem at the factory.
(C) There is a scheduling conflict.
(D) The budget for the party is insufficient.

午前9時54分に、なぜMillerさんは "That's too bad" という発言をしていますか。

(A) 企業は人手不足である。
(B) 工場に問題がある。
(C) スケジュールが合わない。
(D) パーティーの予算が不足している。

新入社員歓迎会を彼らが来る初日に開催しようと考えているAlishaさんに対し、Oliverさんは❷で「彼らは水曜日にAscotの工場を訪問するみたいだ」と新入社員の初日の予定を伝えており、下線部の発言はそれに応答するものである。続く❸では、「それなら、翌日に延期した方がよさそうだ」と日程を変更することを述べている。新入社員歓迎会を水曜日にするのは都合が悪く開催できないため、残念だと述べていると判断できる。よって、(C)が正解。

語彙チェック □ understaffed　人員不足の　□ insufficient　不十分な

150

正解 **B** □□□□

What will Mr. Smith most likely do this afternoon?
(A) Interview a candidate
(B) Place a food order
(C) Respond to an invitation
(D) Make a restaurant reservation

Smithさんは今日の午後に何をすると考えられますか。
(A) 候補者と面接する
(B) 料理の注文をする
(C) 招待に返答する
(D) レストランを予約する

Alishaさんは❶でOliverさんに新入社員歓迎会の準備を頼み、「ケータリングを使っても構わない」と伝えている。❹でOliverさんは「ケータリング会社に電話して注文する」と発言し、予算と人数を聞いた後に❺で「昼食の間にどんなパッケージがあるか調べてみて、それから電話する」と述べている。Oliverさんは昼食後に、新入社員歓迎会用の料理をケータリング会社に頼むと考えられるので、(B)が正解。

👑 **Level Up!**
Smithさんの中盤の発言と最後の発言から分かる情報を組み合わせて解く問題。会話の流れを追い、情報を整理しながら読もう。

To:	All Staff
From:	Ted Dawson
Date:	December 20
Subject:	Tomorrow

To all staff:

❶We have received some reports about intermittent problems with the building's front door. From time to time, it is failing to open automatically. ❷We have called the manufacturer and expect someone to come out to take a look at it tomorrow. The work will probably take all day. **From previous experience,** ❸we have learned that the door and the escalators are on the same circuit. It will almost certainly be necessary to disconnect both. ❹Fortunately, the building's main stairway and the elevator will remain available.

We will post signs at the door to tell visitors to use the manual door at the front of the building. Guests using the basement parking lot will not need to use the escalator or the door, so no notification will be necessary.

I will send an update as soon as we have more information.

Sincerely,

Ted Dawson
Management

問題151-152は次のEメールに関するものです。

受信者：全従業員
送信者：Ted Dawson
日付：12月20日
件名：明日

全従業員へ

ビルのフロントドアに断続的な不具合があるとの報告を受けました。時々、自動で開かなくなることがあります。メーカーに連絡し、明日には誰かが見に来てくれる予定です。作業はおそらく一日がかりになりそうです。以前の経験から、このドアとエスカレーターは同じ回路にあることが分かっています。ほぼ間違いなく、両方を停止する必要があります。幸い、ビルのメインの階段とエレベーターは使用可能なままです。

ビル正面の手動ドアをお客様にご利用いただくよう伝えるため、ドアに看板を掲示する予定です。地下駐車場をご利用のお客様は、エスカレーターやドアをご利用になる必要はありませんので、通知は不要です。

詳細な情報が入り次第、最新情報をお送りします。

敬具

Ted Dawson
マネジメント

語彙チェック □ intermittent 断続的な □ from time to time 時々 □ fail to *do* ～することができない
□ automatically 自動的に □ previous 以前の □ circuit 電気回路 □ certainly 確かに
□ disconnect ～を停止する □ fortunately 幸運にも □ stairway 階段 □ post ～を掲示する
□ manual 手動の □ notification 通知

151

正解 **C** □□□□

What will probably happen tomorrow?

(A) Some important guests will arrive.

(B) A sign will be updated.

(C) Some maintenance will be implemented.

(D) A report will be submitted.

明日におそらく何が起こりますか。

(A) 重要なお客様が到着する。

(B) 看板が更新される。

(C) メンテナンスが行われる。

(D) 報告書が提出される。

❶の1文目で「フロントドアに断続的な不具合があるとの報告を受けた」と述べ、同2文目で「自動で開かなくなる」と不具合の説明をしている。❷では「メーカーに連絡し、明日には誰かが見に来てくれる予定だ」と修理業者が来ることを伝えた後、同2文目で「作業はおそらく一日がかりになる」と述べている。明日に修理業者が来て、ドアのメンテナンス作業が行われると考えられるので、(C)が正解。

語彙チェック □ implement ～を実行する

152

正解 **D** □□□□

What will employees be restricted from doing tomorrow?

(A) Entering through the manual door

(B) Riding on the elevator

(C) Parking in the basement

(D) Using the escalators

明日、従業員は何をすることを制限されますか。

(A) 手動ドアから入ること

(B) エレベーターに乗ること

(C) 地下に駐車すること

(D) エスカレーターを使うこと

❸の「このドアとエスカレーターは同じ回路にある」「両方を停止する必要がある」という内容から、明日のドアの修理作業時にはドアと同じ回路にあるエスカレーターの電源も停止しなければならないと予想できる。続く❹では、「幸い、ビルのメインの階段とエレベーターは使用可能なままだ」と述べていることから、ドアとエスカレーターは使用できないと考えられるので、(D)が正解。エレベーターやビル正面の手動ドア、地下駐車場について言及はされているが、全て利用可能なので(A)(B)(C)は不適切。

語彙チェック □ restrict A from doing Aが～することを制限する □ enter ～に入る

Questions 153-154 refer to the following schedule.

	Workshop: Improving The Client Experience ❶23 June (Day One) 10:00 A.M. ~ 5:00 P.M. $250 per person
10:00 A.M.:	Session 1: Satisfying clients more ❷ Max Fielding from the University of Lancaster will lead a discussion on the kind of issues that cause client dissatisfaction. There are certain themes that many companies fail to consider in staff training.
11:00 A.M.:	❸Session 2: Meeting customers' needs Learn to use various techniques to get accurate feedback from customers in a timely manner. This session is designed to give you the tools you need to identify problems before they become serious.
12:10 P.M.:	Lunch Break ❹ Enjoy a buffet lunch at Salinger's on the conference center's first floor.
1:30 P.M.:	Session 3: Learning from mistakes We will review various case studies from businesses that have had to resurrect their reputations after a client relations mishap. Workshop leaders with years of experience in private enterprise will discuss how these strategies can be adapted to your business.
3:30 P.M.:	Session 4: Raising employees' awareness Learn ways to make your employees more mindful of the client experience, and to maintain that awareness in the day-to-day running of the business.

問題153-154は次の予定表に関するものです。

	ワークショップ：顧客体験の向上 6月23日 (初日) 午前10時～午後5時 お一人様250ドル
午前10時00分：	セッション1：顧客をより満足させる Lancaster大学のMax Fieldingが顧客の不満の原因となる問題点について議論を先導します。多くの企業が職員研修で考慮できていない特定のテーマがあります。
午前11時00分：	セッション2：顧客のニーズに応える 顧客からの正確なフィードバックをタイムリーに得るための様々なテクニックを学びます。このセッションは、問題が深刻になる前に、問題を特定するために必要な手段を提供することを意図しています。
午後12時10分：	お昼休憩 会議場1階のSalinger'sでランチバイキングをお楽しみください。
午後1時30分：	セッション3：失敗から学ぶ 顧客との関係で失敗した後、評判を回復させなければならなかった企業の様々なケーススタディを見直します。民間企業での長年の経験を持つワークショップリーダーが、これらの戦略をどのようにあなたのビジネスに適応させることができるかを議論します。
午後3時30分：	セッション4：従業員の意識を高める 従業員に顧客体験を意識させ、日々の業務運営でその意識を維持する方法を学びます。

語彙チェック □ tool 手段 □ identify ～をつきとめる □ resurrect ～を復活させる □ mishap 災難 □ private 民間の
□ adapt A to B AをBに適合させる □ mindful 注意する □ day-to-day 毎日の

153

Which session is likely to involve the use of surveys?

(A) Session 1
(B) Session 2
(C) Session 3
(D) Session 4

アンケートの利用が伴うと考えられるセッションはどれですか。

(A) セッション1
(B) セッション2
(C) セッション3
(D) セッション4

❸より、セッション2は顧客からのフィードバックがテーマだと分かる。また、「この
セッションは、……問題を特定するために必要な手段を提供する」とあるので、ア
ンケートの利用が伴う可能性が高いと推測できる。よって、(B)が正解。

▼ Level Up!

このような具体的な情報を問う設問には、時
間をかけすぎないことがポイント。
survey「アンケート」に関連する
キーワードがないか、文書を検索
するつもりで読んでいこう。

154

What is NOT implied about the workshop?

(A) It will be led by experts.
(B) It will be held in a convention center.
(C) It is intended specifically for small businesses.
(D) It is a multiple-day event.

ワークショップについて示唆されていないことは何ですか。

(A) 専門家によって指導される。
(B) 会議場で開催される。
(C) 特に中小企業のために意図されている。
(D) 複数日にわたるイベントである。

❷に「Lancaster大学のMax Fieldingが顧客の不満の原因となる問題点について議論を先導する」とあるので、これを専門家による
指導と言い換えた(A)は不正解。❹に「会議場1階のSalinger'sでランチバイキングをお楽しみください」とあり、会場は会議場だと
分かるので(B)も不正解。❶に「6月23日(初日)」とあることから、ワークショップは6月23日以外にも行われると分かり、(D)も示
唆されているため不正解。中小企業向けのワークショップについては言及されていないので、残る(C)が正解。

WILSON ATHLETICA ANNOUNCES NEW FACTORY LOCATION

MONROE, February 7 — Wilson Athletica is a world-renowned brand with many award-winning products in its lineup. It comes as a shock to many when they learn that the company is based in Monroe Oregon, a small rural town far from transportation hubs. In fact, Monroe has been the location of the company's only manufacturing facility. The facility has grown steadily over the years and now employs more than half of the town's population.

❶Today, CEO Don Wilson announced that the company will be building a new factory in Seattle. ❷"We simply can't keep up with demand at our current factory," Wilson explained. "Even if we expanded that plant, there wouldn't be enough people in the area to run it." According to a press release, work on the new factory will begin in March. ❸The company plans to have its grand opening just before the new year. ❹Even though the new factory will be almost twice the size of the current one, the company's headquarters will remain in Monroe.

The company will be hiring new staff in Seattle in early November. Training will be divided between the company's two locations so that staff is ready to start work as soon as the factory opens. The news has excited many local businesses who hope to benefit from partnerships with Wilson Athletica. These include the Seattle Diamonds football team, which is looking for a new sponsor.

問題155-157は次の記事に関するものです。

WILSON ATHLETICA が新しい工場地を発表

MONROE、2月7日―Wilson Athletica 社は、ラインナップに多くの受賞歴のある製品を持つ世界的に有名なブランドである。しかし、同社がOregon 州のMonroe という、交通の中心から離れた小さな田舎町に拠点を置いていることを知ると、多くの人が衝撃を受ける。実は、Monroe は同社の唯一の製造施設がある場所なのだ。この施設は長年にわたって着々と成長し、今では町の人口の半分以上を雇用している。

今日、CEOのDon Wilson は、同社がSeattle に新しい工場を建設することを発表した。「現在の工場では、需要に追いつけないのです」とWilson は説明した。「たとえあの工場を拡張しても、この地域にはそれを管理するのに十分な人員がいないのです」。プレスリリースによると、新工場の建設作業は3月に開始される。同社は新年の直前にグランドオープンを予定している。新しい工場は現在の工場の約2倍の大きさになるが、本社はMonroe のままである。

11月上旬にはSeattle で新入社員を採用する予定だ。工場がオープンしたらすぐに仕事が始められるように、研修は2つの拠点に分けられる。このニュースは、Wilson Athletica 社との提携により利益を期待する多くの地元企業を興奮させた。その中には、新しいスポンサーを探しているフットボールチームのSeattle Diamonds も含まれている。

語彙チェック □ world-renowned　世界的に知られた　□ hub　中枢　□ steadily　着々と　□ simply　単に　□ demand　需要　□ current　今の　□ expand　〜を拡張する　□ divide　〜を分ける　□ benefit　利益を得る　□ partnership　提携

155

正解 B ☐☐☐☐

Why is Wilson Athletica most likely opening a factory in Seattle?

(A) To have access to a larger market

(B) To take advantage of a larger workforce

(C) To facilitate a merger with a major competitor

(D) To be closer to professional sports teams

Wilson Athletica 社はなぜ、Seattle に工場を開設すると考えられますか。

(A) より大きな市場にアクセスできるようにするため

(B) より多くの労働力を活用するため

(C) 主要な競争相手との合併を促進するため

(D) プロのスポーツチームに近づけるため

❶で「同社が Seattle に新しい工場を建設することを発表した」と述べた後に、❷で「現在の工場では、需要に追いつけない」と理由を説明している。また、同2文目では「たとえあの工場を拡張しても、この地域にはそれを管理するのに十分な人員がいない」とあり、田舎町の Monroe では人員が不足していると判断できる。現在より多くの労働力を手に入れるため Seattle に工場を開設すると考えられるので、(B) が正解。

語彙チェック ☐ facilitate ～を促進する

156

正解 D ☐☐☐☐

When most likely will the new plant open?

(A) In February

(B) In March

(C) In November

(D) In December

新しい工場のオープンはいつになると考えられますか。

(A) 2月

(B) 3月

(C) 11月

(D) 12月

❶では新しい工場の建設予定について発表があったことが述べられ、❸には「同社は新年の直前にグランドオープンを予定している」とある。新年の直前ということは12月に工場がオープンすると分かるので、(D) が正解。3月はオープンではなく、建設作業が開始される時期なので (B) は不適切。

157

正解 C ☐☐☐☐

What is implied about Mr. Wilson?

(A) He plans to retire soon.

(B) He wrote the company's press release.

(C) He will remain at the Monroe office.

(D) He sponsors various sporting teams.

Wilson さんについて何が示唆されていますか。

(A) 彼はまもなく引退する予定である。

(B) 彼は会社のプレスリリースを書いた。

(C) 彼は Monroe の事業所に残る。

(D) 彼は様々なスポーツチームのスポンサーをしている。

❹に「新しい工場は現在の工場の約2倍の大きさになるが、本社は Monroe のままである」とあり、Monroe の工場が中心的役割を果たすことに変わりはないと分かる。CEO である Wilson さんは本社に居続ける可能性が高いので、(C) が正解。記事の最終文でスポンサーについて触れられているが、Wilson さんがスポーツチームのスポンサーをしているわけではないので (D) は不正解。

MEMO

To: All Corden Appliances Employees
From: Helen Taylor
Date: September 18

❶The annual employee appreciation banquet will be held on October 10 this year. ❷We have chosen Belvedere Hotel as the location. **The banquet will start at 7:00 P.M.** ❸Cranston City is currently suffering from a parking shortage, so we imagine that many employees might be opposed to attending due to the inconvenience. **For that reason,** ❹we will be providing a bus from the office to the Belvedere Hotel. It will leave here at 5:30 P.M. The return bus will depart the hotel at 9:00 P.M. ❺Alternatively, for people living in the southern suburbs, we will be providing ferry tickets so that they can park their vehicles on Maddon Point and use the ferry service to get to the hotel.

As in previous years, the company will subsidize the event by paying half of the cost. ❻Employees will be charged $30 per head to take part. Please put it in an envelope and hand it directly to Mr. Rose in the General Affairs Department by the day before the event. If you will be unable to attend the banquet, it is necessary to inform him by October 1.

I look forward to seeing you that night!

問題158-160は次のメモに関するものです。

メモ

宛先：Corden 電化製品従業員一同
差出人：Helen Taylor
日付：9月18日

毎年恒例の社員慰安会は、今年は10月10日に開催されます。場所はBelvedereホテルに決定しました。宴会は午後7時から始まります。Cranston市は現在、駐車場不足に悩まされており、不便さから出席を拒む社員が多いのではないかと思います。そのため、オフィスからBelvedereホテルまでのバスを用意することにしました。バスはここを午後5時30分に出発します。帰りのバスは午後9時にホテルを出発します。また、南部郊外にお住まいの方には、Maddon岬に車を停めてフェリーを利用してホテルまで来ていただけるよう、フェリーチケットをご用意する予定です。

例年通り、会社が費用の半額を負担することでイベントの援助をします。社員は一人あたり30ドルの参加費が請求されます。封筒に入れ、イベント前日までに総務部のRoseさんに直接お渡しください。もし宴会に参加できない場合は、10月1日までに彼にその旨を連絡する必要があります。

当日の夜、お会いできるのを楽しみにしています！

語彙チェック □ appreciation 感謝 □ banquet 宴会 □ suffer from ～ ～に苦しむ
□ be opposed to *doing* ～することに反対している □ attend 出席する □ alternatively また □ point 岬
□ subsidize ～を援助する □ per head 一人あたり □ hand ～を渡す

158 正解 D ☐☐☐☐

What is one purpose of the memo?

(A) To thanks employees for their hard work
(B) To announce the commencement of a new project
(C) To inform employees of a change of date
(D) To provide details of transportation options

メモの目的の1つは何ですか。

(A) 従業員の労をねぎらうこと
(B) 新しいプロジェクトの開始を発表すること
(C) 日付の変更を従業員に知らせること
(D) 交通手段の選択肢の詳細を提供すること

❹に「オフィスからBelvedereホテルまでのバスを用意する」とあり、その後も行き帰りのバスの時刻について述べられている。❺では「南部郊外に住んでいる人には、Maddon岬に車を停めてフェリーを利用してホテルまで来れるよう、フェリーチケットを用意する予定だ」とバス以外の交通手段について言及している。バスとフェリーの詳細について知らせていると分かるので、(D)が正解。

語彙チェック ☐ commencement　開始

159 正解 A ☐☐☐☐

What is implied about the Belvedere Hotel?

(A) It is located in Cranston City.
(B) It does not offer guest parking.
(C) It has previously hosted Corden Appliances events.
(D) It will not accept alterations to its reservations.

Belvedereホテルについて何が示唆されていますか。

(A) Cranston市内に位置している。
(B) 来客用駐車場を提供していない。
(C) 以前、Corden電化製品のイベントを開催した。
(D) 予約の変更を受け付けていない。

❷で「場所はBelvedereホテルに決定した」と社員慰安会の会場を伝えている。❸では「Cranston市は現在、駐車場不足に悩まされており、不便さから出席を拒む社員が多いのではないかと思う」とある。よって、社員慰安会の会場であるBelvedereホテルはCranston市にあると判断できるので、(A)が正解。

語彙チェック ☐ alteration　変更

160 正解 C ☐☐☐☐

By when should employees pay the participation fee?

(A) September 18
(B) October 1
(C) October 9
(D) October 10

従業員はいつまでに参加費を支払うべきですか。

(A) 9月18日
(B) 10月1日
(C) 10月9日
(D) 10月10日

❻で、「社員は一人あたり30ドルの参加費が請求される」と参加費について言及された後、「封筒に入れ、イベント前日までに総務部のRoseさんに直接渡してほしい」との説明がある。❶より、社員慰安会は10月10日に開催されると分かり、その前日は10月9日なので(C)が正解。

GEOMAX HOME AUTOMATION
Merchandise Return Instructions

❶Congratulations on your purchase of a quality product from Geomax Home Automation. We are the world's most respected name in voice-operated switches and lights.

❷If you experience any problems with your Geomax device, please call the customer support line before requesting a refund or a return. —[1]— . Our highly trained customer support staff will try to solve any problems you are experiencing with your device. ❸If we are unable to resolve the issue, we will provide you with a reference number which you can pass on to the seller, who will arrange a refund or a replacement. —[2]— .

Please note that the warranty period is 12 months from the date of purchase. —[3]— . ❹Depending on the age of the device and the nature of the problem, customer service staff may ask for proof of purchase. You can do this by providing either your receipt or the warranty card included with these instructions. —[4]— .

Before contacting our customer support line please try the following:
1. Unplug the device and wait 10 seconds before plugging it back in.
2. With the device plugged in, hold down the power button for five seconds.
3. Try using the device on a different power outlet.
4. Look for solutions to problems by visiting the support section of our Web site.

The telephone number for our customer support line is 800 555 3342.
Our customer support page is at www.geomaxha.com/support

問題161-163は次の説明書に関するものです。

GEOMAX ホームオートメーション
商品返品に関する説明書

Geomax ホームオートメーションの高品質な製品をお買い上げいただき、誠にありがとうございます。弊社は、音声で操作するスイッチや照明において、世界で最も高い評価を受けている企業です。

Geomax のデバイスに何らかの問題が発生した場合、返金または返品を依頼する前に、カスタマーサポートラインにお電話ください。高度な訓練を受けたカスタマーサポートスタッフが、お客様のデバイスに発生している問題の解決に努めます。問題を解決できない場合は、参照番号をお知らせしますので、それを販売元にお伝えいただければ、販売元が返金または交換を手配いたします。

保証期間はご購入日から12カ月間となりますのでご注意ください。デバイスの年数や問題の性質によっては、カスタマーサービススタッフが購入証明を求めることがあります。この場合、レシートまたはこの説明書に同梱されている保証書のいずれかを提出することで証明することができます。＊どちらの書類もご用意いただけない場合は、販売元にお問い合わせください。

カスタマーサポートラインにお問い合わせいただく前に、以下のことをお試しください：
1. デバイスのプラグを抜き、10秒待ってから再び差し込んでください。
2. デバイスのプラグを繋いだまま、電源ボタンを5秒間長押ししてください。
3. 別のコンセントでデバイスを使用してみてください。
4. 当社ウェブサイトのサポートセクションで問題の解決策をお探しください。

カスタマーサポートラインの電話番号は、800 555 3342です。
カスタマーサポートページは、www.geomaxha.com/supportです。

語彙チェック □ quality 高品質の □ respected 評判の高い □ resolve ～を解決する □ pass on to ～ ～に伝える □ seller 売り手 □ warranty 保証 □ period 期間 □ nature 性質 □ proof 証拠 □ unplug ～のプラグを抜く □ plug ～のプラグを差し込む □ solution 解決策

161

正解 **A** ☐☐☐☐

For whom is the information intended?

(A) A consumer of electrical goods

(B) A customer support line operator

(C) An online store representative

(D) A repair technician

情報は誰に向けられていますか。

(A) 電気製品の消費者

(B) カスタマーサポートラインのオペレーター

(C) オンラインショップの代表者

(D) 修理技師

❶に「Geomaxホームオートメーションの高品質な製品をお買い上げいただき、誠にありがとうございます」とあることから、製品の購入者へ向けたものであると分かる。その後も、「弊社は、音声で操作するスイッチや照明において、世界で最も高い評価を受けている企業である」とあるので、この企業はスイッチや照明などの電気製品を取り扱っていると分かる。よって、(A)が正解。

162

正解 **A** ☐☐☐☐

What is the purpose of the reference number mentioned in the instructions?

(A) To provide proof that a user has contacted Geomax directly

(B) To show that the device is still covered by its product warranty

(C) To demonstrate the caller is eligible for a discount

(D) To help customer support staff trace the cause of a problem

説明書で言及されている参照番号の目的は何ですか。

(A) 利用者がGeomaxに直接連絡したのを証明すること

(B) デバイスが製品保証の対象であるのを示すこと

(C) 電話をした人が割引対象者であるのを証明すること

(D) カスタマーサポートスタッフが問題の原因を突き止めやすくすること

❷で、「Geomaxのデバイスに何らかの問題が発生した場合、返金または返品を依頼する前に、カスタマーサポートラインに電話してほしい」と述べている。また、❸では「問題を解決できない場合は、参照番号を知らせるので、それを販売元に伝えれば、返金または交換を手配する」とあり、参照番号があることで販売元が返金や交換を行うことができると分かる。参照番号はGeomaxに電話しないと入手できないので、参照番号は直接連絡したことを証明するためにあると考えることができ、(A)が正解。

語彙チェック ☐ proof 証明 ☐ cover ～に適用される ☐ demonstrate ～を証明する ☐ eligible 資格のある
☐ trace ～を明らかにする

163

正解 **D** ☐☐☐☐

In which of the positions marked [1], [2], [3], and [4] does the following sentence best belong?

"If you are unable to supply either document, please contact the seller for assistance."

(A) [1]

(B) [2]

(C) [3]

(D) [4]

[1]、[2]、[3]、[4]と記載された箇所のうち、次の文が入るのに最もふさわしいのはどれですか。

「どちらの書類もご用意いただけない場合は、販売元にお問い合わせください」

(A) [1]

(B) [2]

(C) [3]

(D) [4]

挿入文は、とある書類がない場合は販売元に問い合わせてほしいと述べたもの。説明書の❹には「カスタマーサービススタッフが購入証明を求めることがある」と購入証明について触れている。その後、「レシートまたはこの説明書に同梱されている保証書のいずれかを提出することで証明できる」と、レシートか保証書を提出することで購入を証明できることが書かれている。この後に挿入文を入れると、「レシートも保証書もない場合は販売元にお問い合わせください」という文になり、文脈が自然につながるので(D)が正解。

Travel Maine - July Edition

The Gladstone Inn:
Contemporary Amenities, Classic Luxury
By Rebecca Chow

The Gladstone Inn has been one of Canterbury's most important accommodation providers for more than a century. ❶Originally designed to offer cheap accommodations to traveling salespeople, the hotel is now one of the most luxurious places to stay in Melbourne. Its convenient location, stunning views, and excellent amenities make it a popular destination for celebrities and traveling dignitaries.

❷Recently, the Gladstone Inn has agreed to a partnership with Canterbury Community College whereby students undertake paid internships and learn important skills. Program coordinator Sheryl White has praised the staff at the hotel for the excellent training they are providing. "I'm sure our graduates will be able to find work at luxury hotels anywhere in the world using their experiences," White said. "Many of the interns go on to pursue careers right here, though."

❸The internship program is only available to students in Canterbury Community College's Hospitality course. It is a three-year course with two compulsory internship components, both of which take place in the final year. Intern Melissa Walker said that she felt that the internship and the regular classes were equally important. "It's very helpful to see how the information we are given in the course is used in the real world."

❹The internship program has been running for seven years now, and both the hotel and the college claim to have experienced some additional benefits. The course's popularity has grown to the point where administrators are considering raising their student numbers. Meanwhile, ❺the hotel has a 98 percent occupancy rate throughout the year. They attribute part of that to the goodwill from friends and family of the interns.

問題164-167は次の記事に関するものです。

Travel Maine - 7月号

Gladstone宿：
現代的なアメニティとクラシックな豪華さ
Rebecca Chow記

Gladstone宿は、1世紀以上にわたってCanterburyで最も重要な宿泊施設の1つであり続けている。もともと出張するセールスマンに格安の宿泊施設を提供するために作られたこのホテルは、今ではMelbourneで最も豪華な宿泊施設の1つとなっている。便利な立地、優れた眺望、素晴らしい設備により、有名人や旅行中の要人にも人気のあるホテルである。

最近、Gladstone宿はCanterburyコミュニティカレッジとの提携に合意し、学生が有給インターンシップに参加して重要なスキルを学ぶことになった。プログラム・コーディネーターのSheryl Whiteは、ホテルのスタッフが提供する優れたトレーニングを称賛した。「卒業生たちは、その経験を活かして、世界中の高級ホテルで働くことができると確信しています」とWhiteは述べた。「と言っても、インターン生の多くはここでキャリアを積んでいきます」。

このインターンシッププログラムは、Canterburyコミュニティカレッジのホスピタリティコースの学生だけが参加できるものだ。このコースは3年制で、2つのインターンシップが必修科目として課され、その両方が最終学年で実施される。インターン生のMelissa Walkerは、インターンシップと通常の授業が同じように重要であると感じたと言う。「コースで与えられた情報が、実社会でどのように使われているのかを知ることができ、とても参考になります」。

インターンシッププログラムは7年前から実施されているが、ホテルと大学の双方が、さらなるメリットを実感していると言う。コースの人気は高まり、事務局では生徒数の増加を検討しているほどだ。一方、ホテルは年間を通じて98％の稼働率を誇っている。その理由の1つは、インターン生の友人や家族の好意によるものだという。

語彙チェック   □ design *A* to *do* 〜するようAを設計する □ luxurious 豪華な □ stunning とても美しい
□ dignitary 高位の人 □ whereby それによって □ undertake 〜を引き受ける、〜を始める
□ praise 〜を褒める □ compulsory 必修の □ component 構成要素 □ occupancy 占有
□ attribute *A* to *B* AはBによるものと考える □ goodwill 好意、善意

164

正解 **A** □□□□

What is suggested about the Gladstone Inn?

(A) It has adapted to serve a different clientele.

(B) It was nominated for a hospitality award.

(C) It is the largest hotel in Canterbury.

(D) It recently had its interior renovated.

Gladstone宿について何が分かりますか。

(A) 異なる客層に対応するために適応している。

(B) ホスピタリティ賞にノミネートされた。

(C) Canterburyで一番大きなホテルである。

(D) 最近、内装を改修した。

❶で「もともと出張するセールスマンに格安の宿泊施設を提供するために作られたこのホテルは、今ではMelbourneで最も豪華な宿泊施設の1つとなっている」と、当初のホテルは格安であったが現在は豪華な宿泊施設になっていることが述べられている。同2文目では、「有名人や旅行中の要人にも人気のあるホテル」とあり、客層が有名人や要人に変化したと分かるので(A)が正解。

語彙チェック □ clientele　顧客

165

正解 **B** □□□□

What is implied about the internship program?

(A) It is offered in locations around the world.

(B) It provides a financial reward for its participants.

(C) It is coordinated by an employee of The Gladstone Inn.

(D) It accepts students from a variety of colleges.

インターンシッププログラムについて何が示唆されていますか。

(A) 世界中の場所で提供されている。

(B) 参加者に金銭的な報酬を提供するものである。

(C) Gladstone宿の従業員によって統率されている。

(D) 様々な大学から学生を受け入れている。

❷で「学生が有給インターンシップに参加して重要なスキルを学ぶことになった」とあり、インターンシップには給料が伴うことが分かる。これを「金銭的な報酬を提供する」と言い換えた(B)が正解。

語彙チェック □ reward　報酬　□ coordinate　～をまとめる

166

正解 **C** □□□□

What is probably true about Ms. Walker?

(A) She has stayed at The Gladston Inn on multiple occasions.

(B) She has been offered a permanent position at The Gladston Inn.

(C) She commenced studying at Canterbury Community College over two years ago.

(D) She is a member of the faculty at Canterbury Community College.

Walkerさんについておそらく正しいことは何ですか。

(A) 彼女はGladston宿に何度も宿泊したことがある。

(B) 彼女はGladston宿の正社員をオファーされている。

(C) 彼女は2年以上前にCanterburyコミュニティカレッジで勉強を始めた。

(D) 彼女はCanterburyコミュニティカレッジの教員のメンバーである。

❸の「このインターンシッププログラムは、Canterburyコミュニティカレッジのホスピタリティコースの学生だけが参加できる」や「このコースは3年制で、2つのインターンシップが必修科目として課され、その両方が最終学年で実施される」から、インターンシップに参加するには、Canterburyコミュニティカレッジのホスピタリティコースの学生であること、3年生であることが必須だと考えられる。同3文目からWalkerさんはインターン生であることが分かるので、Canterburyコミュニティカレッジに通う3年生だと判断できる。よって、これを言い換えた(C)が正解。

語彙チェック □ faculty　全教職員

167

正解 **B** □□□□

How has the hotel benefitted from the arrangement?

(A) It is hiring fewer staff members.

(B) It is taking more reservations.

(C) It is getting better reviews.

(D) It is spending less on staffing.

この取り決めによって、ホテルはどのような利益を得ていますか。

(A) スタッフの雇用を減らしている。

(B) 予約の数が増えている。

(C) より良い評価を得ている。

(D) スタッフの人件費が減っている。

❹の「ホテルと大学の双方が、さらなるメリットを実感している」という内容より、インターンシップがホテルに利益をもたらしていることが分かる。❺では「ホテルは年間を通じて98%の稼働率を誇っている」「その理由の1つは、インターン生の友人や家族の好意によるもの」と、利益について具体的に述べられている。つまり、利益とは予約が増えたことだと考えられるので(B)が正解。

Questions 168-171 refer to the following online chat discussion.

Clinton Salazar [3:30 P.M.]:
❶I just got a call from Freeman's Accounting. They are having some trouble with their internal network connection. ❷It's on Sharpe Street in Benowa.

Ignatius Royce [3:31 P.M.]:
❸I installed that network when it first went in so I'm familiar with the setup. **I'm busy all day today, though.**

Maxine Bolton [3:31 P.M.]:
❹I'm at Carter Travel right now. It's a couple of doors down from Freeman's accounting. ❺I could take a look as soon as I'm finished here.

Clinton Salazar [3:33 P.M.]:
Thanks, Maxine. It's fairly urgent, though. ❻How long do you think you'll take?

Maxine Bolton [3:35 P.M.]:
It depends. ❼I'm still tracking down the problem here. It could be something easy or it could take all day.

Dana Alvarez [3:36 P.M.]:
I could be there in 20 minutes, Clinton. Let me know if you need me. I'm at the warehouse right now stocking up on supplies.

Ignatius Royce [3:37 P.M.]:
You should probably take a new router. The one they are using has been there for over a decade. It has reached the end of its lifespan.

Clinton Salazar [3:45 P.M.]:
Good to know. Thanks, Ignatius. Dana, why don't you grab a router and head over there?

Dana Alvarez [3:46 P.M.]:
On my way. ❽Do you know what size they need?

Clinton Salazar [3:49 P.M.]:
Hang on. ❾I'll find out how many employees they have there now.

問題168-171は次のオンラインチャットの話し合いに関するものです。

Clinton Salazar [午後3時30分]：
たった今Freeman会計事務所から電話がありました。社内ネットワーク接続に問題があるそうです。場所はBenowaのSharpe通りです。

Ignatius Royce [午後3時31分]：
そのネットワークを最初に導入したとき、私が設置したので、私はセットアップに精通しています。ですが、今日は一日中忙しいです。

Maxine Bolton [午後3時31分]：
私は今、Carter旅行会社にいます。Freeman会計事務所の2、3軒先です。ここが終わったら、すぐにでも見てきますよ。

Clinton Salazar [午後3時33分]：
ありがとうございます、Maxine。ただ、かなり緊急なんです。どれくらいかかると思いますか。

Maxine Bolton [午後3時35分]：
場合によります。まだここで問題を突き止めているところです。何か簡単なことかもしれないし、一日中かかるかもしれません。

Dana Alvarez [午後3時36分]：
あと20分でそこに行けます、Clinton。私が必要なら知らせてください。私は今、倉庫で補充をしているので。

Ignatius Royce [午後3時37分]：
おそらく新しいルーターを持っていった方がいいですよ。彼らは10年以上前からあるものを使っているんです。もう寿命が来ています。

Clinton Salazar [午後3時45分]：
知れてよかったです。ありがとうございます、Ignatius。Dana、ルーターを持ってそちらに向かってもらえませんか。

Dana Alvarez [午後3時46分]：
すぐ行きます。必要なサイズは分かりますか。

Clinton Salazar [午後3時49分]：
待っててください。彼らの今の従業員数を調べてみます。

語彙チェック ☐ accounting　会計　☐ internal　内部の　☐ fairly　かなり　☐ urgent　急を要する
☐ stock up on ～　～を補充する　☐ lifespan　寿命　☐ grab　～をひっつかむ　☐ head　進む

168

正解 C ▢▢▢▢

Who most likely are the writers?

(A) Accountants

(B) Travel agents

(C) Network engineers

(D) Programmers

書き手たちは誰だと考えられますか。

(A) 会計士

(B) 旅行代理店

(C) ネットワークエンジニア

(D) プログラマー

❶で、Salazar さんは「Freeman 会計事務所の社内ネットワーク接続に問題がある」と伝えている。それに対して❸で Royce さんが「そのネットワークを最初に導入したとき、私が設置したので、私はセットアップに精通している」と返していることから、書き手たちはネットワークを設置する仕事についていると分かり、(C) が正解。

169

正解 D ▢▢▢▢

What is implied about Carter Travel?

(A) It is in the same building as Freeman's Accounting.

(B) It is a newly established business.

(C) It will close soon.

(D) It is on Sharpe Street.

Carter 旅行会社について何が示唆されていますか。

(A) Freeman 会計事務所と同じビルにある。

(B) 新しく設立された企業である。

(C) まもなく閉鎖される。

(D) Sharpe 通りにある。

❹で Bolton さんは「Carter 旅行会社にいる」「Freeman 会計事務所の2、3軒先」と述べ、Carter 旅行会社は Freeman 会計事務所と同じ通りに位置していることを伝えている。❷より、Freeman 会計事務所について「場所は Benowa の Sharpe 通り」であることが分かる。Carter 旅行会社は Freeman 会計事務所の近くにあるので、Sharpe 通りにあると推測でき、(D) が正解。

170

正解 B ▢▢▢▢

At 3:35 P.M., what does Ms. Bolton mean when she writes, "It depends"?

(A) She is not sure what a client is requesting.

(B) She does not know the severity of a problem.

(C) She believes that some equipment is reliable.

(D) She needs to check a map to be certain.

午後3時35分に、"It depends" という発言で、Bolton さんは何を意図していますか。

(A) 彼女は顧客が何を要求しているのか分からない。

(B) 彼女は問題の深刻さが分からない。

(C) 彼女は機器を信頼できると思っている。

(D) 彼女は確信するために地図を確認する必要がある。

Freeman 会計事務所のネットワーク接続の問題について知らされた Bolton さんは、❹と❺で「今取りかかっている Carter 旅行会社での作業が終わったらすぐに見に行く」と申し出ている。その後、Salazar さんは❻で、Freeman 会計事務所に対応できるまでにどれくらいかかるかを Bolton さんに聞いている。それに対して Bolton さんは下線部の発言をした後、❼で「まだここで問題を突き止めているところだ。何か簡単なことかもしれないし、一日中かかるかもしれない」と、Carter 旅行会社での作業にどれほど時間がかかるか分からないことを伝えている。これを「問題の深刻さが分からない」と言い換えた (B) が正解。

語彙チェック ▢ severity　重大さ　▢ reliable　信頼できる

171

正解 B ▢▢▢▢

What will Mr. Salazar most likely do next?

(A) Order a device

(B) Contact a client

(C) Call a branch office

(D) Load a vehicle

Salazar さんは次に何をすると考えられますか。

(A) デバイスを注文する

(B) 顧客へ連絡する

(C) 支店に電話する

(D) 乗り物に積載する

Royce さんが Freeman 会計事務所のルーターは古いものであると伝え、Salazar さんもルーターを持って行くように言ったのを受け、Alvarez さんは❽で「必要なサイズは分かりますか」とルーターのサイズを尋ねている。それに対して Salazar さんは❾で「彼らの今の従業員数を調べてみる」と返している。人数を知るために Freeman 会計事務所に連絡すると考えられるので、Freeman 会計事務所を顧客と言い換えた (B) が正解。

語彙チェック ▢ load　～に荷を積む

225

Questions 172-175 refer to the following advertisement.

Excelsior of Victoria

❶ Finding Buyers for Obscure Items for Over a Hundred Years

❷ Excelsior is where investors in rare antiques and fine artwork come to buy and sell their treasures. Excelsior specializes in high-end items and has a reputation for accuracy in its product descriptions and verification of authenticity. —[1]— . ❸ Our clients receive monthly newsletters describing the contents of our upcoming sales, their estimated sales price, minimum bid amounts, and reserve prices. These are also available from our Web site at www.excelsiorofvictoria.com. —[2]— .

❹ On June 16, we will be selling off a magnificent collection of jazz records, a diary from playwright Tim Cleminson, and a Hudson Dart automobile valued at more than $250,000 among many other things. —[3]— . ❺ You can come and view some of these upcoming items in our exhibition room. ❻ We are in the wonderful Mongomery Building on Regent Street, where Excelsior has been since it was founded.

❼ If you would like to place a bid, you must register in advance. Depending on the item you are wishing to bid on, you may be asked to provide proof of funds to demonstrate your ability to pay. —[4]— . ❽ Please be sure to get a copy from your financial institution before you visit us.

We look forward to serving you soon whether you are buying or selling!

Excelsior of Victoria
100 Regent Street, Victoria
Tel 250-555-4932

問題172-175は次の広告に関するものです。

Excelsior of Victoria

100年以上にわたり、世に知られていない物品の買い手を見つけ続けています

Excelsiorは、希少なアンティークや高級美術品の投資家が宝物を売買するために訪れる場所です。Excelsiorは高級品に特化しており、商品説明の正確さと本物かどうかの実証には定評があります。Excelsiorのお客様には、今後予定されている販売内容、販売推定価格、最低入札額、予約価格などを記載したニュースレターを毎月お受け取りいただいています。これらは、当社のWebサイト（www.excelsiorofvictoria.com）からも入手できます。

6月16日には、素晴らしいジャズのレコードコレクション、劇作家Tim Cleminsonの日記、25万ドル以上するHudson Dartの自動車など、数多くのものを販売する予定です。*少なくとも70名の関係者またはその代理人の出席を見込んでいます。これらの近日発売予定の商品の一部は、当社の展示室でご覧いただくことができます。当店はRegent通りの素晴らしいMongomeryビルにあり、設立当時からその場所にあります。

入札を希望される方は、事前に登録が必要です。入札を希望される商品によっては、支払い能力を証明するために資金証明の提出を求められることがあります。ご来店の前に必ず金融機関からコピーをお受け取りください。

ご購入、ご売却を問わず、お客様のご来店を心よりお待ちしております！

Excelsior of Victoria
Victoria州Regent通り100番地
電話番号 250-555-4932

語彙チェック
□ obscure　世に知られていない　□ antique　骨董品　□ fine　高級な　□ high-end　高級な　□ accuracy　正確さ
□ verification　証明　□ authenticity　本物であること　□ minimum　最低限の　□ bid　入札
□ magnificent　とびきり上等な　□ playwright　劇作家　□ valued at ～　～の価値を有する
□ place a bid　応札する　□ demonstrate　～を証明する

172

正解 A ☐☐☐☐

What is being advertised?

(A) An auction house
(B) An event space
(C) An art gallery
(D) A history museum

何が宣伝されていますか。

(A) オークションハウス
(B) イベントスペース
(C) アートギャラリー
(D) 歴史博物館

❷で、「Excelsiorは、希少なアンティークや高級美術品の投資家が宝物を売買するために訪れる場所である」と、品物の売買が行われる場所であると述べている。❸では「販売内容、販売推定価格、最低入札額、予約価格」について言及しており、オークションをしていると推測できるので、(A)が正解。

173

正解 C ☐☐☐☐

What is implied about the Mongomery building?

(A) It is owned by Excelsior.
(B) It provides parking for registered guests.
(C) It was constructed over a century ago.
(D) It houses a theater.

Mongomeryビルについて、何が示唆されていますか。

(A) Excelsiorによって所有されている。
(B) 登録された来客のために駐車場を提供している。
(C) 100年以上前に建設された。
(D) 劇場が入っている。

❻で、Excelsiorについて「Mongomeryビルにあり、設立当時からその場所にある」とMongomeryビルに位置すると述べている。また、❶では「100年以上にわたり、世に知られていない物品の買い手を見つけ続けている」とあり、100年以上前からExcelsiorは存在していると分かる。つまり、Excelsior設立当時からあるMongomeryビルも100年以上前に建設されたと考えられるので、(C)が正解。

語彙チェック ☐ house 〜を収容する、〜を入れている

174

正解 A ☐☐☐☐

According to the advertisement, what might people be asked to provide when they register?

(A) A bank account statement
(B) A receipt for their purchase
(C) An admission ticket
(D) An invitation from the organizers

広告によると、人々は登録時に何を提供するよう求められる可能性がありますか。

(A) 銀行口座の明細書
(B) 購入時のレシート
(C) 入場券
(D) 主催者からの招待状

❼より、「入札を希望される方は、事前に登録が必要である」と述べた後、「商品によっては、支払い能力を証明するために資金証明の提出を求められる」とある。続く❽で「ご来店の前に必ず金融機関からコピーをお受け取りください」とあり、資金証明を金融機関から用意する必要があると推測できる。選択肢の中で金融機関の書類にあてはまるものは銀行口座の明細書なので、(A)が正解。

175

正解 C ☐☐☐☐

In which of the positions marked [1], [2], [3], and [4] does the following sentence best belong?

"We expect to have at least 70 interested parties or their representatives in attendance."

(A) [1]
(B) [2]
(C) [3]
(D) [4]

[1]、[2]、[3]、[4]と記載された箇所のうち、次の文が入るのに最もふさわしいのはどれですか。

「少なくとも70名の関係者またはその代理人の出席を見込んでいます」

(A) [1]
(B) [2]
(C) [3]
(D) [4]

挿入文は、出席する人数に関する内容である。❹では「6月16日にレコードコレクション、劇作家の日記や自動車などを販売する」とあり、オークションが開催されると分かる。❺では「これらの商品は展示室で見ることができる」と場所を伝えている。❹と❺の間に挿入文を入れると、オークションに出席する人数について言及する流れになり、オークションについて一連の説明をしている文脈になるので、正解は(C)。

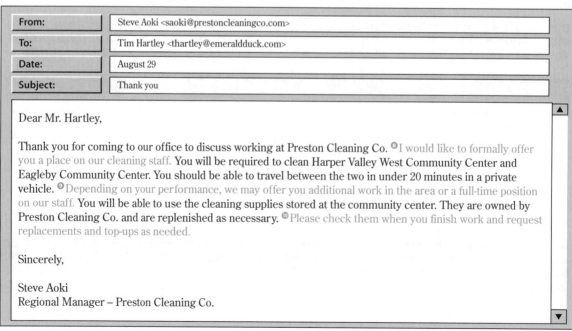

From:	Georgia Paulson <gpaulson@prestoncleanco.com>
To:	Steve Aoki <saoki@prestoncleanco.com>
Date:	August 6
Subject:	New contract

Dear Steve,

❶We have just won the cleaning contract for the Harper Valley community centers. ❷There are a total of 20 community centers that will require cleaning. There is no way that we can accomplish this with our current staff levels. We need to hire additional cleaners on a part-time basis.

According to the contract, the cleaning must be carried out between 6:30 P.M. and 9:30 P.M. Last week, I visited three of the locations to calculate how long it should take. An experienced cleaner should be able to complete the work in around 45 minutes to an hour. Considering travel time, each cleaner will only be able to take care of two locations. The current cleaning company is contracted until September 13. ❸However, the coordinator of the Harper Valley community centers has asked us to start work on September 4. ❹I get the impression that they are dissatisfied with the standard of cleaning they are currently receiving. ❺One problem she mentioned was that cleaners were not completing a checklist she provided. Please make it clear to new hires that the coordinator will be paying close attention to their work. ❻For this reason, we should hire only experienced people with good references from previous employers.

❼Before you advertise the position, I would like you to look at our current work assignments to determine how much of the work current full-time employees will be able to cover. Let's conduct interviews from August 19.

Regards,

Georgia

From:	Steve Aoki <saoki@prestoncleaningco.com>
To:	Tim Hartley <thartley@emeraldduck.com>
Date:	August 29
Subject:	Thank you

Dear Mr. Hartley,

Thank you for coming to our office to discuss working at Preston Cleaning Co. ❽I would like to formally offer you a place on our cleaning staff. You will be required to clean Harper Valley West Community Center and Eagleby Community Center. You should be able to travel between the two in under 20 minutes in a private vehicle. ❾Depending on your performance, we may offer you additional work in the area or a full-time position on our staff. You will be able to use the cleaning supplies stored at the community center. They are owned by Preston Cleaning Co. and are replenished as necessary. ❿Please check them when you finish work and request replacements and top-ups as needed.

Sincerely,

Steve Aoki
Regional Manager – Preston Cleaning Co.

問題176-180は次の2通のEメールに関するものです。

送信者：Georgia Paulson <gpaulson@prestoncleanco.com>
受信者：Steve Aoki <saoki@prestoncleanco.com>
日付：8月6日
件名：新しい契約

Steveへ

我々はたった今、Harper Valleyコミュニティセンターの清掃の契約を獲得しました。清掃が必要なコミュニティセンターは全部で20カ所あります。現在の従業員数では、これを達成することは不可能です。時間給で追加の清掃員を雇用する必要があります。

契約書によると、清掃は午後6時30分から午後9時30分の間に行わなければなりません。先週、私はどれぐらいかかるか計算するために3カ所を訪問しました。経験豊富な清掃員であれば、45分から1時間程度で作業を完了できるはずです。移動時間を考慮すると、1人の清掃員が担当できるのは2カ所だけとなるでしょう。現在の清掃会社は、9月13日までが契約期間です。ですが、Harper Valleyコミュニティセンターの統括者が、9月4日から作業を始めてほしいと我々に依頼してきました。現在の清掃作業の水準に不満があるのではないか、という印象を受けます。彼女が言及していた問題の1つは、清掃員が、彼女が提供するチェックリストを完了させていなかったということでした。新しく雇った従業員に対しては、統括者が彼らの仕事に細心の注意を払っているということを明らかにしてください。このような理由から、我々は前職の雇用者からの推薦状がある経験者のみを採用すべきだと思います。

求人募集をかける前に、現在の業務分担を見て、現在雇っている正社員がどの程度仕事をこなせそうかをあなたに判断してもらいたいです。面接は8月19日から行いましょう。

よろしくお願いします。

Georgia

語彙チェック ☐ there is no way that ～　～することができない　☐ staff level　従業員数　☐ on a part-time basis　時間給で
☐ carry out ～　～を実行する　☐ calculate　～を計算する　☐ experienced　経験豊富な
☐ contracted　契約している　☐ coordinator　責任者、統括者　☐ be dissatisfied with ～　～に不満足である
☐ checklist　チェックリスト　☐ make it clear to A that ～　～ということをAに対して明確にする
☐ hire　雇われた人、～を雇う　☐ reference　推薦状、照会先　☐ cover　～をこなす
☐ conduct an interview　面接を行う

送信者：Steve Aoki <saoki@prestoncleaningco.com>
受信者：Tim Hartley <thartley@emeraldduck.com>
日付：8月29日
件名：ありがとうございます

Hartley様

この度は、Preston清掃会社での勤務についてお話しするためご来社いただきありがとうございました。あなたを正式に清掃スタッフとして採用させていただければと思います。あなたには、Harper Valley西コミュニティセンターとEaglebyコミュニティセンターの清掃をお願いいたします。自家用車を使えばこの2カ所間を20分未満で移動できるはずです。あなたの成果次第では、この地域での追加業務や、正社員としての雇用を提案する可能性もございます。コミュニティセンターに保管されている清掃用具をご使用いただいて構いません。それらはPreston清掃会社が所有しており、随時補充しています。仕事を終えたら確認し、必要に応じて交換や補充を依頼してください。

敬具

Steve Aoki
地域マネージャー – Preston清掃会社

語彙チェック ☐ formally　正式に　☐ place　役割　☐ performance　成果、業績　☐ cleaning supplies　清掃用具
☐ replenish　～を補充する　☐ as necessary　必要に応じて　☐ replacement　取り換え品　☐ top-up　補充

176

What is implied about the work at the Harper Valley community centers?

(A) Some of it will be carried out by existing employees.

(B) Each location will take over an hour to complete.

(C) It will receive a daily inspection from the regional coordinator.

(D) It must be carried out in teams of two.

Harper Valleyコミュニティセンターでの仕事について何が示唆されていますか。

(A) 一部は既存の従業員によって行われる。

(B) 完了するのに1カ所あたり1時間以上かかる。

(C) 毎日、地域統括者の監査を受ける。

(D) 2人1組で実施されなければならない。

1文書目のEメール❶より、Preston清掃会社がHarper Valleyコミュニティセンターの清掃契約を結んだということが分かる。Eメールでは時間給で清掃員を雇うことについて話しており、❼を見ると、Paulsonさんは「求人募集をかける前に、現在の業務分担を見て、現在雇っている正社員がどの程度仕事をこなせそうかを判断してもらいたい」とAokiさんに伝えている。新しい清掃員を臨時で雇うだけでなく、清掃の一部は現在の従業員によって行われるということが示唆されているので、正解は(A)。1文書目に「統括者が細心の注意を払っている」との記述はあるが、毎日とは述べられていないので、(C)は不正解。

語彙チェック ☐ existing 既存の ☐ daily 毎日の ☐ regional 地域の

177

In the first e-mail, the word "impression" in paragraph 2, line 5 is closest in meaning to

(A) imitation

(B) consequence

(C) response

(D) feeling

最初のEメールの第2段落・5行目にある "impression" に最も意味が近いのは

(A) 模倣

(B) 結果

(C) 反応

(D) 印象

下線部分は、1文書目のEメール第2段落の❹にある。I get the impression that ～で「～という印象を受ける」という意味を表す。これと同じ意味を持つのは(D)のfeeling「印象、感じ」。I get(have) the feeling that ～「～という印象を受ける（持つ）」で同じ意味を表す。

178

What is implied about Mr. Hartley?

(A) He will be a full-time employee of Preston Cleaning Co.

(B) He will be reimbursed for cleaning chemicals.

(C) He was vouched for by a previous employer.

(D) He will attend an orientation session on September 12.

Hartleyさんについて何が示唆されていますか。

(A) Preston清掃会社の正社員になる。

(B) 清掃用の化学薬品代を払い戻される。

(C) 以前の雇用主によって保証された。

(D) 9月12日に行われるオリエンテーションに参加する。

Hartleyさんは、2文書目のEメールで登場する人物。❽に「あなた（＝Hartleyさん）を正式に清掃スタッフとして採用させていただきたい」とあることから、Preston清掃会社で雇われるということが分かる。1文書目のEメールの❻に戻ると、「前職の雇用者からの推薦状がある経験者のみを採用すべきだ」と述べられている。つまり、新たに雇用されることとなったHartleyさんは、以前の雇用主からの保証を受けているということが推測できる。よって、正解は(C)。❾で「成果次第では正社員としての雇用を提案する」と述べられているものの、Hartleyさんが正社員になるとまでは示唆されていないので、(A)は不正解。

語彙チェック ☐ reimburse A for B AにB（の費用）を払い戻す ☐ cleaning chemicals 化学薬品 ☐ vouch for ～ ～を保証する

179

When most likely will Mr. Hartley begin working for Preston Cleaning Co.?

(A) On August 19

(B) On August 29

(C) On September 4

(D) On September 13

Hartleyさんはいつ Preston 清掃会社で働き始めると考えられますか。

(A) 8月19日

(B) 8月29日

(C) 9月4日

(D) 9月13日

2文書目のEメールの❽より、HartleyさんはPreston清掃会社で清掃スタッフとして働き始める予定の人物である。さらに1文書目のEメールの❸を見ると、「Harper Valleyコミュニティセンターの統括者が、9月4日から（清掃）作業を始めてほしいと依頼してきた」とある。よって、Hartleyさんはおそらく9月4日から清掃作業に入ると考えられる。正解は(C)。

180

What is NOT a responsibility of the position described in the e-mails?

(A) Cleaning a public facility

(B) Emptying of garbage receptacles

(C) Monitoring inventory

(D) Fulfilling a checklist

Eメールに記載されている職務の責任ではないものは何ですか。

(A) 公共施設を清掃すること

(B) ゴミ箱を空にすること

(C) 在庫を確認すること

(D) チェックリストを満たすこと

Eメールに記載されている職務とは、清掃員が行う作業のこと。❷に「清掃が必要なコミュニティセンターは全部で20カ所」とあることから、(A)の公共施設の清掃は職務の1つとして述べられていることが分かる。次に❿に「仕事を終えたら確認し、必要に応じて（清掃用具の）交換や補充を依頼してください」とあることから、(C)の在庫の確認も職務の1つ。さらに❺に「問題の1つは、清掃員がチェックリストを完了させていなかったということだった」とあることから、(D)のチェックリストを満たすことも職務の範囲内だということが分かる。残った(B)は述べられていないので、これが正解。

語彙チェック ☐ responsibility 責務 ☐ empty of ～ ～を空にする ☐ receptacle 容器 ☐ inventory 在庫
☐ fulfill ～を満たす、～を果たす

Business News

Friday, September 19

Gig Meets Trad

In recent years, the gig economy has been growing steadily, and more and more people have been earning a living by completing tasks of various sizes for a diverse group of temporary employers. There can be problems with this arrangement. Gig workers often have to invest in certain equipment that would ordinarily be supplied by an employer. ❶Also, many people find it hard to focus if they work from home — they get less done because of all the distractions. ❷Another problem is the sense of isolation people feel. They do not benefit from the support networks traditional offices provide.

❸Steven Chan's new company Gigtrad aims to solve this problem by providing a shared workspace for online gig workers. ❹Each site has a wide variety of professional-grade equipment that users of the space can rent for a small additional charge. Users can attend lectures from industry experts.

Gigtrad — The Future of Online Work

❺Everyone loves the freedom gig work provides, but it is not without its downsides. Gigtrad can help alleviate the difficulties of gig work while leveraging the benefits of a shared workspace to improve your productivity.

❻• Get access to a wide variety of high-end equipment at no additional cost.

• Share ideas and collaborate on tasks with other Gigtrad users.

• Broaden your connections within various industries and learn about new opportunities from visiting experts.

❼If you are interested in finding out whether or not Gigtrad is right for your specific situation, you can join our online information session. After listening to a brief rundown of our services by our CEO, you can ask questions and enjoy a guided tour of one of our facilities. There will also be video testimonials by some of our current users. A schedule of upcoming sessions is provided on the Web site.

❽If you are ready to take the next step, visit the Web site and find out if there is a location near you. As a result of our high user satisfaction levels, many of our offices are already at maximum capacity. Nevertheless, you can put your name on a waiting list and be notified when there is an opening.

www.gigtrad.com

ビジネスニュース

9月19日金曜日

ギグ、伝統と交わる

近年、ギグエコノミーは着実に成長しており、多様な臨時雇用主のために大小さまざまな仕事をこなして生計を立てる人が増えてきている。しかし、この取り決めには問題がある。ギグワーカーは、通常は雇用主が提供するであろう特定の機器を購入しなければならないことが多い。また、自宅で仕事をする場合、多くの人が集中力を欠き、気が散って仕事がはかどらないと感じている。もう1つの問題は、人々が抱える孤立感である。彼らは、従来のオフィスが提供していた支援網の恩恵を受けることがないのだ。

Steven Chanの新しい会社であるGigtrad社は、オンラインギグワーカーに共有ワークスペースを提供することで、この問題の解決を目指している。それぞれの場所には、プロ仕様のさまざまな機器が用意されており、スペースの利用者はわずかな追加料金でレンタルすることができる。利用者は、業界のエキスパートによる講義を受けることもできる。

語彙チェック
☐ gig economy　ギグエコノミー（インターネットを通じて単発の仕事を受注する働き方）　☐ steadily　着実に
☐ earn a living by *doing*　〜することで生計を立てる　☐ diverse　多様な　☐ arrangement　取り決め
☐ ordinarily　通常は　☐ distraction　気を散らすもの　☐ isolation　孤立、遮断
☐ benefit from 〜　〜から恩恵を受ける　☐ aim to *do*　〜することを目指す　☐ shared　共有の、共同の
☐ charge　料金

Gigtrad社 — オンラインワークの未来

ギグワークが生み出す自由な働き方は誰もが好むところですが、マイナス面がないわけではありません。Gigtradは、生産性を向上させる共有ワークスペースの恩恵を活用し、ギグワークの難題を軽減します。
• 追加費用なしで、さまざまな種類の高品質機器をご利用ください。
• 他のGigtrad利用者とアイディアを共有し、共同作業をしてみましょう。
• さまざまな業界とのつながりを広げ、訪れる専門家から学びの場を得てください。

Gigtradがあなたの特定の状況に合っているかどうかを知りたい方は、オンライン説明会にご参加ください。弊社のCEOによる手短なサービス概要の説明後、質問や一施設のガイド付き見学ツアーが可能です。また、実際にご利用いただいているお客様の声をご紹介したビデオがございます。今後開催されるセッションのスケジュールは、Webサイトで公開しております。

次のステップに進まれる方は、ウェブサイトにアクセスしてお住まいの近くに施設があるかどうかをご確認ください。利用者満足度が高いため、多くのオフィスはすでに定員に達しております。しかしながら、順番待ちのリストにお名前を登録していただければ、空きが出たときに通知を受け取ることが可能です。

www.gigtrad.com

語彙チェック
☐ downside　マイナス面　☐ alleviate　〜を軽減する　☐ leverage　〜を活用する、〜を利用する
☐ high-end　高品質の　☐ broaden　〜を広げる　☐ rundown　概要、手短な報告　☐ testimonial　顧客の声
☐ capacity　収容量　☐ waiting list　順番待ちのリスト　☐ opening　空き

181

Who is Steven Chan?

(A) A company founder

(B) A customer service representative

(C) A gig worker

(D) A journalist

Steven Chan とは誰ですか。

(A) 会社の創設者

(B) 顧客サービス担当者

(C) ギグワーカー

(D) 報道記者

記事の❸に「Steven Chanの新しい会社であるGigtrad社」とあることに注目。このことからSteven Chanは会社の創設者であることが分かるので、正解は(A)。Steven Chanはギグワーカーに向けたサービスを提供する会社を創設した人物であり、自身がギグワーカーというわけではないので、(C)は不正解。

語彙チェック □ founder 創設者

182

What is NOT mentioned as something experienced by gig workers?

(A) A feeling of solitude

(B) Difficulty concentrating

(C) Enhanced flexibility

(D) Increased earning potential

ギグワーカーによって経験されることとして言及されていないものは何ですか。

(A) 孤独感

(B) 集中することの難しさ

(C) より高い柔軟性

(D) 見込み収入の増加

記事の❷に「もう1つの問題は、人々（ギグワーカー）が抱える孤立感である」とあるので、(A)は言及されている。また❶に「多くの人が集中力を欠き、気が散って仕事がはかどらないと感じている」とあるので、(B)も言及されている。さらに広告の❺に「ギグワークが生み出す自由な働き方は誰もが好む」とあることから、(C)についても言及されている。収入については触れられていないので、残った(D)が正解。

語彙チェック □ solitude 孤独 □ enhanced 強化された □ earning potential 見込み収入

183

Which benefit of Gigtrad has been modified since the article was published?

(A) The service area

(B) The equipment rental option

(C) The management team

(D) The learning opportunities

記事掲載後に修正されたGigtrad社の特典はどれですか。

(A) サービスエリア

(B) 機器の貸し出しオプション

(C) 経営陣

(D) 学びの機会

Gigtrad社が提供する特典として、記事の❹で「プロ仕様のさまざまな機器があり、利用者はわずかな追加料金でレンタル可能」と述べられている。次に2文書目の広告を見ると、❻に「追加費用なしでさまざまな種類の高品質機器をご利用ください」とある。元々機器の利用には追加料金がかかると述べられていたものの、その後追加料金なしで利用できる仕様に変わったということが読み取れるので、正解は(B)。

 **Level Up!**

本問のように、前の部分で述べられていた事実が次の文書で変わっている場合、問題として問われることが多いので注意しよう。

184

正解 B ☐☐☐☐

According to the advertisement, how can people learn more about Gigtrad?

(A) By visiting a local office

(B) By attending an open meeting

(C) By calling a representative

(D) By subscribing to a newsletter

広告によると、人々はどのようにGigtrad社についてもっと知ることができますか。

(A) 現地事務所を訪問することによって

(B) 公開されたミーティングに参加することによって

(C) 担当者に電話することによって

(D) 会報を購読することによって

広告の❼に「Gigtradがあなたの特定の状況に合っているかどうかを知りたい方は、オンライン説明会にご参加ください」とある。open meeting「公開（された）ミーティング」に参加することでGigtrad社についてもっと知ることができると分かるので、正解は(B)。

語彙チェック ☐ newsletter　会報

185

正解 A ☐☐☐☐

What is probably available from the Web site?

(A) A map

(B) A survey form

(C) An app

(D) An employee profile

ウェブサイトから手に入るものはおそらく何ですか。

(A) 地図

(B) アンケートフォーム

(C) アプリ

(D) 社員のプロフィール

広告の❽に「次のステップに進まれる方は、ウェブサイトにアクセスしてお住まいの近くに施設があるかどうかをご確認ください」とある。よって、ウェブサイトにアクセスすると、Gigtrad社が提供する仕事場の所在地が示された地図が手に入ると考えられる。正解は(A)。

Questions 186-190 refer to the following advertisement and e-mails.

▶TRACK_258

Get away from it all at Palazzo Loto Bianco!

Enjoy magnificent sea views from this luxurious seaside resort. ❶We are now offering some special off-peak deals that you can take advantage of from January to March. All guests can take part in free guided tours of nearby Castello di Mola and Villagonia. ❷Stay with us for three nights, and get a fourth night free.

❸International visitors will find that we are a short drive from Catania Airport, and for those traveling domestically, Comiso Airport is very convenient. Valencia Yacht Harbor is within walking distance for those coming by sea.

Palazzo Loto Bianco won last year's Sicily Accommodation Association's award for Best Kept Grounds. Our restaurant Michael's was featured in *Fine Dining Magazine*, which described the menu as "daring", "original", and "delicious".

www. palazzolotobianco.com
TEL: +39 (0)95 555 743

To:	Bruce Towns <btowns@weedontravel.com>
From:	Pietro Messina <pmessina@palazzolotobianco.com>
Date:	February 19
Subject:	Re: 48309432

Dear Mr. Towns,

I am writing about Ms. Tanya Coolidge. ❹She is a customer of Weedon Travel who stayed with us from February 11 to February 16. ❺She locked some valuable items in the room safe and must have forgotten to remove them before she left on the morning of the 16th. We tried contacting her at the number she left with us, but we have been unable to do so. As another guest had reserved the room, we had to have a representative from the manufacturer come to the hotel and open the safe for us. We incurred a fee of US$175.50. As she is a valued customer of Weedon Travel, we are happy to waive that cost.

However, we must insist on sending the items on a paid-on delivery basis. For this reason, it is important that she be home to accept the parcel when it arrives. I suspect that she has not answered her calls because she is still on vacation. ❻Our receptionist remembers her mentioning that she was headed to the airport for a flight to the U.K. ❼Could you <u>pass on</u> this message to her, or provide us with her correct mobile phone number?

Sincerely,

Pietro Messina
❽Hotel Manager — Palazzo Loto Bianco

問題186-190は次の広告と2通のEメールに関するものです。

Palazzo Loto Biancoで日常の煩わしさから解放されましょう！

豪華な海辺のリゾート地から、壮大な海の景色をお楽しみください。1月から3月まで、オフピークの特別料金をご用意しています。ご宿泊いただく全てのお客様には、近隣のCastello di MolaやVillagoniaのガイドツアーに無料でご参加いただけます。3泊ご宿泊いただくと、4泊目が無料になります。

海外からのお客様はCatania空港から車ですぐにお越しになることができ、国内からのお客様にとってはComiso空港がとても便利です。海路でお越しのお客様は、Valenciaヨットハーバーが徒歩圏内です。

Palazzo Loto Biancoは、昨年のSicily宿泊協会Best Kept Grounds賞を受賞しました。当ホテルのレストランMichael'sは、雑誌Fine Dining Magazineに掲載され、そのメニューは「大胆」「独創的」「美味しい」と評されました。

www. palazzolotobianco.com
電話番号：+39 (0)95 555 743

| 語彙チェック | ☐ magnificent　壮大な ☐ luxurious　豪華な ☐ seaside　海辺の ☐ off-peak　オフピークの、閑散時の |
| | ☐ guided　ガイド付きの ☐ domestically　国内で ☐ within walking distance　徒歩圏内で ☐ daring　大胆な |

受信者：Bruce Towns <btowns@weedontravel.com>
送信者：Pietro Messina <pmessina@palazzolotobianco.com>
日付：2月19日
件名：Re: 48309432

Towns様

Tanya Coolidge様について書かせていただきます。彼女は2月11日から2月16日まで当ホテルにご宿泊いただいた、Weedon Travel社のお客様です。彼女は貴重品を部屋の金庫に保管しており、16日の朝出発する前に、それを取り出すのを忘れていたようです。彼女が残していった電話番号に連絡を取ろうとしましたが、できませんでした。他の宿泊客がお部屋を予約されていたため、メーカーの担当者にホテルまで来てもらい、金庫を開けてもらう必要が生じました。その際、175.50米ドルの手数料が発生しました。彼女はWeedon Travel社のお得意様なので、その費用は喜んで免除させていただきます。

しかしながら、品物を着払いでお送りすることに関してはこだわらなければいけません。このため、小包が到着した時に彼女が家にいて受け取っていただくことが重要です。彼女はまだ休暇中なので、電話に応答しないのではないかと思います。当社の受付係は、彼女がイギリスへのフライトのために空港に向かうと言っていたことを記憶しております。このメッセージを彼女に伝えていただくか、彼女の正しい携帯電話番号を教えていただけますか。

どうぞよろしくお願い申し上げます。

Pietro Messina
ホテル支配人— Palazzo Loto Bianco

語彙チェック	☐ valuable item　貴重品 ☐ safe　金庫 ☐ incur　（負債・損失など）をこうむる ☐ valued customer　お得意様
	☐ waive　（権利・請求権など）を放棄する ☐ paid-on delivery basis　配達時の支払い、着払い方式 ☐ parcel　小包
	☐ be headed to 〜　〜に向かう

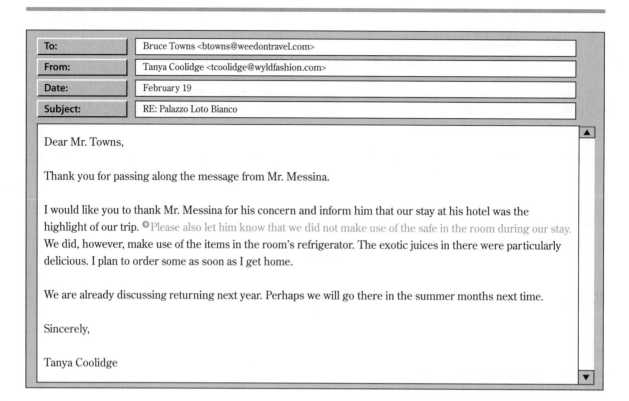

To:	Bruce Towns <btowns@weedontravel.com>
From:	Tanya Coolidge <tcoolidge@wyldfashion.com>
Date:	February 19
Subject:	RE: Palazzo Loto Bianco

Dear Mr. Towns,

Thank you for passing along the message from Mr. Messina.

I would like you to thank Mr. Messina for his concern and inform him that our stay at his hotel was the highlight of our trip. ❷ Please also let him know that we did not make use of the safe in the room during our stay. We did, however, make use of the items in the room's refrigerator. The exotic juices in there were particularly delicious. I plan to order some as soon as I get home.

We are already discussing returning next year. Perhaps we will go there in the summer months next time.

Sincerely,

Tanya Coolidge

受信者：Bruce Towns <btowns@weedontravel.com>
送信者：Tanya Coolidge <tcoolidge@wyldfashion.com>
日付：2月19日
件名：RE: Palazzo Loto Bianco

Towns様

Messina様からの伝言をいただき、ありがとうございました。

Messina様へ、お心遣いへの感謝と、Messina様の働くホテルでの滞在が私たちの旅行で最も思い出に残った旨をお伝えいただければと思います。また、滞在中に私たちが部屋の金庫を使用しなかったこともお伝えください。ただ、部屋の冷蔵庫の中の商品については、利用させていただきました。そこに入っていた外国産のジュースが特に美味しかったです。家に帰ったらすぐに注文するつもりです。

私たちはもうすでに、来年再び戻ってこようかと話し合っています。おそらく、次回は夏の時期に行くことになると思います。

敬具

Tanya Coolidge

語彙チェック　□ pass along ～　～を伝える　□ highlight　ハイライト、顕著な出来事　□ make use of ～　～を使う
□ exotic　外国産の

正解 D ☐☐☐☐

What is suggested about the hotel?

(A) It has a shuttle bus service to the airports.

(B) Its restaurant has won an award.

(C) It has some athletic facilities.

(D) Its rates depend on the season.

ホテルについて何が分かりますか。

(A) 空港へのシャトルバスのサービスがある。

(B そのレストランは賞を受賞したことがある。

(C) いくつかのアスレチック施設がある。

(D) 季節によって料金が変わる。

広告の❶に「1月から3月までオフピークの特別料金をご用意している」とあるので、季節によってホテルの料金が変わるということが判断できる。よって、正解は (D)。Palazzo Loto Bianco というホテル自体は賞を取ったものの、その中にあるレストランについては雑誌に掲載されたという事実しか述べられていないので、(B) は不正解。

👑 **Level Up！**

このような、本文中の具体的な情報を選択肢で抽象的に言い換えるパターンは頻出。よく出るパターンを押さえ、瞬時に言い換えに気付けるようにしておこう。

語彙チェック ☐ athletic 運動の ☐ rate 料金

正解 B ☐☐☐☐

What is implied about Ms. Coolidge?

(A) She has returned to her home in England.

(B) She qualified for one night's free accommodation.

(C) She will be charged for the cost of opening the safe.

(D) She mistakenly brought a piece of the hotel's equipment home.

Coolidge さんについて何が示唆されていますか。

(A) イギリスの故郷に帰った。

(B) 1泊分の無料宿泊の資格を得た。

(C) 金庫を開けるための費用を請求される。

(D) 誤ってホテルの備品を家に持ち帰った。

Coolidge さんについては、2文書目のEメールの❹で「彼女（＝ Coolidge さん）は2月11日から2月16日まで当ホテルに宿泊した顧客だ」と述べられている。また、このEメールの送信者は❽より Palazzo Loto Bianco ホテルの支配人である。Palazzo Loto Bianco の広告である1文書目に戻ると、❷に「3泊ご宿泊いただくと、4泊目が無料になる」とある。2月11日から2月16日まで滞在した Coolidge さんは、4泊目の無料宿泊の資格を得たということが分かるので、正解は (B)。Eメールの第1段落最後に「彼女は Weedon Travel 社のお得意様なので、その費用（＝金庫を開錠するための費用）は喜んで免除する」とあるので、(C) は不適切。

語彙チェック ☐ qualify for ～ ～の資格がある ☐ mistakenly 誤って ☐ bring A home A を家に持ち帰る

正解 A ☐☐☐☐

Where did Ms. Coolidge most likely go on February 16?

(A) To Catania Airport

(B) To Comiso Airport

(C) To Castello di Mola

(D) To Valencia Yacht Harbor

2月16日、Coolidge さんはどこに行ったと考えられますか。

(A) Catania 空港

(B) Comiso 空港

(C) Castello di Mola

(D) Valencia ヨットハーバー

2文書目のEメールの❻に「当社の受付係は、彼女（＝ Coolidge さん）がイギリスへのフライトのために空港に向かうと言っていたことを記憶している」とあり、Coolidge さんは海外へ行く予定があったということが分かる。1文書目のホテルの広告に戻ると、❸に「海外からのお客様は Catania 空港から車ですぐに来られる」とある。これらの情報から、Coolidge さんは Catania 空港へ向かったということが推測できる。よって、正解は (A)。

189

正解 C ☐☐☐☐

In the first e-mail, the phrase "pass on" in paragraph 2, line 4 is closest in meaning to

(A) refuse

(B) go by

(C) convey

(D) determine

最初のEメールの第2段落・4行目にある "pass on" に最も意味が近いのは

(A) 〜を断る

(B) 〜を通り過ぎる

(C) 〜を伝える

(D) 〜を決定する

❼を見ると、pass on の目的語として this message「このメッセージ」が続いている。pass on this[the] message は、「メッセージを伝える、伝言を回す」を意味する。これと同じ意味を持つ単語は、(C) convey。convey は「（ニュース・通信など）を伝える、伝達する」を意味する動詞で、convey a message「メッセージを伝える」という表現でよく用いられる。

190

正解 B ☐☐☐☐

What is implied about the items in the safe?

(A) They were of very high quality.

(B) They belonged to a previous occupant of the room.

(C) They were sent to Ms. Coolidge's home.

(D) They were temporarily kept at a reception desk.

金庫の中の品物について、何が示唆されていますか。

(A) 非常に質の高いものであった。

(B) その部屋の前の利用者のものであった。

(C) Coolidge さんの家に送られた。

(D) 受付で一時的に保管されていた。

2文書目のEメールの❺に「彼女（＝Coolidge さん）は貴重品を部屋の金庫に保管しており、それを取り出すのを忘れていたようだ」とある。これに対して3文書目のEメールの❾で、Coolidge さんは「滞在中に部屋の金庫を使用しなかった」と述べている。つまり、金庫の中の品物は、Coolidge さんが滞在するよりも前にその部屋を利用した人の忘れ物である、と推測できる。よって、正解は (B)。

語彙チェック ☐ of high quality　質の高い　☐ occupant　占有者　☐ temporarily　一時的に

目標5:00

音読 ☐☐☐ 解答時間

: ▶ :

Questions 191-195 refer to the following e-mail, and travel report, and memo.

TRACK_259

To:	Jim Nance <jnance@collinsengineering.com>
From:	Olga Krause <okrause@collinsengineering.com>
Date:	June 10
Subject:	Your trip

Dear Mr. Nance,

I understand that you will be taking your first business trip as an employee of Collins Engineering this month. ❶As you were unable to attend the first day of the new employee orientation, you may be unaware of certain procedures. You are required to submit a travel report within three days of your return. You can obtain an extension if you have special circumstances. The travel report must contain information about your flights, your accommodations, and your ground transportation. ❷You should list any purchases of gasoline separately from the vehicle rental fees. You are not required to include meals in the report, as you will be provided an allowance each day you are away. Every expense mentioned in the report must be accompanied by a receipt. ❸As some employees have misplaced receipts in the past, I recommend that you take a photograph of them with your phone and store them in the cloud. It will still be necessary to print a physical copy to submit with your report.

Please let me know if there is anything else I can assist with. Enjoy your trip.

Sincerely,

Olga Krause
Administration — Collins Engineering

Travel Report

Employee: Jim Nance

Expenses	Cost
Round-trip ticket to Seattle: June 16 Depart Chicago 9:00 A.M. Arrive in Seattle 11:44 A.M. June 20 Depart Seattle 7:00 A.M. Arrive in Chicago 1:01 P.M.	$820.00
Accommodation: ❹June 16 to June 18 — Santa Clarita Inn June 18 to June 20 — Ivory Business Hotel	$950.00 $210.00
❺Other transportation: Rental Vehicle, June 16 to June 18 Shuttle bus from Ivory Business Hotel to Seattle Airport, June 20	$560.00 $14.00

受信者：Jim Nance <jnance@collinsengineering.com>
送信者：Olga Krause <okrause@collinsengineering.com>
日付：6月10日
件名：あなたの出張について

Nance様

今月、Collins Engineering社の社員として初めて出張に行くようですね。あなたは新入社員オリエンテーションの初日に出席できなかったため、特定の手続きについてご存知ないかもしれません。出張報告書は、帰国後3日以内に提出することが義務付けられています。特別な事情がある場合は提出期限を延長することができます。出張報告書には、フライト、宿泊先、地上交通機関に関する情報を記載する必要があります。ガソリンを購入した場合は、レンタカー代とは別に記載する必要があります。旅行中、毎日手当てが支給されるため、報告書に食事代を記載する必要はありません。報告書に記載する経費には、必ず領収書を添付してください。過去に領収書を紛失した社員もいるので、携帯電話で撮影してクラウドに保存しておくことをお勧めします。いずれにしても、報告書と一緒に提出する場合は、物理的なコピーを印刷する必要があります。

他に何かお手伝いできることがあれば、ご連絡ください。ご旅行をお楽しみください。

どうぞよろしくお願いいたします。

Olga Krause
管理部— Collins Engineering

語彙チェック □ be unaware of 〜　〜を知らない　□ procedure　手続き、手順　□ extension　（期限の）延長
□ contain　〜を含む　□ accommodations　宿泊設備　□ list　〜をリストに掲載する　□ gasoline　ガソリン
□ separately　別々に、分けて　□ allowance　手当て　□ be accompanied by 〜　〜が伴う
□ misplace　〜をなくす　□ store　〜を保存する
□ cloud　クラウド（ネットワーク経由でユーザーにサービスを提供する形態）　□ physical　物理的な
□ assist with 〜　〜を手伝う

出張報告書

従業員：Jim Nance

経費	値段
Seattleへの往復航空券： 6月16日 午前9時 Chicago 出発　午前11時44分 Seattle 到着 6月20日 午前7時 Seattle 出発　午後1時01分 Chicago 到着	820ドル
宿泊施設： 6月16日〜18日 — Santa Clarita ホテル 6月18日〜20日 — Ivory ビジネスホテル	950ドル 210ドル
その他交通機関： レンタカー 6月16日〜18日 Ivory ビジネスホテル発 Seattle 空港行きシャトルバス、6月20日	560ドル 14ドル

語彙チェック □ expenses　経費　□ round-trip　往復の　□ inn　ホテル

MEMO

To: Locody Machinery Factory Design Team
From: Jim Nance
Date: June 22
Subject: My trip

❻ I was met by some executives from Locody Machinery at the arrivals gate on June 16. They took me to their manufacturing facility in Lancaster where I was able to view the proposed site of their new facility. The dimensions and their specific requirements have been uploaded to our server for your perusal. I was able to check the ground conditions and take some soil samples, which I sent to Cleminson Labs in Washington for analysis. I am still waiting on their evaluation.

❼ The following evening, I met Jason Paulson from Dunning Projects. Coincidentally, we were staying at the same hotel. It seems that that company has also been asked to make a bid on the project. As a previous employee, I know that they will be working hard to undercut us on price. ❽ They do this by ensuring a speedy construction that will enable them to collect an early completion bonus. It is a risky and aggressive strategy that has worked well for them so far. I know that Collins Engineering does not usually rely on the completion bonus when calculating its profit margin. We should discuss this at our meeting on Monday. I have been assured that the results of the soil sample will be ready by then also.

メモ

宛先：Locody機械工場デザインチーム
差出人：Jim Nance
日付：6月22日
件名：私の出張について

6月16日、到着ゲートでLocody機械会社の重役の方々に出迎えられました。Lancasterにある同社の製造施設に案内いただき、そこで新施設の建設予定地を見ることができました。その規模と彼らの特別な要望は、ご一読いただけるようサーバーにアップロードしてあります。地盤の状態を確認し、土壌のサンプルを採取できました。土壌のサンプルは、分析のためにWashingtonのCleminson研究所へ送りました。現在まだその評価を待っているところです。

翌日の夕方に、Dunning Projects社のJason Paulsonに会いました。偶然にも、同じホテルに泊まっていたのです。どうやら、その会社も当プロジェクトの入札を依頼されているそうです。元従業員として、彼らが価格面で我々を下回るよう努力を行うことは分かっています。スピード施工によって早期完成ボーナスが出る仕組みを保証することによって、彼らは価格を下げられるのです。これはリスクを伴う果敢な戦略であり、これまで彼らにとってはうまくいってきたことです。Collins Engineeringは通常、完成ボーナスを利益率の計算に入れていないことは承知しています。この点については、月曜のミーティングで話し合うべきでしょう。その頃までには、土壌サンプルの結果も出ているはずです。

語彙チェック　□ executive　重役　□ proposed　提案された　□ dimensions　規模、寸法
□ specific requirements　特別な要望・条件　□ perusal　通読、精読　□ ground condition　地盤の状態
□ soil sample　土壌サンプル　□ coincidentally　偶然にも　□ make a bid　入札する
□ undercut　～より安く売る　□ speedy　迅速な　□ aggressive　果敢な、好戦的な　□ calculate　～を計算する
□ profit margin　利益率　□ assure　～に確信させる

正解 D ☐☐☐☐

What is mentioned about Mr. Nance?

(A) He was involved in an employee training program.

(B) He will travel with a colleague.

(C) He was interviewed by Ms. Krause before.

(D) He failed to hear some procedures.

Nanceさんについて何が言及されていますか。

(A) 社員研修プログラムに参加した。

(B) 同僚と出張に行く。

(C) 以前Krauseさんによる面接を受けたことがある。

(D) いくつかの手続きを聞き逃した。

管理部のKrauseさんはNanceさんに対して、Eメールの❶で「(Nanceさんは) 新入社員オリエンテーションの初日に出席できなかったため、特定の手続きについて知らないかもしれない」と伝えている。よって、(D)が正解。fail to doは「～し損なう、～しそびれる」を意味する重要表現。

語彙チェック ☐ be involved in ～　～に関わる

正解 B ☐☐☐☐

What is Mr. Nance advised to do?

(A) Submit a report on the day of his return

(B) Keep digital evidence of his expenditure

(C) Inform a supervisor of changes to his schedule

(D) Attend an orientation session

Nanceさんは何をするように勧められていますか。

(A) 戻った日に報告書を提出する

(B) 支出に関する証拠をデジタル式で記録する

(C) スケジュールの変更を上司に報告する

(D) オリエンテーションに参加する

Nanceさんは、Eメールの❸で「領収書を紛失した社員もいるので、携帯電話で撮影してクラウドに保存しておくことを勧める」とアドバイスを受けている。よって、これを言い換えた(B)が正解。出張報告書は戻ったその日ではなく、戻ってから3日以内に提出するのが決まりだと述べられているので、(A)は不正解。

語彙チェック ☐ digital evidence　電子的な証拠　☐ inform *A* of *B*　AにBを知らせる

正解 C ☐☐☐☐

What required information has Mr. Nance failed to include in the travel report?

(A) Flight details

(B) Meal prices

(C) Fuel costs

(D) Ground transportation

Nanceさんが出張報告書に記載しなかった必要情報は何ですか。

(A) フライトの詳細

(B) 食事の金額

(C) 燃料費

(D) 地上交通機関

Eメールの❷で「ガソリンを購入したらレンタカー代とは別に記載する必要がある」と述べられているものの、Nanceさんの出張報告書❺を見ると、レンタカー代しか記載されていない。よって、正解は(C)。gasolineがfuelと言い換えられている。

語彙チェック ☐ fuel　燃料

👑 Level Up！

Eメールに記載された条件と報告書の内容を照らし合わせて解こう。報告書には食事の金額の記載もないが、Eメールに「報告書に食事代を記載する必要性はない」とあるので、(B)は必要情報にはあたらないことにも注意。

194

正解 B ☐☐☐☐

Where did Mr. Nance encounter Mr. Paulson?

(A) At Ivory Business Hotel

(B) At Santa Clarita Inn

(C) At Seattle Airport

(D) At Locody Machinery

NanceさんはどこでPaulsonさんに出会いましたか。

(A) Ivoryビジネスホテル

(B) Santa Claritaホテル

(C) Seattle空港

(D) Locody機械会社

Nanceさんはメモの❼で「翌日の夕方にDunning Projects社のJason Paulsonに会った」「偶然にも同じホテルに泊まっていた」と述べている。この「翌日の夕方」とは、その前の❻で「6月16日にLocody機械会社の重役の方々に出迎えられた」と述べられていることから、6月17日のことであると分かる。ここで出張報告書の❹を見ると、Nanceさんは6月17日にSanta Claritaホテルに滞在していたことが読み取れる。これらの情報から、Nanceさんが Paulsonさんに会った場所はSanta Claritaホテルであると分かるので、正解は(B)。

195

正解 D ☐☐☐☐

What is implied about Dunning Projects?

(A) Its employment contract restricts staff from working for competitors.

(B) It often collaborates with other firms on large projects.

(C) It promotes its quality assurance policies to potential clients.

(D) Its profitability can be threatened by construction delays.

Dunning Projects社について何が示唆されていますか。

(A) その雇用契約は、従業員が競合他社で働くことを禁止している。

(B) 大きなプロジェクトでは、他の会社と協力することが多い。

(C) 潜在顧客に対して、品質保証の方針をアピールしている。

(D) 工事の遅れによって収益が脅かされる可能性がある。

Dunning Projects社はメモの第2段落目に登場する。❽に「スピード施工によって早期完成ボーナスが出る仕組みを保証することによって、彼らは価格を下げられる」とある。早く施工が終わるとボーナスが出るということは、工事が遅れることによって収益が下がる可能性が示唆されているので、正解は(D)。

語彙チェック ☐ employment contract　雇用契約　☐ restrict *A* from *doing*　Aが～することを禁止する
☐ collaborate with ～　～と協力する、～と共同して働く　☐ quality assurance　品質保証　☐ potential　潜在的な
☐ profitability　収益性　☐ threaten　～を脅かす

Questions 196-200 refer to the following brochure and e-mails.

目標5:00

音読 □ □ □   解答時間   :   ▶   :

▶TRACK_260

Khatri Online Services: India's Premium Outsourcing Agency

❶The name Khatri Online Services (KOS) is synonymous with dependability, accountability, and affordability. We have earned this reputation by consistently putting our clients' needs before our own. Our online workers are highly educated, extremely motivated, and very experienced. They can quickly adapt to your company's culture, learn all of the relevant product specifications, and accurately predict clients' needs.

We offer:
- Consumer-focused technical support by telephone and chat
- Cross-platform software programming
- Web site development

We can supply up to five trained full-time workers with as little as two weeks' notice. ❷There is a ten percent surcharge applicable when workers' start and finish times differ by more than seven hours from Mumbai local time.

To:	Milly Dore <mdore@atlantatech.com>
From:	Sunil Singh <ssingh@khatrionlineservices.com>
Date:	November 4
Subject:	❸Summary of service for October

Dear Ms. Dore,

❹I apologize for the slightly delayed response times your technical support clients reported. ❺There is a 12.5-hour time difference between here and California, which our workers have been struggling to adapt to. ❻In my experience, these problems resolve themselves within the first month.

Summary of service for October

Service	For	Hours
Telephone support line	Smartphone (Model: TGH532)	960
Software programming	❼Tablet (HH673)	N / A
App development	Television Media Box (JS732)	N / A
Online chat support	Laptop Computer (KH864)	480

We will send Atlanta Tech an invoice for these services on November 15. Please let me know if you see any discrepancies.

Sincerely,

❽Sunil Singh
Khatri Outsourcing Agency

問題196-200は次のパンフレットと2通のEメールに関するものです。

Khatri Online Services：インドで最上の外部委託代理業者

Khatri Online Services (KOS) という名前は、信頼性、責任感、そしてお手頃さの代名詞となっています。一貫してお客様のニーズを優先することで、私たちはこのような評判を獲得してまいりました。弊社のオンラインワーカーは高度な教育を受けており、きわめて意欲的で、非常に経験豊富です。あなたの会社の企業文化に素早く適応し、関連する製品仕様の全てを学び、お客様のニーズを正確に予測することができます。

私たちが提供するのは：
• 電話およびチャットによる消費者向け技術サポート
• 異なるプラットフォームに対応したソフトウェアのプログラミング
• ウェブサイトの開発

わずか2週間前までにお知らせいただければ、最大5名まで、訓練を受けたフルタイムの労働者を派遣いたします。業務開始時刻および終了時刻がMumbaiの現地時間から7時間を超えて異なる場合、10パーセントの追加料金がかかります。

語彙チェック
☐ outsourcing 外部委託 ☐ be synonymous with ~ ～の代名詞である、～と同義である
☐ dependability 信頼性 ☐ accountability 責任感 ☐ affordability お手頃さ ☐ earn ～を得る
☐ reputation 評判 ☐ consistently 一貫して ☐ put *A* before *B* B よりもA を優先する
☐ educated 教育を受けた、教養のある ☐ extremely きわめて ☐ product specifications 製品仕様（書）
☐ accurately 正確に ☐ predict ～を予想する ☐ consumer-focused 消費者向けの
☐ cross-platform 異なるプラットフォーム上で使うことのできる ☐ up to ~ 最大～まで ☐ trained 訓練された
☐ notice 予告、知らせ ☐ surcharge 追加料金 ☐ applicable 適用される ☐ differ 異なる

受信者：Milly Dore <mdore@atlantatech.com>
送信者：Sunil Singh <ssingh@khatrionlineservices.com>
日付：11月4日
件名：10月のサービス概要

Dore様

貴社の技術サポートクライアントより報告を受けた、少しの対応遅れについて、お詫び申し上げます。こちらとCaliforniaでは12.5時間の時差があり、従業員が適応するのに苦労しております。私の経験では、これらの問題は最初の1カ月のうちに自然と解消します。

10月のサービス概要

サービス	対象	時間
電話サポートライン	スマートフォン（モデル：TGH532）	960時間
ソフトウェアプログラミング	タブレット（HH673）	該当なし
アプリ開発	テレビメディアボックス（JS732）	該当なし
オンラインチャットサポート	ノートパソコン（KH864）	480時間

これらのサービスに関する請求書は、Atlanta技術社へ11月15日にお送りする予定です。何か相違がございましたら、お知らせください。

敬具

Sunil Singh
Khatri外部委託代理業者

語彙チェック ☐ summary 概要、要約 ☐ slightly わずかに、少し ☐ response time 応答時間
☐ struggle to *do* ～することに苦しむ ☐ resolve *oneself* 自然に解決する ☐ discrepancy 相違、不一致

To:	Milly Dore <mdore@atlantatech.com>
From:	Heath Glenn <hglenn@atlantatech.com>
Date:	November 4
Subject:	Complaints

Hi Milly,

❾There seems to be some system malfunction regarding HH673 and we are receiving quite a few complaints from its users. This problem needs to be addressed as soon as possible. ❿If I remember correctly, Khatri Outsourcing Agency was involved in this. Could you give me the telephone number or e-mail address of the representative you have contacted before? I think it's much faster for me to talk to him or her directly and ask questions on this matter.

Sincerely,

Heath

受信者：Milly Dore <mdore@atlantatech.com>
送信者：Heath Glenn <hglenn@atlantatech.com>
日付：11月4日
件名：苦情

Millyさん

HH673のシステムに不具合があるようで、ユーザーからかなりの数の苦情が寄せられています。この問題はできるだけ早く対処されなければなりません。私の記憶が正しければ、Khatri 外部委託代理業者がこの件に関与していたと思います。以前あなたが連絡していた担当者の電話番号かEメールアドレスを教えていただけませんか。その方と直接話をして、この件について質問した方がより早いと思うのです。

よろしくお願いします。

Heath

語彙チェック　□ malfunction　不具合、不調　□ regarding　～に関して　□ address　～に対処する　□ correctly　正しく
□ directly　直接、直に　□ matter　問題、事柄

196

正解 **B**

According to the brochure, what is KOS known for?

(A) The durability of its products

(B) The responsibility of its employees

(C) The speed of its shipping service

(D) The convenience of its locations

パンフレットによると、KOSは何で知られていますか。

(A) 製品の耐久性

(B) 従業員の責任感

(C) 発送の速さ

(D) 拠点の利便性

パンフレットの❶に「Khatri Online Services (KOS) という名前は、信頼性、責任感、そしてお手頃さの代名詞」と述べられている。2つ目に述べられているaccountability「責任感」と同じ意味を表す(B)が正解。その他の選択肢はどれも本文で述べられていない。

語彙チェック □ be known for ~ ~で知られている □ durability 耐久性 □ responsibility 責任感

197

正解 **A**

What is implied about Atlanta Tech?

(A) It is paying extra for some services.

(B) It was able to reduce costs by using a foreign manufacturer.

(C) It charges its clients an additional fee for technical support.

(D) It relies on outsourcing for device design work.

Atlanta技術会社について何が示唆されていますか。

(A) 一部のサービスに対して追加料金を支払っている。

(B) 海外メーカーを利用することでコストを削減することができた。

(C) 技術サポートに追加料金を請求している。

(D) デバイスのデザイン設計を外部に頼っている。

2文書目のEメールは、Khatri外部委託代理業者が、サービスを利用しているAtlanta技術会社に宛てて送ったもの。❺に「こちらとCaliforniaでは12.5時間の時差があり、従業員が適応するのに苦労している」とあることに注目。1文書目のパンフレットに戻ると、❷に「業務開始時刻および終了時刻がMumbaiの現地時間から7時間を超えて異なる場合、10パーセントの追加料金がかかる」と述べられている。これらの情報から、Atlanta技術会社はKhatri外部委託代理業者に対して10パーセントの追加料金を支払っていると判断できる。よって、正解は(A)。

語彙チェック □ extra 追加料金

198

正解 **C**

What is suggested about KOS?

(A) It sends weekly invoices to its foreign clients.

(B) It manufactures devices for sale in the consumer market.

(C) It has provided Atlanta Tech technical support since October.

(D) It has been notified of an error in its time calculation system.

KOSについて何が分かりますか。

(A) 海外の顧客に週単位で請求書を送っている。

(B) 消費者市場向けのデバイスを製造している。

(C) 10月からAtlanta技術会社に技術サポートを提供している。

(D) 時間計算システムに誤りがあると通知を受けた。

Khatri外部委託代理業者はAtlanta技術会社に対し、2文書目のEメールの❹で、技術サポートに関して対応遅れがあったことを詫びている。また❻では、「経験上これらの問題は最初の1カ月のうちに自然と解消する」と述べている。さらにこのEメールの件名は、❸「10月のサービス概要」なので、Khatri外部委託代理業者は10月からAtlanta技術会社に技術サポートのサービスを提供し始めたということが推測できる。よって、(C)が正解。

語彙チェック □ weekly 週に1回の、毎週の □ manufacture ~を製造する

199

What kind of product does Atlanta Tech receive complaints about?

(A) A smartphone

(B) A tablet

(C) A television media box

(D) A laptop computer

Atlanta技術会社は何の種類の製品について苦情を受けていますか。

(A) スマートフォン

(B) タブレット

(C) テレビメディアボックス

(D) ノートパソコン

Atlanta技術会社のGlennさんは、3文書目のEメールの⑨で「HH673のシステムに不具合があり、ユーザーからかなり苦情が寄せられている」と述べている。HH673とは、2文書目のEメールの⑦に「タブレット（HH673）」とあることから、タブレット製品だと分かる。よって、正解は(B)。

200

What is most likely true about Ms. Dore?

(A) She will apologize to a customer directly.

(B) She has welcomed Mr. Singh to her team.

(C) She received an invoice from Atlanta Tech on November 4.

(D) She will share Mr. Singh's contact details with Mr. Glenn.

Doreさんについて正しいと考えられることは何ですか。

(A) 顧客に直接謝罪をする予定である。

(B) Singhさんを自分のチームに迎え入れた。

(C) 11月4日にAtlanta技術会社から請求書を受け取った。

(D) GlennさんにSinghさんの連絡先を教える。

HH673の製品に苦情が寄せられていることを受け、Glennさんは3文書目のEメール⑩で「私の記憶が正しければ、Khatri外部委託代理業者がこの件に関与していたと思う」「以前あなた（＝Doreさん）が連絡していた担当者の電話番号かEメールアドレスを教えてもらえないか」と尋ねている。2文書目のEメールの⑧より、Doreさんが以前連絡していた担当者の名前はSunil Singhさんだと分かる。よって、DoreさんはGlennさんにSinghさんの連絡先を共有すると考えられるので、(D)が正解。

語彙チェック ☐ contact details　連絡先

990点獲得 全パート模試用マークシート

（コピーしてお使いください）

本書のTEST 1とTEST 2を解くときに使えるマークシートを用意しました。本番さながらにマークシートを使って問題を解くようにしましょう。

TEST 1

Part 1

No.	A B C D
1	Ⓐ Ⓑ Ⓒ Ⓓ
2	Ⓐ Ⓑ Ⓒ Ⓓ
3	Ⓐ Ⓑ Ⓒ Ⓓ
4	Ⓐ Ⓑ Ⓒ Ⓓ
5	Ⓐ Ⓑ Ⓒ Ⓓ
6	Ⓐ Ⓑ Ⓒ Ⓓ
7	Ⓐ Ⓑ Ⓒ Ⓓ
8	Ⓐ Ⓑ Ⓒ Ⓓ
9	Ⓐ Ⓑ Ⓒ Ⓓ
10	Ⓐ Ⓑ Ⓒ Ⓓ

Part 2

No.	A B C	No.	A B C
11	Ⓐ Ⓑ Ⓒ	21	Ⓐ Ⓑ Ⓒ
12	Ⓐ Ⓑ Ⓒ	22	Ⓐ Ⓑ Ⓒ
13	Ⓐ Ⓑ Ⓒ	23	Ⓐ Ⓑ Ⓒ
14	Ⓐ Ⓑ Ⓒ	24	Ⓐ Ⓑ Ⓒ
15	Ⓐ Ⓑ Ⓒ	25	Ⓐ Ⓑ Ⓒ
16	Ⓐ Ⓑ Ⓒ	26	Ⓐ Ⓑ Ⓒ
17	Ⓐ Ⓑ Ⓒ	27	Ⓐ Ⓑ Ⓒ
18	Ⓐ Ⓑ Ⓒ	28	Ⓐ Ⓑ Ⓒ
19	Ⓐ Ⓑ Ⓒ	29	Ⓐ Ⓑ Ⓒ
20	Ⓐ Ⓑ Ⓒ	30	Ⓐ Ⓑ Ⓒ

Part 3

No.	A B C D	No.	A B C D
31	Ⓐ Ⓑ Ⓒ Ⓓ	41	Ⓐ Ⓑ Ⓒ Ⓓ
32	Ⓐ Ⓑ Ⓒ Ⓓ	42	Ⓐ Ⓑ Ⓒ Ⓓ
33	Ⓐ Ⓑ Ⓒ Ⓓ	43	Ⓐ Ⓑ Ⓒ Ⓓ
34	Ⓐ Ⓑ Ⓒ Ⓓ	44	Ⓐ Ⓑ Ⓒ Ⓓ
35	Ⓐ Ⓑ Ⓒ Ⓓ	45	Ⓐ Ⓑ Ⓒ Ⓓ
36	Ⓐ Ⓑ Ⓒ Ⓓ	46	Ⓐ Ⓑ Ⓒ Ⓓ
37	Ⓐ Ⓑ Ⓒ Ⓓ	47	Ⓐ Ⓑ Ⓒ Ⓓ
38	Ⓐ Ⓑ Ⓒ Ⓓ	48	Ⓐ Ⓑ Ⓒ Ⓓ
39	Ⓐ Ⓑ Ⓒ Ⓓ	49	Ⓐ Ⓑ Ⓒ Ⓓ
40	Ⓐ Ⓑ Ⓒ Ⓓ	50	Ⓐ Ⓑ Ⓒ Ⓓ

Part 4

No.	A B C D	No.	A B C D	No.	A B C D	No.	A B C D
51	Ⓐ Ⓑ Ⓒ Ⓓ	61	Ⓐ Ⓑ Ⓒ Ⓓ	71	Ⓐ Ⓑ Ⓒ Ⓓ	81	Ⓐ Ⓑ Ⓒ Ⓓ
52	Ⓐ Ⓑ Ⓒ Ⓓ	62	Ⓐ Ⓑ Ⓒ Ⓓ	72	Ⓐ Ⓑ Ⓒ Ⓓ	82	Ⓐ Ⓑ Ⓒ Ⓓ
53	Ⓐ Ⓑ Ⓒ Ⓓ	63	Ⓐ Ⓑ Ⓒ Ⓓ	73	Ⓐ Ⓑ Ⓒ Ⓓ	83	Ⓐ Ⓑ Ⓒ Ⓓ
54	Ⓐ Ⓑ Ⓒ Ⓓ	64	Ⓐ Ⓑ Ⓒ Ⓓ	74	Ⓐ Ⓑ Ⓒ Ⓓ	84	Ⓐ Ⓑ Ⓒ Ⓓ
55	Ⓐ Ⓑ Ⓒ Ⓓ	65	Ⓐ Ⓑ Ⓒ Ⓓ	75	Ⓐ Ⓑ Ⓒ Ⓓ	85	Ⓐ Ⓑ Ⓒ Ⓓ
56	Ⓐ Ⓑ Ⓒ Ⓓ	66	Ⓐ Ⓑ Ⓒ Ⓓ	76	Ⓐ Ⓑ Ⓒ Ⓓ	86	Ⓐ Ⓑ Ⓒ Ⓓ
57	Ⓐ Ⓑ Ⓒ Ⓓ	67	Ⓐ Ⓑ Ⓒ Ⓓ	77	Ⓐ Ⓑ Ⓒ Ⓓ	87	Ⓐ Ⓑ Ⓒ Ⓓ
58	Ⓐ Ⓑ Ⓒ Ⓓ	68	Ⓐ Ⓑ Ⓒ Ⓓ	78	Ⓐ Ⓑ Ⓒ Ⓓ	88	Ⓐ Ⓑ Ⓒ Ⓓ
59	Ⓐ Ⓑ Ⓒ Ⓓ	69	Ⓐ Ⓑ Ⓒ Ⓓ	79	Ⓐ Ⓑ Ⓒ Ⓓ	89	Ⓐ Ⓑ Ⓒ Ⓓ
60	Ⓐ Ⓑ Ⓒ Ⓓ	70	Ⓐ Ⓑ Ⓒ Ⓓ	80	Ⓐ Ⓑ Ⓒ Ⓓ	90	Ⓐ Ⓑ Ⓒ Ⓓ

No.	A B C D
91	Ⓐ Ⓑ Ⓒ Ⓓ
92	Ⓐ Ⓑ Ⓒ Ⓓ
93	Ⓐ Ⓑ Ⓒ Ⓓ
94	Ⓐ Ⓑ Ⓒ Ⓓ
95	Ⓐ Ⓑ Ⓒ Ⓓ
96	Ⓐ Ⓑ Ⓒ Ⓓ
97	Ⓐ Ⓑ Ⓒ Ⓓ
98	Ⓐ Ⓑ Ⓒ Ⓓ
99	Ⓐ Ⓑ Ⓒ Ⓓ
100	Ⓐ Ⓑ Ⓒ Ⓓ

Part 5

No.	A B C D
101	Ⓐ Ⓑ Ⓒ Ⓓ
102	Ⓐ Ⓑ Ⓒ Ⓓ
103	Ⓐ Ⓑ Ⓒ Ⓓ
104	Ⓐ Ⓑ Ⓒ Ⓓ
105	Ⓐ Ⓑ Ⓒ Ⓓ
106	Ⓐ Ⓑ Ⓒ Ⓓ
107	Ⓐ Ⓑ Ⓒ Ⓓ
108	Ⓐ Ⓑ Ⓒ Ⓓ
109	Ⓐ Ⓑ Ⓒ Ⓓ
110	Ⓐ Ⓑ Ⓒ Ⓓ

Part 6

No.	A B C D
111	Ⓐ Ⓑ Ⓒ Ⓓ
112	Ⓐ Ⓑ Ⓒ Ⓓ
113	Ⓐ Ⓑ Ⓒ Ⓓ
114	Ⓐ Ⓑ Ⓒ Ⓓ
115	Ⓐ Ⓑ Ⓒ Ⓓ
116	Ⓐ Ⓑ Ⓒ Ⓓ
117	Ⓐ Ⓑ Ⓒ Ⓓ
118	Ⓐ Ⓑ Ⓒ Ⓓ
119	Ⓐ Ⓑ Ⓒ Ⓓ
120	Ⓐ Ⓑ Ⓒ Ⓓ

No.	A B C D
121	Ⓐ Ⓑ Ⓒ Ⓓ
122	Ⓐ Ⓑ Ⓒ Ⓓ
123	Ⓐ Ⓑ Ⓒ Ⓓ
124	Ⓐ Ⓑ Ⓒ Ⓓ
125	Ⓐ Ⓑ Ⓒ Ⓓ
126	Ⓐ Ⓑ Ⓒ Ⓓ
127	Ⓐ Ⓑ Ⓒ Ⓓ
128	Ⓐ Ⓑ Ⓒ Ⓓ
129	Ⓐ Ⓑ Ⓒ Ⓓ
130	Ⓐ Ⓑ Ⓒ Ⓓ

Part 7

No.	A B C D	No.	A B C D	No.	A B C D	No.	A B C D	No.	A B C D	No.	A B C D
131	Ⓐ Ⓑ Ⓒ Ⓓ	141	Ⓐ Ⓑ Ⓒ Ⓓ	151	Ⓐ Ⓑ Ⓒ Ⓓ	161	Ⓐ Ⓑ Ⓒ Ⓓ	171	Ⓐ Ⓑ Ⓒ Ⓓ	181	Ⓐ Ⓑ Ⓒ Ⓓ
132	Ⓐ Ⓑ Ⓒ Ⓓ	142	Ⓐ Ⓑ Ⓒ Ⓓ	152	Ⓐ Ⓑ Ⓒ Ⓓ	162	Ⓐ Ⓑ Ⓒ Ⓓ	172	Ⓐ Ⓑ Ⓒ Ⓓ	182	Ⓐ Ⓑ Ⓒ Ⓓ
133	Ⓐ Ⓑ Ⓒ Ⓓ	143	Ⓐ Ⓑ Ⓒ Ⓓ	153	Ⓐ Ⓑ Ⓒ Ⓓ	163	Ⓐ Ⓑ Ⓒ Ⓓ	173	Ⓐ Ⓑ Ⓒ Ⓓ	183	Ⓐ Ⓑ Ⓒ Ⓓ
134	Ⓐ Ⓑ Ⓒ Ⓓ	144	Ⓐ Ⓑ Ⓒ Ⓓ	154	Ⓐ Ⓑ Ⓒ Ⓓ	164	Ⓐ Ⓑ Ⓒ Ⓓ	174	Ⓐ Ⓑ Ⓒ Ⓓ	184	Ⓐ Ⓑ Ⓒ Ⓓ
135	Ⓐ Ⓑ Ⓒ Ⓓ	145	Ⓐ Ⓑ Ⓒ Ⓓ	155	Ⓐ Ⓑ Ⓒ Ⓓ	165	Ⓐ Ⓑ Ⓒ Ⓓ	175	Ⓐ Ⓑ Ⓒ Ⓓ	185	Ⓐ Ⓑ Ⓒ Ⓓ
136	Ⓐ Ⓑ Ⓒ Ⓓ	146	Ⓐ Ⓑ Ⓒ Ⓓ	156	Ⓐ Ⓑ Ⓒ Ⓓ	166	Ⓐ Ⓑ Ⓒ Ⓓ	176	Ⓐ Ⓑ Ⓒ Ⓓ	186	Ⓐ Ⓑ Ⓒ Ⓓ
137	Ⓐ Ⓑ Ⓒ Ⓓ	147	Ⓐ Ⓑ Ⓒ Ⓓ	157	Ⓐ Ⓑ Ⓒ Ⓓ	167	Ⓐ Ⓑ Ⓒ Ⓓ	177	Ⓐ Ⓑ Ⓒ Ⓓ	187	Ⓐ Ⓑ Ⓒ Ⓓ
138	Ⓐ Ⓑ Ⓒ Ⓓ	148	Ⓐ Ⓑ Ⓒ Ⓓ	158	Ⓐ Ⓑ Ⓒ Ⓓ	168	Ⓐ Ⓑ Ⓒ Ⓓ	178	Ⓐ Ⓑ Ⓒ Ⓓ	188	Ⓐ Ⓑ Ⓒ Ⓓ
139	Ⓐ Ⓑ Ⓒ Ⓓ	149	Ⓐ Ⓑ Ⓒ Ⓓ	159	Ⓐ Ⓑ Ⓒ Ⓓ	169	Ⓐ Ⓑ Ⓒ Ⓓ	179	Ⓐ Ⓑ Ⓒ Ⓓ	189	Ⓐ Ⓑ Ⓒ Ⓓ
140	Ⓐ Ⓑ Ⓒ Ⓓ	150	Ⓐ Ⓑ Ⓒ Ⓓ	160	Ⓐ Ⓑ Ⓒ Ⓓ	170	Ⓐ Ⓑ Ⓒ Ⓓ	180	Ⓐ Ⓑ Ⓒ Ⓓ	190	Ⓐ Ⓑ Ⓒ Ⓓ

No.	A B C D
191	Ⓐ Ⓑ Ⓒ Ⓓ
192	Ⓐ Ⓑ Ⓒ Ⓓ
193	Ⓐ Ⓑ Ⓒ Ⓓ
194	Ⓐ Ⓑ Ⓒ Ⓓ
195	Ⓐ Ⓑ Ⓒ Ⓓ
196	Ⓐ Ⓑ Ⓒ Ⓓ
197	Ⓐ Ⓑ Ⓒ Ⓓ
198	Ⓐ Ⓑ Ⓒ Ⓓ
199	Ⓐ Ⓑ Ⓒ Ⓓ
200	Ⓐ Ⓑ Ⓒ Ⓓ

TEST 2

Part 1

No.	ANSWER A B C D
1	Ⓐ Ⓑ Ⓒ Ⓓ
2	Ⓐ Ⓑ Ⓒ Ⓓ
3	Ⓐ Ⓑ Ⓒ Ⓓ
4	Ⓐ Ⓑ Ⓒ Ⓓ
5	Ⓐ Ⓑ Ⓒ Ⓓ
6	Ⓐ Ⓑ Ⓒ Ⓓ
7	Ⓐ Ⓑ Ⓒ Ⓓ
8	Ⓐ Ⓑ Ⓒ Ⓓ
9	Ⓐ Ⓑ Ⓒ Ⓓ
10	Ⓐ Ⓑ Ⓒ Ⓓ

Part 2

No.	ANSWER A B C
11	Ⓐ Ⓑ Ⓒ
12	Ⓐ Ⓑ Ⓒ
13	Ⓐ Ⓑ Ⓒ
14	Ⓐ Ⓑ Ⓒ
15	Ⓐ Ⓑ Ⓒ
16	Ⓐ Ⓑ Ⓒ
17	Ⓐ Ⓑ Ⓒ
18	Ⓐ Ⓑ Ⓒ
19	Ⓐ Ⓑ Ⓒ
20	Ⓐ Ⓑ Ⓒ

No.	ANSWER A B C
21	Ⓐ Ⓑ Ⓒ
22	Ⓐ Ⓑ Ⓒ
23	Ⓐ Ⓑ Ⓒ
24	Ⓐ Ⓑ Ⓒ
25	Ⓐ Ⓑ Ⓒ
26	Ⓐ Ⓑ Ⓒ
27	Ⓐ Ⓑ Ⓒ
28	Ⓐ Ⓑ Ⓒ
29	Ⓐ Ⓑ Ⓒ
30	Ⓐ Ⓑ Ⓒ

Part 3

No.	ANSWER A B C D
31	Ⓐ Ⓑ Ⓒ Ⓓ
32	Ⓐ Ⓑ Ⓒ Ⓓ
33	Ⓐ Ⓑ Ⓒ Ⓓ
34	Ⓐ Ⓑ Ⓒ Ⓓ
35	Ⓐ Ⓑ Ⓒ Ⓓ
36	Ⓐ Ⓑ Ⓒ Ⓓ
37	Ⓐ Ⓑ Ⓒ Ⓓ
38	Ⓐ Ⓑ Ⓒ Ⓓ
39	Ⓐ Ⓑ Ⓒ Ⓓ
40	Ⓐ Ⓑ Ⓒ Ⓓ

No.	ANSWER A B C D
41	Ⓐ Ⓑ Ⓒ Ⓓ
42	Ⓐ Ⓑ Ⓒ Ⓓ
43	Ⓐ Ⓑ Ⓒ Ⓓ
44	Ⓐ Ⓑ Ⓒ Ⓓ
45	Ⓐ Ⓑ Ⓒ Ⓓ
46	Ⓐ Ⓑ Ⓒ Ⓓ
47	Ⓐ Ⓑ Ⓒ Ⓓ
48	Ⓐ Ⓑ Ⓒ Ⓓ
49	Ⓐ Ⓑ Ⓒ Ⓓ
50	Ⓐ Ⓑ Ⓒ Ⓓ

No.	ANSWER A B C D
51	Ⓐ Ⓑ Ⓒ Ⓓ
52	Ⓐ Ⓑ Ⓒ Ⓓ
53	Ⓐ Ⓑ Ⓒ Ⓓ
54	Ⓐ Ⓑ Ⓒ Ⓓ
55	Ⓐ Ⓑ Ⓒ Ⓓ
56	Ⓐ Ⓑ Ⓒ Ⓓ
57	Ⓐ Ⓑ Ⓒ Ⓓ
58	Ⓐ Ⓑ Ⓒ Ⓓ
59	Ⓐ Ⓑ Ⓒ Ⓓ
60	Ⓐ Ⓑ Ⓒ Ⓓ

No.	ANSWER A B C D
61	Ⓐ Ⓑ Ⓒ Ⓓ
62	Ⓐ Ⓑ Ⓒ Ⓓ
63	Ⓐ Ⓑ Ⓒ Ⓓ
64	Ⓐ Ⓑ Ⓒ Ⓓ
65	Ⓐ Ⓑ Ⓒ Ⓓ
66	Ⓐ Ⓑ Ⓒ Ⓓ
67	Ⓐ Ⓑ Ⓒ Ⓓ
68	Ⓐ Ⓑ Ⓒ Ⓓ
69	Ⓐ Ⓑ Ⓒ Ⓓ
70	Ⓐ Ⓑ Ⓒ Ⓓ

Part 4

No.	ANSWER A B C D
71	Ⓐ Ⓑ Ⓒ Ⓓ
72	Ⓐ Ⓑ Ⓒ Ⓓ
73	Ⓐ Ⓑ Ⓒ Ⓓ
74	Ⓐ Ⓑ Ⓒ Ⓓ
75	Ⓐ Ⓑ Ⓒ Ⓓ
76	Ⓐ Ⓑ Ⓒ Ⓓ
77	Ⓐ Ⓑ Ⓒ Ⓓ
78	Ⓐ Ⓑ Ⓒ Ⓓ
79	Ⓐ Ⓑ Ⓒ Ⓓ
80	Ⓐ Ⓑ Ⓒ Ⓓ

No.	ANSWER A B C D
81	Ⓐ Ⓑ Ⓒ Ⓓ
82	Ⓐ Ⓑ Ⓒ Ⓓ
83	Ⓐ Ⓑ Ⓒ Ⓓ
84	Ⓐ Ⓑ Ⓒ Ⓓ
85	Ⓐ Ⓑ Ⓒ Ⓓ
86	Ⓐ Ⓑ Ⓒ Ⓓ
87	Ⓐ Ⓑ Ⓒ Ⓓ
88	Ⓐ Ⓑ Ⓒ Ⓓ
89	Ⓐ Ⓑ Ⓒ Ⓓ
90	Ⓐ Ⓑ Ⓒ Ⓓ

No.	ANSWER A B C D
91	Ⓐ Ⓑ Ⓒ Ⓓ
92	Ⓐ Ⓑ Ⓒ Ⓓ
93	Ⓐ Ⓑ Ⓒ Ⓓ
94	Ⓐ Ⓑ Ⓒ Ⓓ
95	Ⓐ Ⓑ Ⓒ Ⓓ
96	Ⓐ Ⓑ Ⓒ Ⓓ
97	Ⓐ Ⓑ Ⓒ Ⓓ
98	Ⓐ Ⓑ Ⓒ Ⓓ
99	Ⓐ Ⓑ Ⓒ Ⓓ
100	Ⓐ Ⓑ Ⓒ Ⓓ

Part 5

No.	ANSWER A B C D
101	Ⓐ Ⓑ Ⓒ Ⓓ
102	Ⓐ Ⓑ Ⓒ Ⓓ
103	Ⓐ Ⓑ Ⓒ Ⓓ
104	Ⓐ Ⓑ Ⓒ Ⓓ
105	Ⓐ Ⓑ Ⓒ Ⓓ
106	Ⓐ Ⓑ Ⓒ Ⓓ
107	Ⓐ Ⓑ Ⓒ Ⓓ
108	Ⓐ Ⓑ Ⓒ Ⓓ
109	Ⓐ Ⓑ Ⓒ Ⓓ
110	Ⓐ Ⓑ Ⓒ Ⓓ

No.	ANSWER A B C D
111	Ⓐ Ⓑ Ⓒ Ⓓ
112	Ⓐ Ⓑ Ⓒ Ⓓ
113	Ⓐ Ⓑ Ⓒ Ⓓ
114	Ⓐ Ⓑ Ⓒ Ⓓ
115	Ⓐ Ⓑ Ⓒ Ⓓ
116	Ⓐ Ⓑ Ⓒ Ⓓ
117	Ⓐ Ⓑ Ⓒ Ⓓ
118	Ⓐ Ⓑ Ⓒ Ⓓ
119	Ⓐ Ⓑ Ⓒ Ⓓ
120	Ⓐ Ⓑ Ⓒ Ⓓ

Part 6

No.	ANSWER A B C D
121	Ⓐ Ⓑ Ⓒ Ⓓ
122	Ⓐ Ⓑ Ⓒ Ⓓ
123	Ⓐ Ⓑ Ⓒ Ⓓ
124	Ⓐ Ⓑ Ⓒ Ⓓ
125	Ⓐ Ⓑ Ⓒ Ⓓ
126	Ⓐ Ⓑ Ⓒ Ⓓ
127	Ⓐ Ⓑ Ⓒ Ⓓ
128	Ⓐ Ⓑ Ⓒ Ⓓ
129	Ⓐ Ⓑ Ⓒ Ⓓ
130	Ⓐ Ⓑ Ⓒ Ⓓ

No.	ANSWER A B C D
131	Ⓐ Ⓑ Ⓒ Ⓓ
132	Ⓐ Ⓑ Ⓒ Ⓓ
133	Ⓐ Ⓑ Ⓒ Ⓓ
134	Ⓐ Ⓑ Ⓒ Ⓓ
135	Ⓐ Ⓑ Ⓒ Ⓓ
136	Ⓐ Ⓑ Ⓒ Ⓓ
137	Ⓐ Ⓑ Ⓒ Ⓓ
138	Ⓐ Ⓑ Ⓒ Ⓓ
139	Ⓐ Ⓑ Ⓒ Ⓓ
140	Ⓐ Ⓑ Ⓒ Ⓓ

Part 7

No.	ANSWER A B C D
141	Ⓐ Ⓑ Ⓒ Ⓓ
142	Ⓐ Ⓑ Ⓒ Ⓓ
143	Ⓐ Ⓑ Ⓒ Ⓓ
144	Ⓐ Ⓑ Ⓒ Ⓓ
145	Ⓐ Ⓑ Ⓒ Ⓓ
146	Ⓐ Ⓑ Ⓒ Ⓓ
147	Ⓐ Ⓑ Ⓒ Ⓓ
148	Ⓐ Ⓑ Ⓒ Ⓓ
149	Ⓐ Ⓑ Ⓒ Ⓓ
150	Ⓐ Ⓑ Ⓒ Ⓓ

No.	ANSWER A B C D
151	Ⓐ Ⓑ Ⓒ Ⓓ
152	Ⓐ Ⓑ Ⓒ Ⓓ
153	Ⓐ Ⓑ Ⓒ Ⓓ
154	Ⓐ Ⓑ Ⓒ Ⓓ
155	Ⓐ Ⓑ Ⓒ Ⓓ
156	Ⓐ Ⓑ Ⓒ Ⓓ
157	Ⓐ Ⓑ Ⓒ Ⓓ
158	Ⓐ Ⓑ Ⓒ Ⓓ
159	Ⓐ Ⓑ Ⓒ Ⓓ
160	Ⓐ Ⓑ Ⓒ Ⓓ

No.	ANSWER A B C D
161	Ⓐ Ⓑ Ⓒ Ⓓ
162	Ⓐ Ⓑ Ⓒ Ⓓ
163	Ⓐ Ⓑ Ⓒ Ⓓ
164	Ⓐ Ⓑ Ⓒ Ⓓ
165	Ⓐ Ⓑ Ⓒ Ⓓ
166	Ⓐ Ⓑ Ⓒ Ⓓ
167	Ⓐ Ⓑ Ⓒ Ⓓ
168	Ⓐ Ⓑ Ⓒ Ⓓ
169	Ⓐ Ⓑ Ⓒ Ⓓ
170	Ⓐ Ⓑ Ⓒ Ⓓ

No.	ANSWER A B C D
171	Ⓐ Ⓑ Ⓒ Ⓓ
172	Ⓐ Ⓑ Ⓒ Ⓓ
173	Ⓐ Ⓑ Ⓒ Ⓓ
174	Ⓐ Ⓑ Ⓒ Ⓓ
175	Ⓐ Ⓑ Ⓒ Ⓓ
176	Ⓐ Ⓑ Ⓒ Ⓓ
177	Ⓐ Ⓑ Ⓒ Ⓓ
178	Ⓐ Ⓑ Ⓒ Ⓓ
179	Ⓐ Ⓑ Ⓒ Ⓓ
180	Ⓐ Ⓑ Ⓒ Ⓓ

No.	ANSWER A B C D
181	Ⓐ Ⓑ Ⓒ Ⓓ
182	Ⓐ Ⓑ Ⓒ Ⓓ
183	Ⓐ Ⓑ Ⓒ Ⓓ
184	Ⓐ Ⓑ Ⓒ Ⓓ
185	Ⓐ Ⓑ Ⓒ Ⓓ
186	Ⓐ Ⓑ Ⓒ Ⓓ
187	Ⓐ Ⓑ Ⓒ Ⓓ
188	Ⓐ Ⓑ Ⓒ Ⓓ
189	Ⓐ Ⓑ Ⓒ Ⓓ
190	Ⓐ Ⓑ Ⓒ Ⓓ

No.	ANSWER A B C D
191	Ⓐ Ⓑ Ⓒ Ⓓ
192	Ⓐ Ⓑ Ⓒ Ⓓ
193	Ⓐ Ⓑ Ⓒ Ⓓ
194	Ⓐ Ⓑ Ⓒ Ⓓ
195	Ⓐ Ⓑ Ⓒ Ⓓ
196	Ⓐ Ⓑ Ⓒ Ⓓ
197	Ⓐ Ⓑ Ⓒ Ⓓ
198	Ⓐ Ⓑ Ⓒ Ⓓ
199	Ⓐ Ⓑ Ⓒ Ⓓ
200	Ⓐ Ⓑ Ⓒ Ⓓ

著者紹介

株式会社メディアビーコン（Media Beacon）

1999年創業。語学教材に特化した教材制作会社。TOEIC、英検、TOEFL をはじめとする英語の資格試験から、子供英語、中学英語、高校英語、英会話、ビジネス英語まで、英語教材全般の制作を幅広く行う。特に TOEIC の教材制作には定評があり、『TOEIC® テスト新公式問題集 Vol.5』の編集制作ほか、TOEIC 関連企画を多数担当している。出版物以外にも英語学習アプリ、英会話学校のコース設計から指導マニュアルの開発、大手進学塾の教材開発まで、多角的な教材制作が可能な少数少ない制作会社。「語学の力で世界中の人々の幸せに貢献する」をモットーに、社員一同、学習者の笑顔を想いながら教材の研究開発を行っている。また、同時にTOEIC® L&R テストのスコアアップを目指す方のための指導も行っている。

著書に『TOEIC® L&R TEST 990 点獲得 Part 1-4 難問模試』『TOEIC® L&R TEST 990 点獲得 Part 5&6 難問模試』、『TOEIC® L&R TEST 990 点獲得 最強 Part 7 模試』(以上、ベレ出版)、『はじめての TOEIC® L&R テスト 全パート徹底対策』、『TOEIC® L&R テスト 文法集中対策』(以上、新星出版社)、『寝る前 5 分暗記ブック TOEIC テスト単語＆フレーズ』、『寝る前 5 分暗記ブック TOEIC テスト英文法』、『寝る前 5 分暗記ブック 英会話フレーズ集〈基礎編〉』(以上、Gakken) などがある。

YouTube「ビーコン イングリッシュ チャンネル」にて英語学習者のために役立つ情報を配信中。

メディアビーコンの公式 LINE にて、TOEIC テストのスコアアップに役立つ情報を発信中。

◉──カバーデザイン	竹内 雄二
◉──編集	株式会社メディアビーコン（山田優月）
◉──DTP	株式会社秀文社
◉──校正、ネイティブチェック	渡邉真理子、Jonathan Nacht
◉──音声・ナレーション	Andrée Dufleit、Howard Colefield、Nadia McKechnie、Stuart O

［音声DL付］TOEIC®L&R TEST 990点獲得 全パート難問模試

2023 年 9 月 25 日　　　初版発行

著者	メディアビーコン
発行者	内田 真介
発行・発売	ベレ出版
	〒162-0832　東京都新宿区岩戸町12 レベッカビル TEL.03-5225-4790 FAX.03-5225-4795 ホームページ　https://www.beret.co.jp/
印刷	モリモト印刷株式会社
製本	根本製本株式会社

落丁本・乱丁本は小社編集部あてにお送りください。送料小社負担にてお取り替えします。
本書の無断複写は著作権法上での例外を除き禁じられています。購入者以外の第三者による本書のいかなる電子複製も一切認められておりません。

©MediaBeacon 2023. Printed in Japan

ISBN 978-4-86064-737-7 C2082　　　　　　　　　　　　　　　　担当　綿引ゆか

全パート模試

難問模試２セット

目次

ベレ出版

TEST 1

★「大会場バージョン」の特殊音声を使って問題を解きたい方は、トラック番号が "TRACK_S" で始まる音声ファイルをご利用ください。（ダウンロード方法・特殊音声については本冊 P.7 を参照）

正誤記録表（TEST 1）

		1回目		2回目		3回目		4回目	
		日付	○/×	日付	○/×	日付	○/×	日付	○/×
Part 1	1								
	2								
	3								
	4								
	5								
	6								
Part 2	7								
	8								
	9								
	10								
	11								
	12								
	13								
	14								
	15								
	16								
	17								
	18								
	19								
	20								
	21								
	22								
	23								
	24								
	25								
	26								
	27								
	28								
	29								
	30								
	31								
Part 3	32								
	33								
	34								
	35								
	36								
	37								
	38								
	39								
	40								
	41								
	42								
	43								
	44								
	45								
	46								
	47								
	48								
	49								
	50								

		1回目		2回目		3回目		4回目	
		日付	○/×	日付	○/×	日付	○/×	日付	○/×
	51								
	52								
	53								
	54								
	55								
	56								
	57								
	58								
	59								
	60								
	61								
	62								
	63								
	64								
	65								
	66								
	67								
	68								
	69								
	70								
Part 4	71								
	72								
	73								
	74								
	75								
	76								
	77								
	78								
	79								
	80								
	81								
	82								
	83								
	84								
	85								
	86								
	87								
	88								
	89								
	90								
	91								
	92								
	93								
	94								
	95								
	96								
	97								
	98								
	99								
	100								

		1回目		2回目		3回目		4回目	
		日付	○/×	日付	○/×	日付	○/×	日付	○/×
Part 5	101								
	102								
	103								
	104								
	105								
	106								
	107								
	108								
	109								
	110								
	111								
	112								
	113								
	114								
	115								
	116								
	117								
	118								
	119								
	120								
	121								
	122								
	123								
	124								
	125								
	126								
	127								
	128								
	129								
	130								
Part 6	131								
	132								
	133								
	134								
	135								
	136								
	137								
	138								
	139								
	140								
	141								
	142								
	143								
	144								
	145								
	146								
Part 7	147								
	148								
	149								
	150								

	1回目		2回目		3回目		4回目	
	日付	○/×	日付	○/×	日付	○/×	日付	○/×
151								
152								
153								
154								
155								
156								
157								
158								
159								
160								
161								
162								
163								
164								
165								
166								
167								
168								
169								
170								
171								
172								
173								
174								
175								
176								
177								
178								
179								
180								
181								
182								
183								
184								
185								
186								
187								
188								
189								
190								
191								
192								
193								
194								
195								
196								
197								
198								
199								
200								

LISTENING TEST

In the Listening test, your ability to understand spoken English will be tested. The Listening test has four parts and will take approximately 45 minutes. Directions are given for each part. You need to mark your answers on the answer sheet. Nothing must be written in your test book.

PART 1

Directions: In this part, you will hear four statements about a picture in your test book. After hearing the statements, you must select the one statement that best describes what can be seen in the picture. Then mark your answer on your answer sheet. The statements will be spoken only one time and will not be written in your test book.

Answer (C), "They're wearing suits," best describes the picture. You should mark answer (C) on your answer sheet.

1.

2.

GO ON TO THE NEXT PAGE

3.

4.

5.

6.

Directions: In this part, you will hear a question or statement followed by three responses. All of them will be spoken in English. They will be spoken only one time and will not be written in your test book. Select the best response to each question or statement and mark answer (A), (B), or (C) on your answer sheet.

7. Mark your answer.

8. Mark your answer.

9. Mark your answer.

10. Mark your answer.

11. Mark your answer.

12. Mark your answer.

13. Mark your answer.

14. Mark your answer.

15. Mark your answer.

16. Mark your answer.

17. Mark your answer.

18. Mark your answer.

19. Mark your answer.

20. Mark your answer.

21. Mark your answer.

22. Mark your answer.

23. Mark your answer.

24. Mark your answer.

25. Mark your answer.

26. Mark your answer.

27. Mark your answer.

28. Mark your answer.

29. Mark your answer.

30. Mark your answer.

31. Mark your answer.

Directions: In this part, you will hear conversations between two or more people. You must answer three questions about what is said in each conversation. Select the best response to each question and mark answer (A), (B), (C), or (D) on your answer sheet. The conversations will be spoken only one time and will not be written in your test book.

32. Where most likely are the speakers?
    (A) At a restaurant
    (B) At an art gallery
    (C) At a car rental agency
    (D) At a fitness club

33. Why is the woman most likely late?
    (A) She did not check a train schedule.
    (B) She was looking for her telephone.
    (C) She had some car trouble.
    (D) She was in a meeting.

34. What does the man say he will do?
    (A) Provide a map
    (B) Reschedule an appointment
    (C) Call a colleague
    (D) Print out some records

35. Where does the man most likely work?
    (A) At a radio studio
    (B) At a doctor's office
    (C) At an auto repair shop
    (D) At a bakery

36. Why is the woman concerned?
    (A) She will arrive later than expected.
    (B) She does not know the man's address.
    (C) Her phone battery will not last long.
    (D) Her car has broken down.

37. What does the man say the woman should do?
    (A) Call her insurance company
    (B) Rent a vehicle
    (C) Speak with a colleague
    (D) Come on another day

38. What does the man want to find?
    (A) A ticket booth
    (B) An information desk
    (C) A food stall
    (D) A news agency

39. Who most likely is the woman?
    (A) A librarian
    (B) An architect
    (C) A salesperson
    (D) A journalist

40. What does the man suggest?
    (A) Getting something to eat
    (B) Asking for assistance
    (C) Checking a price
    (D) Taking a taxi together

41. What does the woman say she has done?
    (A) Filled out a form
    (B) Installed a device
    (C) Called a store
    (D) Returned an order

42. Why is the man calling?
    (A) To request some assistance
    (B) To recommend some repairs
    (C) To discuss a missing part
    (D) To apologize for a scheduling error

43. Why does the woman say, "I have a meeting near your store in the afternoon"?
    (A) To request delivery
    (B) To turn down an offer
    (C) To reschedule an appointment
    (D) To share an address

GO ON TO THE NEXT PAGE

44. What are the speakers discussing?
    (A) A customer's request
    (B) A news story
    (C) A new regulation
    (D) A party invitation

45. What does the woman mean when she says, "This could be big for us"?
    (A) They have been given an important opportunity.
    (B) They will be very busy in preparation.
    (C) They should hire some additional employees.
    (D) They will have to make an extra order.

46. What will Ms. Day most likely do next month?
    (A) Travel overseas
    (B) Sign a contract
    (C) Expand her business
    (D) Produce a video

47. Why is the man calling the woman?
    (A) To announce a price change
    (B) To suggest some products
    (C) To thank a supplier
    (D) To postpone an appointment

48. What concern does the woman have?
    (A) A software is too complicated to use.
    (B) Few staff members are available.
    (C) An extra cost may be generated.
    (D) There is a traffic congestion.

49. What will the man do next?
    (A) Look for a key
    (B) Repair a vehicle
    (C) Check a deadline
    (D) Set up some equipment

50. What are the speakers mainly discussing?
    (A) A tour of historic places
    (B) A new government regulation
    (C) An office renovation plan
    (D) An opening of a new theater

51. Who most likely is Ms. Wylde?
    (A) A tourist
    (B) A journalist
    (C) An author
    (D) An entertainer

52. What does the man say is available on a Web site?
    (A) The rate for a service
    (B) Comments from customers
    (C) An updated schedule
    (D) A registration form

53. What are the speakers discussing?
    (A) Stage lights
    (B) Printing machines
    (C) A speaker system
    (D) Video cameras

54. What problem does the woman mention?
    (A) The temporary equipment's sound quality is poor.
    (B) The cost is much higher than expected.
    (C) An event may be postponed due to a shipment delay.
    (D) An order form was not completed.

55. What does the man say about the new equipment?
    (A) It is very durable.
    (B) It is more economical.
    (C) It will be shipped from overseas.
    (D) It received positive reviews.

56. What are the speakers discussing?
(A) A business idea
(B) Product availability
(C) A clothing item
(D) A menu update

57. What does Jeff offer to do?
(A) Provide some instructions
(B) Introduce a colleague
(C) Reduce a price
(D) Lend a vehicle

58. What will the woman probably do next?
(A) Write a product review
(B) Check a budget
(C) Place an advertisement
(D) Make a contract

59. What are the speakers mainly discussing?
(A) Shipping difficulties
(B) Work scheduling
(C) Advertising expenses
(D) Product reviews

60. What type of business do the speakers most likely work for?
(A) An accounting firm
(B) An appliance store
(C) A newspaper publisher
(D) A travel agency

61. What does the man ask the woman to do?
(A) Contact a colleague
(B) Attend a conference
(C) Prepare a report
(D) Arrange an event

Madsen Tech — Business Software	
Platinum Pack	$250 per month
Gold Pack	$230 per month
Silver Pack	$200 per month
Bronze Pack	$160 per month

62. According to the woman, why should the company update its software?
(A) It is offering new product types.
(B) It will expand its offices.
(C) There have been some malfunctions.
(D) There is a compatibility problem.

63. What does the woman say about Madsen Tech?
(A) It has a good reputation for customer service.
(B) It is not famous around the country.
(C) It has placed train advertisements.
(D) It is a newly founded company.

64. Look at the graphic. Which package does the man recommend?
(A) Platinum Pack
(B) Gold Pack
(C) Silver Pack
(D) Bronze Pack

GO ON TO THE NEXT PAGE

Tables	
The Spokel	The Objectus
The Giordano	The Retronica

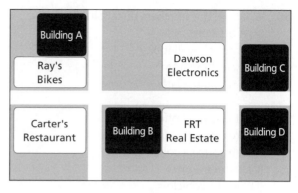

65. Where do the speakers most likely work?
   (A) At a dentist's office
   (B) At a café
   (C) At a publishing house
   (D) At a college

66. Look at the graphic. Which table will the speakers probably buy?
   (A) The Spokel
   (B) The Objectus
   (C) The Giordano
   (D) The Retronica

67. What does the woman ask the man to do?
   (A) Provide a reimbursement
   (B) Help load a truck
   (C) Check a document
   (D) Negotiate a price

68. What will be constructed next year?
   (A) A community college
   (B) A new highway
   (C) An appliance store
   (D) A residential building

69. Look at the graphic. Which building does the man say is not appropriate?
   (A) Building A
   (B) Building B
   (C) Building C
   (D) Building D

70. What will the speakers most likely do next?
   (A) Review a lease agreement
   (B) Tour a vacant building
   (C) Measure a room
   (D) Exchange contact details

Directions: In this part, you will hear talks given by one speaker. You must answer three questions about what is said in each talk. Select the best response to each question and mark answer (A), (B), (C), or (D) on your answer sheet. The talks will be spoken only one time and will not be written in your test book.

71. Where does the speaker most likely work?
    (A) At a travel agency
    (B) At a construction firm
    (C) At an accommodation provider
    (D) At a tour company

72. Why is the speaker calling?
    (A) To recommend a newly released product
    (B) To rearrange the date of a trip
    (C) To promote a campaign for the sea
    (D) To request some assistance for a volunteer

73. What does the speaker want the listener to do?
    (A) Organize an event
    (B) Write a review
    (C) Attend a banquet
    (D) Indicate a preference

74. What is Mr. Arnold's area of expertise?
    (A) Television advertising
    (B) Product manufacturing
    (C) Financial planning
    (D) Exercise and nutrition

75. What has Mr. Arnold recently done?
    (A) Appeared on television
    (B) Gone on a trip to London
    (C) Retired from his job
    (D) Taken a public office

76. What will the speaker most likely do next?
    (A) Announce the winner
    (B) Give a demonstration
    (C) Explain some rules
    (D) Interview a guest

77. What will happen next week?
    (A) Some new employees will start work.
    (B) A security system will be activated.
    (C) An analyst will inspect the facility.
    (D) Some new software will be installed.

78. What benefit does the speaker mention?
    (A) Lower running costs
    (B) Fewer accounting errors
    (C) Easier after-hours access
    (D) More modern appearance

79. What are the listeners asked to do?
    (A) Attend a workshop
    (B) Complete a survey
    (C) Read a manual
    (D) Provide an image

80. Where does the speaker most likely work?
    (A) At a furniture factory
    (B) At a shipping firm
    (C) At a hotel
    (D) At a catering business

81. What was the cause of the delay?
    (A) The company was understaffed.
    (B) A vehicle broke down.
    (C) Some materials ran out.
    (D) A road was closed.

82. What are the listeners asked to do?
    (A) Review a schedule
    (B) Report to work early
    (C) Order extra materials
    (D) Change an estimate

GO ON TO THE NEXT PAGE

83. What items are being promoted?
(A) Beverages
(B) Appliances
(C) Toiletries
(D) Decorations

84. What does the speaker say about the promotion?
(A) It is mainly intended for students.
(B) It offers a 50% discount on the items.
(C) It is conducted once a week.
(D) It will be postponed until tomorrow.

85. According to the speaker, what can customers receive in the mail?
(A) A magazine
(B) A voucher
(C) An invitation
(D) A catalog

86. Why does the speaker say, "We've thrown out two bottles of water this week"?
(A) To explain a decision
(B) To draw attention to an error
(C) To ask for assistance
(D) To introduce a new product

87. What does the speaker say about the newly ordered water bottles?
(A) They are a popular product.
(B) They are not for staff.
(C) They will not expire soon.
(D) They must be removed immediately.

88. What are the listeners asked to do?
(A) Maintain a certain number of refrigerated bottles
(B) Purchase water before scheduling large meetings
(C) Get permission before making large purchases
(D) Keep a record of water usage in the office

89. Why does the speaker say, "It's not an area that has a lot of traffic at any time of day"?
(A) To avoid a misunderstanding
(B) To make a recommendation
(C) To correct some information
(D) To reject a suggestion

90. What is the City Council planning to do?
(A) Hire additional staff
(B) Raise some money
(C) Organize a tour
(D) Build a new complex

91. What will happen next week?
(A) Work on a construction project will begin.
(B) A plan will be discussed.
(C) New equipment will be installed.
(D) A festival will be held for residents.

92. What does the speaker mean when he says, "This'll take a minute"?
(A) A project is easy to complete.
(B) A meeting is near its end.
(C) He does not plan to attend.
(D) His talk will not be over soon.

93. Who are the listeners?
(A) Software developers
(B) Factory workers
(C) Sales representatives
(D) Product designers

94. According to the speaker, what will the company pay for?
(A) Overnight accommodation
(B) Additional training
(C) Building repairs
(D) Transportation costs

Discount Coupon
Indigo Garden Care

1-Month Plan · 5% off

6-Month Plan · 10% off

12-Month Plan · · · · · · · · · · · · · · · · · · 15% off

24-Month Plan · · · · · · · · · · · · · · · · · · 20% off

(Corporate Contracts Only)

Dolby Community Center Entrance Hall

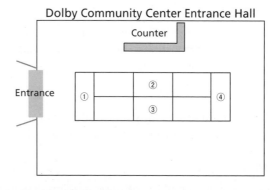

95. Where does the speaker work?
(A) At a factory
(B) At a clinic
(C) At a pharmacy
(D) At a hotel

96. Look at the graphic. What discount will the business receive?
(A) 5% off
(B) 10% off
(C) 15% off
(D) 20% off

97. What does the speaker ask the listener to do?
(A) Provide a price estimate
(B) Visit a residential address
(C) Send some promotional materials
(D) Cancel a gardening contract

98. Who most likely are the listeners?
(A) Students
(B) Bookkeepers
(C) Authors
(D) District center staff

99. Look at the graphic. Where will the recent releases be displayed?
(A) On shelf 1
(B) On shelf 2
(C) On shelf 3
(D) On shelf 4

100. According to the speaker, what will happen tomorrow?
(A) An event will commence.
(B) A shipment will arrive.
(C) A hall will be closed.
(D) A message will be sent.

This is the end of the Listening test.

GO ON TO THE NEXT PAGE

READING TEST

In the Reading test, you will read many kinds of texts and answer several different types of reading comprehension questions. The Reading test has three parts, and directions are given for each part. You have 75 minutes for the entire Reading test and are encouraged to answer as many questions as possible.

You need to mark your answers on the answer sheet.
Nothing must be written in your test book.

PART 5

Directions: In each of the sentences below, a word or phrase is missing. Select the best word or phrase from four choices to complete the sentence. Then mark the letter (A), (B), (C), or (D) on your answer sheet.

101. Customers have shown little ------- to take part in a satisfaction survey unless they are unhappy with some part of the service.
(A) inclination
(B) insulation
(C) consultation
(D) culmination

102. The ------- taken to reduce the annual running costs were more expensive to implement than was expected.
(A) measuring
(B) measurable
(C) measurably
(D) measures

103. Tuffwipes can be used to clean stubborn ------- from all kinds of kitchen appliances.
(A) interim
(B) density
(C) uptick
(D) residue

104. Mr. Cooper was so happy with his new desk heater that he purchased a ------- for his desk at work.
(A) one
(B) further
(C) second
(D) maximum

105. Owing to the mechanical failure, it is ------- impossible to launch the service as scheduled.
(A) barely
(B) virtually
(C) incredibly
(D) indefinitely

106. Five candidates were interviewed for the designer position, ------- of whom had experience in home renovation.
(A) neither
(B) every
(C) each
(D) any

107. The warranty will become ------- if any other party makes alterations to the ice cream maker in any way.
(A) waived
(B) expired
(C) assured
(D) void

108. Even after an exhaustive investigation, no one could say for sure ------- had caused the damage to the machinery.
(A) what
(B) that
(C) where
(D) how

109. Mr. Antilles gave a ------- talk on the use of 3D printers to create parts for antique lamps.
(A) compelling
(B) compelled
(C) compel
(D) compellable

110. Max Leeman has hired a ------- publicist who has a remarkable background to help him prepare for the launch of his latest book.
(A) fatal
(B) seasoned
(C) conceivable
(D) stagnant

111. With this app installed, you can get access to the latest international news ------- in the world you are.
(A) wherever
(B) that
(C) what
(D) however

112. Permission to build a facility in Dolby was dismissed because the land had certain plants ------- to the local wildlife.
(A) vital
(B) vitality
(C) vitally
(D) vitalize

113. Professional photographers from Clearshot Photography ------- at the last meeting to take all of the photographs used in this manual.
(A) have commissioned
(B) would be commissioned
(C) commissioned
(D) were commissioned

114. Although Mr. Porter wanted to sit in the front row, he had to content ------- with being seated in the back row.
(A) he
(B) his
(C) him
(D) himself

115. Mr. Hammond keeps in touch with employees by ------- of a popular social networking app.
(A) way
(B) place
(C) setting
(D) access

116. Mitchum no longer has the ------- force necessary to sustain a business as large as Cox Foods.
(A) laboring
(B) labors
(C) laborious
(D) labor

117. Mr. Clarkson often draws ------- his experience as an engineer when doing maintenance work around the house.
(A) on
(B) about
(C) through
(D) to

118. The East Ridge Apartment complex situated across the river ------- more than 1,000 permanent residents.
(A) house
(B) to house
(C) houses
(D) housing

119. Although Mr. Lin was not considered a ------- candidate for the CEO position, he was chosen unanimously by the board of directors.
(A) likeness
(B) likely
(C) liken
(D) like

120. The sales goal ------- is what they think is achievable considering the recent market trend.
(A) setting
(B) set
(C) to set
(D) sets

GO ON TO THE NEXT PAGE

121. The store featured in MBC magazine and gaining increasing attention now has some new sports apparel ------- the window.
(A) at
(B) up
(C) in
(D) to

122. ------- she has only been with Simpson Animation for two years, Ms. Yeardly is being considered for the CFO position.
(A) Given
(B) Even though
(C) As long as
(D) In case

123. Drummond Enterprises placed an advertisement online ------- to hire an engineer with experience maintaining cargo vessel engines.
(A) arranging
(B) encouraging
(C) looking
(D) recruiting

124. Ms. Walters refused to give any ------- to the idea of merging with a larger company.
(A) considering
(B) consideration
(C) considerate
(D) considerably

125. It is important that user manuals for the photography software be thorough yet -------.
(A) reflective
(B) variable
(C) benevolent
(D) succinct

126. The date for the annual sales conference has been pushed ------- on account of scheduling issues.
(A) away
(B) over
(C) back
(D) along

127. The marketing team discussed their targets and ------- they reach them in the most efficient way.
(A) wherever
(B) how
(C) what
(D) which

128. The client has submitted ------- that will make the arrangement unprofitable for us.
(A) demand
(B) demanding
(C) demands
(D) to demand

129. Although the documentary filmmakers shot hundreds of hours of footage, very ------- of it was used in the series.
(A) few
(B) nothing
(C) little
(D) seldom

130. The way JMB Cooking analyzes recent market trends based on statistical data figures ------- in what is then going to be produced.
(A) inconsistently
(B) simultaneously
(C) prominently
(D) overly

PART 6

Directions: In the following texts, a word, phrase, or sentence is missing. There are four answer choices for each question below the text. Select the best answer to complete the text and mark the letter (A), (B), (C), or (D) on your answer sheet.

Questions 131-134 refer to the following memo.

To: Customer Service Staff

From: Casy Summers

Date: August 2

Subject: Get ready to welcome

This memo is to let everyone know that a new ------- is starting tomorrow. Her name is Nora Timms,
131.

and she ------- the customer service group. Please do your best to make her feel welcome. There is a
132.

morning orientation workshop for her and the other new employees. She is going to take part in the

workshop with them shortly after she reports to work at 9 A.M. She is available ------- that. I am going
133.

to invite her to have lunch with us at Lancelot's. I would like as many people as possible to attend.

Please let me know whether or not you can make it by 5 P.M. ------- .
134.

131. (A) protocol
     (B) acumen
     (C) patron
     (D) associate

132. (A) will be joining
     (B) had joined
     (C) was being joined
     (D) joins

133. (A) because of
     (B) during
     (C) after
     (D) along

134. (A) We need to book tickets as early as
         possible.
     (B) I will make a reservation before I leave.
     (C) I will introduce her to whoever needs her
         help.
     (D) It is only open in the evenings.

GO ON TO THE NEXT PAGE

Questions 135-138 refer to the following e-mail.

To: Jax Ortega <jortega@wyldestalyns.com>

From: Kim Wissler <kwissler@freedomheatmix.com>

Date: May 4

Subject: Your order

Dear Mr. Ortega,

Thank you for your order of an off-peak thermal storage heater for your home. Although it is for ------- use, it weighs in excess of 50 kilograms. We have one in stock, but shipping may take up to two weeks depending on the availability of our shipping company. ------- . Please let me know if you would like us to recommend a qualified electrical technician in your area. The heater ------- in a protective plastic sheet by the manufacturer. Please be sure to remove ------- before turning it on for the first time.

135. **136.** **137.** **138.**

---

135. (A) industrial
(B) domestic
(C) limited
(D) local

136. (A) Unfortunately, we do not have any affiliates near you.
(B) It is light enough for one person to carry with ease.
(C) I noticed that you have not included installation in your order.
(D) As it is a used item, there is only a one-month warranty.

137. (A) was wrapped
(B) had been wrapped
(C) was wrapping
(D) wraps

138. (A) them
(B) him
(C) one
(D) it

Questions 139-142 refer to the following advertisement.

Holland Taban Power (HTP)

HTP can help your business cope with fluctuating ------ requirements. We have a database of over
                                                139.

10,000 highly trained individuals with experience in all kinds of industries. Independent surveys show

that HTP's clients have some of the highest satisfaction scores in the industry. ------ , many express
     140.

interest in making the situation permanent. If both parties are ------ , this can be arranged by paying a
           141.

reasonable one-time introduction fee. If things are not working out as well as you would like, simply

request a replacement. ------ .
       142.

www.hollandtabanpower.com

---

139. (A) staffing
    (B) parking
    (C) funding
    (D) housing

140. (A) Equally
    (B) Naturally
    (C) In contrast
    (D) Similarly

141. (A) desirable
    (B) responsible
    (C) deniable
    (D) amenable

142. (A) You can rest assured there is no one better
        for your organization.
    (B) All placements are final and no further
        requests will be entertained.
    (C) We will make all the necessary
        arrangements with no fuss or additional
        charges.
    (D) Simply give our customer service staff your
        warranty number over the telephone.

GO ON TO THE NEXT PAGE

NOTICE

Attention patrons,

The Moreton Public Library will be closed from April 9 to April 24. During this period, we will be accepting ------- at a mobile building parked by the fountain near the main entrance. There will be a
143.
chute by the front door for after-hours use. Librarians will be present in the office during the library's regular hours of operation. ------- . You will be able to view the online catalog and request books.
144.
------- , staff will require 24 hours to retrieve the books from the collection. Loans ------- at the
145.   146.
previously mentioned mobile building. Further details are available on our Web site. You can view them at www.moretonpubliclibrary.com.

---

143. (A) applications
(B) returns
(C) entries
(D) submissions

144. (A) They will be temporarily halting all services next week.
(B) Our policy on the use of mobile phones in the library has been updated.
(C) Unfortunately, our collection will be unavailable for library patrons to peruse.
(D) Nevertheless, a nearby parking space will be available to our visitors.

145. (A) Accordingly
(B) Otherwise
(C) Therefore
(D) However

146. (A) will be processed
(B) have been processed
(C) processed
(D) to process

PART 7
Directions: In this part you will read a selection of texts, such as newspaper articles, e-mails, and instant messages. Each text or set of texts is followed by several questions. Select the best answer for each question. Then mark the letter (A), (B), (C), or (D) on your answer sheet.

Questions 147-148 refer to the following memo.

WHILE YOU WERE OUT

For:	Don Ayoade
Date:	Tuesday, November 10
Time:	11:23 A.M.
Caller:	Helen Minter
From:	Dainty Software
TEL:	216-555-8543

Message: Tomorrow, Ms. Minter will interview Seth White for a position at her company. She wanted to speak to you because he has listed you as one of his character references. I told her that you were quite busy today, and she assured me that it would only take a minute. She will call back at 3:30 P.M. Otherwise, you could call her whenever you have some free time. Please let me know if you would like a copy of Mr. White's personnel record. I will have someone in HR deliver it to you.

Taken By: Paul Townsend

---

147. What is implied about Mr. White?
(A) He previously worked at Mr. Ayoade's company.
(B) He is currently employed at Dainty Software.
(C) He is a member of the human resources department.
(D) He has moved to a different city.

148. What does Mr. Townsend offer to do?
(A) Speak with an applicant
(B) Schedule a meeting
(C) Deliver a message to Ms. Minter
(D) Request some documents

GO ON TO THE NEXT PAGE

Questions 149-150 refer to the following text-message chain.

Sofia Berger 8:50 A.M.
I'm taking the day off today. Would you mind watering my plants before you leave this evening?

Peter Brown 8:51 A.M.
Happy to. There is a parcel on your desk marked urgent, though. Do you want me to take a look inside?

Sofia Berger 8:53 A.M.
I wasn't expecting anything. You'd better open it up just in case.

Peter Brown 8:54 A.M.
It's a manual for the new 3D printer.

Sofia Berger 8:56 A.M.
That's right! I had to request one because they shipped the printer without it.

Peter Brown 8:59 A.M.
Ok, I'll put it in the cabinet with the printer.

Sofia Berger 9:02 A.M.
Thanks, Peter. The plants will need a little extra water. I won't be in until Monday morning.

Peter Brown 9:03 A.M.
I'll set an alarm, so I don't forget.

---

149. What is one purpose of the text-message chain?
(A) To request time off work
(B) To ask a favor
(C) To announce some changes
(D) To provide feedback

150. At 8:56 A.M., what does Ms. Berger mean when she writes, "That's right"?
(A) She agrees with Mr. Brown.
(B) She wants to encourage Mr. Brown.
(C) She had forgotten what she did.
(D) She knows the answer.

Notice to Camden Town Residents

We have received many calls about trees on public land with branches overhanging private property. Under no circumstances should you attempt to prune or cut down trees in our public parks or any public areas yourself. Town maintenance crews are addressing the issue as fast as they can. Unfortunately, it may take as long as a month before they can respond to your particular request. If you believe that the branches pose a risk to your home, you should take a photograph and send it to the director of the Parks Maintenance Department at pmddirector@ctcc.com.au. If you have trees on your property whose branches are in danger of falling onto any part of your home, you may hire a professional tree surgeon to come and remove those limbs. It is necessary, however, to receive permission from the council if you plan to remove any tree taller than five meters. Please use the form on the council Web site to request a consultation. You will typically receive a response within 24 hours.

151. What is the purpose of the notice?
    (A) To announce a rule change
    (B) To recommend preventative maintenance
    (C) To explain a procedure
    (D) To request volunteer assistance

152. What does the notice say about removing tall trees on private land?
    (A) It can be scheduled using the council Web site.
    (B) It must be carried out by town employees.
    (C) It is required to notify the neighbors of the work.
    (D) It is necessary to obtain prior official approval.

GO ON TO THE NEXT PAGE

Questions 153-154 refer to the following e-mail.

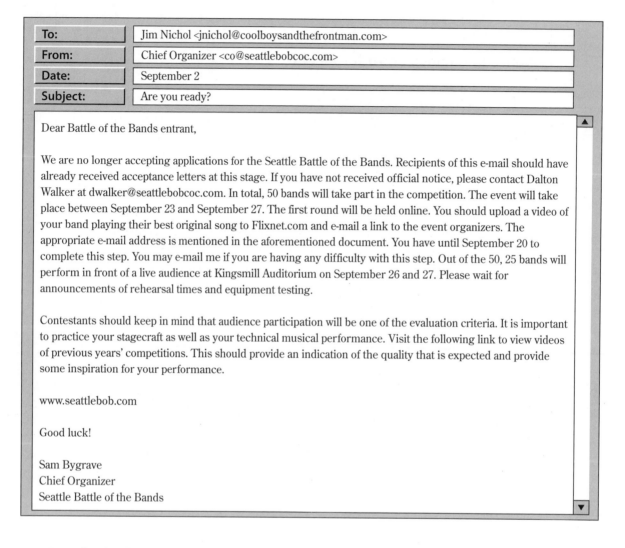

To:	Jim Nichol <jnichol@coolboysandthefrontman.com>
From:	Chief Organizer <co@seattlebobcoc.com>
Date:	September 2
Subject:	Are you ready?

Dear Battle of the Bands entrant,

We are no longer accepting applications for the Seattle Battle of the Bands. Recipients of this e-mail should have already received acceptance letters at this stage. If you have not received official notice, please contact Dalton Walker at dwalker@seattlebobcoc.com. In total, 50 bands will take part in the competition. The event will take place between September 23 and September 27. The first round will be held online. You should upload a video of your band playing their best original song to Flixnet.com and e-mail a link to the event organizers. The appropriate e-mail address is mentioned in the aforementioned document. You have until September 20 to complete this step. You may e-mail me if you are having any difficulty with this step. Out of the 50, 25 bands will perform in front of a live audience at Kingsmill Auditorium on September 26 and 27. Please wait for announcements of rehearsal times and equipment testing.

Contestants should keep in mind that audience participation will be one of the evaluation criteria. It is important to practice your stagecraft as well as your technical musical performance. Visit the following link to view videos of previous years' competitions. This should provide an indication of the quality that is expected and provide some inspiration for your performance.

www.seattlebob.com

Good luck!

Sam Bygrave
Chief Organizer
Seattle Battle of the Bands

153. According to the e-mail, how can readers find the appropriate e-mail address to send video links to?
(A) By downloading the attached document
(B) By checking their acceptance letters
(C) By calling the organizing committee
(D) By visiting the official Web site

154. What is NOT implied about the competition?
(A) Only half of the bands will be invited to perform live.
(B) All of the participants have been decided.
(C) The winners will be selected by the audience.
(D) It will be held over multiple dates.

Questions 155-157 refer to the following article.

MOSCOW (February 7) — Popular social media personality Helga Sanchez has recently announced that she will be moving from New York to Moscow. She informed the five million subscribers to her video blog on Wednesday by broadcasting live from in front of the famous Baranov Theater. She rode on a bus from there to her new apartment in Ananenko Tower all the while talking about her plans for the future direction of her video channel. The tower is one of Moscow's most prestigious addresses. It is famously home to the fashion designer Joe Akimov and international soccer sensation Ivan Oleksiy.

According to one Moscow real estate agent, landlords typically ask between $10,000 and $15,000 per month to rent apartments in the building. So, we can assume that Ms. Sanchez is doing quite well for herself. In recent months, she has switched from touting the products of her sponsors to selling her own line of cosmetics and fashion accessories. Various reports claim that she has more than doubled her monthly income. Her publicist Danny Madsen said that Ms. Sanchez has always wanted to live in Moscow. "This is a permanent arrangement, and she's already quite fluent in the language," he explained. "She plans to create many videos exploring Russian culture and food from her new base here in Moscow." Whether or not she is successful remains to be seen. Her move is an unusual one, but that might work to her advantage. Russia is a largely unexplored region for western video bloggers. Ms. Sanchez has a reputation for being original and extremely entertaining. Undoubtedly, others will be following in her footsteps in the coming years.

155. What is the subject of the article?
(A) A business opportunity for readers
(B) An influencer's recent activities
(C) The popularity of a video streaming site
(D) The rising cost of accommodations in Moscow

156. What is suggested about Ananenko Tower?
(A) It is an expensive place to live.
(B) It is the headquarters of a tech company.
(C) It is close to Baranov Theater.
(D) It is advertised in online videos.

157. What is NOT implied about Ms. Sanchez?
(A) She plans to try Russian cuisine.
(B) She has studied Russian.
(C) She moves on a yearly basis.
(D) She has some famous neighbors.

GO ON TO THE NEXT PAGE

Questions 158-160 refer to the following announcement.

**Important Announcement
From
Redmond Chang, Vice President of Planning and Marketing**

We need product testers.

Anval Inc. is almost ready to start production of its latest Wi-Fi routers. Before we do so, we would like to test the products in the homes of actual consumers. We are looking for 100 households that are willing to install and use our new routers exclusively for a full month. In order to make this a win-win proposition, we are willing to let participants keep the routers valued at around $500 free of charge. Naturally, if we find any bugs or defects, we will provide updates to make sure you are using fully functional equipment.

There are a couple of conditions. First, this offer is not for the households of company employees. As a matter of course, we want to test the products in demanding environments. We need households with four or more members that generate high-volume data traffic. In particular, we are looking for large families with a variety of Internet-connected devices. We are also interested in testing the coverage of our routers. Households making use of their attic, basement, or even a shed are of particular interest. This offer is not limited to the extended families of Anval employees. You are welcome to suggest the opportunity to family friends and acquaintances. Please make it clear, though, that we will be analyzing their usage statistics and keeping logs of errors and anomalies reported by the routers. They will also be asked to take part in a very brief online interview to assess their satisfaction with the devices.

Please ask anyone interested in taking part to contact my assistant Steve Spektor. He will assess their suitability and proceed with their enrollment into the program. We are trying to get the products onto the market by the start of the holiday season, so we hope that you will make this a priority in the coming days.

---

158. Who is organizing the program described in the announcement?
(A) A real estate agency
(B) An appliance store
(C) An Internet service provider
(D) An electronics manufacturer

159. What is a benefit for interested individuals?
(A) Free product samples
(B) Time off work
(C) Additional bonus payments
(D) Expert technical support

160. What is one condition of participation?
(A) People must commit to a year of monitoring.
(B) Homes must have both an attic and a basement.
(C) Households must have a minimum of five members.
(D) People must give their feedback online.

Questions 161-163 refer to the following letter.

Bakersfield Film Appreciation Society
21 Archer Lane, Suite D
Marsden, 80225

May 7

Jack Phipps
134 Sugarwood Road
Woodhill, CO 89237

Dear Mr. Phipps,

This year, the Bakersfield Festival of Film will be held from July 17 to July 19. The Bakersfield Film Appreciation Society is once again fulfilling the role as the event's organizing committee. —[1]—. Last year, when we learned that the rain damage to Thornton Theater would make the venue unusable, we were thrown into a panic. I am sure that if you had not generously offered Carter School of Design's main auditorium for our screenings, we would have been forced to cancel the event. —[2]—.

To show our appreciation for your kind offer, we would like to invite you back this year as a special guest. A special dinner will be held on the first night to welcome representatives of the various production companies. I hope you will agree to sit at a table reserved for friends of the festival. —[3]—. We have also taken the liberty of naming one of the festival awards after you — the Jack Phipps Award for Excellence in Set Design.We would be honored if you would present it to the winner on the final night of the festival. I hope you will agree to say a few words at that time. —[4]—.

Please let me know as soon as possible whether or not you can attend.

Sincerely,

Frida Kruger

Frida Kruger
Chairperson — Bakersfield Film Appreciation Society

---

161. Who most likely is Mr. Phipps?
(A) A business owner
(B) A film club leader
(C) A film producer
(D) A committee member

162. When will Mr. Phipps be asked to speak in public?
(A) On July 16
(B) On July 17
(C) On July 19
(D) On July 20

163. In which of the positions marked [1], [2], [3], and [4] does the following sentence best belong?

"You will be joined by Max Colby, Leanne Hester, and a few other significant contributors."

(A) [1]
(B) [2]
(C) [3]
(D) [4]

GO ON TO THE NEXT PAGE

To:	Stella Evans <sevans@bransonanddavies.co.uk>
From:	Harry Sutherland <hsutherland@stallardem.com>
Date:	23 March
Subject:	Conference

Dear Ms. Evans,

Thank you for agreeing to speak at the upcoming GTX Engineering Conference in London. The work your company has been doing on the Bristol Oil Pipeline project has been gathering a lot of attention, and I am sure attendees will be excited to hear about your progress. We have allocated you 90 minutes on the evening of the first day of the conference. You will be in Room A, which is the biggest of the three rooms we have booked. We imagine you will attract the largest crowd in the time slot.

I understand that you will be coming down to London on the previous day and staying at the Berger Inn across the road. I am sorry to hear that you cannot stay over 11 April for the second day of the conference. Of course, Stallard Event Management will pay for all of your accommodations and transportation. Please remember to send me a copy of the receipts after the conference. As I will be in town on the day before the conference starts to help set up, I was wondering if you would like to have dinner together. If you will be too busy preparing, I understand. I was hoping to discuss an event we are holding in Paris in July. We are looking for a keynote speaker to talk about integrating new technologies into major projects. I think you would be perfect for it. We are offering a very attractive compensation package.

Please let me know if you are interested.

Sincerely,

Harry Sutherland
Stallard Event Management

164. Who most likely is Ms. Evans?
(A) An engineer
(B) An event organizer
(C) A physician
(D) An advertising expert

165. What is implied about the conference?
(A) It will be held over three days.
(B) It will attract attendees from around the world.
(C) Several speakers will be presenting simultaneously.
(D) The venue provides discount accommodations.

166. What is one purpose of the e-mail?
(A) To announce a change of schedule
(B) To discuss a reimbursement procedure
(C) To explain a reservation error
(D) To ask about a venue preference

167. When will Ms. Evans and Mr. Sutherland most likely dine together?
(A) On March 23
(B) On April 10
(C) On April 11
(D) On April 13

Questions 168-171 refer to the following online chat discussion.

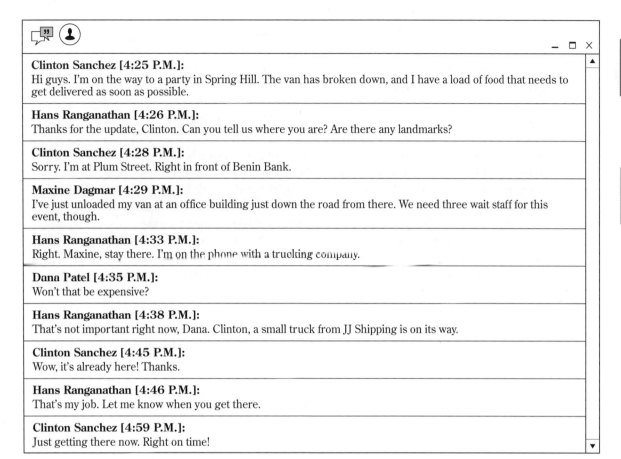

Clinton Sanchez [4:25 P.M.]:
Hi guys. I'm on the way to a party in Spring Hill. The van has broken down, and I have a load of food that needs to get delivered as soon as possible.

Hans Ranganathan [4:26 P.M.]:
Thanks for the update, Clinton. Can you tell us where you are? Are there any landmarks?

Clinton Sanchez [4:28 P.M.]:
Sorry. I'm at Plum Street. Right in front of Benin Bank.

Maxine Dagmar [4:29 P.M.]:
I've just unloaded my van at an office building just down the road from there. We need three wait staff for this event, though.

Hans Ranganathan [4:33 P.M.]:
Right. Maxine, stay there. I'm on the phone with a trucking company.

Dana Patel [4:35 P.M.]:
Won't that be expensive?

Hans Ranganathan [4:38 P.M.]:
That's not important right now, Dana. Clinton, a small truck from JJ Shipping is on its way.

Clinton Sanchez [4:45 P.M.]:
Wow, it's already here! Thanks.

Hans Ranganathan [4:46 P.M.]:
That's my job. Let me know when you get there.

Clinton Sanchez [4:59 P.M.]:
Just getting there now. Right on time!

---

168. Who most likely is Mr. Ranganathan?
(A) A delivery driver
(B) A kitchen worker
(C) A dispatch operator
(D) A banquet participant

169. At 4:29 P.M., what does Ms. Dagmar imply when she writes "We need three wait staff for this event, though"?
(A) She needs some additional help.
(B) A budget is not high enough.
(C) The event may not go smoothly.
(D) She will work as a server.

170. What is Mr. Patel concerned about?
(A) The distance
(B) The cost
(C) The time
(D) The reputation

171. What is probably true about Mr. Sanchez?
(A) He will apologize to his customers.
(B) He had a 5:00 P.M. appointment.
(C) He managed to fix his van.
(D) He will help Ms. Dagmar.

GO ON TO THE NEXT PAGE

Meteor One to Star Francine Lee

LOS ANGELES (February 9) — Fred J Klause's popular science fiction novel *Meteor One* is finally being adapted for the big screen. A press release from Velveteen Production Company announced that it has procured the rights in a $7,000,000 deal. According to the agreement, Klause gets the right of final approval on the cast and the film's creative team. —[1]—. The screenplay is to be written by Odette Xenedez, who was responsible for other high-profile screen adaptations such as *Marionette* and *Double Trouble*. These two films went on to have amazing success making their directors world-famous. *Meteor One* will be helmed by Scott Eastman, a frequent collaborator with Velveteen Production Company.

Production is set to begin in July this year. Because the story is set almost entirely in space, it will be filmed at Velveteen's studios in Middleton, which are currently being used to shoot a television series. —[2]—. Release dates in other countries will be available on the Web site as soon as they are known. You can go to www.meteoronemovie.com although there is currently very little to see.

A few of the cast members have already been announced. Francine Lee will play Dr. Gina Rhodes, and she will be supported by Vance Modine and Pete Cunningham. Extras will be recruited from the community around the studio. Typically, these opportunities are advertised on social media and in local newspapers. —[3]—.

The book has a huge fanbase, which the producers expect to benefit from. However, this can work against the film. If it does not live up to fans' expectations, they may react negatively online discouraging others from seeing it. Mr. Eastman will be under a lot of pressure to keep that group satisfied. —[4]—.

172. What is implied about *Double Trouble?*
  (A) It was directed by Mr. Eastman.
  (B) It was filmed at a studio in Middleton.
  (C) It was first published as a book.
  (D) It was criticized online by fans.

173. What is probably true about Mr. Eastman?
  (A) He has never worked for Velveteen
      Production Company before.
  (B) He has been allocated a budget of just
      $7,000,000.
  (C) His participation was authorized by the
      writer.
  (D) His reputation has spread internationally.

174. According to the article, how can people find
  out about appearing in the film?
  (A) By subscribing to a Middleton newspaper
  (B) By attending an information session
  (C) By sending an e-mail to Velveteen
      Production Company
  (D) By visiting the production company Web
      site

175. In which of the positions marked [1], [2], [3],
  and [4] does the following sentence best
  belong?

  "If everything goes according to plan, the film
  should be in cinemas in time for the school
  holidays in late December in the US."

  (A) [1]
  (B) [2]
  (C) [3]
  (D) [4]

GO ON TO THE NEXT PAGE

TEST 1

TEST 2

GALVESTON (June 19)—Galveston's accommodation shortage is about to be slightly alleviated with the opening of the Tristar Hotel on Sheffield Street. The grand opening will be held on Sunday, June 23. People will be able to view the hotel interior, dine in the restaurants, and even make use of the wellness center and other amenities, but reservations for accommodations will not be taken for dates before July 1. In the meantime, staff will be undergoing intensive training and working to find and resolve any problems before the first overnight guests arrive.

All Tristar Hotels including this one are rated four stars. The Galveston location is unique in that it has the country's largest rooftop swimming pool. The glass walls of the pool allow swimmers to enjoy magnificent views of the city as they relax in the heated water.

To:	Randy Slade
From:	Denis Wainwright
Date:	June 21
Subject:	Update
Attachment:	🖇 PWainwright

Dear Mr. Slade,

I trust things are going smoothly in New York. I can't wait to get back.

I am currently inspecting our Maine location, making sure that the service and facilities meet Tristar's high standards. Naturally, I have not informed the staff that I am a hotel employee or of the purpose of my trip. I think the manager here should be commended for her excellent work. Every member of the staff whom I have encountered has been extremely professional, and my room was immaculate. The same goes for their restaurants. I will be here for one more night. I will send a full report in my next e-mail.

The next hotel I will be inspecting is the new one in Galveston. I cannot get a reservation for the next week and a half, so I have decided to take some time off to catch up with my family in Boston. Naturally, this will require me to purchase an additional airline ticket. I have attached the purchase permission request to this e-mail. Please authorize it as soon as possible because there are only a few seats left.

Sincerely,

Denis

176. According to the article, what problem does Galveston have?
(A) There are not enough hotel rooms.
(B) The transportation system is inconvenient.
(C) The restaurants are too crowded.
(D) The accommodations are not highly rated.

177. When is the final day of intensive training at the Galveston Tristar Hotel?
(A) June 23
(B) June 30
(C) July 1
(D) July 2

178. What is implied about Mr. Wainwright?
(A) He interviewed a hotel manager.
(B) He is staying in a four-star hotel.
(C) He is Mr. Slade's supervisor.
(D) He has trained hotel staff in Maine.

179. What is indicated about the Tristar Hotel in Maine?
(A) It has a rooftop swimming pool.
(B) It is in the city center.
(C) It has more than one restaurant.
(D) It has several vacancies.

180. Where most likely is Mr. Wainwright's next destination?
(A) New York
(B) Galveston
(C) Boston
(D) Maine

GO ON TO THE NEXT PAGE

Questions 181-185 refer to the following online order receipt and e-mail.

Online Order Receipt

Thank you for your order, dated April 4 at 10:20 P.M. The following items are included:

Item	Quantity	Price
McGillicutty Desk Lamp	1	$230.00
Christof Knife Set	1	$120.00
Hanlan Fountain Pen (Blue)	2	$112.00
Giordano Leather Gloves	1	$85.00
Overnight shipping		$26.00
TOTAL		$573.00

These items should arrive on April 6. They have been sent using the following shipping details;

Ms. Donna Tanner
23 Hillview Road
Flint, MI 48006

NOTE: I hope you can take the time to write reviews regarding whether or not you are completely satisfied with your items.
Reviewers who leave comments of 500 words or more will be sent free product samples. They are under no obligation to recommend the products to others, and they may also choose to return the products to us at our expense.

To:	Donna Tanner <dtanner@silvergoose.com>
From:	Miles Poe <mpoe@hanlansm.com>
Date:	April 7
Subject:	Your review

Dear Ms. Tanner,

I hope you do not mind my contacting you directly. I am a member of the sales and marketing team at Hanlan. Beacons Online Shopping has provided me with your e-mail address per your preferences in the service agreement.

Today, I read the review you left on the Beacons Online Shopping Web site. Such a glowing review is sure to affect our future sales.

In the review, you mentioned that the product color did not accurately match the color shown in the product description. Please allow me to apologize for this. Our marketing team is using some new photography equipment which has not been properly calibrated. We will immediately retake the photographs and upload them again. I hope this small difference did not cause too much disappointment.

Lastly, we would be more than happy if you could write a little longer review in the future. We would like you to have a chance to try our free product samples.

Sincerely,

Miles Poe

181. When was Ms. Tanner's order most likely shipped?
(A) On April 4
(B) On April 5
(C) On April 6
(D) On April 7

182. In the e-mail, the word, "per" in paragraph 1, line 2 is closest in meaning to
(A) in accordance with
(B) by means of
(C) for each one
(D) in turn

183. What kind of item did Ms. Tanner leave a review for?
(A) Fashion
(B) Cutlery
(C) Appliances
(D) Stationery

184. What is suggested about Ms. Tanner's review?
(A) It was written on April 7.
(B) It is entirely complimentary.
(C) It was posted anonymously.
(D) It has less than 500 words.

185. In the e-mail, what is mentioned about the equipment the business is using?
(A) It is state-of-the-art.
(B) It was not correctly adjusted.
(C) It will be replaced shortly.
(D) It contains a product defect.

GO ON TO THE NEXT PAGE

https://www.guttenbergprc.com

Guttenberg Painting Restoration and Conservation

Guttenberg Painting Restoration and Conservation is one of Britain's most trusted names for preserving valuable paintings. Our clients include the Baumgartner Museum of Art, Styles Gallery, and Holden Art Fund.

Our highly trained staff can restore your valuable artwork to its original splendor while also ensuring that the art is preserved for many years to come. It is important to do this correctly because paintings preserved using outdated techniques may become damaged by the chemicals used to protect them. We can also correct poorly restored paintings in certain cases.

One of our new services is to create ultra-high resolution digital copies of valuable artwork that can outlive their physical counterparts. This is a free service for artwork at public galleries.

As paintings are restored on a case-by-case basis, it is impossible to publish our rates. Please contact our customer service department to schedule an estimate. We can arrange secure shipment by a special transportation service. We will only come to your location in cases where paintings are particularly valuable or fragile. This will be assessed by analyzing video of your item.

NOTICE

Princeton Gallery regrets that *Battle of Montague* by Daniel Forbes is not available for public viewing. It is currently being restored by a professional from Guttenberg Painting Restoration and Conservation. You can view the progress of the work from a window in the studio on the first floor. The restorer is only active between the hours of 1:00 P.M. and 3:00 P.M. from Monday to Friday.

WORD OUT!

Honest reviews of theaters, galleries, museums, and other attractions.

Princeton Gallery ★ ★ ★ ★ ☆

I would have given Princeton Gallery five stars, but I was unable to properly enjoy *Battle of Montague* — the very painting I was most interested in.I think galleries should use their Web sites to let visitors know when certain works are unavailable. I would have rescheduled my visit. Thankfully, I was able to see two talented restoration workers cleaning the work from a studio window, so it wasn't a complete loss.

Overall, this is one of the best public galleries I have ever visited.

By We Ying Yang

186. What is one benefit of using the service described on the Web site?
(A) Paintings will be less likely to deteriorate over time.
(B) The business offers cheaper rates than its competitors.
(C) Artwork will be easier for investors to sell.
(D) It provides training for gallery employees.

187. What is implied about *Battle of Montague*?
(A) It is on loan from another art gallery.
(B) It was too delicate for transportation.
(C) It is a privately owned artwork.
(D) It will be sold at auction.

188. Why is Ms. Yang disappointed?
(A) Some information was not published online.
(B) A piece of art was not preserved properly.
(C) The art gallery was closed during her visit.
(D) A shipment did not arrive on time.

189. What is suggested about Ms. Yang?
(A) She has a yearly membership at Princeton Gallery.
(B) She viewed an online video of *Battle of Montague*.
(C) She visited Princeton Gallery on a weekday.
(D) She attended an event at Baumgartner Museum of Art.

190. What is indicated about Princeton Gallery?
(A) It is affiliated with the Holden Art Fund.
(B) It received huge funding from Daniel Forbes.
(C) It temporarily misplaced an item in its collection.
(D) It is entitled to receive a digital copy of paintings in its collection.

GO ON TO THE NEXT PAGE

BOSTON (January 21)—The Annual Tiny Home Trade Show will be held in Boston again this year. The term "tiny home" generally refers to homes under 37 square meters. Typically, they can be moved from place to place on wheels built into their bases.

As real estate prices rise, and people's values change, tiny homes are becoming a more and more popular alternative to traditional housing. The market is divided into three main sectors; owner builders, readymade homes, and bespoke homes. At the inaugural Tiny Home Trade Show held last year, Wilson Builds received a lot of interest from the press and the general public. As a manufacturer of readymade homes, Wilson Builds mass produces its homes and sells them at relatively low prices. "Although our homes are readymade, there are a lot of designs for people to choose from," explained CEO Matt Wilson, "No matter which one you choose, you can enjoy the benefits of a fully-equipped, bathroom, kitchen, and laundry."

This year, Wilson Builds will have a lot more competition. Manufacturers from around the United States will be displaying their tiny homes in the Bluewave Convention Center. Manufacturers are not the only businesses the trade show is attracting. A variety of other businesses have sprung up to support the growing community of tiny house enthusiasts. There are building courses people can enroll in, construction plans to buy, and even tiny house rentals available for people who want to experience the lifestyle before they commit. All but the last have been invited to attend this year's trade show.

Carter Homes

Carter Homes has a wide range of tiny homes for rent on short and long-term leases. We can deliver and retrieve them for free to addresses in Boston, Chicago, Dallas, or Sacramento and for a reasonable fee, to anywhere else in the United States. Our supplier Wilson Builds won the Builder-of-the-Year award at this year's Tiny Home Trade Show in Boston.

To:	Helen Hill <hhill@kleemway.com>
From:	Moe Okada <mokada@carterhomes.com>
Date:	January 10
Subject:	Your lease

Dear Ms. Hill,

This is just a brief e-mail to let you know that your lease will expire next month. If you would like to extend the lease for another year, you will need to fill out a new agreement by February 19. I understand that you have relocated the home to Pittsburg. Please keep that in mind when deciding whether or not to extend your lease.

Sincerely,

Moe Okada
Carter Homes

191. What is implied about the Annual Tiny Home Trade Show?
(A) It only caters to traditional homes.
(B) It has reduced its exhibition fees.
(C) It was held in Boston the first time.
(D) It will attract fewer exhibitors this year.

192. In the article, the word "commit" in paragraph 3, line 7 is closest in meaning to
(A) allocate
(B) promise
(C) take into account
(D) go all out

193. What is indicated about Carter Homes?
(A) It won the Builder-of-the-Year award.
(B) It was not eligible for inclusion in the Annual Tiny Home Trade Show.
(C) It manufactures bespoke homes for its clients.
(D) It does not have a customer service office in Boston.

194. Why most likely does Ms. Okada mention Pittsburg?
(A) Her company will build an office there.
(B) It is the location of the next Trade Show.
(C) It is outside the approved usage zones.
(D) There will be a relocation fee.

195. What is probably true about the home Ms. Hill is renting?
(A) It has a laundry area.
(B) It was constructed in Boston.
(C) It was rented on a short-term lease.
(D) It has its own power supply.

GO ON TO THE NEXT PAGE

TRF Business Software

TRF Business Software is an all-in-one accounting, inventory, and payroll package that can help businesses discover inefficiencies and inconsistencies in their workflow. Over time, it can save you millions in wasted time and resources.

We do not provide free evaluation versions of the software, but we do have an informative video that you can watch to see whether or not TRF is right for your business. You are also welcome to read the positive customer testimonials on our Web site.

Subscriptions are paid quarterly, and our rates are reasonable and easy to calculate. We charge $1,500 for the first hundred users and $1,000 for each additional hundred.

Many of our larger clients have dedicated departments constantly monitoring logs and looking for ways to improve profits. For businesses with under a thousand employees, it is generally more economical to hire a consultant with expertise in TRF Business Software. A good consultant will save a company far more money than it costs to hire them. We recommend the following firms:

Osprey Consultants
LeadMax Associates
MDO Analytics

MEMO

To: All Crackersnap Department Heads
From: James Rayhman
Date: October 3
Subject: Consultant

It's been just about two weeks since we hired a consultant from Leadmax Associates. Given the number of our company's employees, I assume it was the right decision to make. The financial benefit of his recommendations will soon exceed the consulting fee.

From September 20 to October 1, the consultant Col Jones immediately reviewed the TRF logs and identified areas that need attention. Please view the advice and write a report on what measures you plan to put in place to solve the issues.

The report is due on the day of our monthly department head meeting. Please submit it to me by e-mail. The contents will be discussed at the meeting.

Sincerely,

James Rayhman

MEETING NOTES

October Meeting of Crackersnap Department Heads

Compiled by Trevor Menzies — Personal Assistant to Mr. Rayhman

Date: October 15   Time: 3:00 P.M. ~ 5:00 P.M.

• Mr. Rayhman reminded department heads of the upcoming employee satisfaction survey.

We must distribute the survey using the TRF Business Software and inform employees that it is to be anonymous. Surveys must be submitted by October 18. The data will be processed by Mr. Jones, and he will present the findings the following week.

196. What is NOT mentioned about TRF Business Software?
(A) It has been praised by its users.
(B) Updates are published regularly.
(C) Customers are charged four times a year.
(D) It enables businesses to improve their work efficiency.

197. What is probably true about Crackersnap?
(A) It has fewer than a thousand employees.
(B) It has provided one of the testimonials on the Web site.
(C) It produced the video mentioned in the information.
(D) It is using a free version of TRF Business Software.

198. When is the deadline for the report mentioned in the memo?
(A) September 20
(B) October 1
(C) October 3
(D) October 15

199. What do the meeting notes say about the survey?
(A) It must be filled out by October 20.
(B) Department heads are not required to submit one.
(C) It is carried out on a yearly basis.
(D) Staff are not required to write their names on it.

200. Which company will process the survey data?
(A) Osprey Consultants
(B) LeadMax Associates
(C) MDO Analytics
(D) Crackersnap

TEST 2

★「大会場バージョン」の特殊音声を使って問題を解きたい方は、トラック番号が "TRACK_S" で始まる音声ファイルをご利用ください。（ダウンロード方法・特殊音声については本冊 P.7 を参照）

正誤記録表（TEST 2）

		1回目		2回目		3回目		4回目	
		日付	○/×	日付	○/×	日付	○/×	日付	○/×
Part 1	1								
	2								
	3								
	4								
	5								
	6								
Part 2	7								
	8								
	9								
	10								
	11								
	12								
	13								
	14								
	15								
	16								
	17								
	18								
	19								
	20								
	21								
	22								
	23								
	24								
	25								
	26								
	27								
	28								
	29								
	30								
	31								
Part 3	32								
	33								
	34								
	35								
	36								
	37								
	38								
	39								
	40								
	41								
	42								
	43								
	44								
	45								
	46								
	47								
	48								
	49								
	50								

		1回目		2回目		3回目		4回目	
		日付	○/×	日付	○/×	日付	○/×	日付	○/×
	51								
	52								
	53								
	54								
	55								
	56								
	57								
	58								
	59								
	60								
	61								
	62								
	63								
	64								
	65								
	66								
	67								
	68								
	69								
	70								
Part 4	71								
	72								
	73								
	74								
	75								
	76								
	77								
	78								
	79								
	80								
	81								
	82								
	83								
	84								
	85								
	86								
	87								
	88								
	89								
	90								
	91								
	92								
	93								
	94								
	95								
	96								
	97								
	98								
	99								
	100								

		1回目		2回目		3回目		4回目	
		日付	○/×	日付	○/×	日付	○/×	日付	○/×
Part 5	101								
	102								
	103								
	104								
	105								
	106								
	107								
	108								
	109								
	110								
	111								
	112								
	113								
	114								
	115								
	116								
	117								
	118								
	119								
	120								
	121								
	122								
	123								
	124								
	125								
	126								
	127								
	128								
	129								
	130								
Part 6	131								
	132								
	133								
	134								
	135								
	136								
	137								
	138								
	139								
	140								
	141								
	142								
	143								
	144								
	145								
	146								
Part 7	147								
	148								
	149								
	150								

	1回目		2回目		3回目		4回目	
	日付	○/×	日付	○/×	日付	○/×	日付	○/×
151								
152								
153								
154								
155								
156								
157								
158								
159								
160								
161								
162								
163								
164								
165								
166								
167								
168								
169								
170								
171								
172								
173								
174								
175								
176								
177								
178								
179								
180								
181								
182								
183								
184								
185								
186								
187								
188								
189								
190								
191								
192								
193								
194								
195								
196								
197								
198								
199								
200								

LISTENING TEST

▶TRACK_131〜▶TRACK_137

In the Listening test, your ability to understand spoken English will be tested. The Listening test has four parts and will take approximately 45 minutes. Directions are given for each part. You need to mark your answers on the answer sheet. Nothing must be written in your test book.

PART 1

Directions: In this part, you will hear four statements about a picture in your test book. After hearing the statements, you must select the one statement that best describes what can be seen in the picture. Then mark your answer on your answer sheet. The statements will be spoken only one time and will not be written in your test book.

Answer (C), "They're wearing suits," best describes the picture. You should mark answer (C) on your answer sheet.

1.

2.

GO ON TO THE NEXT PAGE ▶

3.

4.

5.

6.

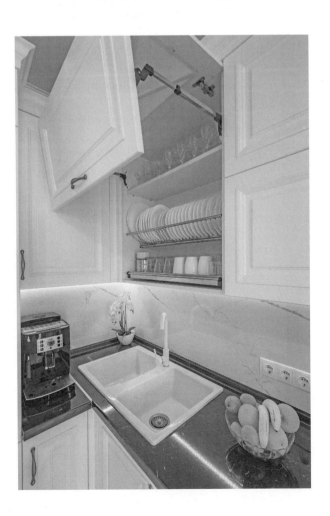

GO ON TO THE NEXT PAGE

PART 2 ▶TRACK_138～▶TRACK_163

Directions: In this part, you will hear a question or statement followed by three responses. All of them will be spoken in English. They will be spoken only one time and will not be written in your test book. Select the best response to each question or statement and mark answer (A), (B), or (C) on your answer sheet.

7. Mark your answer.

8. Mark your answer.

9. Mark your answer.

10. Mark your answer.

11. Mark your answer.

12. Mark your answer.

13. Mark your answer.

14. Mark your answer.

15. Mark your answer.

16. Mark your answer.

17. Mark your answer.

18. Mark your answer.

19. Mark your answer.

20. Mark your answer.

21. Mark your answer.

22. Mark your answer.

23. Mark your answer.

24. Mark your answer.

25. Mark your answer.

26. Mark your answer.

27. Mark your answer.

28. Mark your answer.

29. Mark your answer.

30. Mark your answer.

31. Mark your answer.

Directions: In this part, you will hear conversations between two or more people. You must answer three questions about what is said in each conversation. Select the best response to each question and mark answer (A), (B), (C), or (D) on your answer sheet. The conversations will be spoken only one time and will not be written in your test book.

32. Where most likely are the speakers?
    (A) In a post office
    (B) In a hardware store
    (C) At a car repair garage
    (D) At a hospital

33. What does the woman suggest?
    (A) Buying in bulk
    (B) Visiting a different location
    (C) Trying a new product
    (D) Attending a workshop

34. What does the man request?
    (A) Some directions
    (B) A product demonstration
    (C) Some stationery
    (D) A schedule

35. What is the topic of the conversation?
    (A) A cleaning product
    (B) A Web site update
    (C) A bank transaction
    (D) A computer malfunction

36. What is the woman waiting for?
    (A) An invoice
    (B) Some technical assistance
    (C) An estimate
    (D) Some instruction manuals

37. What will the man do after lunch?
    (A) Attend a seminar
    (B) Meet some clients
    (C) Purchase some tools
    (D) Send a package

38. What are the speakers discussing?
    (A) Room renovation
    (B) Possible event venues
    (C) A construction project
    (D) A furniture shipment

39. What does the woman say she will do?
    (A) Refund some money
    (B) Provide a discount
    (C) Reschedule an event
    (D) Speak with a colleague

40. What does the man ask the woman to do?
    (A) Make a payment
    (B) Arrange a meeting
    (C) Help set up a device
    (D) Provide some information

41. What problem does the woman mention?
    (A) Her office is overly busy.
    (B) Some cleaning work was not carried out.
    (C) She has not received an order.
    (D) She has discovered a product defect.

42. What does the man say about the office in Innesvale?
    (A) The staff there are very helpful.
    (B) It is located near the woman's office.
    (C) It was understaffed yesterday.
    (D) Some guests are headed there.

43. Why does the man say, "It's hard to tell"?
    (A) He has some unfortunate news.
    (B) The situation is very complicated.
    (C) He does not know an answer.
    (D) A colleague is absent from work.

GO ON TO THE NEXT PAGE

44. Why is the woman at the car dealership?
    (A) To have her vehicle serviced
    (B) To purchase a new vehicle
    (C) To test-drive a car
    (D) To pick up some parts

45. What has the woman brought with her?
    (A) An electronic device
    (B) A bicycle
    (C) A beverage
    (D) Some documentation

46. Why is the woman surprised?
    (A) A customer lounge is available.
    (B) She has to wait longer than expected.
    (C) Her appointment was changed.
    (D) The price has been reduced.

47. What is the conversation mainly about?
    (A) A contract bid
    (B) Warehouse cleaning
    (C) A moving service
    (D) Damaged equipment

48. What does the woman ask the man to do?
    (A) Increase a budget
    (B) Order some merchandise
    (C) Update a Web site
    (D) Change a company policy

49. What does the woman suggest doing?
    (A) Searching for an alternative
    (B) Requesting a quotation
    (C) Placing an advertisement
    (D) Offering a discount

50. What does Kate say about Don Hoffman?
    (A) He has left the company.
    (B) He was recently promoted.
    (C) He was an important client.
    (D) He has returned from his vacation.

51. What does Betty offer to do?
    (A) Search for a lost item
    (B) Contact a previous client
    (C) Hire a temporary worker
    (D) Put together a plan

52. What will the man do next?
    (A) Call an ex-employee
    (B) Conduct a training workshop
    (C) Send an e-mail
    (D) Rename a company division

53. What problem does the man mention about the apartment?
    (A) The rooms are too small.
    (B) It is too far from the city.
    (C) The area is too noisy.
    (D) The rent is too expensive.

54. What does the woman imply when she says, "there was a lot to read"?
    (A) Some information was not obvious.
    (B) Ample literature was supplied.
    (C) A process takes a long time.
    (D) People can enjoy various books.

55. What does the man ask the woman to do?
    (A) Negotiate with a landlord
    (B) Help him find a parking space
    (C) Choose some cooking appliances
    (D) Return to a previous apartment

56. What is the topic of the seminar?
(A) Hiring effective workers
(B) Boosting employee morale
(C) Attracting wealthy clients
(D) Reducing running costs

57. Where will the men most likely go next?
(A) To a conference room
(B) To a ticket booth
(C) To a hotel
(D) To a café

58. What does the woman say about the seminar?
(A) It has been rescheduled.
(B) It is held every weekend.
(C) It includes teamwork activities.
(D) It was fully booked.

59. What are the speakers mainly discussing?
(A) Vacation timing
(B) Sales reports
(C) Hiring policies
(D) Running costs

60. Which industry do the speakers most likely work in?
(A) Temporary staffing
(B) Car manufacturing
(C) Clothing design
(D) Real estate

61. What will the man probably do next?
(A) Place an advertisement
(B) Call an applicant
(C) Conduct a survey
(D) Reserve a room

Model	Price	Color	Warranty
Regent A	$1,200	Black	5 years
Regent B		White	5 years
Galant A	$1,600	Black	10 years
Galant B		White	10 years

62. Look at the graphic. Which item did the woman most likely buy?
(A) Regent A
(B) Regent B
(C) Galant A
(D) Galant B

63. What does the man ask about?
(A) A storage plan
(B) A shipping cost
(C) A delivery date
(D) An advertising media

64. What does the man ask the woman to do?
(A) Get help installing some mattresses
(B) Investigate disposal charges
(C) Request a corporate discount
(D) Send in an invoice

GO ON TO THE NEXT PAGE

Annual Revenue by Source

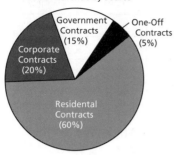

Error Code 662

Recovery Menu:
001 Suspend Program
002 Restart Program
003 Shut Down Program
004 Reboot Computer

65. Look at the graphic. According to the man, what percentage of revenue will likely be lost over the next 12 months?
(A) 5 percent
(B) 15 percent
(C) 20 percent
(D) 60 percent

66. What does the man say the business must do?
(A) Advertise a vacancy
(B) Sell some assets
(C) Negotiate with a client
(D) Reduce its rates

67. What does the woman suggest spending money on?
(A) Advertising their services
(B) Getting financial advice
(C) Investing in real estate
(D) Relocating the business

68. Why are the IT support personnel unavailable?
(A) It is a national holiday.
(B) It is outside office hours.
(C) They are taking a lunch break.
(D) They are at a seminar.

69. Look at the graphic. Which menu option does the man recommend?
(A) Option 001
(B) Option 002
(C) Option 003
(D) Option 004

70. What does the man say he did this week?
(A) Completed a project
(B) Took a vacation
(C) Purchased a new desk
(D) Interviewed an applicant

PART 4

TRACK_191 ~ TRACK_211

Directions: In this part, you will hear talks given by one speaker. You must answer three questions about what is said in each talk. Select the best response to each question and mark answer (A), (B), (C), or (D) on your answer sheet. The talks will be spoken only one time and will not be written in your test book.

71. Where does the listener work?
    (A) At a manufacturing company
    (B) At an advertising firm
    (C) At a newspaper
    (D) At a retail store

72. According to the speaker, what does Stephenson Inc. intend to do?
    (A) Expand into foreign markets
    (B) Renew its public image
    (C) Reduce its product diversity
    (D) Announce a change of ownership

73. What does the speaker mean when he says, "We've invested heavily"?
    (A) His company has confidence in its products.
    (B) His company is short of funds.
    (C) His company will lose a lot of money.
    (A) His company has taken a significant risk.

74. What has caused the delay?
    (A) A late connecting flight
    (B) Difficulty with the boarding gate
    (C) A technical malfunction
    (D) Some missing luggage

75. According to the speaker, what is available to passengers?
    (A) Some refreshments
    (B) An internet connection
    (C) Discount coupons
    (D) Hotel accommodations

76. What will most likely be the topic of the next announcement?
    (A) The weather conditions
    (B) The immigration clearance
    (C) The airport's internet service
    (D) The flight's boarding sequence

77. What are some employees concerned about?
    (A) Career development opportunities
    (B) Noise pollution in the workplace
    (C) Insufficient parking spaces
    (D) Ongoing staffing shortages

78. When does the speaker say a project will probably be completed?
    (A) In two weeks
    (B) In two months
    (C) In six months
    (D) In a year

79. What temporary arrangements have been made for employees?
    (A) Corporate gym memberships
    (B) Staggered work hours
    (C) A shuttle bus service
    (D) Work-from-home options

80. Who are the listeners?
    (A) Art experts
    (B) Corporate donors
    (C) New gallery guides
    (D) Government employees

81. What are the listeners about to receive?
    (A) Refreshments
    (B) Name tags
    (C) Information folders
    (D) Uniforms

82. What will the listeners do next?
    (A) Walk around a building
    (B) Take a break
    (C) Watch a video
    (D) Meet a representative

GO ON TO THE NEXT PAGE

83. What is being advertised?
    (A) A new course
    (B) Discount tuition
    (C) An open house
    (D) Job vacancies

84. What is the college known for?
    (A) Its small classes
    (B) Its excellent equipment
    (C) Its famous graduates
    (D) Its central location

85. According to the speaker, what can the
    listeners do on a Web site?
    (A) Order a brochure
    (B) See student testimonials
    (C) Watch a commercial
    (D) Enroll in a course

86. According to the speaker, what are the
    workshops about?
    (A) Changing services
    (B) Advertising vacancies
    (C) Taking foreign postings
    (D) Choosing domestic suppliers

87. What should the listeners bring with them?
    (A) Flight confirmations
    (B) Health information
    (C) Identification cards
    (D) Trip reports

88. What will the listeners do tomorrow?
    (A) Take a trip
    (B) Roleplay situations
    (C) Fill out forms
    (D) Work in pairs

89. What does the speaker mean when he says,
    "many of us are already working additional
    hours each week"?
    (A) The company is expecting too much.
    (B) It is costing a lot to pay for overtime work.
    (C) Staff are excited to work on a project.
    (D) The employees will quickly complete some
        work.

90. What does the speaker say he will do?
    (A) Check an employee handbook
    (B) Take a trip to the head office
    (C) Promote current employees
    (D) Cover transportation expenses

91. Who most likely are the listeners?
    (A) Section chiefs
    (B) Business investors
    (C) City inspectors
    (D) Equipment suppliers

92. What type of business does the speaker work
    for?
    (A) A food distributor
    (B) A health club
    (C) A furniture warehouse
    (D) An appliance manufacturer

93. What does the speaker ask the listener to do?
    (A) Make a reservation
    (B) Post an online review
    (C) Repair some equipment
    (D) Provide some contact information

94. Why does the speaker say, "A lot of businesses
    are relying on us"?
    (A) To show that her business has a good
        reputation
    (B) To explain the seriousness of a situation
    (C) To offer an excuse for a slow response
    (D) To demonstrate the dependability of an
        appliance

Gettysburg Hotel Restaurant Map

13	Maddison's	
12		Cheers
	Guest Rooms	
4		
3	Red Rock	
2		
Golden Road	1	Reception

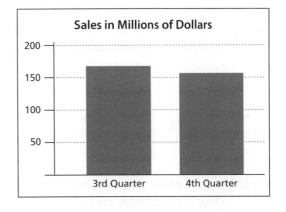

95. Who most likely is the speaker?
(A) A hotel porter
(B) A restaurant worker
(C) A tour guide
(D) A company executive

96. According to the speaker, what will the listeners receive?
(A) A car key
(B) An itinerary
(C) A meal ticket
(D) A product sample

97. Look at the graphic. On which floor will the listeners have dinner?
(A) The 13th Floor
(B) The 12th Floor
(C) The 3rd Floor
(D) The 1st Floor

98. Look at the graphic. What will happen at the company this quarter?
(A) Sales will exceed last quarter's.
(B) An additional bonus will be paid.
(C) Employees will attend a corporate retreat.
(D) A sales target will be revised.

99. Who most likely is Ms. White?
(A) The president of a machinery manufacturer
(B) A writer from a magazine publisher
(C) The chief of the company's accounting section
(D) The manager of the marketing department

100. What will the listeners do after Ms. White speaks?
(A) Vote for a spokesperson
(B) Take a break
(C) Share ideas
(D) Speak with a journalist

GO ON TO THE NEXT PAGE

In the Reading test, you will read many kinds of texts and answer several different types of reading comprehension questions. The Reading test has three parts, and directions are given for each part. You have 75 minutes for the entire Reading test and are encouraged to answer as many questions as possible.

You need to mark your answers on the answer sheet.
Nothing must be written in your test book.

PART 5
Directions: In each of the sentences below, a word or phrase is missing. Select the best word or phrase from four choices to complete the sentence. Then mark the letter (A), (B), (C), or (D) on your answer sheet.

101. The ------- of employment outlined in the employee handbook explain what is expected of workers in various situations.
(A) condition
(B) conditional
(C) conditions
(D) conditionally

102. The museum has an ------- collection of artifacts from local indigenous cultures.
(A) insolvent
(B) eclectic
(C) ultimate
(D) instantaneous

103. According to Ms. Smith's -------, the factory lost power after the new machinery was turned on for the first time.
(A) accountancy
(B) account
(C) accountably
(D) accountable

104. Buffalo brand carpet detergent is ------- most frequently endorsed by industry professionals in light of its quality.
(A) the one
(B) what
(C) its
(D) one of

105. Although sales are below expectations, the new kitchenware is ------- a reputation for excellent usability online.
(A) supplying
(B) granting
(C) enjoying
(D) dedicating

106. The company has arranged a banquet to show employees ------- appreciative it is of their hard work this year.
(A) how
(B) that
(C) however
(D) when

107. ------- stated in the product specifications, the device should be stored in a dry room at below 20 degrees Celsius.
(A) At
(B) While
(C) For
(D) As

108. Some of the board members ------- disapproved of the idea that reduces the development cost.
(A) mildly
(B) narrowly
(C) unanimously
(D) closely

109. Dalton Productions whose latest works are of good repute ------- a documentary on the farming industry every day unless the weather is unfavorable.
(A) to film
(B) have filmed
(C) is filming
(D) filming

110. HR employees usually begin job interviews with general questions and move ------- to the ones about candidates' prior experience.
(A) over
(B) in
(C) on
(D) for

111. Mr. Romanov's ------- to the event attendees was about improving customer satisfaction levels.
(A) addressed
(B) address
(C) addressing
(D) addresses

112. A committee has been commissioned to ------- a plan that will help the business head off competition from international suppliers.
(A) desire
(B) craft
(C) dread
(D) instill

113. The editor requires that the first drafts of articles for the September issue be submitted by August 17 ------- the very latest.
(A) on
(B) in
(C) with
(D) at

114. ------- of the movie production company's directors has experience in a variety of fiction and non-fiction genres.
(A) Some
(B) Every
(C) Each
(D) Both

115. A ------- number of drivers using the road will be compelled to take a detour to lower congestion near the construction area.
(A) respectable
(B) respectably
(C) respectability
(D) respective

116. Mr. Abby, whose first award-winning novel is now getting attention, is planning to hold a talk ------- available online.
(A) substantially
(B) readily
(C) timely
(D) considerably

117. Test audiences for Mick Dunhill's latest film found the production less than -------.
(A) satisfied
(B) satisfaction
(C) satisfy
(D) satisfying

118. Freeman Gym members get 24-hour access and free training consultations, ------- location they choose to use.
(A) where
(B) its
(C) whichever
(D) whose

119. Customers spending over $100 ------- to receive a free set of body towels.
(A) accept
(B) contribute
(C) entitle
(D) deserve

120. Harper Industries has a vacancy at its Waterford Plant for a chemical engineer ------- by the Queensland Industrial Standards Commission.
(A) qualifying
(B) qualified
(C) having qualified
(D) was qualified

GO ON TO THE NEXT PAGE

121. SRT abandoned its plans to expand into Asia
------- concerns that there was not enough
demand for its products there.
(A) amid
(B) within
(C) across
(D) through

122. Departmental budgets will be decided by the
finance director by the end of this week and
------- on January 10.
(A) publishing
(B) publish
(C) publisher
(D) published

123. Many of the items in the exhibition are on
------- from the Metropolitan Museum of
Antiquity in Boise.
(A) care
(B) display
(C) loan
(D) position

124. In order to boost ------- popularity among
young people, Transameri Corp. hired a
marketing agency with a reputation for
innovation.
(A) that
(B) each
(C) those
(D) its

125. Reception staff should monitor the supply of
bottled water in the refrigerator and ------- it
whenever necessary.
(A) alert
(B) replenish
(C) observe
(D) dwindle

126. HGT's decision to relocate will affect
employees, many of ------- purchased their
homes after being hired there.
(A) who
(B) whom
(C) which
(D) that

127. Despite its ------- population, Marsden was
chosen as the location for the new
manufacturing plant.
(A) sparse
(B) imminent
(C) impartial
(D) acute

128. A new dress code policy ------- employees to
wear casual clothes except when meeting
clients will be effective as of March 8.
(A) is enabling
(B) enabling
(C) enabled
(D) enables

129. Ms. Dalton's ------- action saved the company
a lot of money and helped preserve its good
reputation.
(A) time
(B) timing
(C) timer
(D) timely

130. Survey respondents expressed ------- interest
in receiving e-mail updates on special offers
from the hotel.
(A) few
(B) each
(C) little
(D) any

PART 6

Directions: In the following texts, a word, phrase, or sentence is missing. There are four answer choices for each question below the text. Select the best answer to complete the text and mark the letter (A), (B), (C), or (D) on your answer sheet.

Questions 131-134 refer to the following e-mail.

To: Molly Chiang <mchiang@freeducks.com>

From: Greg Smythe <gsmythe@carterindustries.com>

Date: March 23

Subject: Update

Thank you for ------- at Carter Industries. I am happy to inform you that you passed the first stage of
131.
the interview process. We would like to invite you back to meet with the head of our technical writing

department. We have a couple of ------- available. You can come between 9:00 A.M. and 11:00 A.M. on
132.
March 25 or between 1:00 P.M. and 3:00 P.M. on March 26. Please be advised that your appointment

will be made on a first come, first served basis as we are currently in contact with other candidates.

------- . When you come, you should remember to bring your parking receipt from last time. We -------
133.   134.
you for the cost of parking.

131. (A) looking
(B) staying
(C) working
(D) applying

132. (A) vehicles
(B) devices
(C) slots
(D) locations

133. (A) Please let me know your preference as
soon as possible.
(B) At present we are not looking for a new
technical writer.
(C) We will keep your résumé on file in case
another position becomes vacant.
(D) We will have our driver pick you up just
before noon.

134. (A) have reimbursed
(B) will reimburse
(C) reimbursed
(D) have been reimbursing

GO ON TO THE NEXT PAGE

Questions 135-138 refer to the following advertisement.

The Scarborough Inn

The Scarborough Inn is Aberdeen's most ------- hotel. Constructed over a hundred years ago, it boasts
135.
an elegance and charm unlike any other ------- provider in the area. With only 10 guest rooms, we can
136.
afford our guests special attention. This is something our competitors simply cannot ------- . Near the
137.
center of town, we are only 500 meters from Aberdeen Greens Golf Course and a short train ride from
Tullamore Castle. ------- . Visit the Web site to make a reservation or read reviews from our hundreds of
138.
satisfied guests.

www.thescarboroughinn.com
TEL 555 2342

---

135. (A) modern
　　　(B) sizable
　　　(C) luxurious
　　　(D) secluded

136. (A) entertainment
　　　(B) accommodation
　　　(C) transportation
　　　(D) amusement

137. (A) match
　　　(B) charge
　　　(C) spare
　　　(D) retain

138. (A) Neither is accessible from The
　　　　　Scarborough Inn.
　　　(B) The grand opening is scheduled for
　　　　　May 10.
　　　(C) Those who book a room during this period
　　　　　will be offered discounts.
　　　(D) Admission to the latter is included with
　　　　　your stay.

Questions 139-142 refer to the following information.

Wilson Engineering provides some ------ to promote productivity. These can include additional bonus
139.
payments or time off work. This only applies to employees who complete their work ------ it is due. In
140.
addition to early submissions, you may also obtain favorable evaluations through work quality and
general attitude. Supervisors maintain an ongoing record of employee performance. This ------ to
141.
determine eligibility for rewards. ------ . A more thorough description of the evaluation criteria and
142.
the process is available in the employee handbook.

139. (A) incentives
(B) penalties
(C) laws
(D) installments

140. (A) while
(B) when
(C) once
(D) before

141. (A) was being used
(B) is used
(C) has used
(D) is using

142. (A) This generally makes our suppliers more
competitive in terms of service and
pricing.
(B) Unfortunately, the company cannot
provide any financial benefits at this time.
(C) You may contact human resources if you
are unsatisfied with your assessment.
(D) We are unable to share the details about
how this decision is made.

GO ON TO THE NEXT PAGE

Questions 143-146 refer to the following notice.

Notice

------ . We apologize for the short notice. We sincerely regret any inconvenience this causes our
143.
regular customers. Fortunately, the kitchen will remain operational ------ the closure. Therefore, there
144.
will be no interruption to take-out orders. ------ , we will still be accepting delivery orders from our
145.
partners at Deliverystar and NomNoms. You may call our reservations line to make table bookings,
which will be available from June 18. We hope that you come and enjoy our all-new interior and
amenities. To celebrate the improvements, we ------ 20% off all menu items until the end of June.
146.

---

143. (A) Circle Bookstore is moving to a new
location on Hillview Road.
(B) Arena Furniture is looking to hire
temporary staff for the first week of June.
(C) Seashells restaurant will not be open
between June 2 and June 17.
(D) Crystal Café is proud to announce the
opening of its second location.

144. (A) by
(B) during
(C) among
(D) ever since

145. (A) Nevertheless
(B) In contrast
(C) Finally
(D) Furthermore

146. (A) will be offering
(B) had offered
(C) have been offering
(D) will be offered

PART 7

Directions: In this part you will read a selection of texts, such as newspaper articles, e-mails, and instant messages. Each text or set of texts is followed by several questions. Select the best answer for each question. Then mark the letter (A), (B), (C), or (D) on your answer sheet.

Questions 147-148 refer to the following e-mail.

From:	Starwing Online Shopping — Customer Service
To:	Ralph Bennis
Date:	23 June
Subject:	Your order

Hello Ralph,

Have you made up your mind? Your Try-Before-You-Buy one-week try-on period ends tomorrow. If you are not completely happy with your order, you have until 11:59 P.M. tomorrow to send back the unwanted item or items. Otherwise, we'll assume you are satisfied with your items and have decided to keep them. You will be charged accordingly.

Quantity	Description	Unit Price	Item Total
1	Business Shoes	$76.00	$76.00
2	Leather Belt	$34.00	$68.00
1	Business Shirt	$25.00	$25.00
2	Winter vest	$17.00	$34.00
	Merchandise Subtotal:		$203.00
	Goods and Services Tax:		$10.15
	TOTAL:		**$213.15**

*Please note that this does not apply to footwear. Purchases in this category are final and refunds are only issued in cases where the products are defective.

147. What is the purpose of the e-mail?
   (A) To remind a customer of a deadline
   (B) To announce that a shipment has taken place
   (C) To notify a customer of a product recall
   (D) To issue a refund for some goods

148. According to the e-mail, how much has Mr. Bennis already been charged?
   (A) $76.00
   (B) $68.00
   (C) $203.00
   (D) $213.15

GO ON TO THE NEXT PAGE

Questions 149-150 refer to the following text-message chain.

Alisha Miller 9:50 A.M.
I'm thinking of arranging a party to welcome the new employees.

Oliver Smith 9:51 A.M.a
Nice idea. At lunchtime on their first day?

Alisha Miller 9:53 A.M.
Right. Can you take care of it? You can use a caterer if that's easier.

Oliver Smith 9:53 A.M.
Sure, but it looks like they'll be visiting the factory in Ascot on Wednesday.

Alisha Miller 9:54 A.M.
That's too bad. I guess we need to push it back to the day after, then.

Oliver Smith 9:59 A.M.
I'll call the caterer to place an order. What's the budget?

Alisha Miller 10:02 A.M.
$30 per person seems reasonable. I think we have 37 people including us and the new hires.

Oliver Smith 10:03 A.M.
I'll see what packages they have during lunch and then call them.

149. At 9:54 A.M., why does Ms. Miller write, "That's too bad"?
(A) The business is understaffed.
(B) There is a problem at the factory.
(C) There is a scheduling conflict.
(D) The budget for the party is insufficient.

150. What will Mr. Smith most likely do this afternoon?
(A) Interview a candidate
(B) Place a food order
(C) Respond to an invitation
(D) Make a restaurant reservation

To:	All Staff
From:	Ted Dawson
Date:	December 20
Subject:	Tomorrow

To all staff:

We have received some reports about intermittent problems with the building's front door. From time to time, it is failing to open automatically. We have called the manufacturer and expect someone to come out to take a look at it tomorrow. The work will probably take all day. From previous experience, we have learned that the door and the escalators are on the same circuit. It will almost certainly be necessary to disconnect both. Fortunately, the building's main stairway and the elevator will remain available.

We will post signs at the door to tell visitors to use the manual door at the front of the building. Guests using the basement parking lot will not need to use the escalator or the door, so no notification will be necessary.

I will send an update as soon as we have more information.

Sincerely,

Ted Dawson
Management

151. What will probably happen tomorrow?
  (A) Some important guests will arrive.
  (B) A sign will be updated.
  (C) Some maintenance will be implemented.
  (D) A report will be submitted.

152. What will employees be restricted from doing tomorrow?
  (A) Entering through the manual door
  (B) Riding on the elevator
  (C) Parking in the basement
  (D) Using the escalators

TEST 1

TEST 2

	Workshop: Improving The Client Experience 23 June (Day One) 10:00 A.M. ~ 5:00 P.M. $250 per person	
10:00 A.M.:	Session 1: Satisfying clients more Max Fielding from the University of Lancaster will lead a discussion on the kind of issues that cause client dissatisfaction. There are certain themes that many companies fail to consider in staff training.
11:00 A.M.:	Session 2: Meeting customers' needs Learn to use various techniques to get accurate feedback from customers in a timely manner. This session is designed to give you the tools you need to identify problems before they become serious.
12:10 P.M.:	Lunch Break Enjoy a buffet lunch at Salinger's on the conference center's first floor.
1:30 P.M.:	Session 3: Learning from mistakes We will review various case studies from businesses that have had to resurrect their reputations after a client relations mishap. Workshop leaders with years of experience in private enterprise will discuss how these strategies can be adapted to your business.
3:30 P.M.:	Session 4: Raising employees' awareness Learn ways to make your employees more mindful of the client experience, and to maintain that awareness in the day-to-day running of the business.

153. Which session is likely to involve the use of surveys?
(A) Session 1
(B) Session 2
(C) Session 3
(D) Session 4

154. What is NOT implied about the workshop?
(A) It will be led by experts.
(B) It will be held in a convention center.
(C) It is intended specifically for small businesses.
(D) It is a multiple-day event.

Questions 155-157 refer to the following article.

WILSON ATHLETICA ANNOUNCES NEW FACTORY LOCATION

MONROE, February 7 — Wilson Athletica is a world-renowned brand with many award-winning products in its lineup. It comes as a shock to many when they learn that the company is based in Monroe Oregon, a small rural town far from transportation hubs. In fact, Monroe has been the location of the company's only manufacturing facility. The facility has grown steadily over the years and now employs more than half of the town's population.

Today, CEO Don Wilson announced that the company will be building a new factory in Seattle. "We simply can't keep up with demand at our current factory," Wilson explained. "Even if we expanded that plant, there wouldn't be enough people in the area to run it." According to a press release, work on the new factory will begin in March. The company plans to have its grand opening just before the new year. Even though the new factory will be almost twice the size of the current one, the company's headquarters will remain in Monroe.

The company will be hiring new staff in Seattle in early November. Training will be divided between the company's two locations so that staff is ready to start work as soon as the factory opens. The news has excited many local businesses who hope to benefit from partnerships with Wilson Athletica. These include the Seattle Diamonds football team, which is looking for a new sponsor.

155. Why is Wilson Athletica most likely opening a factory in Seattle?
(A) To have access to a larger market
(B) To take advantage of a larger workforce
(C) To facilitate a merger with a major competitor
(D) To be closer to professional sports teams

156. When most likely will the new plant open?
(A) In February
(B) In March
(C) In November
(D) In December

157. What is implied about Mr. Wilson?
(A) He plans to retire soon.
(B) He wrote the company's press release.
(C) He will remain at the Monroe office.
(D) He sponsors various sporting teams.

GO ON TO THE NEXT PAGE

MEMO

To: All Corden Appliances Employees
From: Helen Taylor
Date: September 18

The annual employee appreciation banquet will be held on October 10 this year. We have chosen Belvedere Hotel as the location. The banquet will start at 7:00 P.M. Cranston City is currently suffering from a parking shortage, so we imagine that many employees might be opposed to attending due to the inconvenience. For that reason, we will be providing a bus from the office to the Belvedere Hotel. It will leave here at 5:30 P.M. The return bus will depart the hotel at 9:00 P.M. Alternatively, for people living in the southern suburbs, we will be providing ferry tickets so that they can park their vehicles on Maddon Point and use the ferry service to get to the hotel.

As in previous years, the company will subsidize the event by paying half of the cost. Employees will be charged $30 per head to take part. Please put it in an envelope and hand it directly to Mr. Rose in the General Affairs Department by the day before the event. If you will be unable to attend the banquet, it is necessary to inform him by October 1.

I look forward to seeing you that night!

---

158. What is one purpose of the memo?
(A) To thanks employees for their hard work
(B) To announce the commencement of a new project
(C) To inform employees of a change of date
(D) To provide details of transportation options

159. What is implied about the Belvedere Hotel?
(A) It is located in Cranston City.
(B) It does not offer guest parking.
(C) It has previously hosted Corden Appliances events.
(D) It will not accept alterations to its reservations.

160. By when should employees pay the participation fee?
(A) September 18
(B) October 1
(C) October 9
(D) October 10

Questions 161-163 refer to the following instructions.

GEOMAX HOME AUTOMATION
Merchandise Return Instructions

Congratulations on your purchase of a quality product from Geomax Home Automation. We are the world's most respected name in voice-operated switches and lights.

If you experience any problems with your Geomax device, please call the customer support line before requesting a refund or a return. —[1]— . Our highly trained customer support staff will try to solve any problems you are experiencing with your device. If we are unable to resolve the issue, we will provide you with a reference number which you can pass on to the seller, who will arrange a refund or a replacement. —[2]— .

Please note that the warranty period is 12 months from the date of purchase. —[3]— . Depending on the age of the device and the nature of the problem, customer service staff may ask for proof of purchase. You can do this by providing either your receipt or the warranty card included with these instructions. —[4]— .

Before contacting our customer support line please try the following:
1. Unplug the device and wait 10 seconds before plugging it back in.
2. With the device plugged in, hold down the power button for five seconds.
3. Try using the device on a different power outlet.
4. Look for solutions to problems by visiting the support section of our Web site.

The telephone number for our customer support line is 800 555 3342.
Our customer support page is at www.geomaxha.com/support

---

161. For whom is the information intended?
    (A) A consumer of electrical goods
    (B) A customer support line operator
    (C) An online store representative
    (D) A repair technician

162. What is the purpose of the reference number mentioned in the instructions?
    (A) To provide proof that a user has contacted Geomax directly
    (B) To show that the device is still covered by its product warranty
    (C) To demonstrate the caller is eligible for a discount
    (D) To help customer support staff trace the cause of a problem

163. In which of the positions marked [1], [2], [3], and [4] does the following sentence best belong?

    "If you are unable to supply either document, please contact the seller for assistance."

    (A) [1]
    (B) [2]
    (C) [3]
    (D) [4]

GO ON TO THE NEXT PAGE

13

Travel Maine - July Edition

The Gladstone Inn:
Contemporary Amenities, Classic Luxury
By Rebecca Chow

The Gladstone Inn has been one of Canterbury's most important accommodation providers for more than a century. Originally designed to offer cheap accommodations to traveling salespeople, the hotel is now one of the most luxurious places to stay in Melbourne. Its convenient location, stunning views, and excellent amenities make it a popular destination for celebrities and traveling dignitaries.

Recently, the Gladstone Inn has agreed to a partnership with Canterbury Community College whereby students undertake paid internships and learn important skills. Program coordinator Sheryl White has praised the staff at the hotel for the excellent training they are providing. "I'm sure our graduates will be able to find work at luxury hotels anywhere in the world using their experiences," White said. "Many of the interns go on to pursue careers right here, though."

The internship program is only available to students in Canterbury Community College's Hospitality course. It is a three-year course with two compulsory internship components, both of which take place in the final year. Intern Melissa Walker said that she felt that the internship and the regular classes were equally important. "It's very helpful to see how the information we are given in the course is used in the real world."

The internship program has been running for seven years now, and both the hotel and the college claim to have experienced some additional benefits. The course's popularity has grown to the point where administrators are considering raising their student numbers. Meanwhile, the hotel has a 98 percent occupancy rate throughout the year. They attribute part of that to the goodwill from friends and family of the interns.

164. What is suggested about the Gladstone Inn?
(A) It has adapted to serve a different clientele.
(B) It was nominated for a hospitality award.
(C) It is the largest hotel in Canterbury.
(D) It recently had its interior renovated.

165. What is implied about the internship program?
(A) It is offered in locations around the world.
(B) It provides a financial reward for its participants.
(C) It is coordinated by an employee of The Gladstone Inn.
(D) It accepts students from a variety of colleges.

166. What is probably true about Ms. Walker?
(A) She has stayed at The Gladston Inn on multiple occasions.
(B) She has been offered a permanent position at The Gladston Inn.
(C) She commenced studying at Canterbury Community College over two years ago.
(D) She is a member of the faculty at Canterbury Community College.

167. How has the hotel benefitted from the arrangement?
(A) It is hiring fewer staff members.
(B) It is taking more reservations.
(C) It is getting better reviews.
(D) It is spending less on staffing.

GO ON TO THE NEXT PAGE

Questions 168-171 refer to the following online chat discussion.

Clinton Salazar [3:30 P.M.]:
I just got a call from Freeman's Accounting. They are having some trouble with their internal network connection. It's on Sharpe Street in Benowa.

Ignatius Royce [3:31 P.M.]:
I installed that network when it first went in so I'm familiar with the setup. I'm busy all day today, though.

Maxine Bolton [3:31 P.M.]:
I'm at Carter Travel right now. It's a couple of doors down from Freeman's accounting. I could take a look as soon as I'm finished here.

Clinton Salazar [3:33 P.M.]:
Thanks, Maxine. It's fairly urgent, though. How long do you think you'll take?

Maxine Bolton [3:35 P.M.]:
It depends. I'm still tracking down the problem here. It could be something easy or it could take all day.

Dana Alvarez [3:36 P.M.]:
I could be there in 20 minutes, Clinton. Let me know if you need me. I'm at the warehouse right now stocking up on supplies.

Ignatius Royce [3:37 P.M.]:
You should probably take a new router. The one they are using has been there for over a decade. It has reached the end of its lifespan.

Clinton Salazar [3:45 P.M.]:
Good to know. Thanks, Ignatius. Dana, why don't you grab a router and head over there?

Dana Alvarez [3:46 P.M.]:
On my way. Do you know what size they need?

Clinton Salazar [3:49 P.M.]:
Hang on. I'll find out how many employees they have there now.

168. Who most likely are the writers?
(A) Accountants
(B) Travel agents
(C) Network engineers
(D) Programmers

169. What is implied about Carter Travel?
(A) It is in the same building as Freeman's Accounting.
(B) It is a newly established business.
(C) It will close soon.
(D) It is on Sharpe Street.

170. At 3:35 P.M., what does Ms. Bolton mean when she writes, "It depends"?
(A) She is not sure what a client is requesting.
(B) She does not know the severity of a problem.
(C) She believes that some equipment is reliable.
(D) She needs to check a map to be certain.

171. What will Mr. Salazar most likely do next?
(A) Order a device
(B) Contact a client
(C) Call a branch office
(D) Load a vehicle

Questions 172-175 refer to the following advertisement.

Excelsior of Victoria

Finding Buyers for Obscure Items for Over a Hundred Years

Excelsior is where investors in rare antiques and fine artwork come to buy and sell their treasures. Excelsior specializes in high-end items and has a reputation for accuracy in its product descriptions and verification of authenticity. —[1]— . Our clients receive monthly newsletters describing the contents of our upcoming sales, their estimated sales price, minimum bid amounts, and reserve prices. These are also available from our Web site at www.excelsiorofvictoria.com. —[2]— .

On June 16, we will be selling off a magnificent collection of jazz records, a diary from playwright Tim Cleminson, and a Hudson Dart automobile valued at more than $250,000 among many other things. —[3]— . You can come and view some of these upcoming items in our exhibition room. We are in the wonderful Mongomery Building on Regent Street, where Excelsior has been since it was founded.

If you would like to place a bid, you must register in advance. Depending on the item you are wishing to bid on, you may be asked to provide proof of funds to demonstrate your ability to pay. —[4]— . Please be sure to get a copy from your financial institution before you visit us.

We look forward to serving you soon whether you are buying or selling!

Excelsior of Victoria
100 Regent Street, Victoria
Tel 250-555-4932

---

172. What is being advertised?
(A) An auction house
(B) An event space
(C) An art gallery
(D) A history museum

173. What is implied about the Mongomery building?
(A) It is owned by Excelsior.
(B) It provides parking for registered guests.
(C) It was constructed over a century ago.
(D) It houses a theater.

174. According to the advertisement, what might people be asked to provide when they register?
(A) A bank account statement
(B) A receipt for their purchase
(C) An admission ticket
(D) An invitation from the organizers

175. In which of the positions marked [1], [2], [3], and [4] does the following sentence best belong?

"We expect to have at least 70 interested parties or their representatives in attendance."

(A) [1]
(B) [2]
(C) [3]
(D) [4]

GO ON TO THE NEXT PAGE

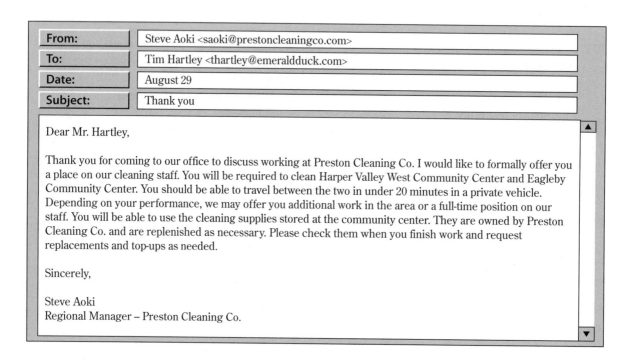

From:	Georgia Paulson <gpaulson@prestoncleanco.com>
To:	Steve Aoki <saoki@prestoncleanco.com>
Date:	August 6
Subject:	New contract

Dear Steve,

We have just won the cleaning contract for the Harper Valley community centers. There are a total of 20 community centers that will require cleaning. There is no way that we can accomplish this with our current staff levels. We need to hire additional cleaners on a part-time basis.

According to the contract, the cleaning must be carried out between 6:30 P.M. and 9:30 P.M. Last week, I visited three of the locations to calculate how long it should take. An experienced cleaner should be able to complete the work in around 45 minutes to an hour. Considering travel time, each cleaner will only be able to take care of two locations. The current cleaning company is contracted until September 13. However, the coordinator of the Harper Valley community centers has asked us to start work on September 4. I get the impression that they are dissatisfied with the standard of cleaning they are currently receiving. One problem she mentioned was that cleaners were not completing a checklist she provided. Please make it clear to new hires that the coordinator will be paying close attention to their work. For this reason, we should hire only experienced people with good references from previous employers.

Before you advertise the position, I would like you to look at our current work assignments to determine how much of the work current full-time employees will be able to cover. Let's conduct interviews from August 19.

Regards,

Georgia

From:	Steve Aoki <saoki@prestoncleaningco.com>
To:	Tim Hartley <thartley@emeraldduck.com>
Date:	August 29
Subject:	Thank you

Dear Mr. Hartley,

Thank you for coming to our office to discuss working at Preston Cleaning Co. I would like to formally offer you a place on our cleaning staff. You will be required to clean Harper Valley West Community Center and Eagleby Community Center. You should be able to travel between the two in under 20 minutes in a private vehicle. Depending on your performance, we may offer you additional work in the area or a full-time position on our staff. You will be able to use the cleaning supplies stored at the community center. They are owned by Preston Cleaning Co. and are replenished as necessary. Please check them when you finish work and request replacements and top-ups as needed.

Sincerely,

Steve Aoki
Regional Manager – Preston Cleaning Co.

176. What is implied about the work at the Harper Valley community centers?
(A) Some of it will be carried out by existing employees.
(B) Each location will take over an hour to complete.
(C) It will receive a daily inspection from the regional coordinator.
(D) It must be carried out in teams of two.

177. In the first e-mail, the word "impression" in paragraph 2, line 5 is closest in meaning to
(A) imitation
(B) consequence
(C) response
(D) feeling

178. What is implied about Mr. Hartley?
(A) He will be a full-time employee of Preston Cleaning Co.
(B) He will be reimbursed for cleaning chemicals.
(C) He was vouched for by a previous employer.
(D) He will attend an orientation session on September 12.

179. When most likely will Mr. Hartley begin working for Preston Cleaning Co.?
(A) On August 19
(B) On August 29
(C) On September 4
(D) On September 13

180. What is NOT a responsibility of the position described in the e-mails?
(A) Cleaning a public facility
(B) Emptying of garbage receptacles
(C) Monitoring inventory
(D) Fulfilling a checklist

GO ON TO THE NEXT PAGE

Business News

Friday, September 19

Gig Meets Trad

In recent years, the gig economy has been growing steadily, and more and more people have been earning a living by completing tasks of various sizes for a diverse group of temporary employers. There can be problems with this arrangement. Gig workers often have to invest in certain equipment that would ordinarily be supplied by an employer. Also, many people find it hard to focus if they work from home — they get less done because of all the distractions. Another problem is the sense of isolation people feel. They do not benefit from the support networks traditional offices provide.

Steven Chan's new company Gigtrad aims to solve this problem by providing a shared workspace for online gig workers. Each site has a wide variety of professional-grade equipment that users of the space can rent for a small additional charge. Users can attend lectures from industry experts.

Gigtrad — The Future of Online Work

Everyone loves the freedom gig work provides, but it is not without its downsides. Gigtrad can help alleviate the difficulties of gig work while leveraging the benefits of a shared workspace to improve your productivity.
- Get access to a wide variety of high-end equipment at no additional cost.
- Share ideas and collaborate on tasks with other Gigtrad users.
- Broaden your connections within various industries and learn about new opportunities from visiting experts.

If you are interested in finding out whether or not Gigtrad is right for your specific situation, you can join our online information session. After listening to a brief rundown of our services by our CEO, you can ask questions and enjoy a guided tour of one of our facilities. There will also be video testimonials by some of our current users. A schedule of upcoming sessions is provided on the Web site.

If you are ready to take the next step, visit the Web site and find out if there is a location near you. As a result of our high user satisfaction levels, many of our offices are already at maximum capacity. Nevertheless, you can put your name on a waiting list and be notified when there is an opening.

www.gigtrad.com

181. Who is Steven Chan?
(A) A company founder
(B) A customer service representative
(C) A gig worker
(D) A journalist

182. What is NOT mentioned as something experienced by gig workers?
(A) A feeling of solitude
(B) Difficulty concentrating
(C) Enhanced flexibility
(D) Increased earning potential

183. Which benefit of Gigtrad has been modified since the article was published?
(A) The service area
(B) The equipment rental option
(C) The management team
(D) The learning opportunities

184. According to the advertisement, how can people learn more about Gigtrad?
(A) By visiting a local office
(B) By attending an open meeting
(C) By calling a representative
(D) By subscribing to a newsletter

185. What is probably available from the Web site?
(A) A map
(B) A survey form
(C) An app
(D) An employee profile

GO ON TO THE NEXT PAGE

Get away from it all at Palazzo Loto Bianco!

Enjoy magnificent sea views from this luxurious seaside resort. We are now offering some special off-peak deals that you can take advantage of from January to March. All guests can take part in free guided tours of nearby Castello di Mola and Villagonia. Stay with us for three nights, and get a fourth night free.

International visitors will find that we are a short drive from Catania Airport, and for those traveling domestically, Comiso Airport is very convenient. Valencia Yacht Harbor is within walking distance for those coming by sea.

Palazzo Loto Bianco won last year's Sicily Accommodation Association's award for Best Kept Grounds. Our restaurant Michael's was featured in *Fine Dining Magazine*, which described the menu as "daring", "original", and "delicious".

www. palazzolotobianco.com
TEL: +39 (0)95 555 743

To:	Bruce Towns <btowns@weedontravel.com>
From:	Pietro Messina <pmessina@palazzolotobianco.com>
Date:	February 19
Subject:	Re: 48309432

Dear Mr. Towns,

I am writing about Ms. Tanya Coolidge. She is a customer of Weedon Travel who stayed with us from February 11 to February 16. She locked some valuable items in the room safe and must have forgotten to remove them before she left on the morning of the 16th. We tried contacting her at the number she left with us, but we have been unable to do so. As another guest had reserved the room, we had to have a representative from the manufacturer come to the hotel and open the safe for us. We incurred a fee of US$175.50. As she is a valued customer of Weedon Travel, we are happy to waive that cost.

However, we must insist on sending the items on a paid-on delivery basis. For this reason, it is important that she be home to accept the parcel when it arrives. I suspect that she has not answered her calls because she is still on vacation. Our receptionist remembers her mentioning that she was headed to the airport for a flight to the U.K. Could you pass on this message to her, or provide us with her correct mobile phone number?

Sincerely,

Pietro Messina
Hotel Manager — Palazzo Loto Bianco

To:	Bruce Towns <btowns@weedontravel.com>
From:	Tanya Coolidge <tcoolidge@wyldfashion.com>
Date:	February 19
Subject:	RE: Palazzo Loto Bianco

Dear Mr. Towns,

Thank you for passing along the message from Mr. Messina.

I would like you to thank Mr. Messina for his concern and inform him that our stay at his hotel was the highlight of our trip. Please also let him know that we did not make use of the safe in the room during our stay. We did, however, make use of the items in the room's refrigerator. The exotic juices in there were particularly delicious. I plan to order some as soon as I get home.

We are already discussing returning next year. Perhaps we will go there in the summer months next time.

Sincerely,

Tanya Coolidge

186. What is suggested about the hotel?
(A) It has a shuttle bus service to the airports.
(B) Its restaurant has won an award.
(C) It has some athletic facilities.
(D) Its rates depend on the season.

187. What is implied about Ms. Coolidge?
(A) She has returned to her home in England.
(B) She qualified for one night's free accommodation.
(C) She will be charged for the cost of opening the safe.
(D) She mistakenly brought a piece of the hotel's equipment home.

188. Where did Ms. Coolidge most likely go on February 16?
(A) To Catania Airport
(B) To Comiso Airport
(C) To Castello di Mola
(D) To Valencia Yacht Harbor

189. In the first e-mail, the phrase "pass on" in paragraph 2, line 4 is closest in meaning to
(A) refuse
(B) go by
(C) convey
(D) determine

190. What is implied about the items in the safe?
(A) They were of very high quality.
(B) They belonged to a previous occupant of the room.
(C) They were sent to Ms. Coolidge's home.
(D) They were temporarily kept at a reception desk.

GO ON TO THE NEXT PAGE

To:	Jim Nance <jnance@collinsengineering.com>
From:	Olga Krause <okrause@collinsengineering.com>
Date:	June 10
Subject:	Your trip

Dear Mr. Nance,

I understand that you will be taking your first business trip as an employee of Collins Engineering this month. As you were unable to attend the first day of the new employee orientation, you may be unaware of certain procedures. You are required to submit a travel report within three days of your return. You can obtain an extension if you have special circumstances. The travel report must contain information about your flights, your accommodations, and your ground transportation. You should list any purchases of gasoline separately from the vehicle rental fees. You are not required to include meals in the report, as you will be provided an allowance each day you are away. Every expense mentioned in the report must be accompanied by a receipt. As some employees have misplaced receipts in the past, I recommend that you take a photograph of them with your phone and store them in the cloud. It will still be necessary to print a physical copy to submit with your report.

Please let me know if there is anything else I can assist with. Enjoy your trip.

Sincerely,

Olga Krause
Administration — Collins Engineering

Travel Report

Employee: Jim Nance

Expenses	Cost
Round-trip ticket to Seattle: June 16 Depart Chicago 9:00 A.M. Arrive in Seattle 11:44 A.M. June 20 Depart Seattle 7:00 A.M. Arrive in Chicago 1:01 P.M.	$820.00
Accommodation: June 16 to June 18 — Santa Clarita Inn June 18 to June 20 — Ivory Business Hotel	$950.00 $210.00
Other transportation: Rental Vehicle, June 16 to June 18 Shuttle bus from Ivory Business Hotel to Seattle Airport, June 20	$560.00 $14.00

MEMO

To: Locody Machinery Factory Design Team
From: Jim Nance
Date: June 22
Subject: My trip

I was met by some executives from Locody Machinery at the arrivals gate on June 16. They took me to their manufacturing facility in Lancaster where I was able to view the proposed site of their new facility. The dimensions and their specific requirements have been uploaded to our server for your perusal. I was able to check the ground conditions and take some soil samples, which I sent to Cleminson Labs in Washington for analysis. I am still waiting on their evaluation.

The following evening, I met Jason Paulson from Dunning Projects. Coincidentally, we were staying at the same hotel. It seems that that company has also been asked to make a bid on the project. As a previous employee, I know that they will be working hard to undercut us on price. They do this by ensuring a speedy construction that will enable them to collect an early completion bonus. It is a risky and aggressive strategy that has worked well for them so far. I know that Collins Engineering does not usually rely on the completion bonus when calculating its profit margin. We should discuss this at our meeting on Monday. I have been assured that the results of the soil sample will be ready by then also.

191. What is mentioned about Mr. Nance?
(A) He was involved in an employee training program.
(B) He will travel with a colleague.
(C) He was interviewed by Ms. Krause before.
(D) He failed to hear some procedures.

192. What is Mr. Nance advised to do?
(A) Submit a report on the day of his return
(B) Keep digital evidence of his expenditure
(C) Inform a supervisor of changes to his schedule
(D) Attend an orientation session

193. What required information has Mr. Nance failed to include in the travel report?
(A) Flight details
(B) Meal prices
(C) Fuel costs
(D) Ground transportation

194. Where did Mr. Nance encounter Mr. Paulson?
(A) At Ivory Business Hotel
(B) At Santa Clarita Inn
(C) At Seattle Airport
(D) At Locody Machinery

195. What is implied about Dunning Projects?
(A) Its employment contract restricts staff from working for competitors.
(B) It often collaborates with other firms on large projects.
(C) It promotes its quality assurance policies to potential clients.
(D) Its profitability can be threatened by construction delays.

GO ON TO THE NEXT PAGE

Khatri Online Services: India's Premium Outsourcing Agency

The name Khatri Online Services (KOS) is synonymous with dependability, accountability, and affordability. We have earned this reputation by consistently putting our clients' needs before our own. Our online workers are highly educated, extremely motivated, and very experienced. They can quickly adapt to your company's culture, learn all of the relevant product specifications, and accurately predict clients' needs.

We offer:

- Consumer-focused technical support by telephone and chat
- Cross-platform software programming
- Web site development

We can supply up to five trained full-time workers with as little as two weeks' notice. There is a ten percent surcharge applicable when workers' start and finish times differ by more than seven hours from Mumbai local time.

To:	Milly Dore <mdore@atlantatech.com>
From:	Sunil Singh <ssingh@khatrionlineservices.com>
Date:	November 4
Subject:	Summary of service for October

Dear Ms. Dore,

I apologize for the slightly delayed response times your technical support clients reported. There is a 12.5-hour time difference between here and California, which our workers have been struggling to adapt to. In my experience, these problems resolve themselves within the first month.

Summary of service for October

Service	For	Hours
Telephone support line	Smartphone (Model: TGH532)	960
Software programming	Tablet (HH673)	N / A
App development	Television Media Box (JS732)	N / A
Online chat support	Laptop Computer (KH864)	480

We will send Atlanta Tech an invoice for these services on November 15. Please let me know if you see any discrepancies.

Sincerely,

Sunil Singh
Khatri Outsourcing Agency

To:	Milly Dore <mdore@atlantatech.com>
From:	Heath Glenn <hglenn@atlantatech.com>
Date:	November 4
Subject:	Complaints

Hi Milly,

There seems to be some system malfunction regarding HH673 and we are receiving quite a few complaints from its users. This problem needs to be addressed as soon as possible. If I remember correctly, Khatri Outsourcing Agency was involved in this. Could you give me the telephone number or e-mail address of the representative you have contacted before? I think it's much faster for me to talk to him or her directly and ask questions on this matter.

Sincerely,

Heath

196. According to the brochure, what is KOS known for?
(A) The durability of its products
(B) The responsibility of its employees
(C) The speed of its shipping service
(D) The convenience of its locations

197. What is implied about Atlanta Tech?
(A) It is paying extra for some services.
(B) It was able to reduce costs by using a foreign manufacturer.
(C) It charges its clients an additional fee for technical support.
(D) It relies on outsourcing for device design work.

198. What is suggested about KOS?
(A) It sends weekly invoices to its foreign clients.
(B) It manufactures devices for sale in the consumer market.
(C) It has provided Atlanta Tech technical support since October.
(D) It has been notified of an error in its time calculation system.

199. What kind of product does Atlanta Tech receive complaints about?
(A) A smartphone
(B) A tablet
(C) A television media box
(D) A laptop computer

200. What is most likely true about Ms. Dore?
(A) She will apologize to a customer directly.
(B) She has welcomed Mr. Singh to her team.
(C) She received an invoice from Atlanta Tech on November 4.
(D) She will share Mr. Singh's contact details with Mr. Glenn.

⇦ この冊子は取り外してご利用いただけます。